DON'T SIGN ANYTHING!

DON'T SIGN ANYTHING!

*How to protect yourself
from the tricks and traps of real estate.*

by
Neil Jenman

Rowley Publications
Sydney

The author accepts responsibility
for the content of this book.

Don't Sign Anything!
by Neil Jenman

First Edition

Published by Rowley Publications Pty Limited ACN 063 990 778
25/7 Anella Avenue Castle Hill NSW 2154 Australia
Telephone: (02) 9894 8988 Facsimile: (02) 9899 8271
www.jenman.com • Toll-Free 1800 1800 18

First published in Australia in October 2002

Printed in Australia by Griffin Press

Designed by GR8 Graphics
2 10/11 Ferguson Road Springwood NSW 2777

Distributed in Australia by Simon & Schuster Australia Pty Ltd
Distributed in New Zealand by Southern Publishers Group

National Library of Australia Cataloguing-in-Publication entry:

Jenman, Neil, 1955

Don't sign anything!
How to protect yourself from the
tricks and traps of real estate.

Bibliography.
Includes index.
ISBN 0 9586517 4 4.

1. Real estate business. 2. House buying.
3. House selling. 4. Home ownership.
5. Real estate investment. I. Title.

333.33

For Lesley, my friend.

It is necessary for us to revise
the whole way of thinking of these people,
and make them understand that they will
only obtain the objects of their desires,
not by trickery and misleading arguments,
but by moral goodness, both in thought and in action.

Cicero, On Duties (II)

List of Contents

Introduction

This book reveals how thousands of consumers are being ripped off in real estate. It shows how the greatest asset of most families is under financial assault from business people who are either dishonest or incompetent – there can be no other explanation for what happens in real estate today. It is a national disgrace.

As a consumer you will probably, in one way or another, be ripped off when you sell or buy a home. But not when you use the idea which is the central theme of this book – **DON'T SIGN ANYTHING**, at least until you are guaranteed that you will be protected. This book will show you, very simply and very clearly, how to protect yourself, financially and emotionally, from the tricks and traps of real estate.

The real estate industry cheats thousands of consumers every year. It happens in every city and in every state all over the country. It happens in Australia and New Zealand. Thousands of decent people, most of whom have worked hard to own their homes, are collectively losing millions of dollars. Increased consumer protection is desperately needed to stop this scandal.

One of the major reasons for this scandal is that the people who advise governments about what is happening in real estate are the people involved in the scandal – the real estate agents and those who represent them. To ask real estate agents how to clean up the real estate industry makes as much sense as asking burglars how to improve home security. And this is why there should be a full *independent* inquiry into an industry that has such a huge impact on so many consumers. Until this happens, your best hope as a consumer is to be as fully informed as possible *before* you buy or sell real estate. The more information you have, the more you will be able to protect yourself.

Please don't think you are too clever to be caught. Many of the victims in real estate are among the most wealthy and affluent people in our society. The traps in real estate are so 'clever' and so deceitful it would take a book to explain them.

This is that book.

Chapter One

An Industry Built on Lies

What is it in the value makeup of our society
that makes it so difficult for us to accept
that whole institutions can be corrupt?

William De Maria, Deadly Disclosures:
Whistleblowing and the Ethical Meltdown of Australia

The death of Richard's wife marked the end of a 57-year marriage. For Richard it also marked an experience with real estate agents he will never forget.

In preparation for his wife's funeral, Richard placed her death notice in the newspaper.[1] He received a call from an agent at 9 am on the day the notice was published. After the funeral two more agents called. They all wanted Richard to sell his home. He asked them to leave him alone. 'Your home must be too big for you,' said one agent, 'You'll have to move into a retirement home soon.'[2]

Richard was distraught. He called the Department of Consumer Affairs in Victoria but was told that nothing could be done. So he called a radio station which led to a storm of controversy about the methods of real estate agents. Victoria's Minister for Consumer Affairs was 'appalled' and promised to investigate the matter.[3]

When governments investigate real estate methods, one of their first contacts are the real estate institutes. But real estate institutes represent real estate agents, not consumers. In Richard's case, the institute gave its usual response about the 'actions of a minority of agents harming the reputation of the majority'. Their spokesperson, Enzo Raimondo, said the institute was 'disgusted' and did not 'condone' agents following up death notices. He promised to 'work with the government on the matter'. He also added that 'adequate training' was needed for agents.[4]

To distance itself from this scandal, the institute wrote to its member agents saying it would launch a campaign to inform the public that agents who were members of the real estate institute were 'ethical, professional and community minded' and that the 'problems' being publicised in the media were caused by either a 'minority' of agents or by agents who were not members of the real estate institute.[5] The campaign began with large newspaper advertisements in which the institute denied that its member agents were involved in harassing recently widowed people.[6]

Two days later, a training manual for agents was purchased from the Real Estate Institute of Victoria.[7] It listed 69 methods to find new business. Method 44 was 'Follow Up Death Notices'. Method 59 was 'Visit Nursing Homes and Retirement Villages'.[8]

This is the real estate industry today. A consumer complains, the government replies and the real estate institutes say they will 'work with the government to investigate'. But it is the people doing the investigating who should be investigated. And so it stays the same – thousands of consumers being deceived by real estate agents.[9]

Emotion

Whether you are a struggling first homebuyer or a multi-millionaire buying a mansion, real estate involves intense emotions. It tears at the heart like few other transactions. The money usually comes second to the emotional feelings involved with home ownership. These feelings are especially sensitive when people feel cheated.

On April 2, 1997 a 63-year-old man walked into a real estate agency in the Melbourne suburb of Avondale Heights. In his arms, hidden by a blanket, was a shotgun. The man felt the agent had cheated him and he wanted his money back. Pointing the gun at the agent, he pulled the trigger. It failed to fire. The agent hid under a desk as the man rampaged through the agency. He confronted another agent who was a partner in the agency and shot her at point-blank range. She died instantly. Later, he claimed he did not intend to kill anyone, he just wanted to scare the agent but he was, as he said, 'out of my head with anger'.[10]

In 1997 in Sydney a young man working in a real estate office was stabbed to death by an enraged tenant.[11] In 2000 in Bunbury, Western Australia, a real estate salesman was convicted of manslaughter after he killed a homebuyer who had threatened him repeatedly.[12] These are the extreme cases where emotions exploded. Nevertheless, thousands of homesellers and buyers know the intense emotional pain or anger that comes from dealing with real estate agents.

The Reason for the Lies

Many agents do not want to cheat their clients. Unfortunately many real estate methods make it hard for agents to act honestly. Typical real estate methods require agents to tell many lies or, at best, to use half-truths. If they tell the complete truth, all the time, most agents would find it hard to survive.

Wherever there is easy money to be made there will be a certain type of person involved. That person is likely to be lazy and unethical. To an outsider, this is how it seems in the real estate industry. Make a quick sale and earn a big commission. With the increase in real estate prices, the average commission earned by many agents is approaching $10,000 per sale. And that is too big for some people to resist. It sounds so easy. Sell a home and get $10,000.

However real estate is not always easy. It is a fiercely competitive world. The reason some agents prey on widowed people is because they are desperate for business. If an unethical person is attracted to real estate because of the appearance of easy money and then discovers that real estate is tougher than it appeared, that person is likely to become more unethical. This is why there are so many unethical real estate agents. The real estate industry is built on lies. But, when you understand the reason for the lies and how they trap consumers, you will be able to protect yourself.

Client Satisfaction in Real Estate

Real estate, unlike most businesses, does not depend on repeat clients. Ordinarily, if business people do the wrong thing, they lose their clients or they are driven out of business – 'run out of town', as the saying goes. But in real estate, the clients of the agents, the homesellers, are the ones who leave town. There is little incentive to keep them happy. The commission on sales can be so big that if an agent has to tell lies to win the business, so what? Even if they stay in the same area, most sellers won't use an agent again for many years.

This is the situation in real estate. The perception of big incomes attracts many unethical people. Some of these people become extremely 'successful' – when success is measured in volume of sales but not client satisfaction.

These apparently successful but unethical people have an unhealthy influence in real estate. They focus on protecting themselves not consumers. Many rise to the top of the industry and design the methods for the others to follow.

Real Estate Methods

Typical real estate methods are filled with slick lines which sound good, but which lead to massive financial and emotional damage to thousands of consumers. Many consumers never realise how badly they have been duped. Even some agents do not realise the harm they are doing to consumers. And, even if they do realise, they feel they have no choice. It's just the way the system works. The tricks are just part of the business. Or, to use the modern excuse for dishonesty, these methods are a 'commercial reality'.[13]

One example is the notorious practice of underquoting the selling price of a home to prospective buyers. The agents will promote a home at a price thousands below its value in order to entice more buyers. Buyers have now become so used to this deceit that many agents feel that they are stuck with it because if they tell the truth the buyers won't believe them anyway. Buyers, knowing that the agents are lying about the likely selling prices, add thousands onto the prices quoted.

And so, in real estate, lying has now become a reality. South Yarra real estate agent Phillipe Batters said on television that he did not believe underquoting was 'a wrong thing to do'. When asked if this meant he was lying to consumers, Batters squirmed.[14]

Honest Agents?

Few agents like telling lies to win business, but fewer still like losing business. Given a choice between telling a lie – which can be justified as a commercial reality or even described as a 'little lie' – and making a sale, or telling the truth and losing a sale, many agents will choose to make the sale. There are not enough sales to go around. It's a tough business.

No matter how honest the agent, if the system is built on lies, it is hard for the agent to do the right thing. Despite their honest intentions, many agents are incompetent because they don't fully understand what they are doing. They are just doing what they have been taught. So, if they don't understand how their systems hurt consumers, then you'd better make sure you understand.

When making the most important financial decision of your life, truth and honesty are very important. If you make financial decisions based on lies you will not only lose money you will most likely be emotionally devastated. And, many times, that's the worst part of dealing with a real estate agent. As the poet Phoebe Cary quipped, 'Of all hard things to bear and grin, the hardest is being taken in.'[15]

Being Sceptical

This book will give you one simple but powerful idea that will make it hard for any agent to cheat you. You will be protected, both financially and emotionally, from the tricks and traps of real estate.

No matter what you hear, no matter what you are told, don't sign anything until you know, for sure, that you can be protected. You are about to see exactly *how* the real estate industry lies to consumers. You can be as sceptical as you like, just don't sign anything. As the essayist, H.L. Mencken once wrote, 'Nine times out of ten, the sceptics are right.'[16] Being sceptical is your first protection against the lies in real estate.

Summary

- Typical real estate methods require agents to tell many lies or, at best, to use half-truths.

- In real estate, lying has become a reality. It is the norm, not the exception.

- Real estate institutes represent agents, not consumers.

- The people doing the investigating in real estate are often the people who should be investigated.

- Typical real estate methods lead to massive financial and emotional damage to thousands of consumers. Many people never realise how they have been duped.

- Many agents don't understand what they are doing. They are just doing what they have been taught.

- A real estate agency, unlike most businesses, does not have many regular clients. Selling and buying a home is, for many people, a once or twice in a lifetime event, so client care is, most often, minimal.

- For most people, real estate is their biggest financial transaction. It also involves intense emotions.

- If you make financial decisions based on lies you are likely to lose money *and* be emotionally devastated.

- No matter what you are told, **don't sign anything** until you know, for sure, that you are safe from the tricks and traps of real estate.

Chapter Two

The Quote Lie

The lie that sets the trap...

Will you walk into my parlor?
Said the spider to the Fly.
'Tis the prettiest little parlor
that ever you did spy.

Mary Howitt, The Spider and the Fly, *1844*

One lie in real estate leads to all the other lies. It is usually the first lie of real estate and it catches almost every homeseller. It leads to frustration, heartbreak and the loss of thousands of dollars. It's the lie told to homesellers about the 'market value' of their home – the 'Quote Lie'.

All the major dangers for both sellers and buyers begin with the Quote Lie.

THE BIGGEST LIAR WINS THE LISTING

The competition between real estate agents is not for buyers, it's for sellers. Almost everything in real estate is focused on finding sellers. Agents need homes to sell (which are called 'listings'). No listings means no sales. The formula is simple: get listings and *then* get sales.

Home-owners who are thinking of selling often speak with several agents in order to find the best one. But the way many sellers choose an agent means they choose the worst agent. They ask the agents to give them a 'quote' on the selling price of their home. This is a big mistake. The most dangerous question you can ask an agent is 'What is my home worth?' Agents know that you will be asking other agents the same question. If they tell you the truth, they know that other agents may tell you a lie and overquote the value of your home. And so the agent who tells the biggest lie about the likely (or more aptly, the unlikely) selling price is often chosen. This is how the biggest liar wins the listing.

BUYING THE LISTING

In the real estate industry, overquoting a price to a seller is called 'buying the listing'. But no matter what it is called or how tough it is for agents to tell the truth, overquoting is deceptive. To entice someone to do business on the basis of a lie is fraud.

However, it is easy for agents to say they made 'an honest mistake', even though the same mistake is made with thousands of sellers. But the truth is that if agents told the truth about the price, they feel they would not be chosen by the sellers.

Most sellers think their home is special and worth more; this is human nature. It is also why sellers want to believe the agent who gives them the highest quote and why they are so easily trapped by the Quote Lie. In his acclaimed book, *Lies! Lies!! Lies!!! The Psychology of Deceit,* Dr Charles Ford explains how lies catch us so easily. 'People who hear what they want to hear do not perceive that information as a lie.'[1]

If the beginning of the sales process depends on a lie, it follows that the entire sales process will be full of lies. One lie leads to more lies to cover up the first lie. This is exactly what happens in real estate.

THE CLEVER CONS

Agents who overquote the price can be very persuasive. The fear of selling too cheaply makes it easy to get caught. You might think you will be able to know when an agent is lying to you. But some of the worst agents are the best liars. Liars don't always look like liars. Charles Whitlock, a world authority on scams, says: 'No good con artist looks like a con artist.' The best con artists are so good that their victims don't even realise they've been scammed which means the best scams rarely get reported.[2] Many tricks in real estate are so deceptive that some homesellers never realise they have been ripped off.

The fear of selling too cheaply makes it easy to get caught

Agents will often use vague statements that sound logical but are very deceitful. They will say they aren't 'sure exactly' what your home is worth. One of the most common tricks is to say a home is 'only worth what the market will pay'. This sounds sensible and that's why so many agents use it. But an agent who works in the market every day should know the market. If you place pressure on the agent, the vagueness will often be replaced with a wonderful story about how so-and-so's home sold for a huge price, much higher than expected. The inference is clear – this could happen to you too. Be careful. Remember that the first aim of every agent, good or bad, is to get your signature on their selling agreement. Don't do it.

Once you have signed with an agent who 'buys the listing' you are caught in a trap from which there is almost no escape. You have legally committed yourself for a long time. No matter what price your home sells for, you have to pay the agent. Thousands of sellers get caught in the 'Quote Trap'.

Don't sign anything until you are sure that the agent, and the agent's system, cannot hurt you or damage the value of your home. Remember, once you sign up with an agent, especially the wrong agent, everything changes. The agent has got the listing. This means the agent has got you.

The Selling Agreement

Most homesellers are too trusting. They have no idea what can happen when they sign a typical selling agreement. They cannot get out of the agreement without heavy penalties or the threat of legal action. Most agents use selling agreements with clauses – usually in fine print – that allow agents to be paid no matter what the selling price. Agents can even get paid if a home is not sold. Thousands of sellers sign with agents under such conditions.

In Melbourne, a minister of religion received a written quote of $185,000 – $195,000 for his home. He signed a selling agreement with an agent who then told him that his home was worth much less. The minister was irate and decided to change agents. Another agent sold the home, but the first agent placed a 'charge' against the minister's home, forcing him to pay almost five thousand dollars for advertising expenses even though this agent had given a false quote and did not sell the minister's home.[3]

Three words can save you from unethical real estate agents. Don't sign anything; at least not until you have a guarantee which protects you from the Quote Trap.

The Quote Trap and Two Common Tricks

Agents are often taught to avoid mentioning a specific price when they first meet sellers. Instead, they use methods which give sellers great hope but are only designed to get them to sign the selling agreement. A common trick has always been the auction method. As you will see in Chapter Seven, thousands of homesellers lose thousands of dollars at auctions without realising it. Auctions are the worst method of selling a home.

Another trick that is becoming increasingly common is the 'bait pricing' strategy. This is where an agent will encourage you to market your home by promoting a price below the value of your home saying that it will attract more buyers. But, remember: agents who use methods to trick buyers will also use methods to trick sellers. These agents are not selectively unethical.

If your home is worth $400,000, the agent will suggest that you market it by saying, 'Buyer Inquiry Range $360,000 to $420,000'. The agent will focus on the $420,000 before you sign the selling agreement. But once you sign you will realise that the price of $360,000 is going to be much closer to your selling price. This is 'bait pricing' and it forces the price down for sellers because it attracts buyers who want to pay the lowest price they see.

Many sellers make plans based on the agent's quote. When their homes sell for less, they feel cheated. The agents will fall back on the common cliché that 'a home is only worth what the market will pay'. But markets don't lie, only agents lie. And the Quote Lie starts all the other lies in real estate.

A Tragic but Typical Case

The Quote Trap, plus an auction, plus a bait price has terrible consequences for homesellers. It's one of real estate's deadliest trifectas.

When Helen and Rodney wanted to sell their home in the Sydney suburb of Sans Souci in 2001, they called two agents. One quoted between $870,000 and $900,000. The other agent said $875,000, but maybe a lot more if they chose what he called 'the best way to sell' – an auction. Helen and Rodney signed up for auction and paid $5000 in advance for advertising expenses. The agent then advertised their home with a bait price of $750,000.[4]

Helen and Rodney saw another home for sale with the same agent. To afford it, they had to sell their home for at least $875,000. They wanted to wait until after their auction. Just in case. The agent assured them that all would be well and so, reluctantly, they agreed to buy the other home before selling their home. They signed a contract and paid a deposit. They were now legally committed to the new home. The agent was certain of making two sales. For Helen and Rodney, the only thing certain was that there was no escape from the effects of the Quote Trap.

At the auction, the bidding stopped at $803,000. The agent said there were many buyers waiting to see if the home was going to be for sale (or placed 'on the market' as agents call it). They were told to announce that the home was for sale at $803,000 and that this would 'bring out the buyers' and increase the price. With just seconds to decide, Helen and Rodney took the agent's advice. There was just one more bid of $2000 more. Their home sold for $805,000. They had been tricked.

Helen felt ill. 'The house, in the opinion of everyone, was a "steal". And steal from us is what this agent did. He took advantage of our commitment to the other home and pressured us into selling for nearly $100,000 less. We lost $20,000 of our deposit on the other home because we could no longer afford it and we had signed a contract to buy it. We lost our advertising money and we are now looking for a place to rent. It was heartbreaking. We have been robbed.'[5]

What happened to Helen and Rodney happens to thousands of sellers. They call some agents, get some quotes and sign up with the agent who quotes the highest price. The fraud of overquoting is so common that nothing short of a full independent inquiry into the real estate industry is likely to prevent sellers continuing to be hurt, both financially and emotionally, from the Quote Trap.

A long-running advertisement placed by the Real Estate Institute of New South Wales said, 'Our ethics and rules of practice guarantee your protection.' Helen wrote to the institute to ask how she could claim on this guarantee.[6] The response was, 'The Institute has no power to award compensation against its members.'[7] Helen wrote back and asked why they advertise a guarantee when there is no guarantee. The institute never replied.[8]

Helen should have demanded a written guarantee *before* she signed with the agent. If the agent had refused to give her a guarantee, Helen should have refused to sign anything.

HOW TO PROTECT YOURSELF FROM THE QUOTE TRAP

The best way to protect yourself from the Quote Trap is to have the agent sign a quotation guarantee. This is what happens when any legitimate business gives you a quotation. They give it to you in writing. They must honour their quote. The same should apply in real estate. If an agent says your home is worth a certain amount, and then sells your home below this amount, you should not have to pay the agent. If an agent will not give you a written guarantee on the price you are quoted, ask 'Why Not?'

Many agents refer to their selling agreement as a 'standard' agreement. The word 'standard' is used to make you feel safe. But the agreement you are being asked to sign is designed by the agents or their representatives – the real estate institutes. These 'standard' selling agreements are designed to protect agents not consumers. If they want you to sign their agreement under their conditions, make sure they sign your guarantee under your conditions.

> **These 'standard' selling agreements are designed to protect agents not consumers**

Honest agents will have no trouble with such a guarantee. Dishonest agents will do all they can to persuade you that you don't need a guarantee. They will say 'real estate is not an exact science' or that you 'need to be realistic'. Don't be fooled. Don't sign anything unless you have a guarantee that if the agent cannot sell your home within the price range you are quoted, the agent will receive no commission. This will sort the good agents from the bad agents. It will protect you from the real estate lie which leads to all the other real estate lies.

HOW TO DISCOVER THE VALUE OF YOUR HOME

There are three ways to discover the value of your home. The first is to use an independent valuer who has no financial interest in a real estate agency. This means the valuer will have no motive to mislead you. Valuers are legally responsible for their valuations. They have to be careful.

Some agents say that valuers are not always accurate. They will be quick to tell you a story about a mistake made by a valuer. But when it comes to the trustworthiness of an agent or a valuer about the price of your home, valuers are a much safer option. Invest in a thorough valuation. Let the valuer know why you want the valuation and make it clear that you expect the valuation to be accurate and not inflated just to please you.

The valuer will have no motive to mislead you

The second way to discover the value of your home is to research similar properties that have sold in your area. This is something valuers will do, but it is also something you can do on your own. Real estate agents refer to this as doing a 'Comparative Market Analysis'. However, be warned: many properties are *undersold* (as you will see in later chapters), so be careful you do not compare the price of your home with homes that have been undersold. And be careful comparing your home with homes that are for sale but not yet sold. Asking prices and selling prices can be very different. Treat a valuation and a comparative market analysis as a guide – often a conservative guide.

The third and best way to discover the true market value of your home is to employ an agent who is a skilled negotiator. In Chapter Five you will see how to get the best market price for your home. Don't sign anything unless you are certain that the agent is capable of getting you the best market price. Almost all methods used by agents are designed to get your home sold at *any* price. Unless you know what is meant by 'best market value', and how to get it, you risk selling your home for thousands of dollars below its best market value.

WHAT IS MARKET VALUE?

The common real estate definition of market value is 'the best price a buyer will pay'. But typical real estate systems are not based on discovering the best price buyers will pay, they are based on the lowest price sellers will accept. The difference between these two 'values' can be huge.

Most agents want to know the lowest price the sellers will accept. This price then becomes the highest the sellers ever receive. For example, let's say a home is for sale for $500,000. The buyers make an offer of $450,000. The sellers refuse and say they won't take less than $475,000. The sellers have now revealed their lowest price. But the buyers have not revealed their highest price.

As a seller you must never reveal your lowest price. If you do, this price will become the highest you get. Thousands of homesellers get caught in this trap. Just ask any buyers what they paid for a home and then ask them how much they would have paid. Most would have paid more. When asked why they didn't pay more, they will say the agent did not ask for more. It's incredible that agents, who are employed by sellers to get the best market price, rarely discover what they themselves define as market value – the highest the buyers will pay.

Agents have one focus after they get the listing – get the sale. And the simplest way to get a sale is to discover the sellers' lowest price. The most common example is auctions. At an auction the sellers' lowest price is always known before a property is sold. But the buyers' highest price is seldom known. The highest bid made by buyers at auctions is rarely the highest they were prepared to pay.

Thousands of sellers are fooled into believing that auctions get higher prices. But big ticket items – such as homes and highly valuable merchandise, rarely get the best price at auction. Sure, they can get a high price, but there is a big difference between a high price and the best price, as the following story shows.

In 1999, Marilyn Monroe's dress was auctioned in New York.[9] This was the dress in which she sang 'Happy Birthday' to President Kennedy in Madison Square Garden in New York in 1962. It was expected to sell for 'about $500,000'. It sold for $1.15 million.[10]

Those who don't understand auctions thought the auction was responsible for the great price. But buyers do not buy because of an auction, especially with big ticket items; they buy because they want what is being sold. In this case, the buyers for Marilyn Monroe's dress were prepared to pay $3 million. 'We got the bargain of the century,' said one of the buyers. 'We stole it,' laughed his partner." This is a perfect example of how auctions get lower prices. The owner of Marilyn's dress missed out on almost two million dollars.

Many agents and most sellers do not understand what is meant by 'market value'. Is it the sellers' lowest price or the buyers' highest price? If you are selling, you want the buyers' highest price. And that should be your only definition of market value.

If you are selling your home, it is vital that you understand and avoid the tricks and traps of the typical methods which get you a lower market price. Until then, don't sign anything.

PROTECTING YOURSELF FROM FALSE QUOTES

Homesellers should insist that an agent is responsible for the quote given to them when they sign the selling agreement. As a seller, you should say, 'If you sell my home for less than the price you are quoting me, you will not be paid.' These words should be written down and the agent should sign them *before* you sign the agent's agreement. If the agent refuses to sign, don't sign anything with that agent.

Sure, no one can know exactly, to the precise dollar, what any home will sell for; but the agent can give you a price range, from a low point to a high point, and if your home sells below the lowest point of the price range, the agent should not be paid. Honest agents will agree to this condition. If not, don't sign anything, no matter how much pressure is placed upon you.

Sellers who believe the false quotes given to them by the agents – and then sign up with the agents – are placing themselves in grave danger. They are caught in the Quote Trap. They have signed a legal agreement with the agent. And now, before their homes are sold, they must endure a real estate method called 'conditioning'.

Summary

- The agent who tells the biggest lie when quoting the likely selling price is often chosen to sell the home.

- Overquoting a selling price to a home-owner, in order to be chosen as the agent, is known as 'buying the listing'. In reality, it's fraud.

- Because the beginning of the sales process depends on a lie, the entire process becomes full of lies. More lies are needed to cover up the first lie.

- Many victims don't realise how they are caught. The best con artists seem very plausible.

- One of the most common tricks is to claim that a home is 'only worth what the market will pay'.

- An agent should know the market prices.

- The Quote Lie catches thousands of sellers in the Quote Trap.

- Once sellers sign up with an agent, everything changes. No matter what price a home sells for, the agent still wants to be paid.

- Most sellers do not realise that they cannot get out of the selling agreement without costs or legal action.

- As a seller, you should say, 'If you sell my home for less than you are quoting me, you will not be paid.'

- If an agent won't give you a written guarantee on the price quoted, ask 'Why Not?'

- **Don't sign anything** unless you get a guarantee on the quoted price. Honest agents will give such a guarantee.

Chapter Three

Conditioning

How the Quote Trap leads to a series of lies

Falsus in uno, falsus in omnibus.
(Untrue in one thing, untrue in everything.)

Crocodiles can't chew. They drag their victims underwater until they drown. And then they take them to their den where they leave them to rot until they can break off pieces and swallow them more easily.[1] This 'softening up' process is the nature of crocodiles. And real estate agents.

Agents can't tell you the truth about the price of your home, otherwise they'd never catch you. And so they sign you up on their selling agreements by promising you a high price. You are trapped in their den where they 'condition' you until you are ready to sell at a lower price.

DEFINING CONDITIONING

After the Quote Lie comes the conditioning which has one purpose: *to convince sellers to lower their prices* to the point at which their homes can be easily sold. Many sellers never realise what happens. They don't know that almost every strategy suggested by the agent is done to cover up the lie of the false quote.

The purpose of any lie is to hide the truth. When the selling process starts with a lie, more lies are needed to cover up the first lie. Soon, the whole process involves an intricate system of lies. In the world of modern real estate selling, lies are well-woven into the system. And conditioning is a huge part of the system.

THE CONDITIONING STAGES

There are two stages to the conditioning process. The first is Activity conditioning where the agents do, or appear to do, lots of work. The 'activity stage' can last for several weeks, sometimes months. It depends on your resistance or how urgently you need to sell.

You may think all this activity is to sell your home, however, its sole purpose is to soften you up for the second stage of the conditioning process – Crunch conditioning. Intense pressure is used to get you to accept a lower price. The crunch occurs when you are desperate to be rid of the pain of conditioning. If you are not ready, the agents have a number of high pressure tactics to make you see reason or, as they often call it, be 'realistic'.

Activity Conditioning

The agent will commence a 'campaign' – advertising, lots of inspections – all aimed at getting lots of people to see your home. It's called 'exposure'. And it seems so sensible. But it's just part of the conditioning process, designed to soften you up for the 'crunch'.

Activity conditioning damages the value of your home and is one of the major reasons why homes sell for thousands of dollars below their best market value. Of all the traps in real estate, activity conditioning is probably the least understood by homesellers. It is widely used because it seems to be a logical part of the selling process. It allows agents to disguise the Quote Lie by shifting the blame to something called 'the market'.

THE MARKET MYTHS

To hear agents talking about 'the market', it almost seems as if they are discussing another person. Early in the sales process, perhaps even before you have signed up, agents will talk about 'the market'. Their conversation will go something like this: 'It depends on what the market says', or 'No one knows, for sure, how the market will respond', or 'We need to give your home lots of exposure to the market', or 'Once we take your home to the market, we'll see what the market tells us'. The agents will promise to tell you 'what the market is saying'. This is one promise they always keep.

Once you have signed up with an agent, your home is 'on the market'. Those crocodile jaws are locked on to your home. And the conditioning begins. At first it's so subtle you barely notice. The agent will tell you about the 'marketing campaign': where and when your home will be advertised so that you don't miss it; other salespeople from the office may inspect your home; the photos will go in the agency window; the open inspection dates will be set; some buyers may come through (people who have been 'in the market' for a while). All looks promising. Your hopes will be high.

It won't be long before you begin to receive 'market feedback'. That's when you start to realise that things aren't as good as you expected (some agents refer to conditioning as 'managing the owners' expectations'). In the early stages the agent will calm your fears by saying that this activity is 'part of the plan'. You may be told that 'it's only early days yet'. The market feedback will go something like this, 'There were some positive inspections and we are waiting to hear back from a few people.' Nothing. You are told not to worry – there are 'more ads booked' and 'more inspections lined up'.

And then comes more feedback – not quite as positive this time. It depends on what the agents feel you can handle; your anxiety level is a big factor. In the early stages the feedback will focus on your home. 'The buyers don't like the position', or 'They want a bigger block', or 'They need more space inside', or 'It's too far from the station'. The worst feature of your home is the one you get most feedback about. Your anxiety level will increase. If you ask the agent why there is no mention of your home's good features, you could get any of a dozen standard answers, the most common of which is, 'I'm just telling you what the market is saying.'

The agents are shifting the blame to the buyers – the 'market'. And you can't blame the agents for what the market is saying can you? Yes you can, because if the buyers are not buying your home it probably means the price is too high. And the reason the price is too high is because the agent told you at the time you signed up that you could expect a high price. The agent will begin to remind you about 'the market'. 'Yes, of course, I want you to get a good price. And we still might. There's plenty of time. I am just letting you know what the market is saying, just like I told you I would.' You may feel you are being unreasonable and that perhaps you should, after all, leave it to the agent. This is a big mistake. From this point onwards, things only get worse.

About three weeks after your home has been on the market, you will start to receive the next stage of market feedback. The focus will shift from your home's features to your home's price. It doesn't matter what method of sale you are using, the conditioning to lower the price will be similar. It is all based on 'what the market is saying'. And it comes straight from the real estate training courses where agents learn excuses such as: 'The buyers think it's overpriced based on what they have seen', or 'They bought something else which was a bit cheaper', or 'The buyers are indicating it is worth $X'. And this is where you will often receive what some agents call the 'kick in the guts' or the 'belt around the head' – an absurdly low offer. Of course, the agents, being quick to show they are 'on your side' will tell you to 'reject this offer'. They will agree that such a low price is ridiculous.

It is easy to find buyers who offer low prices, and agents are bound by law to pass on all offers to a homeseller. To pass on an offer that is absurdly low is just another opportunity to condition you. It's all part of the system. The agent tells the lies, the market tells the truth. To the agents, it's beautiful.

They are in the clear. To the sellers, it's a disaster. They are in the jaws of the crocodiles.

At this point, many sellers agree to reduce their price. Often it's too late – the damage has been done. The buyers are beginning to wonder why the home hasn't sold. The sellers, too, are thinking the same: 'Something is wrong with the house'. But no, there is rarely anything wrong with the house, there is just something seriously wrong with the way it is being marketed. Many sellers, even many agents, do not understand how to market a home. One of the essential laws of marketing is to protect the value of the product being sold. Even the agents who genuinely want to do the right thing fall for the myths of real estate marketing. They use the market in the wrong way and in doing so they damage the value of their clients' homes, wiping thousands of dollars from the final selling prices.

'SOPHISTICATED' CONDITIONING

Few homesellers understand just how sophisticated modern real estate conditioning has become. This is why so many sellers are caught. Methods that were once part of the legitimate selling process have been manipulated to such an extent that they are now used against sellers rather than to sell the house.

If you think that conditioning simply means giving you bad news about your home to persuade you to lower your price, think again. The bad news is only part of the process. Conditioning has become so clever that many sellers thank the agents for their 'efforts'. These sellers never realise they have undersold their homes by thousands of dollars.

Please realise this: if your home sells for less than the agent quoted you, it does not matter how much effort the agent appears to have made, *you have sold for less than you were quoted*. Whether you are happy with the outcome or not, you have been conditioned to accept a lower price.

THE STRESS OF CONDITIONING

Thousands of homesellers feel that dreadful disappointment as the agent creates more and more activity and brings more and more bad news. The more activity, the more convinced you are that your home is too highly priced. And the more likely you are to 'crack' and reduce your price when the crunch comes. The crunch is a nightmare for sellers. No matter how tough you are, the steadily increasing pressure of having a home for sale is hard to withstand. It's like a vice tightening on your mind. The pressure builds to the point where you will feel like screaming, 'Enough'. As *Money Magazine* once reported, conditioning can reduce the toughest homeseller to 'a blubbering jelly'.[2]

When you understand what is happening you will know how to avoid the pressure of conditioning altogether. And, best of all, you will know how to get the best market price for your home without damaging its value.

THE REALITY OF CONDITIONING

Agents often tell sellers, 'You need to be realistic.' But the reality is that these sellers have been duped: duped into signing a selling agreement with an agent who lied about the quoted selling price; duped into believing that all the activity was to help sell their homes, when in reality it was to condition them to accept a lower price; and, finally, these sellers must pay a commission regardless of the price or the level of service they have received. Agents get paid no matter how much a home sells for and no matter how much financial and emotional pain is inflicted on sellers. It's not pleasant, but it is reality.

PROTECTION AGAINST CONDITIONING

As a homeseller you can never be totally sure whether or not you are going to be conditioned by an agent – but you can protect yourself. Don't sign anything until the agent gives you a guarantee that you will not be conditioned.

There are two classic signs of conditioning. The first is when the agent praises your home and mentions its good features before you sign; and then, after you sign, the agent criticises your home and points out its bad features. The second is when the price the agent quotes you becomes less after you sign. In both cases, you should have the right to dismiss the agent. No matter how tough it may be to ask for a guarantee against conditioning, it is not as tough as being stuck with an agent who is conditioning you to lower the price. It is your home, you probably worked hard to buy it, you should work just as hard to protect its value. Don't sign anything unless you are protected from conditioning.

CONDITIONING TIME

Many sellers are shocked to discover that they are legally committed to stay with an agent they don't like. Even if an agent has lied or given you dreadful service, it doesn't matter – once you have signed you are 'locked-in' to that agent for the time period of the selling agency agreement. The 'standard' time is between 90 and 120 days. Some agents may try to sign you up for longer. The longer the time, the more time the agent has to condition you. Agents refer to this as 'tying up' the homesellers.

It is also referred to as 'controlling the listings' because the agent now has control over a large aspect of your financial life. A Real Estate Institute of Australia publication informs agents how to 'condition' sellers once they are 'controlled'. It says, 'Don't be afraid to tell vendors under a controlled listing that their property is overpriced.'[3] Once agents have a 'controlled' listing, they can tell the sellers anything, because the sellers can't escape. This is why they are known as 'controlled'. They cannot sell their homes without paying the agent, no matter what the agent tells them.

The time period of an agent's agreement can cause enormous harm to sellers. The agent can give you a false quote, sign you up for a long period and then just wait for you to crack and sell at a lower price. The longer the time, the longer the agent has to condition you.

This trap has caught so many sellers that legislation has been introduced in Queensland which sets the maximum period of an agent's agreement at 60 days. This legislation was passed despite the protests of agents who are now denied a basic ingredient of conditioning – plenty of time.

Don't sign anything that ties you to an agent for more than 49 days. This is ample time to find a buyer for most homes. The longer a home is on the market for sale, the less chance there is of getting the best price for it.

If the agent won't agree to accept a maximum seven-week contract, don't sign anything. Find another agent.

Conditioning is not Necessary

If there was more honesty in real estate, there would be no need for conditioning. If homesellers obtained an independent valuation before signing with an agent, they would have a better idea of the value of their home. They would know which agents were using the false-quote trap to win their business. In these cases, the sellers would not only avoid the Quote Trap, they would also avoid the conditioning used to cover up the lie of the Quote Trap.

The correct way to sell a home is to find an agent who will not 'buy the listing' by overquoting the price. You should speak with several agents. Tell these agents that you will not punish them for telling you the truth about the likely price. You don't want the biggest liar. You want the truth.

Let the agents know, in advance, that you require a written guarantee on several points that will protect you from the typical lies, tricks and traps of real estate. It is no good asking agents not to lie to you – you have to make it hard for them to lie. You have to make sure that only the agents who tell you the truth can sell your home. Until this happens, don't sign anything with any agent, no matter what they tell you. Real estate is not just a big financial event, it is also one of the most emotional events of any person's life. Take the time to get it right before you choose an agent.

The Emotional Impact of Conditioning

No one is immune from the impact of conditioning, but those who are most vulnerable are often the elderly who seem more willing to trust agents. These people can have their lives shattered by the typical real estate sales process. Imagine the trauma when you are told your home is worth $420,000 and you are then conditioned over several weeks to accept $355,000.

These figures describe what happened to one couple when they decided to sell their home in the Melbourne suburb of Camberwell. They fell victim to almost all the conditioning methods you will read about in the following chapters: expensive advertising campaigns, auction, open inspections, bait pricing to attract buyers at a lower price, negative feedback, pressure from the agent to be 'realistic' about their price. The husband died soon after the home was sold. His wife was described as being 'venomous' with the agent and 'beside herself with grief'. Her words left no doubt about her feelings: 'It was an incredibly distressing experience and I will never auction again as long as I live.'[4]

An 88-year-old man was described by his daughter as being 'shattered and destroyed' after the auction of his home in the Sydney suburb of West Ryde.[5] A few weeks later the agent distributed a newsletter saying that 'consumers can have complete confidence in the auction process' and that they 'shouldn't be influenced by the overly emotive media reports'.[6] Like many agents, he did not understand (or did not care) how typical real estate systems hurt consumers.

Sure, typical systems sell real estate, but the damage in social cost to the community is something few agents consider. Consumers have little protection from the excuses given by agents to justify typical real estate systems. But when it comes to protecting their right to the commission, many agents are ruthless. They will not hesitate to take legal action against consumers.

The reported case of a World War II veteran and invalid pensioner is a classic example of what happens to many homesellers. When his first agent did not sell his home in Cairns, he signed with a second agent. His home was sold and he moved to a retirement home at the Gold Coast. A few weeks later he received a letter from the first agent demanding $5500 in commission. He protested that he had already paid this first agent several hundred dollars for a failed auction. It didn't matter. He had signed a 'standard' agreement and because the buyer of the home had seen the home with both agents, he had to pay both agents. He paid two commissions for selling one home.[7] Both agents were members of the Real Estate Institute of Queensland.[8] As you will see, one of the biggest traps is to believe that dealing with a member of a Real Estate Institute means you are protected.

In the absence of adequate consumer protection laws, your best protection is this: don't sign anything until the agent gives you a guarantee that you will be protected.

Summary

- Conditioning is done to convince sellers to lower their prices so that their homes can be sold more easily.
- There are two stages to conditioning: Activity conditioning and Crunch conditioning.
- Activity conditioning damages the value of homes causing them to sell below their best market value.
- Conditioning allows agents to disguise the Quote Lie by shifting the blame to 'the market'.
- Conditioning is part of the game. The agent tells the lies, 'the market' tells the truth. To the agents, they are in the clear. To the sellers, it's an emotional and financial disaster.
- An essential law of marketing is to *protect the value* of the product being sold. Activity conditioning ignores this law and damages the product – your home.
- Thousands of sellers feel dreadful disappointment as the agent brings more and more bad news.

- There are two signs of conditioning. The first is when an agent praises your home before you sign, and then, after you sign, the agent criticises your home. The second is when the price the agent quotes becomes less after you sign. In both cases, you should have the right to dismiss the agent.

- The time period of an agreement is critical. The longer the time, the more the agent can condition you.

- The longer a home is for sale, the less chance there is of getting the best price for it.

- **Don't sign anything** that binds you to an agent for more than seven weeks.

- If an agent won't agree to a seven-week period, **don't sign anything.** Find another agent.

Chapter Four

Protecting the Value of Your Home ...

before it's sold

In the old days, the most quoted maxim
in real estate was 'caveat emptor',
Latin for, 'Let the buyer beware'.
Today, that's all changed.
Today's slogan should read, 'Let the seller beware'.

Robert Irwin, Tips & Traps When Selling a Home

Your home is special. It is one of a kind. It is not a mass-produced product such as a car with thousands of identical models for sale. Even if your home is similar to others, it still has a feel to it – something special which sets it apart from other homes. And that's how you should market it: *as something special,* not as something that everyone else has rejected. Once you understand the importance of your home being seen as special, you will understand how to protect its value. To do this, you have to understand how typical real estate marketing – with its large conditioning component – damages the value of your home.

The Damage of Activity Marketing

As you have seen, the main way that agents convince sellers to reduce their prices is by creating lots of activity. Lots of people see (or hear about) your home. If no one buys it, the agent blames the market, you lower your price and the agent makes a sale. Your home sells below its best market value and you lose thousands of dollars. The reason you lose is because the marketing activity damages the value of your home and causes buyers to either reject it or to pay less for it. Because you have only one home to sell, you can only have one buyer for it. Agents who tell you that they will get 'more buyers interested' are using a clever trick. They say that the more buyers who are interested, the more money you will get. It sounds so logical. And it would be if all the buyers who saw your home (or heard about it) *wanted* to buy it. But most of the people who see your home will not want to buy it. Most of them won't even be buyers. By creating lots of activity, the agent will tell you that your home has been 'exposed'. But exposure to the wrong people does not sell your home, it damages the value of your home, because, and remember this as it's one of the most important points when selling a home: the more people who hear about your home, and the longer the time, the harder it is to get the best price.

The Right Buyers

The only buyers you want are the ones who will pay you the best market value. These buyers must feel that your home is special, not a home that they perceive as rejected by hundreds of other buyers. If the right buyers think there is something wrong with your home, there is only one way to entice them: a lower price.

You only need one buyer for your home. And the right buyer will be the one who 'loves' your home. When buyers love a home they pay the best prices. Buyers love homes that are special and unique. They rarely love rejects.

In every area, there are a limited number of genuine buyers at any one time. Depending on the size of the area, the variety of homes in the area, or the economic climate, there is usually only a handful of buyers suited to your home. Oh sure, there will be plenty of buyers 'if the price is right' – but that means the right price for them, not for you. Bargain-hunters are not the buyers you want. You want buyers who love your home or, at the least, like it enough to pay the best market price for it.

STALE HOMES

When a home has massive exposure to the market, it quickly becomes stale. There is a saying used by many agents, 'You can't keep it a secret.' But your home should never be exposed to hundreds or even thousands of people who do *not* want to buy it.

Real Estate Institute training courses teach agents how to 'sell' the benefits of exposure to homesellers. But the truth is evident with this statement from an institute text book, 'An advertisement repeated week after week elicits questions about what is wrong with the property.'[1]

One of the first questions buyers ask is, 'How long has this home been for sale?' The next question is, 'Why hasn't it sold?' Even if they love the home, they will rarely want to pay a high price if they think it has been rejected by other buyers. As a seller, this puts you in a position of weakness. It's not the *quantity* of buyers you want, it's the *quality.* Quantity gets you a lower price. Quality gets you a higher price. Insist on quality.

QUALITY MEANS QUALIFIED

People who are not in a position to buy your home cannot be called buyers. At best, they are 'lookers'. And lookers are not buyers, at least not for your home. Lookers are often 'knockers'. They find fault with your home. They are the people from whom the agents get the negative 'feedback' to pass on to you. You should not let these people near your home. They should not even know that your home is for sale.

An agent who understands marketing will protect the

value of your home by only bringing it to the attention of buyers who are likely to buy it. The agent won't go to the market and yell out, 'Hey, look at this home I have for sale, it's beautiful, it's great value, you'll love it,' because next week, if your home is not sold, it will no longer be seen as special. It will be stale.

The best agents will attract the buyers to the agency or, as you will see, the best agents keep careful track of buyers in the area, and will 'qualify' those buyers. The agent will ask the buyers to describe the home they are looking for. If their description matches your home, the agent will bring them to see it. If the agent has properly qualified the buyers, they will like your home. And then, if the agent is a competent negotiator, you will get the best market price.

Compare this with what typically happens. The agent arranges a public 'open for inspection' where there are dozens of 'lookers' at the home. Among these lookers, there may be some genuine buyers. Later, the agent calls the genuine buyers to see if they are interested. This creates the impression that no one else is interested. After all, the buyers saw other 'buyers' inspecting the home – why weren't they interested and why hasn't it sold? The buyers have probably seen advertisements for the home – perhaps for several weeks. And now the agent is chasing them to see if they are interested. The message is clear: no one else wants the home.

One lady, who was looking to buy a home in the Dandenong area of Victoria, said what many buyers think, 'The more they advertise them, the less interested I become.'[2] The only people who should see or hear about your home are those who are likely to buy it, no one else. You need as many 'qualified' buyers as possible. You do not need useless activity. Thousands of sellers get lower prices because of the twin marketing mistakes of too much time and too much exposure. When added to the poor negotiation skills of most agents, it's a recipe for complete disaster, as the following case proves.

The sellers wanted $690,000 for their home. Its true market value was around $500,000. Nevertheless, it was widely advertised. Nothing happened. After several months, with no genuine buyers, the sellers were worried. They reduced the price to its real value, but all the activity had damaged the value and it was becoming known as the 'local lemon'. No one seemed interested. Finally, a buyer made an offer of just $390,000. The sellers refused. They were 'not that desperate'. But more time passed and still no one was interested. The sellers were now really desperate. And then another buyer offered $360,000. The sellers accepted. Incredibly, the buyer who offered $390,000 (and who was still interested) was not contacted by the agent before the home was sold for $360,000.[3] Constant exposure combined with incompetence led to a disaster for these sellers. The buyers got a bargain.

And that's the way it is – bad marketing and incompetent negotiation damages the value of a home.

BACK AT THE OFFICE

Agents know that most sellers want to 'see something happening' before they will agree to drop their prices. And many sellers walk straight into the activity trap by demanding that agents 'do something'.

Real estate salespeople often beg each other to 'take someone through' various homes so that the owners can be persuaded to lower their prices. This explains why many buyers are shown homes that are completely different from what they asked to see. The agents need inspections so they can say to the sellers, 'We have shown it to lots of people and no one's buying it. You have to lower the price.' Meanwhile the longer a home remains unsold the worse it looks. The price gets lower. As stated, this is why agents like long time periods on their selling agreements because it gives them time to condition the sellers. And this is why sellers should remember this – don't sign any selling agreement that lasts more than seven weeks.

A real estate salesperson in Victoria resigned from one

agency after being told to mislead sellers about the number of inspections at 'open houses'. At the agency's sales meeting, the subject of seller feedback was being discussed. No one had come through one of the homes open for inspection at the weekend. The salesperson told the owners what had happened. Her sales manager was irate. 'Never tell the sellers that no one came through,' he said.[4]

In New South Wales, an agent teaching a real estate course was asked, 'What happens if we don't get any inspections?' He was reported to have said, 'Just get names out of the phone book.'[5] As far back as 1986, another real estate teacher had taught, 'your mother's maiden name or the name of the receptionist will do'.[6]

One homeseller who has sold several times said, 'I have lost so much money through ignorance that I shudder to think about it. It happens just like you say.' On his last move, when he was transferred interstate, his wife, who had stayed behind to sell their home, was being pressured by the agents. She was in tears. When their selling agreement was close to expiring, the agent used a common ploy – taking stooges through the home. The seller explained: 'As the agent left with this so-called woman buyer, my wife heard them joking. The woman said to the agent, "Well, how was that? Was I convincing enough for you?" The agent later rang to tell me that the "buyer" wasn't interested. Is there nothing that these people will not stoop to?'[7]

Some agents engage in what's known as 'card bombing'. They visit your home, with or without a buyer (or a looker), when you are not home. They leave their own business card plus the cards of other salespeople to create the impression that buyers have inspected your home.

At sales meetings, agents discuss which properties 'need' to be advertised. Agents know that the more they advertise a home, the easier it is to get the sellers to reduce the prices. They must create the impression that they are 'doing something'. And they are; they are making the homes stale, while charging homesellers for advertising which promotes the agent.

Homes which sell for the best prices are like the best paying jobs – they are rarely advertised.

Don't sign anything to sell your home until you understand how typical real estate advertising gets lower prices (see Chapter Six).

THE SAD TRUTH ABOUT LIES

For many sellers, it is heartbreaking to discover that their homes are worth less than they expected. They feel cheated. A common reaction is, 'Why didn't the agent just tell me, in the beginning, what my home was really worth?' But if the agents told the truth they may not have been chosen as the agent. Sadly, the biggest liars often win the business. As marketing expert Roy Williams explains, 'The honest business people of yesterday assumed all they had to do was tell the truth. The result, all too often, was a dramatic loss of business to deceitful competitors. With their family's future on the line, the reluctant response of honest business people was often to fight fire with fire.'[8]

Williams points out that it is not enough to tell the truth. It's more than that – consumers have to 'realise the truth'. Or, to quote one agent, 'It would save sellers a lot of money if the agents who lied to get them to sign up, called the sellers when they got back to their office and admitted they'd lied.'[9] Something like, 'Look, I know I said you'd get $500,000 but the truth is you're going to be lucky to get $450,000.'

So long as agents get away with telling lies to catch homesellers and then use 'the market' to cover up their lies, they will continue to tell lies to make sales. Lying is an integral part of real estate sales.

THE QUICK SALE IS OFTEN THE BEST

Most homes do not need a long time to sell. The number of genuine buyers for any home will almost always be greatest when a home is first placed for sale. The home will be fresh, it will be special, and there will be several buyers who are already looking in the area. If these buyers see the home – and if they do not buy it – the sellers could be in for a long wait until new buyers come into the area.

If your home does not sell in the first 30 days, even in the first 14 days, it may take months to sell. The best price often comes in the first few days that the home is for sale. But this is when many sellers make a critical error – they reject an offer the likes of which they may never see again. All this assumes, of course, that the sellers know the true value of their home.

Many sellers think a quick sale means their home is too cheap; they think that if they get a good price early, they will get a better price later. But this rarely happens. The best price usually comes early. If it's what you want and your agent is competent and has a list of the genuine buyers who are looking in the area, and these buyers have been contacted about your home, often the best advice is to take the best offer, before your home becomes stale.

Many times, especially with auctions, buyers make an early offer on a home. The offer is refused and then later they buy the same home at a lower price. The longer your home is exposed, the weaker your negotiating position becomes.

Agents are often scared by early offers. It creates the impression that they have not 'done enough'. But agents are paid to get the highest market value, not to take the longest amount of time to do it. A member of a government board which hears disputes about agents' commissions tells the following story.

A home was sold in two days. The sellers objected to the agent being paid his full commission.

'Were you happy with the price?' the seller was asked.

'Very happy,' came the reply.

'Did the agent tell you, before you hired the agent, how much commission you'd have to pay if your home was sold?'

'Yes, but what we're objecting to is paying all this money for two days work. It's not fair.'

A board member said, 'You are asking us to punish this agent for being efficient.'

The matter was dismissed.[10]

When you hire an agent, you should expect that the agent will have a number of buyers who are known to the agent. Efficient agents keep in regular contact with buyers. If you hire an agent who already has a buyer at a great price, you are fortunate. You will save yourself time as well as money. And you will avoid the pain of weeks of useless activity and conditioning, all of which can get you a lower price. The commission you pay for a quick sale can be great value.

TWO VALUES FOR YOUR HOME

One thing cannot be overstated: there are two market values for your home. First, the lowest price you will accept and, second, the highest price a buyer will pay. These two values can be thousands of dollars apart.

Anyone can find a buyer for your home if the price is low enough. But it takes great skill in both marketing and negotiation to get the best market price. Anything less means you lose. It doesn't matter whether or not you accept the price, if you sell below the best market value, you have lost money.

Don't sign anything to sell your home until you know how to sell for the best market value.

Summary

- When your home is considered special, its value is enhanced. You must protect the value of your home.

- Overexposure can quickly damage your home's value. The more people who hear about it and the more time that passes, the harder it becomes to get the best price.

- When buyers love a home they pay the best price. Buyers love homes that are special, not homes that have been rejected by other buyers.

- To protect the value of your home, remember it's not the *quantity* of buyers who see it, it's the *quality*. Quantity gets you a lower price. Quality gets you a higher price.

- There are *two* market prices for a home: the lowest a seller will accept or the highest a buyer will pay. These two prices can be thousands of dollars apart.

- The value of homes is damaged because of the twin marketing mistakes of too much time and too much exposure. Added to the poor negotiation skills of most agents, it's a recipe for financial disaster.

- If the agent is a competent negotiator, sellers will get the best market price.

- The number of genuine buyers is usually higher when a home is first placed for sale. The home will be fresh, it will be special, and there will be several genuine buyers who are already looking in the area.

- If a home does not sell in the first 30 days, it may take months to sell. The longer it takes to sell, the greater the risk of damage to its value.

- As a seller, do not focus on the lowest you will accept. Focus on the highest a buyer will pay.

- **Don't sign anything** to sell your home unless you are sure that its value is protected.

Chapter Five

Selling Your Home for the BEST Market Value

*The agent said $440,000 was the highest we could get.
And so we sold. A few weeks later,
we discovered that the people who bought our home
would have willingly paid $480,000.*

*It will take five years to save
what we lost in five minutes.*

Peter & Leanne Dawson, Moonee Ponds, 2002

Thousands of homesellers undersell their homes. They don't do it on purpose, they just don't know how to protect the value of their homes. Many sellers never realise how much they lose. It's as if they move out of their homes and, unknowingly, leave behind a suitcase full of cash.

THE VALUE OF YOUR HOME

The best market value of your home is the highest price a buyer is prepared to pay for it. The problem for you is that most buyers pay *less* than they were prepared to pay. Your loss is the difference between the amount the buyers paid for your home and the amount they were prepared to pay. Those three words – *prepared to pay* – are critical words. Remember them, and don't sign anything until you are sure you have received the best market price.

Think about when you bought your home. Would you have paid more? What if you were going to lose it unless you did pay more? How much more would you have paid? When you have answered these questions, ask yourself one more question. If you had been asked to pay just *another* thousand dollars, would you have done so? Try these questions on other home-owners, your friends or family, and you'll see that most sellers undersell their homes. If you ask another question, 'Why didn't you pay more?', the answers will make you realise just how incompetent most agents are at negotiating the best price for sellers.

One of the most dangerous traps is the question, 'What will you take?' Most sellers fall into the trap and say, 'We won't take less than $X,' (whatever is their lowest price). The first rule for protecting the value of your home is *never tell anyone your lowest price*. Don't think you can avoid this trap by increasing the amount of your lowest price. Some sellers add on a few thousand dollars expecting that agents (and buyers) will attempt to knock them down on price. But this still misses the major point: as the seller, you have to *discover the buyers' highest price*. Your lowest price is nobody's business but your own.

THE ART OF NEGOTIATION

Most agents are dreadful negotiators. If they weren't, they could not possibly make such blunders which damage the value of their clients' homes. Agents usually focus on one thing – making sales. To the agents, the sales come first. The price, *any price,* comes second. And most sales are made when sellers reveal their lowest price. 'That's as low as I can get it for you,' is a common statement made by agents to buyers. Or worse, agents will encourage buyers to make offers well below what the buyers were willing to pay. The agents then go to the sellers and say, 'We've got this great offer. You should take it.' And sometimes it *is* a great offer. Sometimes it is more than the seller's lowest price. But the *big* question is rarely asked: Is it the most the buyers are prepared to pay? And, if so, how do you know? How can you be sure that the price you are offered for your home is the highest the buyers will pay?

THE 'WALK AWAY' PRICE

A common system of buying and selling real estate works like this. The sellers set an asking price and the buyers make an offer. If the sellers reject the offer, the buyers increase their offer. And on it goes. This process of going back and forth is known as 'counter-offers'. It stops when one of two things happens. First, the sellers and the buyers agree. However the sellers still don't know if the buyers would have paid more. There is a lot of bluffing in real estate. Or, second, the buyers walk away. This almost certainly means they offered their highest price – or they just got fed-up. The trouble is they have now gone, perhaps for good. When negotiating, nothing looks worse than having to chase buyers. If you appear desperate you get a lower price.

As a seller your aim is to discover the buyers' highest price without losing the sale. But the more you go back and forth in the counter-offers game, the more you risk either selling too low or losing the buyers. What you have to do, therefore, is discover the price at which the buyers are prepared to walk away. And you have to do this before they walk away. This is done by refusing to consider any price until the *buyers declare in writing* that the price they are offering is indeed the highest they will pay. Here's how you do it.

THE BUYERS' PRICE DECLARATION

When buyers are interested in buying your home, instead of revealing your lowest price, your agent asks the buyers to reveal *their* highest price. This is done by politely asking the buyers to sign a Buyers' Price Declaration which says the price they are offering is the highest they will pay, and, if their price is *not* acceptable to you, they will not require you to notify them should you decide to sell to another buyer who offers a higher price.

This does not normally happen in real estate which is why homesellers lose thousands of dollars. As mentioned, the typical focus is on the seller's lowest price. For example, at auctions, sellers reveal their lowest price – the 'reserve price'. A competent negotiator knows that such a strategy is madness. As a seller, if you have to reveal your lowest price and the buyers never have to reveal their highest price, it is virtually impossible for you to get the best market price. The Buyers' Price Declaration makes it the right way around. It could be called a 'Buyers' Reserve'.

It's simple. If the buyers don't want to reveal their highest price, you know that any offer they make is not their best. If this happens, you would be silly to accept. The buyers will realise this. They will also realise there is little point in bluffing; they either make their best offer – their walk-away price – or you do not consider their offer. If they really do want to buy your home, they will reveal their highest price rather than risk losing the home.

Most genuine buyers are happy to avoid haggling. When they find a home they love at a price they can afford they want to buy it. They don't want to play games, they just want to buy the home they love.

THE RIGHT HOME IS MOST IMPORTANT

The most important factor to homebuyers is finding the right home. If buyers love a home, most will pay the highest they can afford to pay. Of course, they want to buy as cheaply as possible and if given the chance to do so, no one can blame them for paying less. But homebuyers – especially those buying a family home – place far more importance on buying the right home than on buying a bargain. They all have a maximum price they can afford. You are not asking them to pay more than they can afford; but you are making sure that your home is not sold to someone who would have paid more for it. You are protecting the value of your home by making sure you get the true market value – *the highest any buyer is prepared to pay.*

BEHIND THE SCENES

Most agents know that homes are often sold for less than their best price. The Real Estate Institute of Victoria had a course topic on what to say to sellers who discover that their homes had been undersold.[1] More effort goes into covering up the damage done to the value of homes than fixing the systems that cause the damage.

With so many systems and methods that damage the value of homes, it is easy for buyers to buy properties for lower prices. This is evidenced by the growth in agents who act for buyers (buyers' advocates). These agents use their knowledge of the typical systems to save thousands of dollars for buyers. *'We know the tricks of the trade,'* say their advertisements. Some are advertising the specific amounts that sellers are losing as well as the names of the buyers and where they bought. One can only imagine how the sellers feel when they see advertisements showing exactly by how much their homes have been undersold.[2]

THE SELLERS' AGENT

When you hire an agent to sell your home, you are hiring that agent to get you the best market price. It is vital that your agent understands the art of negotiation and will protect your financial interests. The agent does not need to use any tricks; the truth is powerful enough. Buyers appreciate the truth. And the truth is that the agent's job is to get the best price for you, the seller. If the buyers like your home, the agent will ask them to reveal their highest price with a Buyers' Price Declaration. Sure, the buyers might have to pay more for your home, but if they can afford to pay more – and they are not being deceived about its worth – there is nothing wrong with them paying more than you were prepared to accept. The alternative is that you, the seller, get less.

When you sell a home, it is your last chance to get any financial return from it. Most buyers will have many years to enjoy capital appreciation. Any extra they pay by giving you their maximum price should be returned to them when they sell. The buyers understand this truth. While many buyers are pleased to buy at a lower price, they are unlikely to use the same agent when they sell their home. This is exactly how Julia and her husband felt after they bought a home in the Brisbane suburb of Strathpine. Said Julia, 'We were appalled with *all* the agents we saw. The agent selling the house saved us $10,000 with the answer to one simple question: "Why are the owners asking this price?" He said, "I know they're negotiable within $10,000." We absolutely loved this house and were quite prepared to pay more than the asking price if it came to that! Following the agent's comment about being negotiable within $10,000, our first offer was $10,000 less than the asking price and was accepted the same day (the agent told us he'd had to convince the sellers to accept the offer). We feel like we should be paying this guy, not the sellers!'[3]

Had the agent been competent, the negotiation might have gone something like this:

Julia: We love this home, what price will they take?

Agent: They will take the highest price you are prepared to pay, provided it is better than any other buyer is prepared to pay, and provided they like the price you are prepared to pay.

Julia: What do you mean?

Agent: If your price is the best price available and they like it, they will sell it to you. If you love the home, I suggest you offer the best price you are prepared to pay, which gives you the best chance of buying the home.

Julia: But what if I want to start off by making a lower offer?

Agent: You can do that if you wish, but I must tell the owners that I believe you have not paid your best price.

Julia: But if I tell you that it is my best price – how will you know?

Agent: I will ask you to give me your walk-away price in writing, saying that if your offer is not accepted you will not object if the home is sold to someone else for a higher amount than your offer.

Julia: But I want to be notified if my offer is not accepted and if someone makes a better offer?

Agent: Why?

Julia: So that I have the chance to pay more.

Agent: You have that chance now.

Julia: The other agents don't do this.

Agent: The other agents must sell homes too cheaply. If you want to buy the home, just offer the most you can afford. If you won't sign the Buyers' Price Declaration, that's okay, but the sellers will not consider any offer unless the buyers have stated that it is their best price. If it was your home would you sell it for less than you could?

Julia: No, but I want to buy for less than I can.

Agent: Well, you have come to the wrong agent. I suggest you try the auctions. That's where you know the seller's lowest price before you buy and no one ever gets to know your highest price. You just have to make the highest offer, which is different from paying your highest price.

Julia: But this is the home we want to buy.

Agent: Good, then tell me your best price and you'll have the best chance of buying it.

Julia: Okay, I understand.

Anyone who has studied negotiation knows that every buyer has a walk-away price – the highest they are prepared to pay. Many agents have urged sellers to accept a price by saying it's 'the best price you'll get' and then, when the sellers refuse, the agent has got a higher price from the same buyers. Had the sellers taken the agent's advice they would have lost thousands.

PROTECTING YOURSELF

If agents had to forfeit their commission when they undersold homes, less homes would be undersold. As a seller, you must insist that your agent focuses on the highest a buyer is prepared to pay for your home. This is easy. Just tell the agent that you require a written guarantee that your home will not be knowingly sold to a buyer who was prepared to pay more, and that the agent will make sure your home is not undersold.

If the first rule to protect the best market value of your home is never tell anyone your lowest price, then the second rule is this: don't sign anything unless the agent gives you a written guarantee that your home will not be undersold.

If you won't sign a written guarantee to protect the value of my home, I won't sign anything with you

Many agents will tell you that this is not 'normal' or ask you 'How are they supposed to know what a buyer will pay?'. But if the agent does not know how to get the highest price for your home, you have to ask yourself: 'Is this the agent I want to sell my home?'

Don't be pressured into signing any agent's 'standard' selling agreement. It is your home, you are employing the agent. You can, and you should, set the conditions under which you hire the agent. You are the employer, the boss. Take control. Protect your asset from being undersold. Say to the agent: 'If you won't sign a written guarantee to protect the value of my home, I won't sign anything with you.' If you can't find an agent prepared to sign such a condition, you might be better off selling your home privately with no agent. After reading this book, you'll be more qualified – in so far as negotiation and marketing skills are concerned – than most agents.

Commissions and Expenses

Don't sign anything unless you have a guarantee that you will not have to pay anything until after your home is sold. Accept no excuses with this condition, no matter what agents tell you. Break this rule and, as many sellers discover, you will pay money you don't have to pay. You will almost certainly be ripped off.

Advance Fee Scams

One of the most notorious ways that people are conned, worldwide, is with Advance Fee Scams. Consumers are duped into paying money before they receive a product or service. This money is usually disguised as a fee – such as an application fee or an order fee. Like most 'good' scams, it seems perfectly reasonable – that's why so many people fall for it.

In real estate, the advance fee scam comes in the guise of advertising fees. Agents will say they need to advertise your home and that 'advertising costs money'. True, but it's your money and, as you will see in Chapter Six, some of the greatest rip-offs in real estate relate to advertising. An agent may tell you that advertising is 'separate from the commission'. Don't fall for this trap. Tell the agent that *all* fees, whether they be for commission or advertising or any 'fee' associated with the sale

If you get nothing, you should pay nothing

of your home, will only be paid after your home is sold. That's how it should be. If you get nothing, you should pay nothing.

When you confront an agent with this condition, some of the slickest sales lines will be thrown at you. No matter how logical it all sounds, don't be swayed. Don't sign anything if you are asked to pay any fees in advance. And, also, don't sign anything that requires you to pay fees later if your home is not sold. One of the most common traps is when agents say they will pay the costs and you only pay when your home is sold or if you withdraw from sale or choose another agent. Beware: small print means BIG danger.[4]

THE ARREARS FEE SCAM

This scam is as common as the advance fee scam, but it is much harder to detect. The agent says that you 'do not have to pay anything in advance'. You think this means that you do not have to pay until after your home is sold. Wrong. Here's how the Arrears Fee Scam traps homesellers: The agent signs you up and then, when you refuse to lower the price and decide either not to sell or to choose another agent, you receive a bill for 'advertising expenses'. You are trapped, you can't get out of the agreement unless you pay the advertising 'fees'. As real estate agent James Tostevin teaches agents, 'With a large advertising budget the client will be loyal to you for longer. If they owe $4000, $5000 or $6000 they often believe that taking the property away from you will mean they have to pay the advertising owing immediately!'[5]

The warning cannot be over-stated: don't sign anything unless you do not have to pay anything until your home is sold. And make sure that the fee or commission (or whatever they call it) is one fee which includes *everything*. There must be *no* hidden extras.

You are hiring an agent to sell your home. Do not pay unless your home is sold. It's that simple.

You are also hiring an agent to sell your home for the best market value. If the price is low enough, anyone can sell your home. You can do it yourself, quite easily. It is bad enough to have your home undersold by thousands of dollars, but it's worse when you also have to pay thousands of dollars in commission as well.

Thousands of sellers are being ripped off in two ways – their homes are undersold and they pay huge commissions. It's like the crooked shop-keeper who taught his son, 'Always overcharge the customer and short-change them as well. They'll never catch you on both.'

HOW MUCH DO YOU PAY AN AGENT?

In most states, agents can charge whatever you agree to pay. But in states where fees are controlled by law, agents have a maximum amount they can charge. This makes many homesellers believe they cannot negotiate with the agent. This is incorrect. While agents are not allowed to charge more than the maximum fee, there is no law to stop them charging less.

The standard method of paying an agent is a percentage of the selling price. In effect, the agent gets a percentage of the value of your home, a slice of your equity. And this is why it is so important that the agent gets you the highest market price. The fee you pay to a competent agent is worth it if the agent's result more than covers the fee. Competent agents understand how to get the best market value. They will also protect the value of your home before it sells. Incompetent agents *cause* your home to be sold for a lower price, and many of them charge high commissions. Incompetent agents are bad value at any price.

To get value from an agent you must get the best market value. You have to be certain that the selling price you receive is directly attributable to the skill of the agent.

As for the amount you should pay – once your home is sold and you are satisfied that you have received the best market value – that can vary from around two to four per cent. Sometimes a little more, sometimes a little less. The major point is this: you must not pay anything until your home is sold and you are completely satisfied with the price. A good negotiator can easily increase the market value of your home by as much as ten per cent. And so, if you pay five per cent you are in front by five per cent and you have got good value. But if you hire an agent who charges you one per cent (as some do) and your home sells for ten per cent less, you are nine per cent behind. That's $9000 for every $100,000. It soon adds up.

COMMISSION TRAPS

There are four commission traps for homesellers. The first is paying money in advance. Don't do it. The second is signing anything that requires you to pay money if your home is not sold. Don't do it. The third is an agent who too quickly agrees to give you a discounted rate. If the agents discount their own price you can be sure they are going to discount the price of your home. Be careful. If you want to negotiate the commission, do it at the time of the sale, not when you hire the agent. Remember that all fees charged by agents are negotiable, no matter what they tell you – even the regulated agents can negotiate down.

The Bonus Commission Scam – The Fourth Trap

The fourth commission trap is a nasty one. It's the Bonus Scam. On the surface, it seems fair. It requires homesellers to pay far more commission if their homes sell for more money.

This scam goes under a variety of names – the 'bonus commission', the 'accelerator fee', the 'split the difference', 'getting the overs' – but whatever they call it, here's how you can recognise it. Agents will suggest you pay their standard fee; some will offer you a lower fee to entice you to sign up. Then, if your home sells for a higher price than they quoted, you pay a bigger percentage. This is where it gets nasty.

Let's say the agent says your home should sell for $400,000. The agent offers to charge you a flat rate of two per cent up to $400,000. If you say you'll be happy with $400,000, the agent then says, 'If I can get you more than $400,000, you'll be even happier won't you?' (This is one of those trick selling questions to which the only answer can be 'yes'.) The agent then suggests you pay a 'bonus' for any amount above $400,000. How much bonus? One real estate trainer, David Pilling, suggests 30 per cent. On a promotional CD urging agents to use his services, he speaks with several agents who can be heard gleefully saying that this scheme has doubled or trebled their commission on each sale. It depends on the gullibility of the homesellers.[6]

For example, if the agent's standard rate is three per cent and the agent discounts the fee to two per cent but adds a 'bonus' commission of 30 per cent and the home sells for $450,000, the commission goes from the 'standard' rate of $12,000 to the new rate of $23,000 (two per cent on $400,000 and 30 per cent on $50,000). You might say 'so what?'. The agent got you extra so you don't mind paying extra. But this is why these agents love this scam, it *seems* fair. It has even fooled some media commentators. But unless you're involved in the industry it can be hard to know what's really going on. What's really going on is that the agent underquoted the value of the home; it was already worth $450,000. The home simply sold for its true market value.

No agent should be entitled to a 30 per cent share of any part of the value of your home. But even 30 per cent might be a conservative example. As more agents get away with this scam – and as their greed increases – there is no telling how many homesellers will be ripped off. The warning is clear – don't sign anything with any agent who suggests you pay a bonus fee.

The following example shows how nasty the bonus fee can become.

A real estate salesperson who worked for an agency in the Melbourne suburb of Hampton Park described how they pulled off this scam: 'We would receive an offer on a property, but would "condition" the sellers on a lower price than the offer we held. We would "condition" the sellers several times at lower amounts, working our way up slowly to the real offer. Sometimes the sellers would accept one of these lower amounts. We would then put it to the sellers that if we could get any more money from the buyers, would the sellers agree to split the difference 50/50, even though, of course, we already knew we had more. So, in total, we received our normal fee plus half the difference between the offer and what the sellers agreed to accept.'[7]

In another example, an inexperienced seller had two properties. He wanted $180,000 for one and $190,000 for the other. The agent suggested that the commission should be all of the amount by which the properties could be sold over the figures suggested by the seller. The seller agreed. But, in reality, the first property was worth about $210,000 and the second $220,000, which meant that the agent was charging $60,000 in commission for selling $430,000 worth of real estate.[8]

Don't sign anything with any agent who suggests you pay a bonus commission. And remember, no matter what any agent tells you, the golden rule for paying agents is this: never pay any money for any reason until your home is sold for the price you want.

THE METHOD OF SALE

The wrong method of sale can wipe thousands of dollars from the value of your home. But what is the wrong method? With so many different methods, it is confusing. You have to decide which method is right for you. But you can only make the right decision with the right information. This is why it is so important that you examine each method before you sign anything. The value of your family home is on the line. Choose carefully.

Each selling method has a number of tricks and traps that can severely damage the value of your home. Even if you choose the best method, you will get a lower price unless you know how to avoid the tricks associated with all of the methods – or unless your agent has that rare combination of honesty and competency. The best agents always guarantee their service.

Don't sign anything unless you are confident that the agent you are employing is the best for you. And, no matter how confident you feel, don't sign anything unless you receive a guarantee that you can dismiss the agent if you discover that he or she is dishonest or incompetent.

Summary

- The best market value is the highest price a buyer is prepared to pay.

- A seller's aim is to discover the buyer's highest price.

- As a seller, if you reveal your lowest price and the buyers never reveal their highest price, it is almost impossible for you to get the best market price.

- To discover the buyer's highest price, the sellers ask the buyers to sign a Buyers' Price Declaration.

- Anyone who has studied negotiation knows that every buyer has a walk-away price – the highest they are prepared to pay.

- If buyers love a home, most will pay their highest price rather than risk losing it.

- By requiring a Buyers' Price Declaration, sellers are not asking buyers to pay more than they can afford; they are just reducing the risk of underselling their homes.

- If you hire an agent to sell your home, the agent should know how to get you the best market price.

- When you sell, the price is paramount. It is your last chance to obtain any financial return from your home.

- If agents had to forfeit their commission when they undersold homes, less homes would be undersold.

- Sellers should say to the agent: 'If you won't sign a guarantee to protect the value of my home, I won't sign anything with you.'

- **Don't sign anything** unless the agent gives you a written guarantee that your home will not be undersold.

- The fee you pay to a competent agent is worth it if the agent's result more than covers the fee.

- *All* fees are negotiable, no matter what agents tell you – even the regulated agents can negotiate down.

- If you want to negotiate the commission, do it at the time of the sale, not when you hire the agent.

- **Don't sign anything** with any agent who suggests you pay a 'bonus fee'.

- **Don't sign anything** unless you are guaranteed in writing that you will not have to pay until your home is sold and you are happy with the service from the agent.

Chapter Six

Real Estate Advertising

One of real estate's greatest traps

It is the wisdom of the crocodiles that
shed tears when they would devour.

Francis Bacon

Thousands of homesellers fall into the advertising trap. They do not realise that advertising *does not* sell their homes, or that one of the main reasons for advertising is to promote agents, not homes. They do not realise that agents can earn thousands of dollars from kickbacks, or that advertising is one of the agents' best conditioning weapons to convince sellers to lower their prices.

But worst of all, few sellers realise how advertising damages the value of their homes. As you will see, typical real estate advertising often leads to lower prices.

A CLOSE LOOK AT REAL ESTATE ADVERTISING

Open a major newspaper on Saturday and you will see thousands of real estate advertisements. Find a local newspaper and you will see pages of glossy advertisements.

Unlike television, with limits on advertising content, there is no limit on advertising in newspapers. Often 80 per cent of local newspapers can be taken up with real estate advertising.[1] And yet, usually less than two per cent of readers are looking to buy homes.[2] Something doesn't add up.

The legendary advertising expert, Claude Hopkins, said that 'the only purpose of advertising is to create sales'.[3] Real estate advertising does not *create* sales. And agents know it. As far back as 1982, one overseas study showed that less than one home in five hundred is sold because of an agent's advertisement for the home.[4]

Homebuyers do not buy because they like the advertisements, they buy because they like the homes. If there were no real estate advertisements, homes would still be sold. Homebuyers would do what they have always done – and what they still do today – they would choose an area, go to the area and visit real estate agents.

Agents say that advertising attracts buyers. However, most buyers never buy the homes they first called about. Even those who do buy homes they see in advertisements would still have bought the homes had they been found in another manner.

One of the most basic principles of marketing is cost efficiency. There are many ways of finding customers, and the essence of intelligent marketing is to find the least expensive way. It's a simple business principle – how much is spent compared with how much is returned. The costs of typical real estate advertising just don't stack up. The cost to homesellers far outweighs the benefits, which are virtually nil. Therefore, as a marketing strategy, most real estate advertising is a complete failure – for the sellers, that is. For the agents, it's another story; they promote their real estate agencies at the expense of the sellers.

All over Australia and New Zealand, sellers are cheated out of thousands of dollars with real estate advertising. Auckland lawyer Greg Tower says advertising is attractive for agents because their names are 'plastered' all over the ads. He says the best thing for agents is that they are not paying for advertising, which can be between $4000 and $7000 'on top of commission'.[5]

All this is well known in the real estate industry. The Real Estate Institute of New South Wales says, 'Sellers might be alarmed to learn that the advertising they are paying for has a slim chance of selling their homes.'[6] So, why so much real estate advertising? The institute's quote reveals why: *sellers are paying*. Agents can promote themselves at the sellers' expense. Add this to the sweetheart deals, kickbacks, discounts or rebates from many newspapers and the recipe is complete – an explosion of advertising and the fleecing of thousands of homesellers.

However, despite this explosion of real estate advertising in the past 20 years, the number of homes sold has barely changed. In many areas, sales numbers have fallen. The huge costs of selling and buying often makes staying put a more attractive option for home-owners.

PROFILE, PROFIT AND PROPAGANDA

Real estate advertising has almost nothing to do with selling homes. It's all about profile and profit. The Real Estate Institute of Victoria's journal for its agents had an article that said, 'If you create massive profile and at the same time reduce your advertising costs, you are achieving massive profits for yourself and your agency.'[7] One book written for agents explains the true reason agents advertise, 'We advertise to achieve many various things, but in all cases the end result is the same – we are advertising our businesses.'[8]

The Real Estate Institute in Victoria also teaches agents 'The more ads you have with your name on them, the more successful you will look.'[9] When giving advice to consumers, institutes often tell sellers to choose the agent who does the most advertising. The inference being that the agents doing the most advertising are the best agents. It could be more accurate to say that agents who do the most advertising are fleecing the most homesellers.

Newspapers often display advertisements about the

'success' of advertising which fools more homesellers into believing that advertising is essential to sell their homes. Newspapers earn millions of dollars from real estate advertising. Their classified sections are referred to in the trade as 'rivers of gold'. Many newspapers sponsor real estate awards for agents. The awards focus on the amount of money spent on advertising. This, of course, is money spent by consumers who believe the propaganda about advertising.

Few homesellers realise what is going on behind the scenes with advertising. Fewer still are aware of the damage to the value of their homes. And almost no one seems to realise that typical real estate advertising is a major part of 'conditioning' – persuading sellers to lower their prices so their homes can be sold more easily.

Before showing how real estate advertising gets lower prices, it is important to realise how agents make huge profits from advertising and why there is so much misleading information about advertising.

A Brief History of Real Estate Advertising

In 1970, in the Queensland coastal town of Yeppoon, a real estate agent called Reg Baglow would advertise each week in the local paper. Most of the agents did the same – a few homes in the paper each week. When the buyers came to the office, Reg listened to what they wanted, and then he took them out in his car and showed them homes. Often they'd buy one. The buyers would move in, the sellers would move out, and Reg would get a commission. Everyone was happy. Handshakes and best wishes all around. It was simple and honest business. Sure, it was old-fashioned compared with today's real estate business. But Reg was doing nicely.

Reg didn't mislead sellers by saying the ads created the sales. Besides, if he said that, the sellers might wonder why they needed an agent. If all he did was put an ad in the paper, wait for a call and then make a sale, what was he doing that the sellers couldn't do? Reg often said he didn't really need to advertise because 'all the buyers come to the area anyway'.[10] And the way buyers were treated in those days is the way many buyers would like to be treated these days. What genuine buyers want, most of all, is to find the right home. They want agents who will listen to them and treat them with respect. Just like Reg used to do. Reg advertised because other agents advertised and because, when he started in real estate, his boss advertised. And his boss advertised because his boss advertised. It had been that way for decades.

Just as the purpose of a real estate office is to sell real estate, the purpose of a newspaper is to sell advertising. In the 1970s many agencies sold a lot more real estate than today's real estate agencies. And most newspapers sold a lot less real estate advertising than they are selling today. But, during the real estate booms of the late 1970s, more real estate offices opened. Agents began to compete with each other based on the amount of advertising they were doing. The newspapers would convince agents to take a full-page advertisement and this would make other agents want to do the same. One page led to two pages and so on. The agents doing the most advertising began to say to homesellers, 'Look at us. We must be successful.'

Advertising became a 'listing tool' to attract sellers and soon the real estate industry was addicted to massive advertising. Many newspapers made huge profits. But, once booms ended, many agents battled to survive, especially in Victoria where regulated commission rates were among the lowest in Australia. Agents struggled to pay the huge advertising costs, but they needed their advertising 'fix' to keep up with their competitors. The legendary advertising man, Howard Gossage, once said, 'As the immunity to ads builds up, it costs more and more to advertise each year. It's like narcotics, it must be taken in ever-increasing doses to achieve the same effect.'[11]

And then came a solution – auctions. With auctions, sellers paid for the advertising. The newspapers supported auctions. And advertising increased again.

Another method was soon introduced for sales not by auction. It was called VPA – vendor pays advertising. And now agents could do almost unlimited advertising because the sellers were paying for it. This is how advertising really exploded.

Today, homesellers are being deceived on a grand scale. And almost no one is doing anything about it because most people, other than agents and newspapers, do not realise what is going on. Homesellers have been fooled into thinking that advertising is essential. Many agents are fooled too. They believe modern marketing is more 'sophisticated'. But, as one agent said, 'What is sophisticated about spending more money to make less sales? That's not sophisticated, that's stupid.'[12] It is also dishonest because one of the duties of any professional in charge of consumers' finances is to protect those finances.

Back in Reg's day, he paid his advertising bills from his commission. He didn't asked homesellers to pay for advertising. According to today's agents, Reg's methods are old-fashioned. But Reg was honest. Perhaps honesty is old-fashioned.

ADVERTISING KICKBACKS AND SWEETHEART DEALS

In 2001 Australia's Prime Minister, John Howard, announced a royal commission into building rorts. He said Australians deserved a 'clean building industry'.[13] The commission's role was to examine 'kickbacks and sweetheart deals'. He did not mention the real estate industry where sweetheart deals and kickbacks cost homesellers millions of dollars. So far, there has been no independent inquiry into real estate rorts which hurt thousands of consumers.

The spark that ignited the explosion of advertising in real estate was the vendor paid scheme. But the flames of advertising have roared since kickbacks and sweetheart deals between agents and advertisers took off in the 1990s.

Today it's like a raging bush fire that is burning millions of dollars of homesellers' money every year.

Kickback schemes work like this. When agents advertise homes the sellers, who are paying for the advertising, are charged the casual rate. The agents receive a 'volume discount' for the advertising which is not passed on to the sellers. For example, the casual rate for a big glossy advertisement may be $1700. But the discount or 'volume' rate for agents is $1050.[14] The agents pocket the $650 difference. The round-robin book-keeping methods used to receive these discounts go as close to the legal line as possible. Effectively, advertising kickbacks mean that agents can earn a higher percentage of commission for selling advertising than for selling real estate. The commission on home sales averages about three per cent, but the commission on advertising can be up to 40 per cent. This fans the flames of advertising. The money to be made is too tempting for many agents. It is easy because the agents just have to say that 'marketing is important'. The slick sales lines plus the increasing number of sweet deals offered to agents has seen real estate agents become more like advertising agents.

Disclosure and Consent

Agents are quick to say, 'We're not doing anything illegal.' Technically, provided they tell homesellers about it, kickbacks – which agents and newspapers prefer to call 'rebates', 'volume discounts' or 'marketing packages' – are legal. But, despite the legal disclosures, few sellers are aware of the kickback scams. The property editor of *The Australian*, Maurice Dunlevy, wrote, 'What they [agents] don't tell you is that they receive huge kickbacks from advertisers.'[15]

The fact that many sellers don't know about kickbacks does not mean agents haven't told them. It's all there, in the selling agreement, usually 'disclosed' in the fine print and a swift whisper. As one seller explained, 'If you look closely enough or if you listen carefully, they do mention it.'[16]

Look at standard selling agency agreements and you will see – usually in six point writing – a clause which reads like this: 'The

Principal acknowledges that the agent may be entitled to receive volume contract payments from particular suppliers of services relating to the volume of advertising placed by the agent with suppliers which may include the advertising of your property and the seller agrees to the retention by the agent of all such volume contract payments.'[17]

The translation is simple: the more advertising money sellers pay, the more the agent is paid.

The Real Estate Institute of Australia's Code of Conduct requires its agents to obtain 'written consent' from homesellers before being able to 'demand, retain or receive a discount or rebate' for advertising.[18] 'Written consent' means the sellers have signed the standard selling agreement designed by the real estate institutes. The fine print in these agreements is often deliberately small. In 2002, the Real Estate Institute of New South Wales went one step further than fine print. It issued agency agreements with important conditions in feint print as well as fine print.

This is why it is so important that all sellers remember – don't sign anything which allows an agent to receive any kickbacks for any reason. Sellers should make the demand, *no kickbacks*. It does not matter if the agent has 'disclosed' that kickbacks are to be paid. As one lawyer said, 'Telling someone in advance that you are about to do the wrong thing does not make it right. It just makes it legal.'[19]

Public and Private Comments by Agents

Publicly, agents claim that rebates compensate them for the cost of 'arranging the advertising'. But one agent in Melbourne revealed the truth behind the wink-wink-nudge-nudge world of real estate advertising when he bragged to his mates, 'These rebates pay for the lease on my Porsche.'[20]

Many agents use a common trick. If a seller pays for advertising for a five-week period and a buyer is found in the first week, the agents encourage the sellers to keep the advertising going. They use the argument, 'It might help us to find more buyers.' It also makes sure that the agents get their maximum exposure and their full kickback.

The Fight for Legislation to Protect Consumers

Some agents have opposed kickbacks for years. These agents cross out the kickback clauses in the real estate institute agreements. However, the anti-kickback agents struggle to oppose the powerful forces of self-interest.

The 1999 president of the Real Estate Institute of Victoria, Garry Nash, described kickbacks as 'unethical' and accused agents of 'profiteering'. He said homesellers were being 'hoodwinked by agents who offer a low commission rate, knowing they will be compensated with advertising kickbacks.'[21] Despite becoming unpopular with many agents, Nash pushed hard for kickbacks to be banned.

In 1999, the Victorian government came close to passing legislation to abolish kickbacks. But then a new government was elected. The institute also had its elections and a new president was elected. The Institute's CEO, Norman Huon, resigned in 1999.[22] By 2000, with a new state government, a new real estate institute president and a new institute CEO, the fight to ban kickbacks was lost. Today homesellers continue to lose millions of dollars through needless advertising from which agents, all over Australia, continue to pocket huge kickbacks.

Without an independent inquiry into the real estate industry, the chance of legislation to protect homesellers is slim. Kickbacks are hidden under the guise that they are perfectly legal. But, as any ethicist knows, legal and ethical are not the same. 'Legislation is usually passed after there is an awareness that a problem exists. In other words legislation is passed after the damage has been done,' wrote John Dalton.[23] Legislation to ban kickbacks seems a long way off. Agents fight hard to protect their profits no matter how these profits are obtained. Meanwhile, thousands of sellers are duped. Their lack of experience makes them easy prey for agents who are just as keen to sell advertising as they are to sell real estate. Many agents openly admit what is happening. As one wrote, 'In my opinion, the biggest problem with rebates is that they are called rebates. In fact they are payments for carrying out the task of selling advertising space on behalf of various media companies such as *The Age*.'[24] This agent claimed that agents who oppose kickbacks are 'jealous' of agents who earn up to $500,000 a year from kickbacks. He made no mention of the thousands of home-owners who lose money while agents earn thousands of dollars in advertising commissions. Home-owners like Mr and Mrs Bebarfald, pensioners, who became classic kickback victims. When their home didn't sell, they were faced with a $5000 advertising bill and the threat of legal action. They were forced to borrow money from their children to pay the agent, Tim Fletcher.[25] It was all perfectly legal – the agreement they signed clearly showed that Fletcher was entitled to advertising kickbacks and the right to 'demand' payment for advertising.

Agents profit while sellers lose. It goes on all the time. Real estate institutes rarely focus on issues which lower the profits of agents. And institutes influence government policy. In the absence of legislation, the best protection for homesellers is don't sign anything unless the agent guarantees that any money from advertising kickbacks will be paid to the sellers.

The Legal Line

The line between legal and illegal with kickbacks is thin. It seems to depend on the terminology or how the kickbacks are paid to the agents. Many agents sign contracts with newspapers guaranteeing that they will obtain a minimum amount of money from homesellers. The more money paid by homesellers, the sweeter the deals for the agents.

Some contracts contain clauses in case kickbacks become illegal. One Sydney newspaper's contract contained these words, 'in the event that the rebate scheme is not permissible as a result of any Federal and/or State legislation which may be passed subsequent to this Deed, then the parties will negotiate in good faith as to how, if possible, any similar scheme will be administered in the future.'[26] A consumer protection lawyer translated this to mean, 'If we get caught and new laws are passed to stop us, then we agree to find a way around the new laws.'[27]

The agents and the advertisers take great pains to stay on the right side of that thin legal line.

In 2000 one of Melbourne's newspapers, *The Age*, decided to start a real estate magazine in competition with another newspaper, *The Melbourne Weekly*, which, for years, had been packed with real estate advertisements. To entice agents to 'jump ship', huge deals were offered in the form of cash bonuses. Agents were offered 'payments' (which turned out to be a wrong *legal* choice of word) of $20,000 for committing to a minimum number of pages per year. Some of the bigger agents were reputedly offered up to $80,000 in cash payments.[28] Another newspaper, Melbourne's *Herald Sun*, which does not offer rebates to agents, exposed this scandal.

The ABC's *Media Watch*, then hosted by Paul Barry, aired the story. It was revealed that most of the big real estate advertising papers offer kickbacks under the guise of 'volume discounts' or 'rebates' plus sweetheart deals. Adelaide's *Advertiser* was giving free holidays to agents. Barry quipped, 'Fancy that. Do you think the agents take their clients along?'[29]

A spokesperson for *The Age* admitted they 'might have erred' in their wording. Instead of saying 'payments', they should have said 'rebates'. The real estate institute issued a statement saying *The Age* had done nothing 'improper'. A spokesperson for *The Age* said he was 'pleased that the position is now better understood'.[30] The 2000 President of the Real Estate Institute of Victoria, Jeff Gole, reportedly used a common excuse for questionable business methods. He said, 'Advertising rebates have been commonplace in the industry for a long time.'[31]

Following the arrest of agents in a United States kickback scam involving building materials, the chief investigator said, 'Kickbacks have been a way of life for many years in the residential real estate industry.'[32] But he did not accept this as an excuse. The city's police commissioner added, 'Economic crime is just as important as street crime. These arrests in a kickback scheme show that this type of corruption still plagues the industry, costing innocent consumers millions of dollars in inflated costs.'[33]

Real estate consumers are losing millions because of advertising kickbacks.

Sellers Lose While Agents Win

When Bryan and Anne paid $16,000 in advertising expenses to an agent to sell their home in Brisbane, they were assured that this would attract lots of buyers.[34] When their home did not sell, Bryan and Anne lost most of their money. Like thousands of homesellers, they were now in a worse position – no sale and a huge expense.

They went to a lawyer in the hope of getting their money returned based on misleading statements by the agent. However, the cost of the legal fees was prohibitive. Having signed a standard real estate selling agreement, their chance of compensation was slim.

This is why it is so important that homesellers don't sign anything unless the agent gives a guarantee in writing that there will be no charges unless the home is sold and the sellers are happy with the price. No excuses.

THE GREAT CONDITIONING TOOL

Behind the scenes, advertising is known as a 'great listing tool' because it tricks sellers into believing that agents who do the most advertising must be the best agents. But, once you sign up with the agent, advertising becomes a 'great conditioning tool'. It is one of their major weapons to persuade you to lower your price.

Agents will tell you that advertising is 'essential'. They will say, 'The more people who hear about your home, the more likely you are to get a good price.' It sounds so sensible. But it is not true. By advertising your home – on the pretext of attracting buyers – agents can show lots of activity. And then, within a few weeks, when you have been sufficiently 'conditioned' to the 'reality' of the market, the pressure is applied to persuade you to lower your price. Your home is sold and the agent gets paid.

If advertising really was the cause of selling your home, you would not need an agent. You could advertise and attract the buyers for yourself. Why pay twice – once for advertising and once for commission? If the agents are taking your money and placing ads in the papers with their names emblazoned on the ads, they are doing nothing you could not do. You can place an ad in the paper, without the agent's name. You can sit at home and wait for buyers to turn up.

Agents say that advertising finds buyers, but if agents really are 'looking for buyers', why are they so notorious for failing to follow up buyers who contact them? Agents often boast about the number of calls they receive or the number of people who inspected a home. But, as only one buyer can buy each home, what happens to all the other buyers? For example, during a real estate institute awards presentation, it was announced that more than 800 people inspected a property advertised by one of their agents.[35] This agent received an award for an advertising 'campaign' that cost the sellers more than $6000.[36] But what happened to the other 799 people? Why don't the agents contact these other 799 'buyers' for the other homes they have for sale? The answer is simple: these agents are advertising to promote themselves and to profit from advertising at the expense of the sellers. This wastage of money is of no concern to these agents. It is not their money and, besides, it is a great way to condition sellers down in price by creating lots of activity. That's what activity conditioning is all about.

> **Homesellers are slowly waking up to what's really going on**

Advertising Gets Agents Out of the Quote Lie

Homesellers are slowly waking up to what's really going on – agents are advertising to promote themselves, to attract more sellers and to condition sellers who are their clients. When the homes don't sell, the agents have the perfect excuse – the 'market'. Sometimes the agents will feign surprise as they talk about 'what the market is saying'.

Advertising is a major part of the Activity Conditioning

(mentioned in Chapter Three) to convince sellers to lower the price of their homes. But what's worse is that all this advertising often damages the value of their homes and causes sellers to get a lower price than if their homes had not been advertised.

Advertising is so important for the conditioning process that many agents will even waste their own money advertising. They need to create the appearance of activity. It's activity conditioning.

ADVERTISING: COMMON THEORY AND HIDDEN REALITY

The common theory with real estate advertising is that to sell your home you *must* advertise in a newspaper. Many agents will argue that you need to advertise as widely as possible because they do not know where the buyers are going to come from. This is true. But these agents are displaying their ignorance of marketing. Of course, they may not know what areas the buyers are coming *from,* but they know what area they are coming to. They are coming to your area.

Typical real estate advertising damages the value of homes. In so many cases, if the home had not been advertised, the final selling price could have been much higher. The advertising ruined the market for the home. And that's the hidden reality of real estate advertising.

The Maths of Marketing and Advertising

When you advertise in a big city newspaper, it costs you a lot of money. This is because the newspaper has many readers and you will reach a bigger audience. But you don't want *readers,* you want *buyers.* In fact, you only want one buyer. It breaks one of the fundamental financial rules of marketing to pay money to reach a market that has no interest in what you want to sell.

When selling your family home you have a smaller product range than, say, a major corporation. For instance, Colgate advertises to millions of people because millions of people use toothpaste and Colgate has millions of tubes of toothpaste to sell. A homeseller has one home to sell and is only looking for one buyer. To advertise one product to millions of people, when you only have one item in your product range, is mathematical madness. The tiny percentage of buyers who buy a home they see advertised, would still have bought that home if they had found it in another manner – and a manner which could easily have been more cost effective.

At best, typical real estate advertising is an expensive lottery method. At worst, it gets lower prices

At best, typical real estate advertising is an expensive lottery method. At worst, it gets lower prices.

The Right Buyers Must See Your Home

The right buyers are the ones who pay the best market price for your home. They will almost always be the buyers looking for a *family* home. But they have to *see* your home. They have to come inside, they have to feel the atmosphere or, if it needs repair, they have to feel its potential. They cannot get this feeling from an advertisement. Advertising kills atmosphere. It spoils the joyous surprise. Many buyers are turned off by the look of an advertisement and don't inquire about homes which may have been perfect for them. This is how you can miss out on the right buyer and have to accept a lower price from another buyer.

Disappointment and Anger

Agents are notorious for using 'puffery' in advertising. Good features are exaggerated and bad features are ignored – or at best, played down. As one buyer commented, 'These advertisements double the good news and halve the bad news. We are sick of looking at homes which are nothing like what is described in the ads.'[37]

Puffery makes buyers angry. Even if they like the home, they will not like feeling tricked. When a home does not live up to the expectation created by the advertising, it is automatic to think it is overpriced. If the buyers are still interested, they will almost certainly offer a lower price – almost as revenge for being deceived. Trust is an important ingredient to a successful negotiation. Typical real estate advertising kills trust.

One real estate agent said, 'In our area Wednesday was 'Argument Day'. That's when the local paper comes out. We would get lots of calls from buyers, all of whom had been attracted by something good in the ads for the homes. And then, when they saw the homes or found out where they were located, they got annoyed. This did incredible damage to the value of the homes. Once we realised what was happening and we explained it to the sellers, they also realised how advertising was hurting their chances of getting the best price.' This agent no longer advertises in the typical manner. Not only does his office make more sales, the sellers are getting better prices and the buyers are happier.[38]

The only people who should know that your home is for sale are genuine buyers

Comparisons Cause Huge Damage to the Value

Typical real estate advertising allows buyers to make inaccurate price comparisons. Many homes look similar from the outside. But some owners have spent thousands of dollars internally, while others have spent nothing. When homes look similar in advertisements it damages the value of the better homes. The buyers compare the prices and judge the value of homes before they see them.

Advertising to Non-buyers

By mass advertising a home it comes to the attention of thousands of people who do not want to buy it. Aside from the wastage of money in reaching these non-buyers, this leads to criticism of the home. People who have no interest in buying a home are unlikely to praise it. On the contrary, many people denigrate the home, saying such things as, 'They must be kidding. They'll never get that price.' This is common in small communities. The opinions of non-buyers influence real buyers. Big mistake.

This is especially true with agents. When your home is advertised, other agents often work against you. They will say such things as, 'Oh, I know that place, let me tell you what's wrong with it.' The only people who should know that your home is for sale are genuine buyers. An agent who understands the difference between advertising and marketing will know how to market your home to the right buyers instead of damaging its value by advertising it to thousands of people who don't want to buy it.

What's Wrong with the Home?

The more a home is advertised the less chance there is of getting the best price for it. It quickly acquires the lemon tag.

When Bruce placed his home for sale, he was approached by a television lifestyle program. The television channel spent thousands of dollars to improve his home to make it easier to sell. Bruce thought he had struck the jackpot. But as far as getting a sale at a better price was concerned, it never happened. Over several weeks the home was exposed to millions of viewers. However, no one wanted to buy it, despite it being well priced in the opinion of the agent. The more publicity it received the more people wondered why no one had bought it. According to the agent, it became a famous lemon.[39]

Another well-publicised incident was an auction for a home which was to be broadcast live on television. The home had been advertised for several months and failed to sell. The owners wanted $400,000, but the best they were reportedly offered was $352,000. Along came the television show with its extra publicity and a massive budget of $40,000 to improve the home. It sounded great. But on the night of the live auction, the home sold for a mere $345,000. The buyer was a relative of the agent.[40]

Agents often say there are only two reasons a home does

not sell – either it is not advertised enough or the price is too high. Once your home has been advertised – lots of 'exposure' – then, according to the agents, that only leaves one reason if it doesn't sell – the price. And presto, you lower your price and the agent makes the sale. But it's rarely the price; it's the advertising that has damaged the value of your home by giving it too much exposure. Don't be fooled with the 'exposure' line. It's like sunburn. The more you expose your home the more you burn your price.

The more you expose your home the more you burn your price

Many agents who have stopped doing typical real estate advertising have noticed three things: one, they save their clients thousands of dollars in wasted advertising costs; two, they get better prices; and, three, they sell more homes.

More Advertising Warnings

Sure, agents get calls about the homes they advertise, but these calls benefit the agents. Agents have many homes to show buyers. If a buyer enquires about your home but buys another home, the agent does not pay you for using your home to attract other customers. On the contrary, unless you are paying advertising money to the agent, many ignore your home. As one seller described it, 'When the advertising money runs out, so does the agent.'[41]

One agent explained what happens, 'Typically, agents get sellers to pay for the ads so they can create activity to condition the sellers down to the price they should have been told at the start. It would have been much cheaper for the sellers to get a valuer.'[42]

When sellers refuse to be bullied or realise they have been tricked, many refuse to pay. They then find themselves locked in to the selling agreement and can't leave the agent without paying a big advertising account. This is exactly what many agents plan to do. It is what they have been taught in the real estate courses.[43]

The Bait Advertising Trap

One of the most distressing things to happen to homesellers is to see their homes advertised with a bait price. Agents will advertise a 'price from' or a 'price range' thousands below what the sellers want. The agents justify this by saying it attracts more buyers. But it attracts buyers who want to pay a lower price.

When Lisa sold her home in the Melbourne suburb of Kensington, this is how she described bait advertising, 'I wanted $370,000. The agent advertised it as 'price range from $230,000'. I had to pay the bill for an ad which was an absolute lie and which brought the wrong buyers to my home. The agent said this is normal practice. How can it be normal to lie to me *and* the buyers? I couldn't believe it. But then, later, I found out that this is what lots of agents do.'[44] Lisa demanded that the agent stop using bait advertising for her home.

It attracts buyers who want to pay a lower price

A newspaper advertisement, written by a branch president of the real estate institute, Lou Rendina, urged consumers to complain to the institute about false price advertising. He described it as 'scandalous'.[45] But Rendina was the agent using false pricing for Lisa's home. In real estate, those doing the investigating are often the ones who need to be investigated.

Because real estate institutes represent real estate agents not consumers, and because these deceits are so common, agents get away with blatant breaches of the law. However, a lawyer who worked with the Australian Competition and Consumer Commission (ACCC) said, 'Many agents are unaware that they face massive fines for practices they consider 'normal'. It seems just a matter of time before real estate agents start to feel the full force of the law.'[46]

In New Zealand, the Commerce Commission launched prosecutions against some agents who advertised misleading prices. The commission was especially concerned with the practice known as 'Buyer Inquiry Range', which is also referred to as 'Price Banding'.[47] Incredibly, even agents who are convicted of breaching fair trading laws are still able to keep trading as agents, many seeing it as a joke.

One convicted agent urged other agents not to worry too much, saying that after he was convicted he had enjoyed a 'fantastic' holiday in Fiji knowing that he could keep trading as an agent. The President of the Real Estate Institute of New Zealand said, 'They can't be tried twice for the same crime.'[48] But as one observer quipped, 'That's like allowing drunk drivers to *keep* driving.'[49]

Meanwhile, thousands of agents continue to cheat consumers with a series of clever tricks followed by the same excuses. 'We have to advertise to get buyers. It is not our fault if the market says your home is worth less. We advertised for you, so you have to pay the advertising expenses.' Most consumers are not prepared to spend the time, the money or the emotional energy needed to stand up to unethical agents, some of whom can get really nasty.

Bullying and Intimidation:
The Nasty Side of Real Estate

An advertisement for a debt collection agency in the Real Estate Institute of Victoria's Journal had the heading, 'Stress Free Debt Collection. Let us take the stress of debt collection away from your staff and place it in the hands of our professional collection agents.' This collection agency offers to chase homesellers for 'unpaid advertising'.[50]

Another debt collection company tells agents, 'Your staff spend ages chasing reluctant home-owners whose properties haven't sold'.[51] Their advertisement talks about 'hard case' sellers, meaning those who are the most annoyed about being ripped off. Many homesellers are intimidated by demands from agents. Incredibly, sellers are made to feel they are the crooks when they don't want to pay agents. Some receive threats and harassment.

When Greg and Victoria tried to sell their home, the agent advertised their home with a bait price which was $170,000 less than the price he quoted them. After a few weeks, they were being pressured to accept an offer $60,000 below the agent's initial quote.

Greg and Victoria were locked in – both with the agreement and an advertising bill (payable on demand) if they left the agent. But Victoria was determined. She wrote to the agent saying she and her husband had been induced to sign up with the agent based on deception. She refused to pay the advertising bill. She told the agent she was going to write to the authorities.

Within an hour of receiving her letter, an angry real estate salesperson called her husband and said, 'I am going to f--- you like I have never f----- anyone before. You are going to find out what I do to people who don't pay their bills. You know what happens to their families.'

Greg and Victoria were terrified. They were so scared they not only stopped complaining, they agreed to pay the agent and give him a good reference.[52]

Agents bullying and threatening sellers over fees is common. The change in personality from sweet and charming before they sign up to aggressive and threatening after they sign up can defy belief. Jim and Enza were stunned at the treatment they received when they tried to sell their home in South Australia. The agent indicated they could get $600,000 at auction.[53] The pressure began the moment they signed up. As the real estate trainer, David Pilling, teaches agents, 'Your strongest position in the selling process is one second after the vendor has signed the listing authority'.[54]

Jim and Enza's home was advertised as, 'Bidding from $350,000'. And, just as it says in the real estate text books, they were bombarded with bad news as part of the conditioning process. At the auction, the highest bid for their home was $405,000 which, naturally, they refused. A few weeks after the auction, with their home still not sold, the agent demanded payment for the advertising expenses and the full commission. They couldn't believe it. And then came a letter from a solicitor with threats, such as, 'You are indebted to our client for the agreed commission and marketing costs of $16,492.00.' The letter also said that the agent 'will not hesitate to lodge a caveat over your property' and ended with the words, 'We trust you will appreciate the seriousness of your position in this matter.' Jim and Enza said, 'Now that our home has failed to sell, the agent is demanding payment for being highly deceptive and greatly misleading. This is madness!'[55]

Maximum Financial Danger: The Trap of Maximum Coverage

There are a multitude of places to advertise. Naturally, each has a price. Attempts will be made to convince you that they all help you to get 'maximum coverage'. This means maximum profit for the companies who own the advertising mediums – and for the agents who receive kickbacks. They all want to drink from the 'river of gold'. There are major city newspapers, local papers, specialty papers, feature sections or liftouts in papers and, of course, real estate magazines. Plus, many agents now produce, at great expense, their own magazines, each vying to be bigger, better and more frequent than the next.

As a homeseller, you can have colour brochures, floor plans, flyers, mammoth signboards filled with detail – even colour photos on the signs. Some agents charge for specialist copywriters to write advertisements. And then there may be the cost of a professional photographer. There are even talking signs so buyers can park outside your home, tune their car radio to the FM frequency displayed on the signboard and hear a professional announcer smoothly describe your home. There are the timeless window displays, even talking windows where a code number is displayed on each home and by pressing the numbers onto a pad, people can listen to a description of a selected home. They can use a speaker to record their details for the agents. (School children often leave colourful messages.)

But let's not forget the Internet with its coverage of a potential 876 million people. Try beating that one. And, just to make sure you are totally 'sold' on all of these places to advertise, each has its own reason why you must use it. 'It can get you that one buyer which can make all the difference. Look at the value. You have a home worth hundreds of thousands of dollars and, for a few hundred or just an extra thousand or so, you can have all this exposure,' say the agents.

Be prepared, also, for that great sales convincer – a story of someone who sold for a great price with one of these methods. If you don't use it, you could miss out. It's only a few hundred more for each method. But it all adds up to a multi-million-dollar fleecing of thousands of sellers every year. Like the great stories about lottery winners which never mention the millions of losers, you will be given similar stories with advertising.

You are the seller of a home, not the buyer of advertising

One seller described real estate advertising sales pitches as a 'litany of lunacy'. When an agent prepared a marketing plan listing all his recommended ways of marketing her home together with an estimated 'investment' (which means 'cost'), she laughed. 'Wait a minute,' she said, 'I want to sell my home, I don't want to buy advertising.'[56]

You go to a real estate agent to find a buyer for your home. Real estate agents should have buyers, just as butcher shops have meat. One of the best analogies to describe how sellers are conned into paying for advertising is this, 'Going to a real estate agent and being asked for money so that the agent can find a buyer makes as much sense as going to a butcher shop and being asked for money to find a cow.'

You are the seller of a home, not the buyer of advertising. It cannot be stressed enough – all these advertising methods are not designed to benefit sellers. They are designed to benefit agents. It's all about exposure for the agent, kickbacks and, finally, activity conditioning to soften up the sellers for the second stage of the conditioning process – the crunch.

Maximum exposure means maximum profit for everyone except homesellers. For sellers, it means maximum danger, both in the cost of the advertising and in the damage to the value of their homes. As thousands of sellers fall for these advertising traps, more and more ways to get more and more money from sellers keep being discovered. Forget it. Don't sign anything unless the agent agrees on no charges until your home is sold.

Agents of Mass Deception

The worst agents – those who can do the most damage to you financially – don't look like bad agents. Like most 'good' con artists they look credible. They build images based around their advertising and their profile. They often win awards from real estate institutes which makes them seem all the more credible. Some even hire public relations companies or 'image specialists' to maintain their profiles. They build a perception of great success. But this perception is based on deception. They deceive the society upon which they prey.

If they can deceive governments and journalists, they can certainly deceive inexperienced consumers. Many 'prominent' agents are just miniature versions of the notorious corporate crooks of recent decades. They say one thing publicly but another thing privately.

The Internet Sell

The industry's love affair with the Internet is the love of profit. It has little to do with better service for homesellers. As a real estate teacher explained to his students, 'The Internet generates listings not sales.'[57] But that's not what sellers are told. On the contrary, they are told that the Internet is another 'essential' marketing tool.

Despite the claims of sales being made 'because of the Internet', buyers rarely buy because of the Internet. They buy because they inspect the homes. Of course, many buyers look at the Internet, but most want information. They will soon pick the 'stale' homes on the Internet, which are being overexposed, just as they do with typical advertising.

The Internet can be a big money earner for agents. And that means more glib sales lines as consumers are talked into wasting more money to increase the profits of agents.

In 2000, Philip Harris, an agent in the Sydney suburb of Balmain, claimed that many agents would load the Internet charges to increase their profits, just as they do with newspaper advertising. This was immediately denied by an Eastern Suburbs agent, John McGrath. In an interview given to a national magazine[58], McGrath, who was a director of a major real estate Internet site[59], said he doubted Harris's claim. This was his public message. Privately, within the industry, he was giving a different message. In a cassette mailed to agents throughout Australia urging them to use the Internet site with which he was involved, he told agents they could pay $150 per month to use the site but they could have as many homes as they liked on the site and charge each seller $45. He boasted that his agency gets $5500 or $6000 'out of' most of their sellers. Even if other agents couldn't get as much as his agency, then at least they could 'get a $45 cheque' from each seller. As an example McGrath said, 'We have like a hundred listings that go on there in a month so we make a lot of money out of it. If you get 20 listings per month that's $900 and the cost is $150. Be in it for net profit.'[60]

There are two sides to the world of real estate, especially with advertising. And consumers are not likely to hear both sides. The two major newspaper groups – Fairfax and News Limited – both own shares in major real estate Internet sites.[61]

Protect Yourself

The family home is a source of huge profit for agents and advertisers. By allowing their homes to be mass advertised, sellers unwittingly play straight into the hands of agents who are either dishonest or incompetent. It's bad enough to have the value of your home damaged through advertising, but it's worse if you are tricked into paying for it. Don't sign anything unless the agent can show you how to sell your home without damaging its value. And don't sign anything that requires you to pay any money for advertising at any time for any reason.

All costs should be included in the agent's commission which should only be paid after your home has been sold for the best market price. As one savvy homeseller commented, 'I pay an agent to deliver a service – the sale of my home for the best price. It's the way I do business. It's called COD – cash on delivery.'[62]

The protection message to sellers is clear and simple: Unless you receive a written guarantee that you will not have to pay anything until your home is sold, don't sign anything.

REAL ESTATE ADVERTISING SOLUTIONS

Consumers – and many agents – are so brainwashed into believing that advertising is essential to selling a home their first reaction to 'advertising gets lower prices' is, 'But how can you sell a home without advertising it?' Research shows that 98 per cent of homebuyers cite the area as their first and major reason for buying.[63] They all come to the area before they buy. All an agent has to do is *attract the buyers who are looking to buy in the area.*

What Buyers Do When They Want to Buy

Serious homebuyers go to real estate agents. They know that real estate agents sell homes, just as supermarkets sell groceries. Buyers shop around. They look in agents' windows. If they don't see a home they like in the window, they may not even go into the agency; they will look in another window. They may do this for quite a while. They have to run the gamut of many agents. But, if they find an agent who listens to them, and keeps in contact with them, or even searches for a home for them, they will be attracted to this agent.

When buyers see homes in windows or in the paper, they know which homes are not selling and which ones are being reduced in price. Some agents cross out the prices of homes in their window and write a new, lower price. This tells buyers which homes are becoming stale.

Attracting the Buyers

Agents who understand marketing know how to attract buyers to their offices. They know that one of the first principles of marketing is to make it easy for buyers to buy. These agents will make themselves readily available to genuine buyers. They are open seven days a week often until late in the evening. Incredibly, most agents are closed when most buyers are available.

Competent agents attract buyers into their offices and then they discuss the homes they have for sale. They do not want the buyers to make the wrong judgement about homes without talking to the agent. Wrong judgments are made when homes are advertised in the window, in the papers or on the Internet and the buyers make a decision without meeting the agent or inspecting the homes. Many buyers say, 'We've seen that home and we don't like it.' But they have only *seen* the advertisement. Such incompetence costs sellers dearly.

One of the best examples of marketing incompetence is virtual tours on the Internet. A virtual tour can never be as effective as a real tour. The right buyers are often lost because the agents never meet them. The best agents want to meet the best buyers. To do this, they use intelligent marketing.

Imagine an agent has 30 homes for sale. If the agent advertises all those homes, as most agents do, then unless buyers see something they like, they have no reason to contact the agent. Dan Gooder Richard, an expert in real estate marketing, says 'The single biggest reason that property advertising is less effective is its limited appeal.'[64] Each ad only appeals to a very small number of buyers. When these buyers call about these homes, they almost never buy them. This leads to immense frustration and disappointment.

If, instead of advertising full details of all the 30 homes, the agency advertises that it has many homes for sale, this appeals to all buyers. They will want to know what is for sale. Another way that agents attract more genuine buyers is by offering free home-buying information; again, this is appealing to *all* buyers.

The best agents accumulate lists of buyers, just as they have lists of sellers (listings). Many times, the best agents will find the right buyer quickly because the buyers are already 'on their books'. This is intelligent marketing, the opposite to what most agents do.

Homes that appear to have been rejected by many buyers are hard to sell

Homebuyers spend an average of 85 days searching for the right home.[65] These buyers are *in* the area, looking around. If an agent can't find buyers without typical advertising, there is something seriously wrong with the agent's ability.

Keep the Home Special

Freshness attracts buyers. Homes that appear to have been rejected by many buyers are hard to sell. For example, the biggest lemons are often homes which fail to sell at auction. The same principle applies in most selling situations – fresh stock gets the best price. Old stock gets the lowest price.

Advertise to Buyers Only

To protect the value of the homes for sale, an agent should only discuss each home with buyers who are likely to buy it. This is the opposite to the 'hit and miss' method typically used by agents where they allow anyone to inspect homes and hope that someone says yes.

One advertisement, which made perfect sense to buyers, said, 'Our homes are so special we have decided only to show them to homebuyers.'[66] Another advertisement that appealed to all buyers said, 'Sometimes the best homes are not advertised.'[67] And that's intelligent marketing as compared with typical advertising.

Once a competent agent attracts buyers, the agent discovers what they want and discusses homes that might be suitable. The agent may produce photographs and some details about each home. The more interest the buyers show, the more information the agent will reveal. This is 'advertising' to buyers only. It is allowing the agent to protect the value of homes by keeping them special.

Everyone is happy – the sellers who got the best market price, the buyers because they found an agent who found them a special home and the agent who is paid for doing what the sellers want. It's good honest business where everyone wins and no one gets hurt.

The Purpose of an Agent

You hire an agent to sell your home for the best price. You do not hire an agent to advertise your home, take kickbacks, damage the value of your home and then demand payment when your home does not sell or if it sells for thousands below what you expected. This is madness.

An agent should be your ally, the person who takes care of your greatest asset, the person you can trust. If not, you should dismiss the agent and get another one or, if you can't find an agent worth trusting, use the ideas in Chapter Nine and do what many sellers do – sell without an agent.

You can protect yourself from the tricks and traps of real estate advertising. Don't sign anything unless you are guaranteed that the agent will not damage the value of your home with typical real estate advertising. It's your home. Protect it.

Summary

- One of the major reasons for advertising is to promote agents, not to sell homes.

- Many agents pocket thousands of dollars in kickbacks, and earn a higher percentage commission from advertising than from selling real estate.

- Advertising is a big part of the conditioning process.

- Buyers do not buy because of advertisements, they buy because they like the homes.

- Advertising can quickly damage the value of a home.

- The more a home is advertised the more buyers wonder what is wrong. It often becomes known as a lemon.

- If advertising really did cause sales, as many agents claim, sellers could advertise their own homes and save paying the agents' commissions.

- At best, most real estate advertising is an expensive lottery method. At worst, it gets lower prices.

- 'Exposure' is like sunburn. The more you expose your home, the more you burn your price.

- Home-owners should be the sellers of homes not the buyers of advertising that promotes the agents. Never pay any money to an agent before your home is sold.

- Always check the fine print. **Don't sign anything** with any agent who has a kickback clause in the agreement.

- **Don't sign anything** unless you are guaranteed that the agent will not damage the value of your home through advertising. Often, the agents doing the most advertising are the worst agents for sellers.

Chapter Seven

Auctions

Trickery and deception on a massive scale

Auctions are all about loot and hope.
They are fundamentally larcenous rituals,
with buyers hoping to steal a bargain,
while sellers hope to extort a ridiculous price.
It is the auctioneers' job to glide between
these two irreconcilable illusions,
extracting their own commission ...

Robert Lacey, Sotheby's – Bidding for Class

Attend any real estate auction and you'll see it for yourself – agents in dark suits hovering around the crowd. You will see the bidding start low. You may not spot the 'dummy' bidders, but you'll usually see the 'crunching'.

When the bidding slows, agents will approach people in the crowd. You will see them whispering urgently. They are trying to coax sellers down in price and buyers up in price. You will see people squirming, many will be sweating. Often you will see women sobbing as the pressure mounts. As one agent described it, 'The wife was crying so much that we couldn't get her to shake her head yes or no when we were trying to convince her to accept an offer below the reserve price.'[1]

THE MOST COMMON FRAUD

Auctions are real estate's most common fraud. They involve deceit on a massive scale. From the poorest pensioners to the wealthiest millionaires, no consumer is safe. But inexperienced consumers, such as the elderly and first-time homebuyers, are especially vulnerable. They lose money and have their hearts broken by this cruel and heartless method of selling real estate.

The deceit with auctions starts with the prices quoted to buyers and sellers. If a home is worth $500,000, the agent may tell the sellers, 'You could get $600,000.' The agent then tells the buyers, 'You might buy it for $400,000.' The agent then manipulates both parties to either go up or down in price.

Auctions give agents massive control

If the sellers and buyers later complain that the price is different from what they were first told, the agent blames 'the market'.

As the auction gets closer, the manipulation increases. And so does the pressure. During the auction, it becomes extreme. Sellers and buyers are crunched into making instant decisions. There is no cooling-off period in the auction furnace. The pressure at auctions makes it easier for agents to make sales. It forces consumers to make instant decisions. It is one of the major reasons agents use auctions.

The real estate industry has created an elaborate system of deceit to cover up the truth about auctions. Publicly, consumers are told that auctions are successful, or that they have a long and respected history, or that they are a popular method of selling. But as you will see, auctions are successful for agents more than consumers. As for being popular, most consumers despise real estate auctions.[2] Homesellers rarely choose auctions voluntarily, they are tricked by a series of slick statements. At best, they are told half-truths; at worst, they are the victims of fraud.

Real estate auctions are all about conditioning sellers down in price, pushing buyers up in price and making sure agents get paid no matter what the price. Auctions give agents massive control because sellers and buyers are trapped in an atmosphere where they can be hammered into submission.

CONSUMER CONFUSION

Melbourne lawyer Peter Mericka said, 'The auction system is just one gigantic scam and everyone in the industry, other than consumers, seems to be in on it.'[3] Mericka's view is contradicted by auction agents who always have a story about how a home sold at auction for a record price and how the sellers were delighted. Auction agents will say it is their job to get the highest price for their clients, the sellers, and that auctions are 'the best way to get the best price'. On the surface, this seems logical.

> **The auction system is just one gigantic scam**

But there are many stories about bargains at auctions, when buyers paid thousands less than they were prepared to pay. The buyers will be delighted but the sellers will be distressed. For every story about a high price, there is a story about a low price. It's confusing.

Two different agents may give two different views. One will say auction is the best way to sell because 'auctions get higher prices' and the other will say it is the worst way to sell because 'auctions get lower prices'. Both will make persuasive arguments. It is hard to know which view is correct. Are auctions always bad? Do they get high prices or low prices? Are they really a fraud as the critics claim; or are they a fair way to buy and sell as the supporters claim?

The American newspaper columnist, Robert Lentz, is fascinated by auctions. Although he writes about general auctions – such as antiques and clearing sales – his words could apply equally to real estate auctions in Australia and New Zealand. Describing how consumers are puzzled by auctions, Lentz writes, 'As a seller, you can watch in horror as your possessions are practically given away, or you can exult as maniacs empty their pockets for them. As a buyer, you can exult as you load up on treasures for a small fraction of their worth, or you can feel the menthol in your stomach as you discover you have paid far too much.'[4]

Consumers are puzzled by auctions. But, as Lentz says, 'Puzzlement is a loss of control, understanding is control'.[5] In real estate the agents have control because they understand what is happening. Most consumers do not understand what is happening. They do not have control. Consumers have heard good stories and bad stories. Although they don't fully understand the system, they can often be lured into auctions by agents who tell them the good stories. 'Look what happened to this lucky seller. It can happen to you too.' And the bad stories, well, they are 'isolated' or happen to someone else.

When you understand auctions, you will be able to protect yourself from the tricks, the traps and the fraud.

CONSUMERS: WINNERS OR LOSERS AT AUCTIONS?

Some consumers do win at auctions, but how do they win? And who are they – sellers or buyers? Was it the auction that made them win or was it chance? As you will see, the only certain winners at auctions are real estate agents. This is because agents control the auctions. The first thing they control is the risk. If someone loses, it is not the agent, it's the consumer.

Auctions strip consumers of three of their most basic rights

Auctions strip consumers of three of their most basic rights: the right to safety, the right to information and the right to redress. There are no guarantees with auctions. If there were, the typical real estate auction system in Australia and New Zealand could not exist. Most information about auctions is deliberately one-sided and misleading. Auctions are dangerous places for consumers.

The auction system is designed to suit agents. It makes it easier for them to win listings and then to quickly condition the sellers to lower their prices. And that is the essence of the auction system – it is a conditioning method.

How Auctions Condition
Real Estate Consumers

The Real Estate Institute of Australia published the *Real Estate Office Manual*. It stated that auctions are 'the fastest and best conditioning method'.[6]

Although the Institute denies that auctions are used to condition consumers[7], their manual reveals the truth. It teaches agents how to condition sellers after they have signed up for auction: 'Being nice to sellers about the price they want will not get results. At least three letters, three office meetings, ten telephone calls and six home visits will condition the sellers.'[8]

The real estate institute's manual supplies a series of standard conditioning letters with statements such as: 'The response to the marketing has been certainly below expectations.' In discussing the price, the letters say, 'We believe there is little likelihood of achieving a sale at or near this figure.' To condition the sellers for auction day, there is this statement: 'Unless we have a realistic reserve in line with the market, there is little likelihood of a sale eventuating.'[9]

Auction conditioning is not only taught by the real estate institutes, it is taught by most of the real estate networks. It is also taught in government colleges where one teacher described auctions as a method that gives sellers what they need – 'a kick in the guts'.[10]

As explained in Chapter Three, conditioning begins once a seller has signed up with an agent. It's how agents convince sellers to 'accept reality'. This means that sellers have to stop believing what the agents told them before they signed up – which was the Quote Lie – and start believing what 'the market' is now telling them. Auctions give agents the perfect excuse for getting out of the Quote Lie. When the highest price offered at the auction is lower than the sellers expected, the agents blame 'the market'.

As you have seen, the first stage of conditioning is activity. And activity begins with advertising. In real estate, the word auction is almost a synonym for advertising. With auctions, agents get free advertising for themselves, huge kickbacks and discounts on the advertising money paid by the sellers, and then, on top of this, auctions are the 'fastest and best conditioning method'. It's a triple win for agents even before the home is sold. The sellers take all the risk. If their home is not sold or if it sells for a lower price, the agent still wins.

Buyers' agent David Morrell says that sellers have 'better odds at the casino'.[11]

According to Melbourne's *Herald Sun*, Martin Bartlett, an agent from Rowville in Victoria, admitted that advertising kickbacks (he called them 'incentives') increased his number of auctions. Since advertising promotion 'came in', his auctions trebled from 100 to 300 per year.[12] Advertising kickbacks are a huge incentive for agents to push auctions.

As stated, conditioning is an integral part of the auction system. First there is activity conditioning and then, as you will see, there is the crunch conditioning on auction day. No seller is immune. It catches everyone.

When New Zealand broadcaster Brian Edwards wanted to sell his home, he was astonished at the price he was quoted. The agent assured him the price was correct. But, once he was signed up for auction, the activity conditioning began – advertising, open inspections and lots of feedback. And, as Brian told it: 'Within days the agents began talking the price down. Bye-bye 200 grand! In each of the next four weeks it drops by a further $75,000. We're now at a figure $500,000 less than they assured us in writing we could get for the property. This, the agents calmly inform us is what "the market" is telling them. We wonder what "the market" was telling them when they appraised the property. This is typical of what happens at auctions. It's the norm. Thousands of people reading this will be saying: "That's exactly what happened to us".'[13]

For years, agents have been taught how to condition sellers with auctions. One real estate institute textbook teaches, 'The conditioning process must start early. It's no good telling them the bad news the day before the auction.'[14]

After committing to thousands of dollars in advertising money, after weeks of activity conditioning, the sellers are softened up, ready for the auction day. This is when extreme pressure is placed on them to lower their prices. It is when they suffer the trauma of crunch conditioning. There is barely time to think about what they are doing. The agents have control over the nervous sellers. As Graham White, a former training officer of L.J. Hooker, taught back in the 1980s, 'It's your job to wander around and keep them nervous.' White revels in the fact that sellers are 'terrified'. To get them to drop their price, he teaches agents to pressure sellers to take the highest bid. The property is then sold and, as he gleefully taught, 'The fee is yours.'[15]

Agents pressuring consumers at auctions is one of the most shameful sights in real estate

Agents pressuring consumers at auctions is one of the most shameful sights in real estate. As Brian Edwards says, the emotional distress, the feelings of disappointment, anger and despair are 'simply not worth it'.[16]

AUCTIONS: THE REALITY OF PRICES

One of the most important principles of negotiation is that to get the highest price you must start high, from a position of strength. Auctions start low which places sellers in a position of weakness. Agents will say, 'If you put a price on your home, the price can only go down.' This is not true. Many homes, especially in boom times, sell for more than the price displayed. As shown in Chapter Five, if there are two or more buyers, each buyer declares their best offer, in private. The sellers can choose the highest offer. This is not what happens at auctions. The highest price at auction is rarely the highest the buyer was prepared to pay.

Imagine you want to buy a home at auction and the most you can afford is $400,000. You are the only one who knows your highest price. The seller's lowest price – the reserve – is $340,000. Although you seldom know the reserve price before the auction starts, you will know it before the auction ends. But no one will ever know your highest price.

Typically, the following is what happens at auctions. The bidding starts at $300,000 and goes up in amounts of $10,000. First $310,000, then $320,000, then $330,000, then $340,000. Then it to slows to amounts of $1000. Now, imagine there is only you and one other buyer bidding. When the other buyer bids $350,000, how much more do you bid? Another $1000. And then, there are no more bids. Do you bid again? Of course not. You are the highest bidder. And the agent says 'Sold!' You buy for $49,000 below your highest price. As the buyer, you are the big winner. The sellers do not know that they are the losers.

Is the market price the sellers' lowest price or the buyers' highest price?

Because the reserve price was $340,000, the agent says the home sold for '$11,000 above reserve'. You know it sold for $49,000 below your highest price. Everyone, except you, thinks the auction got the best price.

Some people will say that this is the market price. But is the market price the sellers' lowest price or the buyers' highest price? Sellers employ agents to get the highest price, not a price tens of thousands below what the buyers are prepared to pay. The market price they want is the highest price a buyer is prepared to pay.

When Martin paid $675,000 for a home in the Sydney suburb of Clovelly he reportedly said, 'I would have gone to $700,000.'[17] The agent, John McGrath, was quoted as saying the home sold for a 'higher price' because it was 'expected' to sell for $650,000. But it did not sell for the best market price because the seller missed out on $25,000. In addition, she also paid commission and advertising costs.

Newspaper reports about sales above reserve disguise the reality that auctions get lower prices. One of thousands of examples was a home in the Melbourne suburb of Cheltenham. It sold for $235,000. Its reserve was $200,000. But the buyer had stated in writing that she was prepared to pay $260,000. Again, another of the thousands of homes which are sold for less than the buyers were prepared to pay – and reported in the papers as selling 'above reserve'.

An agent in the Melbourne suburb of Brighton advertised that he gets 'higher prices'. At the time his advertisement appeared, a buyer bought a home from him at auction for $83,000 below what the buyer was prepared to pay. Sure, the home sold above the reserve. But that's the catch for sellers. By allowing the agent to focus on their *lowest* price instead of the buyers' highest price, sellers lose thousands of dollars.[18]

Agents who claim that auctions get the highest price are either incompetent or dishonest

Agents who claim that auctions get the highest price are either incompetent or dishonest. The nature of auctions makes it almost impossible for sellers to get the highest price.

Auctions Get the Second Best Price

As accountant Ian Eldershaw explains, 'Auctions get you second best – never the best. The second best price level is set by the second best bidder. An auction stops when the second best bidder drops out and you never know how much you could have really got. For instance, imagine two people called Ken and Helen both want to buy your home. Ken is prepared to pay $340,000 and Helen is prepared to pay $320,000. But what will happen in an auction? You'll get a little over $320,000. When Helen stops bidding at $320,000, Ken will bid $321,000. And the bidding stops! The auction is over. It's an anti-climax. Ken grins in triumph because he paid $19,000 less than he expected. You missed out on $19,000. You got *second* best.'[19]

Ian points out that a skilled negotiator would have got the best price of $340,000. To get the best price, each buyer would have been asked to declare their best price one time and one time only. Helen would have declared $320,000. And because Ken would not have known Helen's price, he would have no option but to declare his best price. The big trouble with auctions, for sellers, is that the prices being offered are done in public. Every buyer knows exactly what other buyers are offering. Everyone knows the sellers' lowest price, but no one knows the buyers' highest prices. This is like playing cards where one person has to turn the cards face up and the others are allowed to keep them face down. The people who see all the cards have a huge advantage.

Marilu Hurt McCarty, Professor of Economics at Georgia University, says that when bidding is transparent – meaning that each bidder can see what other bidders are offering – buyers hold their bids below what they are prepared to pay. This means they are 'paying less to the sellers'.[20] And this is why auctions do not get the best price, they get the second best price. But still, thousands of sellers are tricked by the one-sided arguments of the auction agents.

David Slade is a real estate agent in Timaru, New Zealand. His agency was considered for the sale of a prime lake-front site on Lake Tekapo.[21] David advised against auction, but he was not selected as the agent. The sellers signed up for an auction with a large real estate network.[22] At the auction, the bidding commenced low, as it always does, and then, when it reached $192,000, it stalled. No further bids. The property was sold. A newspaper wrote a story about the success of this auction with the agent boasting, 'It's a lot of money.'[23] Yes, it was a lot of money. But, not in the way that most readers were led to believe. The buyer had been prepared to pay $315,000.[24] But the second highest buyer had only been prepared to pay $191,000. And so the sellers received $192,000, which was one thousand dollars above the second best price. Had they followed the advice of David Slade and not chosen auction, they would have received an extra $123,000 – from the same buyer. They would have received the best price, not the second best price.

The Reserve Price Trap

The reserve price is the lowest price the sellers will accept. Publicly, sellers are told, 'The reserve is there to protect you. Your property cannot be sold below your reserve. This means you are safe.'

But, as one agent says, 'The reserve price is basically a joke. A lot of auctions never reach the reserve.'[25] For sellers, the words 'going, going, gone' take on a whole new meaning on auction day.

Here's what typically happens. The agent, through activity conditioning, convinces the sellers to lower their reserve *before* the auction. If the home does not reach their reserve at the auction, sellers are placed under extreme pressure – usually in front of a crowd of onlookers – to further lower their reserve. Often the sellers are mentally exhausted. They will do anything to relieve the pressure. In real estate terms, the sellers 'crack'.

The Real Estate Institute of Australia teaches agents how to maintain the pressure on sellers at the auction. Its published training manual says: 'The pressure on them is starting to become intense and your persistency will win out in the end.'[26] Sellers are told that the reserve protects them from selling too low. But, on the auction day, the sellers will need protection from the agent. They are about to be crunched.

AUCTION DAY: THE CRUNCH

High pressure is the hallmark of an auction. The crunching process is pre-planned and deliberate with scant regard for the suffering of people who are bullied and tricked. Thousands of decent people are financially and emotionally devastated by this form of real estate terrorism. People like Sharon Wilkes, who was told that she could expect up to the 'high $500,000s' when she was persuaded to auction her home in the Sydney suburb of Wahroonga.

The 'On the market' Trick

When the bidding for Sharon's home reached $495,000, the agent used a common crunching trick. He told Sharon that to 'stimulate the bidding' and get the price higher she would need to put her home 'on the market'. Many sellers do not realise that 'on the market' is industry jargon for 'selling at the price offered'. It means the home can now be sold for the highest bid whether the sellers are happy or not. These sellers are confused, they feel their home is already 'on the market' because they want to sell it. They do not realise they are about to be tricked into selling for thousands below what they expected. Under pressure they are extremely vulnerable.

Thinking that 'on the market' meant that negotiations would start at $495,000, Sharon agreed. Almost immediately, her home was being sold at $495,000. When she realised what was happening Sharon yelled, 'No! That's not right. We can't sell at that price'. The agent ignored her and called out, 'Sold!'.[27] Sharon, sobbing with grief, felt forced to sign the contract. 'We were devastated,' she said. 'I cried for the next hour and was physically sick.' Despite being assured by the agent that she would find another home, Sharon discovered that this, too, was a lie. Having sold too cheaply, she was unable to buy again in the same area.[28]

No Time to 'Dwell on the Price'

The aim for most agents is to make the sale at the auction by using high-pressure tactics before consumers realise what is happening. A manual published by the Real Estate Institute of Australia teaches agents what to do. It says, 'Move quickly! Don't give them time to dwell on the price.'[29]

The trauma to consumers lasts long after the agents have spent their commissions. Today, Sharon still has nightmares and says she can burst into tears just thinking about what happened. Agents may use methods that don't give consumers time to dwell on the price or on the consequences of instant decisions but, later, consumers have plenty of time to dwell on what happened. For many people the trauma is so severe they never recover. They suffer for the rest of their lives from a system which has always exploited sellers and buyers. The real estate industry has known for years the pain inflicted on consumers with auctions. Horror stories are denied or covered up. Meanwhile, the industry still touts auctions as a fair way to sell or buy property, never mentioning the grave risks or that there are no second chances when making such a mammoth financial decision, usually alone and unprotected on a weekend.

The most staggering aspect of auctions is the lack of consumer protection. On March 11, 2002 the Australian Government introduced the Financial Services Reform Act which made it mandatory for consumers to be given 14-day cooling-off periods for all financial services and products.[30] There was only one exception – real estate. The biggest financial product of all was exempt from the legislation.

No Second Chances

John was a dairy farmer, a fit, hard-working and careful man with a wife and three young-adult children.[31] When he saw a dairy farm that was being auctioned, he decided to make an offer before the auction. His offer, $1.15 million, was refused; however the agent pushed him to pay more. John wanted to wait until the auction. But still the agent persisted, calling day and night badgering John to increase his offer. Some evenings, the family would return home to find the agent waiting for them. They were harassed for almost a month. On the day of the auction, John and his wife made a bid of $1.15 million. Theirs was the second bid after a first bid of $1.1 million from someone they couldn't see or hear. And then came a third bid, again from an unknown person, for $1.2 million. John then increased his bid to $1.25 million. Again, another bid was made from an unknown person for $1.3 million at which price the farm was passed in as unsold. To John's surprise the agent approached him and invited him to come inside the home to talk about the price. Said John's wife, Janice, 'We were surprised at this strategy, because we knew we weren't the last bidders. At no time did the agent approach any other person.'

Inside the home, John and Janice were confronted by three agents and the owners of the farm. They were pressured to increase their offer above $1.25 million. John refused because it was more than he could afford, and, besides, he needed time to sell his other property. The agent told him not to worry and that everything would be okay. He was crunched until he finally caved in and agreed to pay $1.285 million. He signed the contract and then parted with a cheque for a deposit of $128,500.

On the way home, John was agitated and kept saying to Janice, 'We shouldn't have done it.' From then on, something changed. He was barely eating or sleeping. Some days he wouldn't get out of bed. His solicitor had told him that he could not get out of the contract. Unable to sell his other property, he became more depressed. His dairy business began to suffer. One night, after dinner, John said he had to go out. He never returned. Early the next morning, his two sons found his ute, parked in a machinery shed with the engine running. John was inside. He had killed himself - carbon monoxide poisoning.

Weeks later, Janice tried again to cancel the sale, but the sellers had to be 'compensated for their loss' now that John could not buy the farm. Janice had to pay another $71,500 to get out of the contract. In all, she and her three children lost $200,000 and a husband and father.[32]

There are no cooling-off periods with real estate auctions. No second chances, no matter what.

DUMMY BIDDING:
THE TRUTH ABOUT AUCTION'S NOTORIOUS FRAUD

Dummy bidding is false bidding. It is done to fool genuine buyers into thinking real buyers are bidding. But, as you will see, dummy bidding is also used to get sellers to lower their prices.

Dummy bidding happens in two ways. First, the auctioneer calls out bogus bids, pretending someone in the crowd has made the bids. This is referred to as 'pulling bids', often from trees or walls. Second, stooges are planted in the crowd who call out bids. Many auctioneers use secret signals to tell stooges when to bid.[33] It happens at thousands of auctions. But for years the public message from the real estate industry has been to say it is 'isolated'. Or even to deny it with statements such as 'Dummy bidding? I don't know what you're talking about.'

In 2001, John Hill, the President of the Real Estate Institute of New South Wales was quoted as saying, 'There would be tricks of the trade out there but I've never experienced dummy bidders.'[34] The CEO of the Real Estate Institute of Victoria, Enzo Raimondo, in an interview on ABC Radio, said, 'I'm not sure what is meant by dummy bids. I haven't heard anyone explain to me what a dummy bid is.'[35] The announcer explained it to him: 'Someone standing in the audience pretending to be a real bidder and they're not.' Raimondo said, 'The auction process has been around for a long, long time.'[36] When he used similar statements on Radio 3AW, the announcer said, 'Enzo, you are treating me as an idiot here.'[37]

Dummy bidding is also used to get sellers to lower their prices

Anita Roddick, the founder of The Body Shop and a fierce critic of corporate dishonesty, once wrote, 'When you take the high moral road, it is difficult for anyone to object without looking like a complete fool.'[38] The defenders of dummy bidding were beginning to look very foolish.

Dummy Bidding Goes to Court

In June 2001, an auction agent sued a buyers' advocate for calling him 'an idiot'.[39] The buyers' advocate, Justin Dunne, saw the agent, Tim Fletcher, using dummy bids at an auction. Mr Dunne, who was representing a genuine buyer, refused to bid when dummy bids were being made.

The home did not reach its reserve price. The auction stopped and Mr Fletcher went inside the home with another genuine bidder (who had been bidding against the dummy bidders). Reportedly, Mr Dunne banged on the door, demanding the right to negotiate. Mr Fletcher refused to negotiate with Mr Dunne's buyer even though Mr Dunne's buyer was apparently willing to pay more money.[40] The home was sold to the other buyer at a lower price. Not only did Mr Dunne's buyer lose the home, but the seller almost certainly lost several thousand dollars. Mr Dunne was reported to have said, 'The owner's relatives think you are an idiot. I am going to report you to the fraud squad.'[41] Fletcher said it was 'absolutely fundamental' for his reputation that he be viewed as 'an upstanding person'.[42] And so he sued Dunne for defamation.

In July, the case was dismissed. The magistrate said, 'I find that Mr Fletcher, in using what on evidence, sadly, is a common practice, was indulging in a deceitful, misleading and fraudulent stratagem to boost bids.' The magistrate described fictitious bidding as 'evil'.[43] Mr Fletcher, with his reputation in tatters, continued to defend dummy bidding. He said his father had done it and so had his grandfather. He said the magistrate was wrong and that the decision was 'an attack on the vendors of this state'.[44] Enzo Raimondo from the Real Estate Institute of Victoria referred to dummy bids as 'vendor bids' and said they were 'clearly designed to protect the vendor's interest'.[45]

Fletcher claimed it was 'almost a civil liberties issue' as sellers had the right to protect themselves with dummy bids.[46] But as one consumer said, 'Since when has fraud been a civil liberty?'[47]

Defending Dummy Bidding: The Reality Comes to Light

With Fletcher's public disgrace, it was hard for the real estate industry to keep denying what had been known for years – dummy bidding goes on in all states of Australia and in New Zealand.

Many agents pay dummy bidders to attend auctions. The deceit had become so blatant that some agents were even sending invoices to sellers for the cost of dummy bidders.[48]

The Century 21 network once sent an urgent fax to its salespeople demanding that they stop asking homesellers to bring dummy bidders to auctions, inferring that this was giving away their secrets. 'Do not tell the vendor any more about the processes we use to achieve a sale than is absolutely necessary,' was the instruction. The network wanted to have its own dummy bidders – which it referred to as 'helpers'. The message ended by saying, 'They are to be OUR HELPERS not the vendors.'[49]

The public exposure of dummy bidding drew a common corporate response to questionable business methods – change the name. Just as killing whales is called 'harvesting', or gambling is called 'gaming', dummy bidding is called 'vendor bidding'.

The Real Estate Institute of Queensland issued a statement saying consumers were being confused based on 'spurious evidence'. The president, Mark Brimble, attacked 'self-appointed consumer advocates' for damaging the 'integrity' of auctions. He said, 'We all know that no matter how many "vendor bids" are made before the reserve is reached, none are going to result in a sale.'[50] Enzo Raimondo from the Real Estate Institute in Victoria repeated the common excuse made by many agents: that vendor bidding is 'protecting the vendor's interest'.[51] They claim that dummy bids are only made below the reserve price so that homes will not be undersold.

Then why have them? If the property is not going to be sold below the reserve price, there is no need to have any bids below the reserve price. The auction can just start at the reserve price. Melbourne lawyer Peter Lowenstern said, 'There is no need for vendor bids at all.'[52] His comments upset many agents, and again, Raimondo from the institute leapt to the defence of dummy bidding arguing that legal advice given to the institute was that vendor bidding was not misleading.[53] But another lawyer, Neil McPhee, who lectured in business law at the University of Melbourne had written as far back as 1993 that 'a reserve price offers far better protection' for sellers than dummy bidders.[54]

The defence of dummy bidding comes from the real estate industry, not from consumer advocates, lawyers, magistrates or consumers. Research shows that 84 per cent of consumers do not support dummy bidding.[55] The typical real estate industry response is that the critics 'do not understand'.

To most consumers, the standard arguments in support of vendor bidding don't make sense. There must be other reasons, reasons they are not being told.

A major reason that agents start the bidding below the reserve price is because they have been *underquoting* the price **Real estate** to buyers. If the reserve is $500,000 the agents may have told buyers 'bidding to start from **auctions** $400,000'. Imagine the reaction of buyers if the **depend on** auctioneer said, 'Ladies and gentlemen, the reserve price on this home is $500,000. That is **deceit** the lowest the seller is prepared to accept, so we will start bidding at $500,000.' The buyers would know instantly that they had been duped.

If auctions began at the reserve price, then, by the agents' own admission, there would be no need for dummy bidding. There would also be no need to tell lies to buyers about the expected selling price. But less buyers would be lured to auctions by the falsely quoted cheap prices. Auctions would not work as well for the agent. Real estate auctions depend on deceit.

Dummy bidding is a fraud on all consumers. Many consumers may not understand it completely, but they do understand one thing – it doesn't *feel* right. As Marsha Bertrand, author of *Fraud! How to Protect Yourself from Schemes, Scams and Swindlers,* points out, 'Often when [consumers] don't understand something, they think it's because they're stupid. But the truth is that they don't understand something because it doesn't make sense.'[56]

How Dummy Bidding Traps Sellers

Agents use the dummy bidders to get the bidding up to the price at which they feel the sellers will crack. If there is only one genuine buyer at an auction – which is often the case – the agents will want to sell the home to that buyer, whatever the price. But, without dummy bidders, they will not be able to get the auction going. The dummy bidders allow the agents to fool the buyers into thinking they are bidding against other buyers.

Dummy bidding also hides from the sellers the fact that there is only one bidder. It makes sellers think that the crowd (read, 'the market') is saying their home is worth what is being bid. Sellers have no idea that there is only one genuine bidder. They see the crowd, they hear lots of bidders and they think, 'With all these "buyers", this must be the best market price for my home.' This is exactly what agents want sellers to think.

As it becomes harder to get more bids from real bidders, the auction will slow down. The agent will pause the auction at a real bid and then pressure the sellers to lower their reserve. As one textbook teaches agents, 'You shouldn't worry if the reserve seems a little high because when the bidding slows down, the reserve can be lowered immediately to the amount of the highest bid.' This teacher than adds these words in bold letters, **'Bingo! Another sale.'**[57]

Agents start bidding below the reserve price because they intend to make sales below the reserve price. It's a fairly obvious point that most sellers don't understand – until it's too late.

Agents start bidding below the reserve price because they intend to make sales below the reserve price

If bidding began at the reserve price this would protect the sellers. But the agents have lied to the sellers about the likely selling price and they use dummy bidding, followed by high pressure and the statement, 'This is what the market is saying,' to manipulate sellers into lowering their prices. Dummy bidding looks like it is helping sellers, but it is dragging them into the jaws of the crocodiles. They get crunched. As Douglas Rushkoff, author of *Coercion,* explains, 'The better and more sophisticated the manipulation, the less aware of it we are.'[58]

Dummy bidding brings to a horrible conclusion weeks of conditioning and false information. Typical real estate selling is all about making the sales and getting the commission. And, because of the lies told to sellers and buyers, the best way to make sales is to find the best method of conditioning.

This is why the Real Estate Institute of Australia describes auctions as 'the fastest and best conditioning method'.

PRESSURE, TERROR AND HEARTACHE

Auction day is the agent's best chance to make a sale. Most agents seize that chance in a big way. The financial and emotional wellbeing of consumers is cast aside by the agent's fervent desire to get the sale and get the commission.

Bullying

One prominent Melbourne auctioneer had an advertisement with six action photos of himself and the heading, *'Ladies and Gentlemen, I am a brutal auctioneer.'*[59] The Macquarie Dictionary defines brutal as 'savage', 'cruel', 'inhuman', 'crude', 'coarse', 'harsh', 'irrational' and 'unreasoning'. A brute is defined as a 'selfish or unsympathetic person'.[60] The advertisement ends with the words, 'You'll like our approach'. But few consumers like the approach of agents at auctions. They feel trapped, powerless and intimidated.

Radio personality Greg Evans tells how his agent stood over him. 'I was sitting on a bench in my garden with the agent standing over me yelling that I was an idiot for not dropping my reserve.' Greg was shaking but wasn't sure whether it was from fear or anger.[61] Television personality and former model Deborah Hutton described the auction of her apartment as 'one of the worst experiences of my life'. She said, 'The whole thing was a total sham.'[62]

When a Melbourne barrister sued an auction agent for more than $200,000 for underselling his home, the claim was dismissed.[63] The judge described the auction system as a 'farce' and inferred that the barrister, being a 'well-educated person', should have known better. As usual, real estate institute spokesperson Enzo Raimondo was quoted as saying that the judge showed 'a lack of understanding of the system'.[64]

A Sydney couple who reportedly sued an agent for bullying them into dropping their reserve price got a different result. The agent's insurers agreed to pay $60,000 in an out-of-court settlement.[65] The president of the Real Estate Institute said the agent was a 'valued member' who had the 'full support' of the institute. The president was reportedly concerned that the case may encourage other sellers to take a 'similar course of action'.[66] But given that the couple's legal costs were reported to be $53,000, it was not likely to inspire other sellers to take such action.[67]

Bullying is endemic to auctions; it has been going on for years. In 1991, journalist Gordon Broderick described how 'the fat real estate agent with unkempt hair and 'Zapata' moustache [was] shuttling between two competing bidders urgently whispering encouragement into their respective ears'. He noticed a young woman who was 'reduced to a sobbing wreck'. Broderick's companion described auctions as 'sleazy'. Many people also describe them as sad.[68]

After Melbourne agent Tim Fletcher had his dummy bidding practices described as 'evil' by a magistrate, he appeared on television and radio defending dummy bidding, saying he did it to protect sellers. He told the audience, 'I've always been a passionate vendor's man.'[69]

However, at the same time as Fletcher was telling viewers about his commitment to protect sellers, he was suing one of his own sellers, Mr and Mrs Perryman, who claimed Fletcher had attempted to 'trick' them into selling below their reserve price. At the auction of their home, the pressure became so intense that the police were reportedly called to remove Fletcher from the premises. Although he did not sell their home, Fletcher wanted a commission of $12,104.00.[70] While justifying dummy bidding with the standard industry statement that it 'protects vendors', one of Fletcher's vendors was being sued by Fletcher even though he did not sell their home.[71]

The law is either too expensive or too stressful for most consumers

Auctions have no guarantees other than those available under the law – and the law is either too expensive or too stressful for most consumers. The best guarantee of protection for consumers is three words – don't sign anything. At least not until the agent signs a guarantee stating that there will be no conditioning at any stage.

Again, Remember, there are No Second Chances!

On one of the most financially important days of their lives, and one of the most emotional times, mums and dads, professionals, pensioners, celebrities – everyone who is involved in a real estate auction – feels the pressure. And there are no second chances. If a decision is made in the heat of the moment, and it turns out to be the wrong decision, too bad. Once the auction is over and the contracts are signed, that's it. The deal is done. There are no cooling-off periods.

The real estate industry has convinced governments that cooling-off periods and guarantees are not required with auctions. In the hottest selling environment when people are making the most important financial decision of their lives, they are denied one of their most important consumer rights – a cooling-off period.

In 2000, the Queensland government enacted legislation making it mandatory for a cooling-off period to apply to 'all residential property sales', *except auctions*.[72] And yet probably more consumers are hurt by auctions than any other method of selling real estate. But the government, as governments in each state do, received advice from the state's real estate institute.

If governments saw some of the industry training material on auctions, they may consider stronger legislation to protect consumers. At the very least, they may consider withdrawing government funding given to institutes for training agents and for giving public information. The Real Estate Institute of Australia, in one of its training books, teaches agents how to crunch sellers at auctions, saying, 'Take control: they are usually numb.'[73] Stunned and terrified consumers are easy to control at auctions.

At an auction, you are a captive. The agents do not want you escaping without signing. The Real Estate Institute of

Victoria tells auctioneers, 'Remember, when signing a client up, make sure you keep an eye on them and always look for possible escape routes.'[74]

How Auctions Remove the 'Pause Button'

When agents push consumers into making spur-of-the-moment decisions, they remove one of the most fundamental safety points in negotiation – the ability to be able to think it over. In negotiation, this is called being able to 'push the pause button'.[75] When this gambit is taken away, consumers are at the mercy of agents.

At auctions, agents place tremendous pressure on consumers to 'act now'. When the bidding pauses, sellers have the eyes of the crowd upon them. The auctioneer may yell, 'We are just getting instructions from our vendors.' But the vendors, who gave the instructions before the auction, are now being publicly pressured to change their 'instructions'. The agent wants a sale. Now.

Embarrassment and intimidation is a deliberate manipulation strategy at auctions.

Typical Auction Training for Agents

One auctioneer who teaches salespeople how to 'work an auction' taught the procedure:

'Make sure you get the reserve price down. Visit the owners the night before the auction. If they are being stubborn, get them as low as you can and then leave the rest to me. We'll meet before the auction and work out how we will play it. You tell me what genuine buyers you've got. If you've only got one buyer, don't worry, I'll just take it up to whatever price you think the buyer will pay. And then, if this is below the reserve, which it usually is, here's what we'll do – I will stop the auction and ask you to 'get instructions'. You must go to the owners and tell them that this is their one chance to sell. Make sure you get them to sell it now. If you let them go without selling, you'll blow it. You'll get nothing. When they are at the auction, when the pressure's on, when all the eyes are watching them, they'll crack.'

This teacher showed the salespeople how to walk over to the sellers so that there was 'no mistake' about who they were. He recommended standing above them and as close as possible. He then said: 'While you are crunching them, I'll be asking you to please hurry up because there are other people waiting for other properties. This will embarrass the hell out of them. Most of them will crack. If they don't, then you must tell them to put it "on the market" so that this will add urgency to it and get some more bids. All you have to do – remember this – is to get them to say "yes" to putting it on the market. It doesn't mean they will be selling at this price – but even if it does sell, you will get the sale. They can't change their minds once they say it's on the market. I will stop pulling bids so that the real bidders are the highest bidders. And if no one else bids, it's all over and we all get paid. Believe me, I have been doing this for years and it works. If you do it properly. Don't lose your nerve. Don't stand there with your arms folded. Go right up to them, point them out to me and the crowd and then get them to put it on the market.'[76]

This is auction training school where agents are taught to stage-manage the entire event. The Real Estate Institute of Australia's training says: 'At the fall of the hammer, the auctioneer should congratulate the purchasers and all sales staff should applaud; this will always result in general applause from the attendees.'[77] No matter what happens, the impression must be given that the auction was a success.

But success for an agent so often means distress for a consumer. As one agent remarked, 'Those smiles you see at the end of an auction are rarely the smiles of people who were happy with the auction. They are the smiles of people who are glad that the trauma is finally over, no matter what the result.'[78]

Words of Caution

Consumers who feel trapped at auctions should remember the slogan from the anti-drugs campaign: 'Just say no'.

Many people have someone attend the auction with them; there is strength in numbers. Or, better still, you should make your decision before the auction and then do not attend. Send someone as your representative or be available by phone contact. The agents will want you at the auction because they intend to crunch you. Don't let yourself be dragged into the crocodile den. Stay away and stay safe.

The word auction only needs to have the 'C' taken from the middle of it and moved to the front. It then becomes 'caution'. And that's what you need at an auction – extreme caution.

Extra Stress Needs Extra CAUTION

One of the golden rules of auctions is: *Believe nothing until you check everything.* But you should check everything and make your decisions *before* the auction. Under stress, you can easily make the wrong decisions.

Some agents focus on what's called 'The Three Ds' – Death, Debt and Divorce. The greater your need to sell, the easier it is to persuade you to sell for a lower price. With personal stress and the stress of the auction, you will be at your most vulnerable. You are going to have an auctioneer yelling at you with a hammer in his hand. You are going to have salespeople sidling up to you and urging you to make a decision. This is the time for extra caution.

When Roz auctioned a family member's home in the Sydney suburb of Enmore, the bidding stopped below her reserve. The agent approached her and whispered that the buyers had a pest report and the home was infested with termites. Roz was shocked, but agreed to drop the reserve. Her home was immediately sold. Three months later she visited the new owners and asked to see the pest report. It had never existed.[79]

When Judith auctioned her mother's home in Adelaide the agent assured her the price would 'definitely' reach the 'high 200s'. At the auction Judith was crunched and lowered her reserve to $245,000. To her horror, she then saw the agent wink at the bidder.[80]

In Victoria a buyer refused to sign the contract even though she was the highest bidder. The agent's conduct was so bad that a report stated, 'The conduct of the agent was potentially dangerous as the purchaser could have charged the agent with assault, battery and false imprisonment.'[81]

Publicly, the real estate industry says that bad stories are isolated. This is nonsense. Bad stories are denied or hushed up. The newspapers are filled with auction success stories. The bad stories, of which there are thousands, are rarely mentioned. It is not in the interests of most newspapers to report bad stories about real estate.

In May 2001 Cindy Martin, the property writer for the Sydney *Sun-Herald*, asked readers to tell their auction stories. The response was 'overwhelming'. As Cindy wrote, 'most of them were tales of horror'.[82]

One couple who had owned their home for 60 years were quoted 'more than $1 million' by the agent. Based on this, they bought an apartment for $750,000. They expected to receive $250,000 from their 'changeover'. They thought they had 'won the lottery'. But their home sold for $720,000. Instead of having $250,000 extra, they found themselves in debt for $30,000.[83]

Another couple, who had lived in their home for 40 years, were told that the reserve would 'protect' them. When the bidding stopped below the reserve, the agent asked them to 'put their home on the market'. They did not realise that 'on the market' means 'your home can be sold at this low price'. Their lawyer said, 'This story highlights one of the really annoying aspects of real estate – agents' incessant use of industry jargon.'[84]

Despite the 'overwhelming' response of 'tales of horror' only two appeared in the paper.[85]

Journalists, however noble their intentions, are often at the mercy of editors, who, in turn can be influenced by advertisers. Profit often rules what consumers read. As one consumer lawyer says, 'Those who promote and profit from the auction process are very powerful and influential within government and the media.'[86] As many consumers only buy or sell once or twice in their lives, the chance of discovering the truth about auctions is slim.

When it comes to auctions, remember the three-word message – don't sign anything. At least not until you understand how to protect yourself, emotionally and financially from the tricks and traps of auction.

MORE AUCTION TRICKS

Here are a dozen common auction tricks which trap thousands of sellers. Don't let them trap you.

1. The Frenzied Buying Trick

Agents say that buyers get swept up in the emotion of the auction. This rarely happens. Sure, at some auctions for low cost items, such as bric-a-brac or clearance sales, people might get carried away. Auctions for family homes are entirely different to clearance sale auctions.

Buyers cannot bid more than their financial limits. The way agents talk about the 'frenzy' at auction, it appears that buyers have unlimited funds. Buyers do not buy because of the auction. They buy because they want the home. The method of sale does not increase their ability to spend.

2. The Attract Buyers Trick

Agents say that auctions attract more buyers. This is not true. Auctions repel buyers. Buyers generally detest auctions. They often say, 'We do not want to look at anything for auction.' They only turn up to auctions if it is the only choice for them. It makes no sense to offer a home for sale using a method that most buyers detest.

This is especially true in areas which agents call 'auction areas'. The agents will tell sellers, 'In this area, everybody uses auction. If you don't auction, people will wonder why.' This is even more reason to avoid auction because more buyers will be available to look at homes which are not being auctioned. In 'auction areas' buyers want to buy homes, just as they do in all areas. Buyers aren't attracted to auctions, they are attracted to homes.

> Melbourne agent Tim Fletcher uses a common real estate statement to entice sellers to auction their homes, especially when the real estate market is hot. He says, 'Anyone who does not auction their home is committing financial suicide.'[87] But, as many sellers have discovered, it is more truthful to say that anyone who does auction their home is committing financial suicide. The best price at auction for Mr and Mrs Perryman's home was $406,000.
>
> This followed weeks of advertising, open inspections and pressure so severe that the police were involved.[88] Later, without an auction and without Fletcher, they sold their home for $427,000. However they still had to pay commission to Fletcher because they had signed his selling agreement which meant he was legally entitled to commission regardless of whether or not he was responsible for selling their home.[89]

This is why it is so important that sellers don't sign anything unless they have a guarantee that the agent will not charge them unless their home is sold for the price they were quoted – or more.

3. The Lots of Buyers Trick

The reason there are often lots of buyers at auctions is not because the buyers are eager to pay a high price. On the contrary, the buyers have been tricked into attending auctions by being told that they 'may' get a bargain. It is easy to have lots of buyers if the price is low. They are eager to pay a lower price, not a higher price.

A home can only be sold to one buyer. When one buyer – who can pay the best price – is surrounded by buyers who want to buy for a low price, the best buyer is influenced to pay less, not more. One agent explained it this way, 'Sometimes it's hard enough to find one buyer for a home, never mind having to find two which is what is needed with auctions. The only way to get two buyers is to lower the price. This does not help the sellers.'[90]

The more buyers who want to buy for a low price, the more likely you are to get a lower price. It is not buyers (plural) that you want for your home, but one buyer who will pay the *best* price. The best buyers pay less *because of* the auction. As New Zealand broadcaster Brian Edwards explained, 'The aim of the auction process is to flush out all the prospective buyers. This argument is deeply flawed. You aren't, of course, flushing out all the prospective buyers, only that elite group of cash buyers who can afford to commit themselves unconditionally on the day.'[91]

Don't be fooled by the 'lots of buyers' trick. You need the best buyers, not lots of lookers or bargain-hunters. As shown with advertising, the more people who see your home and do not buy it, the more you damage the value of your home.

4. The Definite Date Trick

Auction agents will say you get a set date when your home will be sold. But why wait weeks? Many buyers want to buy immediately. If they see an auction which is weeks away, they can lose interest. This is especially true if agents insist that the home 'goes to auction'. The reason agents like homes to be sold at auction is because it makes auctions look successful.

Some agents, if they get a buyer before the auction, will not want the home to be sold because they have not spent all the seller's advertising money. This is common. 'We have to keep our profiles high,' say the agents.

Many buyers make offers before an auction which are declined. The agent will tell the owners, 'You might get more at auction.' But the sellers often get less at the auction. As one buyers' advocate boasted, 'I have bought homes for $100,000 less than my clients offered prior to the auctions – it happens all the time.'[92]

5. The Set Time Trick

Brian and his partner were devastated. They arrived 25 minutes late at the auction and the home had been sold. But what really hurt was the selling price. It was $155,000 below Brian's maximum price of

$480,000. But there was still hope. Brian spoke with the buyer who had just paid $325,000. He offered him $50,000 to back out of the sale. The buyer refused, saying that he, too, had been prepared to pay much more. Brian then offered the buyer $100,000 to pull out of the sale. He still refused.[93]

For the sake of 25 minutes, the sellers missed out on having two buyers bidding for their home. If Brian had arrived on time, he would have bid to $480,000. Twenty-five minutes cost the sellers $155,000.

There are many stories of people not making it to an auction on time – an accident, a speeding ticket, a wrong time printed in an advertisement, bad weather. There are hundreds of ways a set time can backfire on the sellers. Sellers never know who does not show up. According to one report, a homebuyer speeding to an auction tooted his horn as he overtook an unmarked police car. The police gave chase but the buyer kept going, driving on footpaths and on the wrong side of the road. Finally, the police cornered him but he still tried to escape. Senior Constable James McCashney told the court that the driver's excuse was that he was 'running late for an auction'. He was fined $1200 and disqualified from driving for six months. Apparently he did not make it to the auction.[94]

The Real Estate Institute of Victoria is aware of cases where the auctioneer arrived so late that the crowd had gone or, worst of all, where the auctioneer never showed up.[95]

6. The Quicker Sale Trick

Saying that auctions sell homes more quickly than other sale methods is one of the biggest lies in real estate. It's not the auctions which make the homes sell more quickly, it's the prices and the pressure. As with the definite date trick, many homes would have sold sooner if the buyers did not have to wait for the auctions. If the homes that sold at auction had not been auctioned, almost all of them could have sold just as quickly. And for better prices.

7. The Percentage Sell Trick

Many agents fudge auction results to make auctions appear more successful. They will ignore properties which are passed in (meaning they failed to sell); they will count sales made before the auction and after the auction as sales made at auction; they will include sales made by private treaty as auction sales; they will misreport the names of suburbs to create the perception that they have a bigger market share.[96]

And, of course, they will always report the amount by which properties have sold above the reserve and never mention how much the properties sold below the price the buyers were prepared to pay.

The fudging of auction results is common

United States criminal investigator George Allen tells how auctioneers manipulate the results at auctions by 'failing to disclose the numbers or values of items that did not sell. This practice may lead customers to misjudge market trends.'[97] The fudging of auction results is common in real estate.

8. The Competition Trick

To say that competition forces up prices is only part of the truth. If the competition is in public, as happens at auctions, each buyer sees what other buyers are offering. Instead of offering their highest price, each buyer only offers a small amount above what the other buyers offer. As already explained, this is how auctions get the second best price, not the best price. The bidding is *comparative* because each buyer compares their bid with that made by other buyers. The price then stalls when the final bidder sees the others stop. Such public comparisons cost sellers thousands.

9. The Buyer Bait Trick

When an agent says, 'bidding to start from', then whatever price is being advertised is the price at which buyers will be attracted. If you want $500,000 and the agent attracts buyers who want to pay 'from $400,000', it can be hard to get them to pay $500,000. At the auction you will have a crowd of buyers attracted by the $400,000 bait price. Of course, the agent can push them up in price. But to what level? If the bidding stalls at $450,000, the agent will say, 'This is what the market is telling us your home is worth.' But the agent has been looking in the *wrong* market. If you want to sell a home for $500,000, the first thing you need is a buyer who can pay $500,000.

10. The Conditions Trick

Agents will say that when you sell by auction you can set the conditions. You can put whatever you want in the contract and the buyers can't change it. Aside from this not being true (the buyers can ask for anything to be changed before the sale), when you put tough conditions in a contract you risk repelling the best buyers.

11. The Three Stage Trick

Agents say you can sell before the auction, at the auction or after the auction. They call it a 'three stage' process.

The agent has been looking in the wrong market

But this is just an excuse for when the home does not sell at the auction.

And herein lies one of the biggest auction traps – homes that do not sell. Everyone wants to know what happened. 'With all that advertising, with all those inspections and that huge crowd at the auction, you mean it didn't sell?' say the astounded buyers. And then comes that price-killer question, 'What's wrong with it.'

The major thing wrong with a home that doesn't sell at auction is the agent who recommended the auction.

12. The Fall of the Hammer Trick

Agents say that one of the benefits of auction is that buyers cannot change their minds. Neither can the sellers. If either the sellers or the buyers make a mistake at the auction, they are both caught. This trick benefits the agents more than the sellers and buyers. It means that once the hammer falls the agents get paid, no matter how the sellers or buyers feel.

Or does it?

When journalist Amanda Hodge was the final bidder on a St Kilda home, the auctioneer yelled, 'Sold'. He shook her hand. Suddenly another bidder emerged. The auctioneer restarted the auction and the home was sold to another buyer.[98] Amanda's 'purchase' lasted mere seconds. She discovered what many agents have always known – the fall of the hammer is a charade. It means nothing. It is now – and always has been – one gigantic bluff on the part of the agents.

> **The fall of the hammer is a charade. It means nothing**

Until a contract is signed by both the sellers and the buyers, no sale is certain. As one lawyer commented, 'The fall of the hammer is meaningless.'[99] Other lawyers agree. One said that auctioneers who tell bidders they are legally committed to proceed are 'perpetuating a fraud' because no one is legally committed to anything until they have signed a contract.[100] If you are selling or buying at auction and you have been pressured into making an instant decision, the rule is simple: do not sign any contract until you seek independent legal advice. Even if the agent says you are legally committed, don't be bluffed. Don't sign anything. Just walk away and find a lawyer. Agents who don't keep their word are often quick to force you to keep yours. Morally, if you have given your word under duress or trickery you should not sign anything. Just remember that at every auction a consumer loses. Make sure it is not you.

> **Do not sign any contract until you seek independent legal advice**

How Consumers Always Lose at Auctions

Take any auction, consider any outcome and you'll discover the truth – consumers always lose.

Outcome 1.
The Home Sells for More Than the Reserve Price

The first loser is the seller because most winning bidders

would have paid more. The seller will also lose the advertising money – which can be as much as two per cent of the sale price. Rarely does the advertising money create the sale. It just creates profile for the agents.

The second loser (or losers) are the unsuccessful buyers who miss out on the home. These 'underbidders' may have paid hundreds of dollars for building reports and legal expenses, even loan expenses. Some will have paid for valuations. Sometimes the same building inspectors will have been hired by different buyers, all of whom are interested in the same property.

When Jeff Hercz was looking at a home, a building inspector arrived. The inspector spent five minutes at the home because he had already inspected it for another buyer. The cost for each inspection was $420. As Jeff asked, 'Is it legal to charge for the same service twice?'[101] The inspector had been employed by two different buyers, so it is legal. Although this can happen in any type of sale, it is much more common with auctions because buyers are led to believe they will get the home for a low price. This means more buyers waste more money.

Outcome 2.
The Home Sells for Less Than the Reserve Price

In this case, the sellers lose their advertising money in addition to the amount their home sold below its value or what the sellers were expecting. Many sellers make financial commitments based on the price they were quoted and therefore expected. The Quote Lie does a lot of damage.

Outcome 3.
The Home Does Not Sell

In a manual published by the Real Estate Institute of Australia, agents are told, 'Should the property not sell, don't apologise to the sellers.'[102]

Even such obvious failures as homes not selling at auctions are not admitted by many agents. They say it is part of the three stage process where a sale can be made before the auction, at the auction or after the auction. This is nonsense. The sellers lose their advertising money, the value of their home is damaged and it is seen as a lemon.

Again, all the buyers lose their inspection money. Many are furious because the agent gave them a false quote about the likely selling price. They wasted their time and their money trying to buy a home they never had a chance of buying.

BUYING YOUR FAMILY HOME AT AUCTION

If the home you want is for sale by auction, you have to play the auction game. The first thing you have to ask is: Can I afford the home? You don't want to spend money and time, plus get your hopes up, only to find out later that you never had a chance.

Three Prices

There are three prices you have to discover about any home. First, *what the home is worth* – its approximate 'market value'. Second, *what the home is worth to you*. And third, the *price at which the sellers will sell the home*.

You can find the answer to the first question by comparing the home with other homes sold in the area. Be careful though. In a rising market recent sales may be lower than today's prices. Conversely, the same applies in a falling market. The sales of yesterday may be higher than the sales of today. No matter what agents tell you, real estate prices do drop.

Nevertheless, comparing the home you want to buy with similar homes that have sold recently will give you some idea of the current market value of the home. Also, you should consider hiring an independent valuer. It may cost you a few hundred dollars, but it is well worth it.

But, before you pay any money – on a valuation or an inspection or on anything – you have to decide what the home is worth *to you*. If you love the home and you intend to live in it for many years, be prepared to pay more than the current market value, if necessary.

Michael and Lesley found the home they loved. Its market value was around $850,000. But to them it was worth more because they loved it. The maximum they could pay was $892,500. And that's what they paid for the home. As Michael said, 'Our happiness is not for sale. We did not want to risk losing this home. We loved it and we knew we would live there for the rest of our lives. If we pay more than the market value, it won't matter in a few years. And they will be very happy years.'[103]

So, what is the home you love worth to you? Answer that question and you will be in the best position to buy it. You will be able to give it your best attempt.

Finally you have to discover *the price at which the owner will sell*. You must know if you are in with a chance. With auctions, this can be hard. But it's not impossible. Most agents will either be vague about the price or they will underquote the price to entice you to the auction. If the price the agent quotes is the most you can afford, chances are that you will miss the home. With auctions, many agents who quote a likely selling price to buyers are lying.

It is better to spend days researching than to spend years regretting

How do you know if the agent is lying? You don't. You have to know the prices at which similar homes have sold. This involves research. The more knowledge you have, the more likely you are to win with auctions. It is better to spend days researching than to spend years regretting.

Let's say your research leads you to believe the home is worth $500,000. And let's say the agent is quoting 'from $450,000'. If the most you can afford is $555,000, you are in with a big chance. So, go back to the first question and hire an independent valuer. Also, get *independent* legal advice. And then go to the auction, preferably with a friend who knows what to do, and bid.

Risks

The biggest fear with trying to buy a home you love is the thought of losing it. Maybe it will be sold before the auction to someone else. This is a risk you want to eliminate. First, ask the agent if the home is likely to be sold before auction. If the agent says yes, you then have to consider if you will make an offer before the auction. This is a form of mental torture. If you make an offer, do you make your best offer? If so, this will mean revealing your best price. If the offer is rejected, what do you do then? Do you still go to the auction? Yes.

In a typical example, one couple made an offer of $720,000 before an auction. It was rejected. Because it was their maximum price, and it was refused, they did not go to the auction. Later, they were shocked to discover that the home sold for $680,000.[104] This happens often. If you make an offer before an auction and that offer is rejected, *go to the auction.* It might sell for less.

You can rarely offer a low price and have the best chance of buying the home

If the agent says that offers will not be considered before the auction, how can you be sure? John was told that no offers would be considered before auction. But a week before the auction, he saw a sold sign outside the home. When he called the agent, he was told that someone had made a 'good offer'. But it was $22,000 less than he was prepared to pay.[105]

If an agent says that no offers will be considered before auction, ask, 'What about a good offer?' At this point you have to decide how much you want to risk losing the home. Which is more important to you – the home itself or the price you pay? You can rarely offer a low price and have the best chance of buying the home. What you can do, however, is make a good offer – below your best – and keep in close contact with the agent in case another offer is made which is above your offer.

What you need, most of all, is assurance that the home will not be sold without you having a chance to increase your offer. You should give the agent a letter insisting that you be given the right to make another offer before the home is sold. If the agent signs a receipt for this letter, the implication is clear. However, understand that offering any price below your best price can be dangerous. You could still lose the home you love.

There are many factors in this mental chess game. But the major points of buying your family home at auction are:

1. Discover the three prices – the market price, your price, and the sellers' price.

2. Get independent legal advice.

3. Get an independent valuation.

4. Discover if a sale before auction is possible.

5. Decide whether to make your best offer or a good offer. Give the agent a letter to reduce the risk of another buyer paying less than your best offer.

6. Buy the home, either before the auction or at the auction.

Planning Your Maximum Buying Price

Your main aim at auction is to buy the home *at a price you can afford*. You must set a maximum limit beyond which you will pay no more. The joy of buying the home you love can be wiped out by the pain of paying more than you can afford. Set your limit, before the auction, and stick to it. If the bidding goes beyond your limit, stop.

It is better to put the pressure on yourself before the auction, when you have time to think clearly

Remember, if you get into financial trouble later, the agent will do nothing to help you. Once you buy, you are on your own. Be very careful of the line, 'It's only another thousand dollars.' It could be the thousand dollars that breaks you. Set your limit and stick to it. No matter what.

When setting your limit, work out the most you are prepared to pay. Take your time. Consider everything –

especially your *future* capacity to repay a loan. And then, in a sort of mental rehearsal, ask yourself: 'What if I have to pay a little bit more?'

If your limit is $550,000, could you pay $551,000? What about $552,000? How about another $500 making it $552,500? Do you see where this is leading? It is better to put the pressure on yourself before the auction, when you have time to think clearly. Be certain before the auction so that you can be firm at the auction. Set your limit and stick to it. No matter what. If you do not buy the home, perhaps it was not meant to be. It might hurt, but it will never hurt as much as not being able to make the payments and, later, being forced out of your home.

> **It's agony when another buyer pays less than you were prepared to pay**

Bidding at the Auction

The golden rule of bidding at auctions – never bid until the property is on the market (meaning the home is going to be sold at or above the price currently being bid) – has been tarnished in recent years. When the bidding stops below the reserve and the home is passed in, the agent will negotiate with the highest bidder. Sometimes the other bidders never get a chance.

When Marcello attended an auction in Essendon[106], the auctioneer, Lou Rendina, who was the local branch president of the Real Estate Institute of Victoria, became annoyed with buyers asking if the home was on the market. One buyer yelled out, 'Just answer the question.'[107] Rendina stopped the auction and took the highest bidder inside the home. A few minutes later, he emerged from the home. With a smirk, he stuck a sold sticker on the sign. The home had been sold for $370,000. Marcello was prepared to pay $400,000.[108]

Such incompetence is common, so be careful. It's heartbreaking to lose a home you love, but it's agony when another buyer pays less than you were prepared to pay.

Bidding Tricks

At the auction, you will be told this is a 'rare opportunity', it is the 'best time to buy' and 'make sure you don't miss out'. Ignore clichés; they are similar at every auction. Just stay focussed on your aim – to bid within your limit. The auctioneer may think he has control. But you know something he doesn't. You know what you are prepared to pay. Keep your maximum amount confidential.

The auctioneer will call for an 'opening bid'. You can either remain silent – the longer it takes to get the auction started, the more other buyers may wonder what is wrong – or you can do what some bidders do, open the bidding at a low figure. This may cast doubts in the minds of other bidders and make them lower their maximum.

There are a lot of 'maybes' with auctions, but the best advice, if you are inexperienced, is to act calmly and bid slowly and confidently. Yes, it may bother you to think that you are bidding against stooges. But that's the way of auctions. If you feel you are bidding against a dummy bidder, or you suspect that the auctioneer is inventing bids, you can ask, 'Is that a real bid or a dummy bid?' The auctioneer will not like this, but you have the right to ask if you are being deceived.

One buyer was told, 'No, madam, it is not a dummy bid, it is a "vendor" bid. The lady said, 'Well, to me, that's the same thing, so please let me know when it is a real bid because I only want to bid against real bidders.' The auction stopped and she bought the home for $22,000 below her maximum price.[109] At another auction, the auctioneer said, 'I do not take dummy bids, Sir.' The bidder said, 'Are you telling me that you have never taken a dummy bid?' The auctioneer went red. The bidding slowed.[110]

You should stand either at the back of the crowd or, if you are assertive, stand at the front, close to the auctioneer, facing the crowd. You want to see clearly what is going on. It makes it harder for the auctioneer if he knows that you can see where the bids are coming from.

Once the bidding starts – and assuming you are bidding against genuine bidders – don't be afraid to keep bidding. You can bid fast or slow. If you bid fast, it may create the impression that you are determined. As the price climbs, this can make the other bidders think there is no point going on – you are going to buy it no matter what. Or, you can bid slowly, making the auctioneer work for each bid.

You can 'cut' the bidding. If it is rising in $10,000 amounts, cut it to $5000. And then, at the next bid, cut it to $1000. And then to $500. Even to $100. It's worth a try.

Buyers' advocate David Morrell seems to enjoy the intimidation at auctions. In one reported instance, when he was bidding on behalf of a buyer, the bids were going up in $50,000 amounts. Morrell increased his bid by one dollar. The auctioneer refused to accept such a low rise in the bidding. Morrell approached the auctioneer, placed his arm around his shoulders, looked out at the crowd and said, 'Show me your bidder.' There was no other bidder. The auctioneer accepted Morrell's one dollar bid.[111]

Some bidders like to use what's called the 'knockout bid' which means you suddenly make a big bid to frighten off the other bidders. However, if you win the auction with a knockout bid, you will always wonder if you could have won with a lower bid.

But, remember, the main aim is to buy below your limit and, having achieved this aim, don't worry about what could have happened. Just be happy that you bought the home, probably below your maximum.

You have the right to ask if the home is 'on the market'. If not, you can remain silent. There is no need for you to bid if others are bidding. But make sure you start bidding when the auction is slowing down. Keep asking if the home is 'on the market'.

Once the bidding stops, the agents will put pressure on the sellers. This is where you should appear very firm, even if the price is still below your maximum. The pressure comes hardest on the person the agents believe is softest. The tougher you are on the agent, the easier they will be on you – and the harder they will be on the seller. It may sound harsh but, as a buyer, you don't choose the way the home is sold. Auction is the agents' game. If you play it well you can win well.

If, after speaking with the sellers, the agent says, 'It's on the market, it's going to be sold,' then just wait. Your heart will be pounding as you wait to hear that word, 'Sold'. If other bidders start bidding now, just follow the same rules. Keep bidding, either fast or slow, whatever you feel is best. Stop bidding when you reach your limit. Remember the promise you made to yourself before the auction. Walk away. If you must stay, do not bid past your limit.

The tougher you are on the agent, the easier they will be on you

If you follow this advice, you will have the best chance of buying. It is almost certain that if you do buy, you will buy below your maximum. Auctions can get high prices but they get lower prices than most winning bidders were prepared to pay. This is some compensation for the trauma buyers have to endure. For sellers, auctions are almost always a losing proposition.

Someone to Watch Over You

When Bill and Reyna bought a home at auction, their maximum price was $650,000. A friend, who was a critic of auctions, well known for saying that auctions get lower prices, bid on their behalf. The home sold for $615,000. Bill and Reyna were delighted because they saved $35,000.[112]

For sellers, auctions are almost always a losing proposition

The reserve on the home was $600,000, and, because it sold for $15,000 above the reserve, a newspaper trumpeted that the auction critic had been proved wrong, saying that the golden rule of real estate is to 'always get the best price for the seller'.[113] The golden rule of auctions, which newspapers often ignore or do not understand, is that auctions get lower prices.

The friend did not charge Bill and Reyna for saving them $35,000. He didn't really do anything they could not have done. The main reason to have someone bid for you is moral support. You can tell your friend your maximum price and just stand in the background. Or stay away.

If you don't have a friend who can bid for you – and you want moral support (and maybe someone who knows what's going on) you can ask a friendly and competent agent to bid for you. Many agents will do this at no charge, especially if you are selling your current home with their agency.

Or you can consider using an agent who specialises in acting for buyers – a buyers' advocate.

Buyers' Advocates

With so much deceit in real estate, especially at auctions, some buyers are employing an agent to act on their behalf. These buyers' agents, or buyers' advocates, claim to be able to save buyers thousands of dollars. They don't come cheap, usually charging between one and two per cent of the home's price. With sellers and buyers both paying commission, this adds substantially to the cost of home sales.

Buyers' advocates know the tricks of real estate. In many cases, they have used them. These agents have switched sides. They now act for buyers instead of sellers. And when there is an agent acting for the seller and another agent acting for the buyer, it becomes a contest as to who is the better negotiator. If the seller is using an auction, the buyers' agent will almost certainly be the winner. Buyers' advocates are doing what sellers' agents have been doing for years – advertising how much money they make for their clients at auctions. Some even advertise the addresses of homes and the amounts saved by buying at auction.

Buyers' advocates are often unpopular with auction agents. They have been accused of being 'hostile' and 'intimidating' – the same accusation levelled at auction agents for years. 'I am not here to make friends,' says advocate David Morrell, who says he is employed to buy homes for buyers at the lowest possible price. He knows the auction system well. He says 'most auctions involve misrepresentation and deceptive conduct and are a fraud.'[114] Morrell also says that professionals 'love auctions' because they can save thousands of dollars for buyers. It is well known in real estate circles that he will even pay competing bidders to stop bidding. 'Sometimes we'll go to a bidder and offer them large sums of money to stop bidding,' Morrell reportedly said.[115]

A buyers' advocate makes it even more certain that sellers will get lower prices at auction.

Paying a Buyers' Advocate

In the United States, buyers' advocates are common. But in Australia and New Zealand, they are just beginning to emerge. If they negotiate and save you money, they are worth considering. However, their standard method of charging makes no sense. It works against the interests of the buyers. The job of a buyers' advocate is to buy a home at the lowest price. But they charge a percentage of the purchase price, which means the more you pay for your home, the more you have to pay the advocate.

Don't hire someone to get you a lower price and then pay them extra if you pay a higher price

Don't hire someone to get you a lower price and then pay them extra if you pay a higher price.

The best way to pay a buyers' advocate is from a percentage of *what they save you* on the price of the home. If your maximum price is $550,000 and the agent gets the home for $550,000 they should not be paid. They saved you nothing so they should be paid nothing. However, if they negotiate a price for you of $530,000, they have saved you $20,000. You should pay a percentage of the $20,000. How much? Between 25 and 50 per cent would be fair.

Buyers' advocates often perform another role: finding you the right home. One part-time advocate in Melbourne began charging $500 for searching for a home and 35 per cent of the amount saved on the price. The demand for his services was so high that he couldn't handle it all.[116]

Don't sign anything unless the advocate agrees to charge you only after the job is complete. Most honest business people will agree to payment on completion of their service. They do not ask for money in advance.

Auction Bargains

Many agents use the fact that government departments sell by auction to infer that auctions are the best way to sell. But many sellers who would normally criticise governments for wastage don't consider that the same governments waste money with their real estate sales. Those in charge of the public purse are notorious for wasting money. In real estate, their financial incompetence is common. From Cairns to Hobart – and all over Australia – government departments are costing taxpayers millions by selling real estate at auction. At these auctions, there are bargains galore.

In 2001, the Cairns City Council, in a clamp-down on unpaid rates, commenced an 'aggressive' campaign to sell properties for overdue rates. Their initial target was 64 properties. All were to be auctioned. The first was a home in the suburb of Earlville. It sold for $51,500. One agent, just by driving by the home, said its value was 'around $75,000'.[117] It was in poor condition, but another home in the same street had recently sold for $162,000. The CEO of the Cairns Council was reported as saying their actions had 'reaped rewards'.[118]

In Hobart, the government owned a property in the Lower Sandy Bay area. Before its scheduled auction, a buyer offered $1.4 million. The agent said the property must be sold at auction, not before. The property then sold at auction for $1.075 million, $325,000 less than the offer before the auction. As one agent commented, 'Taxpayers lost $325,000.'[119]

In the Melbourne suburb of Melton, the Department of Human Services wrote to an agent asking him to sell a property by auction. The agent, who had sold more than 7000 properties in the district, wrote to the department with evidence that auctions get lower prices. He said it would be unethical of him, as an agent acting for a seller, to use a method which did not get the best price. He believed he could sell the property for 'close to $200,000' – but not at auction. He was ignored. The property was given to another agent. It sold by auction for $145,000.[120]

Another agent was asked by the same government department to auction three homes. The agent said, 'Auction is the worst method of selling. We could not be involved in something that would deliberately lose thousands of dollars for the Department of Human Services and taxpayers.' In his area, the majority of homebuyers need a loan approval which, the agent claims, means they find it difficult to buy at auction. 'The auction system discriminates against battling homebuyers,' he said.[121]

There are bargains galore at auctions, despite the denials of auction agents. The chief executive of a real estate chain said, 'Auction bargains? Nothing could be more of a myth.' He made the usual claim that 'the reserve price protects the seller'.[122] Buyers' advocate David Morrell responded, 'This man must have blinkers on.'[123] As for the reserve price 'protecting' sellers, Morrell revealed what most agents know, but what they hide from homesellers, 'It is similar to stealing ice cream from babies.'[124]

One of the most financially successful property developers in Australia is Harry Triguboff of Meriton Apartments. He is ranked sixth of ten billionaires in Australia.[125] He has sold thousands of apartments but has never used the auction system to sell.[126] The most successful investors know that auctions are not the place to sell real estate for the highest market price.

However, some auction agents truly believe that auctions get the best prices. One New Zealand agent, Michael Boulgaris, who also hosted a real estate program on television (where he was caught on camera arranging dummy bidders)[127] fell into the auction trap. When he sold his own home, he paid $10,000 for a huge advertising campaign. The auction failed.[128] He admitted his home became a lemon, saying, 'I'm stuck with a home that I'm not going to be able to sell through over-exposure.' Five months later he was forced to sell at a loss of $60,000.[129] Incredibly, as a real estate agent, Boulgaris continued to recommend auctions to homesellers. He blamed his own auction failure on the honesty of his agent. She told buyers the truth about how much he wanted. 'You were supposed to feed people's greed,' he told his agent, who obviously did not agree that buyers should be deceived by a false low quote.[130] But, as Boulgaris says, 'You have to let people have that sense of a bargain and think that they might get the property for their hoped-for price.'[131] With auctions, you have to trick buyers with a fraudulent bait price.

Trickery has always been the nature of auctions.

AUCTIONS: A HISTORY OF MISERY AND TRICKERY

'Auctions have been around since Roman times,' or so agents say in an effort to make them seem respectable. But the length of time something has been around does not make it respectable. History shows that it would be more correct to compare auctions with domestic violence than respectability.

Auctions began with the abuse of women. About 2500 years ago (in Ancient Greece, not Rome), men formed a circle around groups of young women who were rounded up for annual village sales. The most attractive ones were sold first, usually to the wealthier men. This was all legal. But unlike today, the law in those early auctions required a 'guarantee'. If a man did not like the woman he bought at auction, he was entitled to a refund of his purchase price.[132]

Auctions have always been associated with misery. When Roman armies went into battle, the old style auction agents followed them. After the battle, the agents would auction captured prisoners who were to be used as slaves. They would also sell captured goods. These auctions were known as *sub hasta* – Latin for 'under the spear'. Hence the origin of the term 'under the hammer'.[133]

Dummy bidding existed in ancient auctions. The Roman statesman Cicero felt it was necessary to 'revise the whole way of thinking' of some business people. He said 'trickery and misleading arguments' hurt society because they were contrary to one of the essential components of a healthy society – 'moral goodness'. Cicero opposed dummy bidding, saying 'a vendor must not employ a puffer to raise the price'.[134]

In 193 AD, 236 years after Cicero died, the entire Roman Empire collapsed and was auctioned as one lot. There were only two bidders. It is not known if one of them was a dummy bidder. Auctions disappeared for almost 1400 years.

It was misery once again that saw their revival in France in 1556. A group of 'bailiff' auctioneers had the exclusive rights to sell the property of people who had been executed. These auctioneers, who all wore black, were often caught selling property at low prices to their friends.[135]

When King Charles I of England was beheaded in 1649, the government auctioned his art collection which was bought at bargain prices by foreign investors and collectors.[136]

The slave traders who captured Africans and shipped them in chains to America needed a quick return on their 'investments'. The treatment of these people – or 'chattels' as they were often called – was brutal. Prior to being sold at auction, they were split into groups based on age, sex and condition. As screaming family members were being separated forever the auctioneer would yell, 'Bring up the niggers.'[137]

The early auctions mostly involved misery, trickery and low prices. Auctions were a business of exploitation and sudden opportunity. They were rarely a serious part of traditional business.

Auctions in Business

Auctions made their way into the business world in the 1700s. The goods sold were generally cheap and of poor quality, often coming from bankrupt or deceased estates. The crowds at these early auctions were mostly poor or working-class people. Auctions were not the domain of the rich.

Auctions are a form of theatre, with an almost intoxicating mood of excitement. Their fast pace gives victims little time to think. Like mental drunks, consumers are easy prey for the auction hucksters. In the early business auctions, sellers and buyers were described as being 'reduced to a state of imbecility'.[138]

In 1766, a charismatic Englishman, James Christie, wanted to attract the wealthier classes to auctions. Whatever Christie auctioned, it was billed as the finest – horses had pedigrees, tulips were exclusive. His goods often came from a 'noble personage'. He was also discreet. When wealthy people fell upon hard times, Christie would lend them money which he would recover from the auction of their goods. It became acceptable for the upper class to be seen at auctions.[139]

Another auctioneer of the same period was Samuel Baker, a book dealer who held his first book auction in 1744. When Baker died in 1778, his nephew, John Sotheby, inherited the firm which then became known as Sotheby's. Although Sotheby's claims to be have been 'founded in 1744', author Robert Lacey, who wrote a book about Sotheby's, describes this claim as typical of the auction business where 'nothing is ever quite what it seems'.[140]

Dummy bidding, or 'puffing' as it was then called, was an essential part of auctions. In 1776, the British peer Lord Mansfield ruled that using a 'puffer' was fraudulent and amounted to swindling.[141] (In 2001, 225 years later, Melbourne Magistrate Colin MacLeod used almost the same words to describe dummy bidding.)[142]

In America in the early 1800s, the alleged evils of auction were exposed in a series of speeches, letters and pamphlets. Anti-auction meetings were held throughout the country. Auctioneers were described as people of 'meanness and cunning'. Auctions were branded as 'immoral' and 'highly injurious of consumers'. One publication described auctions as 'a delusion, a mockery, and a snare, benefiting no one whatever but the auctioneers, the commission agents and the auctioneers underlings.'[143]

Sellers were encouraged to use auctions due to higher prices gained. And buyers were encouraged to buy due to lower prices paid. Auctions confused consumers. Said one report, 'auctions create complicated deceptions'.[144] Higher prices were alleged to have occurred mostly when property belonged to the auctioneer. But, 'when the property does not belong to the auctioneer it is sold cheap to encourage attendance'.[145]

'Auctions create complicated deceptions'

Auctions fooled thousands of inexperienced consumers. Another report stated, 'The system can only exist upon the stupidity of mankind.'[146] Consumers were ignorant about auctions. They were fooled by the hype and the glib lines. And they were among the poorer people in society. It was known that 'substantial and really valuable goods are not often seen at auction'.[147]

The auction system was cheap, seedy and grubby. It was not respected. The wealthy classes knew they could sell for better prices at private sales.

How Auctions Tricked the Rich

Until the middle of the twentieth century it was accepted that auctions were most suited to goods of poor or average quality. If something was of high quality, it was sold privately. But if speed and need were more important than price, auction was the choice. Auctions were not the place for quality items because auctions got lower prices. And the public knew it.

In 1937, an ambitious young man, Peter Wilson, began working for Sotheby's as a porter. Two years later, Wilson's wife inherited some money and helped Wilson to buy a share in the ownership of the company.[148] When war broke out, Wilson left to serve his country, eventually working in military intelligence for MI6. His code number was 007.[149] He was so good at subterfuge that he considered becoming a full-time spy. But the love of auctions lured him back to Sotheby's after the war.

It was Wilson's dream to lift the image of auctions by selling expensive goods. Despite his determination to capture a whole new market, both in England and the United States, his more traditional and conservative partners were not so sure. The last major change at Sotheby's was when they had moved from book auctions to general auctions in the eighteenth century.

In June 1956, Wilson saw his big chance. A retired naval officer, Commander Beauchamp, wanted to sell a magnificent painting that was part of an inheritance he had received. The painting, *The Adoration of Shepherds* by Nicolas Poussin, had last sold in 1792.[150] Its sale would be a major event. Wilson convinced the naval commander to auction the painting. It would be the feature of Sotheby's July sale. Wilson believed the publicity would launch Sotheby's into the world of high priced art. It was a major coup for Wilson. He was delighted.

But when Beauchamp received an offer of 10,000 pounds from a private dealer, he decided not to auction his painting. Wilson tried to convince him to stay with the auction sale. The private dealer then increased his offer to 15,000 pounds. Wilson was desperate. Once again an expensive work of art was to be sold privately. The issue that had foiled auctioneers for years – that auctions get lower prices for quality items – looked set to foil Wilson.

Wilson decided to take a huge risk. He told Beauchamp that Sotheby's would guarantee him a price at auction which was at least as good as the private offer. If the painting sold below 15,000 pounds, Sotheby's would make up the difference. If it sold for more, Beauchamp would receive more. Such an offer had never been made in the history of auctions. Beauchamp could not lose. The deal was done. The famous Poussin was ready for auction.

But then disaster struck for Wilson. Commander Beauchamp wanted more money. A friend had told him the painting was worth at least 35,000 pounds. Unless Sotheby's would increase its guarantee, he would withdraw the painting from the auction.[151] The Sotheby's partners were nervous. One said 'This is not how auctioneers should behave.'[152] But Wilson was determined. It would be a terrible loss of face for Sotheby's to lose its star attraction. He persuaded the board to increase its guarantee to 35,000 pounds. As the auction day loomed, the deal was finally done.

At the auction, the painting sold for 29,000 pounds. It was a record price for a painting at auction. The publicity was enormous. All the auction houses were delighted. Wilson had done the impossible. He had shown that high prices for quality goods can be achieved at auctions.

On that day, July 11, 1956 the auction world captured a market which had eluded it for years. And no one realised what had happened. Sotheby's quietly gave Commander Beauchamp a cheque for six thousand pounds and discreetly wrote it off as a loss in their books. But it was a loss that proved to be a magnificent investment for the auction houses. Consumers, rich and poor, were tricked into believing the greatest lie of auctions – that auctions get the highest prices.

Soon after the Sotheby's auction, the Poussin painting was resold. The sale was arranged privately at a much higher price. It was bought by the National Gallery[153] where it hangs today – a symbol, perhaps, of how auctions tricked the rich.

The Modern History of Auction Deceit

After the Poussin sale, with sellers of all ranks fooled into believing that auctions get higher prices, the auction business really took off. Suddenly it had respect. Headlines reported high prices at auctions and the myth took hold. Just as people once knew that auctions got lower prices, they now believed that auctions got higher prices.

In London in 1962, the esteemed writer W. Somerset Maugham, nearing the end of a long life, placed his art collection with Sotheby's for auction. Maugham was told by Sotheby's that he could expect $2,240,000.[154] With Maugham's name attached to it the sale created a blaze of publicity. Although the final selling price was $1,466,864, well short of the estimate (and almost certainly the value), Maugham, at 88 years of age, did not seem worried, saying only that the selling price was 'a lot of money'.[155]

As has been the trend ever since with auctions, most observers focus on the celebrities involved, the items being sold and the selling prices, not whether these selling prices are the highest prices. In 1999 when Marilyn Monroe's dress sold for $1,150,000 at auction, the focus was on Marilyn, the dress and what seemed a huge price. Hardly anyone noticed that the buyer was willing to pay up to $3,000,000 for it.[156]

From Somerset Maugham in the 1960s to Marilyn Monroe in the 1990s, the public has become dazzled with the spectacle of auctions without realising what goes on behind the scenes. Auctions get lower prices, especially with quality items, such as works of art and real estate.

Back in 1779, Christie's had sold Robert Walpole's art collection.[157] They didn't sell it by auction. They sold it by private negotiation for what was certainly the highest price. More than 200 years later, in 2000, Christie's sold a manuscript of a book by another Walpole, Sir Hugh Walpole. This time the sale was by auction. The buyer paid $1500. He was prepared to pay $27,750.[158]

In art auctions, dummy bids come from chandeliers. In real estate, they come from trees

The nature of auctions makes them susceptible to deceit; people are easily fooled. No matter what product is sold, the principles are the same. Deceit is built in to the system. In art auctions, dummy bids come from chandeliers. In real estate, they come from trees. Cheating is not only irresistible, it is often unavoidable. When there is only one buyer for an item, a dummy bid is almost essential. A dummy bid is to an auction what a spark plug is to an engine.

No matter what the product, or the time in history, auction and deceit go together. Of the 'Top 10 Internet Frauds', auctions rank number one, accounting for 78 per cent of all Internet fraud.[159]

Today, the two largest auction houses in the world are Sotheby's and Christie's. Together, they control 90 per cent of the world's auctions.[160] In October 2000, Sotheby's in the United States was fined 45 million dollars after pleading guilty to price-fixing. Christie's confessed to the same scam.[161] In December 2001, the former chairman of Sotheby's, Alfred Taubman, was found guilty of conspiring with the chairman of Christie's, Sir Anthony Tennant, to fleece millions of dollars from sellers. In April 2002, Taubman was sentenced to a year in jail.[162] Tennant lives in England and cannot be extradited to the United States. He is described as 'an international fugitive'.[163]

Real Estate Auctions

After Peter Wilson convinced the world that high-priced items could be sold at auction, it was inevitable that real estate would become a target. Before he joined Sotheby's, Wilson was an advertising salesman. Attracting publicity was his skill. The auction 'theatre' with crowds of people, excitement and perceived high prices was a magnet for the media. The back-stage antics were rarely understood, let alone reported.

Such conditions were perfect for real estate where, aside from early land sales and distress sales during the Depression, auctions were rare. But for sales of family homes, auctions meant free advertising and a method to condition the sellers. As newspapers were benefiting from the increased advertising revenue, they had every reason to support real estate auctions. And they did. They filled their pages with tales of great auction success.

Today, real estate auctions are reported as a 'proven method'. But stories that show that auctions are a proven fraud are almost never reported. Many newspapers refuse to accept advertising which is critical of auctions. Agents who want to place an advertisement with the heading 'Auction – the BEST way to sell a home' are welcomed. But agents who want to change one word in the heading – the word 'best' to the word 'worst' – face having their advertisements banned.

Freedom of the press means freedom to ban advertisements that harm the profits of the press.

However, when auctions of family homes first began – long before the cloak of cover-up descended – many agents opposed auctions. And so did the bodies that represent real estate agents, similar bodies that today praise auctions.

Stories that show that auctions are a proven fraud are almost never reported

In the early 1970s, in answer to the question from a home-owner, 'Could you tell me the pitfalls (if any) attached to selling by auction?' An official industry response was, 'The agent who persuades you to sell by auction is the beneficiary. You pay for the free advertising of the agent's name included in your advertisements in the daily press. The cost of the auction to you, Mr and Mrs Citizen, is money you have wasted when no sale is effected.'[164]

This was the response before the industry realised that when 'citizens' lost money, agents and newspapers made money. And then the official response changed.

Whether it's the art world or the real estate world, the history of auctions is a history of misery and trickery. In real estate, auctions are the industry's most common fraud. Few people – other than agents – understand what's going on behind the scenes. But you know.

You know the truth about real estate auctions. And you know this – don't sign anything unless you are safe from the traps of auctions. Be careful. Be extremely careful.

Summary

- Auctions involve massive deceit. Inexperienced consumers are the most vulnerable with this cruel and heartless method of selling real estate.
- The deceit with auctions starts with the false prices quoted to both sellers and buyers.

- Thousands of sellers are tricked into choosing auction. At best, most sellers are told half-truths; at worst, they are the victims of fraud.

- Auctions are about conditioning sellers down in price, pushing buyers up in price and making sure agents get paid no matter what the selling price.

- Auctions give agents massive control because consumers are trapped in an atmosphere where they can be hammered into submission.

- Thousands of decent people are financially and emotionally devastated by this form of real estate terrorism.

- Auctions do not get the best price, they get the second best price.

- Agents who say that auctions get the best prices are incompetent or dishonest. It is almost impossible to get the best market price at auction.

- There are no cooling-off periods with real estate auctions. No second chances, no matter what, once you sign the contract.

- The pressure at auctions forces consumers to make instant decisions. It is one of the major reasons agents use auctions.

- If you are selling, don't auction. If you are buying, understand how easy it can be to buy below your limit.

- If you are pressured, **don't sign anything** no matter what. Auctions are a bluff. Until a contract is signed, no sale is certain. Wait until you get independent legal advice.

Chapter Eight

Inspections

Finding the right buyer when you sell, finding the right home when you buy

Our house is small,
no mansion for a millionaire,
but there is room for love
and room for friends,
that's all we care.

Common saying

Welcome to the world of home inspections. If you've tried to buy a home, especially in a major capital city, you'll be familiar with the routine. Often it goes something like this.

You call an agent. There will be 'nobody in'. You leave a message. No one calls you. At first you are puzzled, perhaps even forgiving. And so you call again. They are 'out' or 'in a meeting'. The receptionist can't tell you anything. You might be given a mobile number for the person handling that property. When you call, you get a message service. You leave your details again. Nothing.

Finally, when you contact someone, your request to look at a home will be met with a sigh. 'It's open on Saturday between two and three,' will be the bored response. If that doesn't suit you, too bad. Or come to next week's open house. At first, this attitude will amaze you. But this is the beginning. You haven't seen anything yet.

When Sally Richmond was searching for her first home, she wanted 'compassion, understanding and honesty'. Instead she found her 'dreams shattered' at the way she was treated. 'Having invested that amount of time, energy and petrol, you'd expect some straight answers and a degree of sincerity. Ha! Ha! – wrong industry. This is real estate baby and you are fresh flesh.'[1]

Sally's verdict on agents: 'In six months, you've sparked levels of defensiveness, suspicion and aggression in me that 15 years of dating is yet to match.'[2]

THE NATURE OF AGENTS

To understand why so many agents treat buyers badly, you must remember the nature of agents. It's rarely buyers that agents want – especially when the real estate market is hot – it's sellers. Agents are paid by sellers. Sure, a buyer has to buy before an agent is paid, but once an agent has been hired by a motivated seller, the agent knows that a sale is certain. There is an expression in real estate, 'Well listed and it's already sold.' The seller is tied up on a selling agreement, usually for several months. All the agent has to do is get the price down and the home will be sold. If you don't buy it, someone else will.

When you understand what motivates agents you will know how to play their game.

It's the Quote Lie – Again

Almost every real estate trick can be traced back to the Quote Lie. Having given sellers a false quote about the selling price, agents must now condition the sellers down in price. To do this, an elaborate charade is played out. The inspection process is part of the charade. As you've seen, it ends when the sellers are ready to be crunched.

INSIDE THE WORLD OF HOME INSPECTIONS

In the world of real estate inspections, nothing is as it seems.

As a homeseller, the last thing you want is people coming through your home who are not going to buy it. As a homebuyer, the last thing you want is to see homes you don't want or you cannot buy. But, in thousands of cases, this is exactly what agents do – they allow anyone to inspect homes for sale. Just as agents have dummy bidders at auctions, they also have dummy inspections. It's all aimed at fooling sellers into thinking their homes have been 'exposed to the market'. Agents need lots of inspections so they can blame the market when the price has to be lowered.

Agents need lots of inspections so they can blame the market when the price has to be lowered

The Inspections Charade

The average homebuyer spends around three months looking for a home.[3] Sometimes, over a period of weeks, hundreds of people wander through homes for sale. With most salespeople averaging around two sales a month, something doesn't make sense. Who are all these people looking at homes? And what are real estate salespeople doing if they are only selling two homes a month? They are playing the inspection game to fool sellers.

Types of Inspections

There are two types of inspections for homes. First, there are private inspections where buyers come through one at a time and at different times. And second, there are open inspections where lots of buyers come through at the same time. Most agents prefer open inspections. But, for both sellers and buyers, open inspections are the worst method of inspection.

Open inspections are the worst method of inspection

OPEN INSPECTIONS

To discover the real reasons for open inspections, you only have to compare what agents say publicly with what they say privately. Publicly, agents say that open inspections get more buyers and are more convenient. But, as you will see, open inspections help agents and harm homesellers. Privately, agents know the real reasons for open inspections, because they learn them from real estate courses, manuals and books. And they discuss them regularly in their offices – when consumers are not listening.

Open inspections allow agents to find more prospects – especially sellers. They allow agents to condition the sellers by showing lots of activity and they allow agents to promote themselves. These are the three main reasons agents use open inspections.

James Tostevin, an agent who claims to be the most successful in Victoria, boasts at seminars that open inspections enable him to find 50 new homesellers each year.[4] This amounts to around $500,000 a year in commission from sellers he meets at open inspections. That's right – *sellers*, not buyers.

As far back as 1986, one real estate trainer taught that open inspections are such a good source of leads that, 'The worst thing you can do is sell the home which is open for inspection.'[5] This cuts off the source of leads for the agent. The Real Estate Institute of Australia's publication, *Real Estate Office Manual,* says that with open inspections 'the sellers perceive a service is being provided', meaning that the sellers see lots of activity and are therefore more likely to be 'realistic' about their price. The manual also says that open inspections allow 'the profile of the office to be heightened'.[6]

Open inspections are an American phenomenon that first emerged in Australia and New Zealand in the late 1970s, but really took off in the 1990s. Before then, agents used to meet buyers at their offices, discuss their needs, decide which homes might be suitable and then show those homes to the buyers. It was called 'qualifying', which is one of the essential ingredients of any true sales professional. It is an ingredient that has been all but lost in the modern world of real estate sales. Today, many agents do what qualifies as the best money earner. The needs of the customers take second place to agents' profits.

American sales trainers showed their down-under colleagues the real reasons for open inspections – *to find more homes to sell*. America's most famous real estate trainer, Mike Ferry, makes it clear when he shouts, 'The real reason you hold an Open House – you're looking for prospects who will either list or sell property.'[7]

Open inspections rarely sell homes. In 1993, the Real Estate Institute of Queensland printed an article by an American trainer who wrote, 'open houses are often better for listing than for selling.'[8] The Aussies were hooked. In 1996, the Real Estate Institute of Queensland's journal for its agents said, 'The principal reason for running an open inspection is not to sell the property, but to find sellers.'[9] In his book for consumers, American author Terry Eilers reveals the results of a survey of open inspections. It showed that 70 per cent of visitors had no intention of buying a home.[10]

Open inspections are a magnet for future homesellers. As one home-owner said, 'When I looked closely, I discovered what happened at the open inspections. I paid the agent to be there to sell my property, not to spend his time securing listings for himself. The advertising I paid for was there to promote his business. Agents know they can sell homes for better prices without open inspections but they would miss out on the opportunity to get more homes for sale.' Another home-owner said that agents should pay the sellers who allow their homes to be used as sources of business for agents.

As with advertising and auctions, open inspections are rarely the *reason* a home is sold.

HOW OPEN INSPECTIONS GET LOWER PRICES

Most homesellers would be horrified to realise how open inspections damage the value of their homes. By allowing open inspections, sellers are playing straight into the agents' hands. The price of their home goes down and this, of course, makes it easier for agents to sell the homes. The agents get paid, but the sellers get a lower price.

• Inconvenient for Buyers

Your home is open for one hour (sometimes it's just half an hour) on one day. If this time does not suit the best buyers they don't show up. Many will never come back. They will buy something else.

If you owned a shop you wouldn't tell customers they could only buy for an hour each week

If you owned a shop you wouldn't tell customers they could only buy for an hour each week. Don't have your home open for inspection for an hour a week. It makes it too hard for the best buyers to see it. Have it open at any time to suit the best buyers. One of the golden rules of winning customers is: *Make it easy for people to buy.* Open inspections make it hard for buyers.

• Attracts the Wrong People

Most people who visit open inspections are lookers, not buyers. Some even class visiting open inspections as their hobby.

John knows his home city of Adelaide well. He was a contributing author to *The Jubilee History of South Australia*. He was also a taxi driver who used to take tourists on guided tours of the city. One day his passengers were two Japanese tourists who asked if they could see how Australians lived. 'No problem,' said John, 'Hop in.' Starting in Port Adelaide and working his way through the suburbs, John stopped at all the real estate open inspections. 'They thought it was wonderful.'" The agents didn't mind because the more people who inspected the homes, the easier it became to condition the sellers with the line, 'This is what the market is saying.'

Some homesellers wonder at the hordes of strangers traipsing through their homes. One seller on Sydney's North Shore noticed a man filming her home. She said, 'Open inspections never felt right but the agent said they were normal. But when I saw that creepy guy with the video camera it didn't feel normal. I said no more. That was the end of open inspections for me.'[12]

Many lookers make rude remarks about your home in the presence of genuine buyers. Imagine genuine buyers arriving at your home at the same time as lookers are leaving. The genuine buyer thinks, 'This is a nice home.' But the lookers have a scowl on their faces. The buyers wonder what is wrong. This will either scare the genuine buyers away or cause them to offer you a lower price. You must keep lookers and sticky-beaks out of your home. If an agent doesn't know the difference between lookers and buyers, get another agent. You hire an agent to sell your home, not to wave people through your home. You could do that yourself and not have to pay an agent.

If an agent doesn't know the difference between lookers and buyers, get another agent

• Too Many People

The more people who see your home and the longer your home is for sale, the more likely you are to get a lower price. With dozens, even hundreds, of people coming through and no one buying it, people begin to wonder what's wrong. A common thought is: 'Why is everyone rejecting this home.'

Many people do not like to buy a home that has been on display to the neighbourhood. It spoils the intimacy of the home. Homes are private places and open inspections destroy one of the big selling points of a home – its uniqueness, that feeling of being special.

Suellen and her husband bought an ex-display home. It was a beautiful home, but it had languished unsold for months. 'I didn't realise that so many people don't want to buy homes that all the world has been looking at,' Suellen said. 'Now I know why. I get sick of strangers telling me they have been inside my home.'[13]

Homes inspected by too many people are like fruit touched by too many fingers. To attract buyers the price has to be slashed.

• Too Few People

As a homeseller, you rarely win with open inspections. If no one shows up, agents have a prepared script. 'Do not apologise,' says one training manual. 'Explain to your sellers that the advertising copy was good, but that you cannot create a market if it is not there.'[14] Once again, the market is the excuse for incompetence. But if no one turns up to the open inspection, the home can become the joke of the area. It means the price has to be lowered to attract buyers.

• The Best Buyers are Ignored

For an agent to get the best price for your home, the agent has to know the buyers. At open inspections there is not enough time to get to know the buyers. The agent should spend time pointing out the best features of your home, not just letting buyers wander around on their own. Chances are they will miss some of the best features. Many buyers complain that the agent is too interested in getting to the next open inspection to answer their questions.

Agents rarely follow up the people who come to open inspections

It is well known by real estate agents and buyers that agents rarely follow up the people who come to open inspections. This reveals one of the real purposes for open inspections: to create the impression of activity so that the sellers can be conditioned to lower their prices.

As one real estate teacher explained in the topic, 'Getting the Price Down Painlessly', it works like this: 'After several weekends of open houses your sellers are going to feel down and out. They may not have been willing to listen to you before, but now you have the public's response.'[15]

• It Makes Your Home Look Smaller

The more people you have in your home, the smaller it looks. Try putting a dozen people into your lounge room or kitchen and you'll realise how your home looks smaller. The smaller the home, the smaller the price. It's an obvious point that most sellers do not realise.

• Price Comparisons

Your home has to compete with other homes that are open for inspection. If your home is similar to others, the buyers will go from one home to another comparing prices. The price of your home is dragged down to the *lowest* price of similar homes.

Your home will often be used to 'switch' buyers to less expensive homes. It's one of the oldest real estate tricks – have some overpriced homes to show buyers so that other homes look good in comparison. Meanwhile, just wait a few weeks until the sellers of the overpriced home have been conditioned to become 'realistic'.

With all these reasons against open inspections, you may wonder why so many agents do them. It comes back to the three reasons agents like open inspections – to meet other homesellers, to create lots of activity conditioning and to promote the agent.

As one real estate trainer admitted, 'The odds are at least 250 to 1 that any given person or couple walking into an Open House will buy it.'[16]

THE DANGER OF OPEN INSPECTIONS

In January 2001, Seattle real estate agent Michael Emert was murdered in a home he had been showing to buyers. In a 12-year period in the United States, 70 real estate agents were murdered in similar circumstances.[17] Aware that almost identical conditions exist in Australia, one real estate group issued safety guidelines for agents.[18] But no safety guidelines were issued for consumers, especially homesellers. If sellers knew the dangers, they might not allow their homes to be open for inspection. And that would not be good for agents.

Open inspections are an open invitation to anyone. The Australian columnist Danny Katz wrote, 'It's incredible; you can just walk in off the street and spend up to an hour in the home of a complete stranger.' Katz points out that agents don't care who comes into a home. 'A guy could show up in a blood-spattered smock with a swastika tattooed on his forehead and the real estate agent would say, "Come in Mr Manson, have a look around …".'[19]

Publicly, the real estate industry scoffs at the dangers of open inspections. Incidents of theft are denied or referred to as isolated. People who warn consumers are described as alarmist. The usual response is, 'We have been doing open inspections for years and never had a problem.' But most problems occur *after* the agents have gone. Few crimes happen during the open inspections. The thieves 'inspect' the homes and come back later. Victorian Police Detective Adrian Woodcock said, 'I wouldn't have my home open for inspection full stop.'[20] As far back as 1998, the Queensland Police reported an 'alarming increase in the number of reports of robbers posing as buyers.'[21]

The disregard for the safety of sellers is evident with celebrities. In 2001, after robberies at the homes of AFL stars, one of the victims, Richmond footballer Brendon Gale, said that players and managers were concerned at the breach of security. Manager Ron Joseph believed 'real estate agents should be made more responsible'.[22] When actor Kate Fischer sold her Bondi apartment, the agent boasted that it 'attracted a flood of celebrity spotters'. The agent reportedly said, 'We noticed one of the pillows missing from the main bedroom. Someone must have taken it for a souvenir.'[23] Just weeks after the death of one of Australia's most loved actors, Ruth Cracknell, her home was for sale. The agent, unable to resist talking about such a celebrity, attracted hundreds of people to the home, but admitted to a reporter that, '99.9 per cent of them have just come because it was Ruth's place'.[24]

When Claire Browne lost her jewellery during an open

inspection, she received an extra shock. No insurance. Consumer advocate and television reporter Helen Wellings has often warned consumers that their homes are not insured for thefts at open inspections.[25]

Despite warnings from the police, Neighbourhood Watch, insurance companies and consumer advocates, agents continue to laud open inspections as a benefit for consumers. But, just as agents use open inspections to target new sellers, criminals use them to target family possessions for theft. Some agents hand out floor plans of homes, others will even show strangers how the security system works.

The *Fraud Identification Handbook* published in the United States says, 'Some sneaky criminals enter homes-for-sale by posing as potential buyers.' And it's not just petty crime. John Douglas, the legendary FBI profiler, believes two of the major kidnapping crimes of the twentieth century – the Lindbergh baby and the JonBenet Ramsay case – may have been linked to open inspections.[26]

This is not an American problem, it is a worldwide problem. Open inspections are dangerous, despite agents saying they have 'never had a problem' or that they 'always get the names' of people who inspect homes for sale. A study in 2002 conducted in the Australian cities of Brisbane, Sydney, Melbourne and Adelaide revealed the following: only 48 per cent of agents asked for the names of the people visiting the homes. No agents requested formal identification. In 98 per cent of cases, strangers were allowed to wander unsupervised through the sellers' homes.[27]

Criminals use them to target family possessions for theft

The Real Estate Institute of Victoria told its member agents to tell homesellers that agents are not responsible for theft during an open inspection.[28] But agents *should be* responsible for their clients' safety. If an agent will not accept such responsibility, don't sign anything. Get another agent.

Financial Protection for Homesellers

The two major parts of activity conditioning are advertising and inspections. Open inspections depend on advertising. When open inspections first appeared on the Australian real estate scene, some newspapers offered to publish free open inspection guides in their real estate sections. Agents became hooked on open inspections which meant they also became hooked on advertising.

As real estate trainer David Pilling explains, 'It's impossible to separate press advertising from open inspections.' He teaches agents that open inspections are used to 'milk the buyers to get listings'[29] because buyers often have a home to sell before they buy.

Efficiency

The advertising of homes for sale and the massive numbers of inspections are just a charade to condition sellers and make them think the agent has worked hard. But hard work is not the same as efficiency. The hallmark of an efficient agent is one who can find the most genuine buyers willing to pay the best price in the shortest time and with the least cost to the homeseller. That's efficiency.

The Bank of Buyers

Efficient agents keep records of genuine buyers searching for suitable homes. They have a 'bank of buyers'. Just as buyers go to agents expecting to find homes, sellers should go to agents expecting to find buyers. Sellers should ask, 'Do you have any buyers for my home?' The agent will then look through the bank of buyers for the best prospects.

Most agents do not keep accurate records of buyers. Some even tell buyers to 'watch our advertisements'. But if agents watched buyers instead of advertisements, there would be no need for advertisements. The main purpose of advertisements and massive numbers of inspections is not to search for buyers, it's to condition the sellers with lots of visible activity.

The Arithmetic of Inspections

You only have to do some simple sums to discover the inefficiency of most agents with the so-called 'search for buyers'. You can apply these sums to any area.

As an example, take an average suburb in a major city. The number of sales per year rarely exceeds 500.[30] This is approximately 42 sales a month. If the average buyer spends three months looking for a home, there will be approximately 126 buyers actively looking in the area all the time. This means, when your home first comes for sale, there are a maximum of 126 fresh prospects. But these buyers have to be shared among *all types* of properties for sale. Just as there are different properties, there are buyers with different requirements. This narrows the prospect base for each home.

The number of buyers for your home will diminish, not increase, as time goes on

Within a month, 42 buyers will have bought, but there will still be 126 buyers looking to buy because 42 new buyers will enter the market. It really is like a bank of buyers. Those who buy are 'withdrawals' from the bank. They come off the market. And those who start looking are 'deposits'. They come onto the market.

The greatest number of new buyers for your home will be when your home is new to the market. You will never have a better chance to get the best price than when your home first comes up for sale because the number of buyers for your home will diminish, not increase, as time goes on. If your home does not sell to any of the large number of existing buyers in the bank, you have to wait for new buyers to enter the market.

How Inspections and Time Make Your Home Stale

Let's say a home is worth $480,000. The sellers may want $500,000, perhaps more. If the agent has led them to believe they might get more than $500,000, the agent then has to condition them down to the real price. Meanwhile, buyers will make excellent offers which can seem like low offers. The sellers will reject these offers. In a few weeks, when the home has been 'exposed', the sellers start to become more 'realistic'.

Stale homes get lower prices

What this really means, of course, is that they are starting to realise the truth – that their home was worth $480,000 all along. Only now the exposure has damaged the value of their home. Instead of it being worth $480,000 it may only be worth $460,000, perhaps less. In the beginning, when their home was fresh they may have received $500,000, but with all the exposure they may struggle to even get $450,000. Time can be expensive. Stale homes get lower prices. It's that simple.

Fresh is Best

Genuine buyers will be excited by a 'fresh' home – one that has just come for sale. If they like it and the agent is a good negotiator, they will buy it immediately and pay the best price. Interest is at its peak when a home is fresh. If you want to create competition among buyers, do it early when there are more genuine buyers. When buyers know the home is fresh, they know that other buyers will be coming to see it. Many times they will pay a premium for your home, sometimes more than your asking price.

Advertising tells buyers that your home is not sold. Often, the homes that sell for the best prices are never advertised

It cannot be stressed strongly enough – the best buyer for your home is almost always the early buyer. Every day that your home is for sale it becomes more stale. Advertising does not make buyers buy – they were already intending to buy. Advertising tells buyers that your home is not sold. Often, the homes that sell for the best prices are never advertised. When your home is not advertised it is seen as special and special homes get higher prices.

There are thousands of stories of people who had their homes for sale for months and who were forced to accept a lower price. How many times do you hear of sellers having their homes for sale for a long time and getting a higher price? Almost never. High prices come early. Low prices come late. This is why you should never sign with an agent for a long time period. Some marketing experts believe the maximum time you should give an agent is 30 days. This gives the agents an incentive to sell your home for the best price. It does not give them enough time to condition you down in price. It forces agents to be truthful, from the beginning, about the likely selling price of your home.

The more that buyers see your home being advertised and inspected by hordes of people, the more inclined they are to pay less. But nothing can beat a home which is fresh. This is the time to get the best price. Fresh is best.

FINDING THE RIGHT HOME

As a homebuyer, your major aim is finding the best home within your price limit. Later, you can worry about negotiating the price. First, find the right home, then negotiate the best price.

Your Financial Limit

The first thing you must do is set your financial limit. And stick to it. Be careful you do not borrow the absolute maximum you can afford. Something always goes wrong. Allow for it.

No mortgage means no worry

The most important goal in life is happiness – peace of mind. One of your happiest days will be when you pay off your home. No mortgage means no worry. Sure, this is the opposite to what some financial advisers suggest. But for the sake of your happiness and personal security your family home should be sacrosanct – untouchable to the tentacles of debt that ensnare many families.

In his book *Simple Truths*, author Kent Nerburn says that

debt, not poverty, is the enemy of peace of mind. As for the financial advisers, he has this to say, 'There are massive forces in the world to tell you of the great benefits of debt. They will tell you that you can have tomorrow's pleasures at today's prices. They will present arguments that are convincing and seductive. But it all comes down to the same thing: you have mortgaged your future to pay for your present, and this is something you don't ever want to do.'[31]

Your aim with the debt on your home should be to get rid of it. The smaller the debt, the sooner it will be gone. And once that debt is gone, never get it back. If you want to invest in real estate, do it without debt on your family home.

Once you set your financial limit, you are ready to search for a home.

Real Estate Advertisements

Many real estate advertisements are misleading – both in price and description. When you inspect homes that you have seen advertised, you will soon discover that most are nothing like their descriptions. Most real estate advertisements leave out the bad features of homes.

The odds of finding your home from an agent's advertisement are slim. Use these advertisements for research. You can compare asking prices. You can discover which homes are becoming stale. If you find a home you like, you can check back through weeks of advertising and discover if the home was advertised – perhaps with another agent. Maybe the price is too high or there is something wrong with the home. The more it has been advertised, the more likely you are to buy it for a cheaper price.

Find an Agent and then Find a Home

Finding a good agent is one of the main keys to finding a good home. Whether it's just by making a phone call or seeing the same agent at different open inspections or going to inspect homes with an agent, you can meet most of the agents selling homes in your chosen area. If you meet one that you like, try to build rapport. Sit down with the agent and discuss what you want. The more time the agent spends with you, the more the agent may help you find a home. Buying is much easier if you find an agent who helps you. If the agent knows what you want, the agent should call you the moment the right home comes for sale.

Many good agents will search for a home for you. If they know you are serious, they know that all they have to do is find the right home and they will make a sale. If you like the agent, be frank about what you want and what you can pay. There is a common expression among agents: 'All buyers are liars.' But buyers believe agents are liars. Such distrust is no way to do business, especially for something as important as your home. If everyone is truthful with each other, it becomes much easier to do business. Trust is important.

On Your Own

If you can't find an agent you like, then, aside from hiring a buyers' advocate, you have to search on your own. Be patient and persistent. Go to all the agents as often as you can. Pester them. When the right home comes for sale, make sure you are there, on the spot. If a home is fresh on the market, and it's what you really want, be prepared to make your best offer.

You will also need to check everything carefully. Never take the agent's word, especially when it comes to price. When you find a home you like, use the same strategies discussed in buying a home that is for auction. Make sure you learn the basics of negotiation in the next chapter. And always follow the golden rule of buying real estate: don't sign anything until you receive *independent* legal advice.

The Time to Buy

Agents always seem to say 'now is the time to buy'. But the right time to buy a family home is when you find the right home. Of course, you may get a better deal when the market is slow, but no one really knows what the future holds. The experts are often wrong. Real estate goes up in price and it goes down in price. Often it remains stagnant for years. But this is not the main issue when you are buying your family home. You are not an investor, you are a family homebuyer. The right time to buy a family home is when you can afford it and when you find a home you love.

Put your family needs first and you'll usually discover, later, that your home was a great investment.

You will find the home you love if two factors are present: first, if your price range is suited to the area and, second, if you are willing to persist. Keep looking until you find the home you love. Once you find that home, it's not hard to buy for less than you are prepared to pay.

Finding the right buyer when you are selling, or finding the right home when you are buying, is the first step. The next step is to be safe when you negotiate.

Summary

- Often, the inspection process is part of an elaborate charade to condition sellers down in price.

- For sellers and buyers, open inspections are the worst method of inspection.

- As a seller, the last thing you want is people inspecting your home who cannot buy it. As a genuine buyer, the last thing you want is to inspect homes you don't want or you cannot buy.

- Lots of inspections enable agents to blame the market when the price has to be lowered.

- Aside from conditioning sellers, one of the main reasons for open inspections is for agents to find more sellers, not more buyers.

- Open inspections destroy one of the big selling points of a home – its feeling of being special.

- Homes inspected by too many people are like fruit touched by too many fingers. To attract buyers the price has to be slashed.

- Open inspections are dangerous. Criminals use them to target family possessions for theft.

- Most sellers are not aware that their homes are not insured against theft resulting from open inspections.

- At most open inspections, the security is appalling. Strangers are allowed to wander around unsupervised.

- The best buyer for a home is almost always the early buyer. The more inspections, the higher the risk of damaging the value of the home.

- As a seller, the only people who should inspect your home are those who are identified and qualified. **Don't sign anything** unless your home is secure – in all ways.

Chapter Nine

Safe Negotiating

How to sell and buy at the right price

There is nothing so costly as ignorance.

Horace Mann

I t's one of the most quarrelsome questions in real estate: what is the right price? The standard answers are that sellers want the highest price and buyers want the lowest price. And so begins a form of war between agents and sellers and buyers. Suspicion and distrust are common. Lies become both weapons and shields in these negotiating battles.

Agents try hard to convince everyone that they got a good deal. 'This is a great price, you should take it,' they will tell sellers. At the same time, they will tell buyers, 'This is great value.' When it comes to haggling, real estate lies can reach fever pitch. But it doesn't have to be this way.

THE RIGHT PRICE

In real estate valuation there is a theory known as 'willing seller/willing buyer'. This theory says that the true value of a property is the price a willing seller accepts from a willing buyer where everyone is fully informed and not under any undue pressure or influence. This technical theory can be summed up in one word – fairness. The basis of all ethical negotiation is that both sellers and buyers get a 'fair deal'. In his book *The Seven Habits of Highly Effective People*, Stephen Covey, the business philosopher, calls this 'Win/Win' negotiation.

Sadly, this is more idealistic than realistic in real estate where 'right price' usually has little to do with fairness and more to do with what's right for one person and wrong for another. As Covey says, 'Most people have been deeply scripted in the Win/Lose mentality since birth.'[1] Even the expression, 'We got a real bargain,' is an admission that someone else lost money.

The real estate world creates distrust. With everyone focused on self-preservation, few people consider others. Honest people are often transformed into a type of werewolf in a real estate negotiation. It all seems to be justified on the basis of hurt or be hurt. The thought is, 'For me to win someone has to lose. What choice do I have?'

And this is the basis of much real estate negotiating: people foxing with each other, hiding or twisting the truth to suit their own ends. Sellers who are willing to sell for one price insist on a higher price. Buyers who are willing to pay a higher price will offer a lower price. And the agents float alongside like crocodiles, watching the effects of their systems and waiting for the right moment to crunch both sellers and buyers.

This is the typical real estate world. It can tear you apart emotionally, leave you financially wounded, make you bitter and angry, and maybe even guilty at what you did in order to survive. It is a horrible world – unless you understand how to deal with it *before* you enter it.

UNDERSTANDING REAL ESTATE NEGOTIATION

There are two ways to play the real estate negotiation game – honestly or dishonestly. If you want to play it honestly, as most people prefer, then you must understand the dishonesty that is built in to real estate. You must be prepared to handle whatever you encounter. One of the key elements to a successful negotiation is *preparation*. If you are prepared, if you have the knowledge, even the most *basic* knowledge, you can be safe. You can get the 'right price'. But first, you have to understand the roles of the people in the negotiation.

The Role of the Agents

Technically, the role of an agent is to get the best price for a home. Agents are paid by sellers which means they have a legal and a moral duty to protect sellers. In reality, this rarely happens. Most agents are dreadful negotiators. Their incompetence costs sellers thousands of dollars and, at the same time, does incredible damage to the buyers; often the damage to both sellers and buyers is as much emotional as it is financial. Agents are not dealing with property as much as they are dealing with people. And people have feelings.

One of the key elements to a successful negotiation is preparation

These feelings are especially sensitive when it comes to making not just one of their biggest financial decisions, but also one of their biggest *emotional* decisions.

Sometimes it is not the agent who is to blame, but the system. It is hard to do the right thing with the wrong system. Agents are virtually forced to tell lies. From the very beginning, when they want to win the rights to sell a home, they feel forced to give a false high quote in order to be selected as the agent. They, too, are trapped. Their only escape is to continue down a path which requires

Agents are virtually forced to tell lies

them to lie or, at best, to twist the truth. The agents have been given a set time to sell the home – usually three months. If they don't sell the home, the sellers will choose another agent.

And so, here is what agents are faced with: a home which is overpriced and a deadline to sell the home. The typical role of an agent is to get the sellers to lower their price and make the sale before the agent's time period expires.

Many real estate salespeople are paid commission-only. If they don't make sales, they don't get paid. Sales are crucial to their survival. Being nice, offering good service, or even being truthful can come second to their hunger for sales.

Real estate is not a business where the same customers come in every day. Many are one-time customers, especially sellers who move out of the area. Even the buyers who move into an area may not need an agent again for many years. So, with the combination of a commission reward system, and customers who may never come back, salespeople have few incentives to offer wonderful service. The nature of real estate makes it hard for even the most honest salespeople to do the right thing. This is why so many salespeople quit the industry, never to return.

The Role of the Sellers

The role of the sellers is to get the *best market price* for their homes. When they sell, it is their last chance to recoup what may have come from years of struggle. The best market price is vital. On this there can be no compromise.

However, many homesellers ask for too much money, especially in the beginning when their home is first offered for sale. There are two main reasons why this happens. The first is the fear of selling too cheaply, which comes from a distrust of agents – and often buyers. A common statement sellers make is, 'I am not going to give it away.'

As sellers, we tend to see only the good in our homes. Rarely do we see the faults and, if we do, we tend to under-estimate their significance while, at the same time, overestimating the features of our homes. In economics this is known as 'the endowment effect', the natural tendency to place an unrealistically high value on something to which we are personally attached. The sale of a family home is the classic example of the endowment effect.[2]

Harvard Professor and author of *Smart Money Decisions* Dr Max Bazerman explains it this way, 'The husband and wife who are about to sell the home in which they raised their family may find it difficult to objectively assess the selling price of something to which they have a strong emotional connection.' Bazerman says the endowment effect harms sellers, because it causes them to reject early offers only to 'regret the decision after their home gets stuck on the market'. Not only do sellers end up losing financially, they must also endure the emotional pain of having 'a cherished belonging rejected over and over again by potential buyers put off by an unrealistically high price.'[3]

When homesellers, whose role is to get the highest price, meet the agents, whose role is to make sales, it's a recipe for deceit and disaster. All the agent has to do is tell the sellers what they want to hear – 'It's a wonderful home and you'll get a phenomenal price' – and the sellers sign up with the agent. This is why many homes come onto the market with sellers who want too much money and with agents who have to use tricks to get the sellers to reduce the prices, and tricks to get the buyers to look at the homes. Tricks and dishonesty become part of the process.

Unfortunately, the solution is rarely about honesty alone. If agents are honest and tell sellers the truth about the value of their homes, many will choose another agent – one prepared to lie by saying what sellers wanted to hear. Dr Bazerman's solution is simple. He says sellers 'should seek out an unbiased assessment' of the home from 'a knowledgable but disinterested third party.'[4] This means that homesellers, unless they have complete trust and confidence in an agent, should engage an independent and reputable valuer *before* their home is placed for sale. The valuation is their guide to the right price.

The valuation is their guide to the right price

Armed with this knowledge, sellers can make decisions devoid of emotional attachment. They can remove the danger of the endowment effect. They can make sure that their role – to get the best market price – is more likely to be successful. They will know what to say when agents or buyers try to lower their price. But they will also be able to select the agent who is being honest about the price of their home. With an honest agent, there is no need for tricks.

As one homeseller put it, 'Having a valuation was the smartest thing we did. It was like having inside knowledge. We ended up selling for more than the valuation price. But without the valuation we would definitely have started too high and ended up having our home rejected by buyers. I will never sell a home in the future without using a valuer.'[5]

If they resist the urge to overprice their home because of their emotional attachment, sellers can find the best agent and have the best chance of getting the best market price.

The Role of the Buyers

Aside from investors, developers and bargain-hunters, the first role of most homebuyers is to find the right home at a price they can afford. With family-home buyers, the home comes first; the price comes second. Sure, no buyers want to pay too much; but, if the home is what they want – if they love it and they can afford it – they will gladly pay a fair price for it. In some cases, they will pay extra. A family home is something most buyers will live in for years. The price they pay will be repaid in two ways – years of happiness and years of capital appreciation.

Of the three roles in negotiation, the buyers' role is usually the most emotional. Most buying decisions are made with the heart. But lack of respect for the feelings of buyers makes them angry and upset. The lies about the prices, the availability or the condition of homes can make buyers despise agents. This is why buyers hide their feelings; it is why they rarely say what they can pay or what they want. They do not want to 'open their hearts' in case their hearts are broken. And so buyers, too, get swept up in the deceitful ways of real estate.

But the buyers, like the sellers, do not understand how the typical systems work and this is why the systems work against them. They don't know how to play the game and so they get played by the game. The agents understand the game. They know the tricks. And many don't care who gets hurt as long as they make the sales and get their commissions.

In the three roles in real estate, there are agents who often do anything to get a sale. And then there are the sellers and buyers who don't trust agents and try to protect themselves. With this combination, the chances of someone being hurt are high. And that's why, for sellers and buyers, understanding the typical systems is so important. Sellers just want the best market price and buyers will be happy if they get the best home they can afford. If an honest agent is involved, the process can be happy for everyone.

THE BASICS OF REAL ESTATE NEGOTIATION

The great truths in life are always simple. And the basics of real estate negotiation are all based on simple truths.

Fairness

A major principle of negotiation is fairness. If you go into a negotiation with a win/lose attitude, it will rarely be pleasant. As the saying goes, 'If you get involved in the rat race, even if you win, you are still a rat.'

So, don't be a rat. Don't tell lies. Just state the truth plainly. Make your intentions clear, but make it clear, also, that you want to be treated fairly. Being fair does not mean being soft. It means being fair *and* firm. Don't treat people as if they are dishonest, no matter how cynical you may feel. Be friendly. Act as if you expect to be well treated.

Being fair does not mean being soft

If people see you as honest and fair, you are more likely to be treated honestly and fairly. If you are also seen as competent, you are even more likely to be well treated. Your best chance of being treated fairly is to have a fair attitude. In short, you should be fair, firm and friendly.

Nick and Therese found a home which had failed to sell at auction. The reserve price had been $320,000. They felt it was great value. But the home had been overexposed; too much advertising and too many inspections had damaged its value. It was the proverbial lemon. The agent said the sellers were desperate.

They made an offer of $310,000 which the agent persuaded the sellers to accept. Later, in a conversation with Nick, the agent said that even though the sellers had accepted his offer, they were 'not happy'. And so Nick *increased* his offer to $315,000. The agent was stunned. 'You don't have to do that,' he said, 'They have signed the contract. The home is yours.' The agent seemed annoyed because it meant changing the paperwork. But Nick was adamant. He did not want to buy at the expense of someone else's misfortune. It didn't feel right.[6]

There is an inherent goodness in many people which is more common than most of us believe

There is an inherent goodness in many people which is more common than most of us believe. It surfaces when people are fair with each other, regardless of the attitudes of agents. In real estate you are dealing with people's feelings. If you respect others and treat them fairly, you may be delighted at how they treat you.

The most successful negotiations are where buyers and sellers are both satisfied. Make fairness your aim in a negotiation. It will make you feel good; and that's a good deal in itself.

Even though you are fair, you may find that fairness is not immediately given back to you. This is why it is important to know the traps in real estate negotiation. This includes the *self-inflicted* traps.

Be Realistic

One of the main causes of distress in real estate is trying to do the impossible. People often stretch themselves too far financially or try to buy or sell at levels not possible for their situation. This is one of the most common *self-inflicted* real estate traps.

The market can only give you the best price on offer in the market

For instance, you cannot base the selling price of your home on your personal needs. Too many sellers set their asking price based on what they 'have to do' in the future. This is not realistic. The real estate market cannot give you your personal needs. The market can only give you the best price on offer in the market. Whether or not this price matches your needs is another issue. Don't say, therefore, that you 'need' a certain price. Say, instead, that you want the best market price. If that price matches your needs, you can sell. If not, you can stay.

If you are buying, don't say that you have to buy in a certain area at a certain price. First decide on the maximum price you can afford and then find the area to fit your price. Most buyers select the area first and then try to buy at their price. This is the wrong way around. It is like trying to make two go into one. It won't go. It is better to afford comfortably most of the homes in an area than to search for one home at an impossible low price. If you can't find a home within your price range, you are probably looking in the wrong area. You can't expect homesellers to lower prices to match the price you can afford. That is not fair.

If you can't find a home within your price range, you are probably looking in the wrong area

You have to compete with other buyers in the marketplace. Be one of the best buyers. This will make sure you get one of the best homes.

The same applies when you are selling. Your home competes with other homes for sale. If you price your home too high, buyers will buy better priced homes. And, as we have already seen, the longer your home is for sale, the lower your selling price becomes. Unless, of course, you are prepared to wait for the market to increase to match your asking price; however, this may take years.

So, be realistic. As a buyer, make sure your best price will give you the best range of homes to inspect. As a seller make sure your home is priced to attract the best buyers.

Your home cannot be *on* the market unless it is priced *in* the market

Asking an unrealistic price and not attracting buyers is the same as not having your home for sale. Your home cannot be *on* the market unless it is priced *in* the market. Of course, some agents will say they can 'get your price'. But they may ask you to pay for advertising or ask you to sign up for long periods of time. Why? Because they intend to talk you down in price.

Sell when you are ready to sell and buy when you are ready to buy. And, in both cases, if you are realistic and you understand the process, you will nearly always get the best price when selling and the best home when buying.

Emotion

Almost every decision you make is based on emotion. People do what makes them feel good. If you are not comfortable, if something does not feel right, there is a reason. Either you do not have enough information or you are making a mistake. Listen to your feelings, they are your best guide. But, at the same time, try not to get emotionally caught. If you fall in love with a home, be prepared to pay the top price.

A home is a place where you should be happy. And you should love the home you want to buy. Some first-time homebuyers have no choice other than to buy whatever they can afford. They have to get a foot on the real estate ladder. They may not love the home, but they should, at least, love the *situation* of being a home-owner.

But, no matter what type of buyer you are, how do you avoid being emotionally caught? If you look for a home in an area that you can *easily* afford, you might love two or more homes. One of the most powerful points in negotiation is *alternatives*. If you love more than one home, the sellers will have to compete for you financially. You could buy the home you love at a price below what you would have paid. This is even better. A home you love at a good price.

The same applies when selling. If you have two or more buyers interested in your home, you can sell to the buyer who pays the best price. But always be aware of the emotional feelings of others.

Commitment

Be careful with verbal commitments. This is not only because of legal reasons, but also emotional reasons. If you have more than one buyer for your home, you may cause emotional harm to the buyer who does not buy.

When Penny and Greg bought their home at auction, another buyer, a woman, was bidding against them. Penny and Greg won the auction. The woman then said to Penny, 'I hate you.'[7]

Penny was devastated. 'What a welcome to our new home,' she said. Later, the woman apologised, saying she had felt assured she could buy the home because the advertised price was within her budget. She had been looking for months and loved this home which the agent had quoted at a starting price $100,000 below the selling price.[8] Again, it was the bait price trick.

Do not create false hope in people. Never mind what the agent says, if you show respect in negotiations, this alone can increase your chance of success. People like to deal with nice people. And nice people respect the feelings of others.

Remember, however, that until a legal contract is signed by the sellers and the buyers, *nothing* is certain. Something can still go wrong. No matter how careful you are, or no matter how much respect you show, you can still be hurt. The best you can do is play fair and, at the same time, be aware of the tricks which can be used against you.

> **Until a legal contract is signed by the sellers and the buyers, *nothing* is certain**

THE TRICKS AND TRAPS OF REAL ESTATE NEGOTIATION

The tricks in real estate range from carelessness and innocent misrepresentation through to criminal fraud. Agents who deliberately engage in fraud are rarely caught and prosecuted. They use well-rehearsed excuses to disguise their deceit. Unethical conduct is often legal. And illegal conduct is often hard to prove.

> **Unethical conduct is often legal**

Consumers who have been cheated often feel powerless. Sure, they can 'take legal action', but the trauma and expense frightens most people. Consequently, they are left with nothing but mental and financial scars from their real estate experiences. Knowledge of the following tricks and traps will help you to avoid them before they catch you. Be aware of them all.

First, some advice for investors selling a tenanted property.

Keep your Tenants

Be careful of the 'get the tenants out' trick. An agent may say it is easier to sell a vacant property. This is rarely true. If your tenant moves out, you are under financial pressure to sell more quickly. Lots of landlords are caught with this trick. If a vacant property does not sell, they only have two choices – cut their losses and drop their price, or cancel the sale and find another tenant.

The solution is to keep the tenants and negotiate a lower rent while the property is for sale. The reduction in rent is given for two reasons. First, to compensate the tenants for the inconvenience of inspections and, second, to encourage the tenants to allow inspections at times to suit prospective buyers. Be sure to give the tenants plenty of notice if the property is bought by someone who wants to live in it. Good tenants deserve good treatment. Help them and they will help you in return. You rarely need to have your investment property vacant while it is being sold.

Dummy Offers

A dummy bidder at an auction is replaced by a dummy buyer in a normal sale. Here's how it works. Sellers will be given a ridiculously low offer. Often the agent will appear to be the sellers' friend, saying something like, 'I do not recommend you take this offer.' But it is all part of the softening up process. Agents know that one of the best ways to condition sellers is to hit them with a very low offer. Often such offers are just dummy offers.

The Lowering the Offer Trick

This is a common trick. The buyers make an offer and the agent submits an even lower offer to the sellers. For example, if a buyer offers $450,000, the agent may say that the buyer offered $430,000. The sellers will be left to stew, while the agent says something like, 'I'll see if I can get more out of them.' Later, the agent says, 'Good news, I have got them up to $450,000.' This makes the sellers feel relieved while the agent appears to be the hero.

The same trick is sometimes used on buyers, but the other way around. If the sellers say they will accept $450,000, the agent will tell the buyers that they want $460,000. If the buyers agree to pay, again the agent is the hero. Agents justify this trick by saying they are 'acting in the best interests of the seller'. To tell lies because it is best for the seller does not lessen the deceit.

Verbal Offers

Verbal offers can be a big trap for both sellers and buyers. Some buyers will say to an agent, 'Find out the lowest they will take and if I like the price, I will buy it.' The sellers, in good faith reveal their lowest price and the buyers change their mind. Suddenly, like wildfire, everyone knows the sellers' lowest price. All future offers are usually even lower.

As a seller, if you tell someone the lowest price you are prepared to accept it can easily become the highest price you ever get. You should not negotiate unless you are sure the buyers are serious. Serious buyers make offers in writing, usually with a substantial cheque.

As a homebuyer, sellers will take more notice of your offer if it is in writing.

The Other Buyer

Be careful. If you make an offer below the maximum you are prepared to pay, you risk losing the home to a buyer prepared to pay more than you. This really hurts if you were prepared to pay more than the other buyer.

When Bruce Connelly tried to buy a block of land, he made a verbal offer. The agent said it was 'not sufficient'. Bruce said he would increase the offer if he could have more details about the land. The agent promised to call him back. But no call came. When Bruce finally spoke to the agent the land had been sold. He was told there was no 'legal reason' for the agent to call him. A few weeks later Bruce discovered that the land was sold for $5000 less than he was willing to pay. The buyer was a builder known to the agent.[9]

How could Bruce have protected himself? When the agent did not return his call, he should have contacted the seller directly – or told his lawyer to contact the seller's lawyer. But Bruce, like many consumers, was playing fair and expecting the agent to do the same. He did not realise that the word of an agent is often meaningless. Like police officers who must carefully follow the rules while dealing with criminals who follow no rules, honest consumers often find they are dealing with dishonest agents who follow no rules. In these cases, buyers and sellers should bypass the agents and contact each other.

This is not being underhanded. It is showing agents that if they will not honour their words, then something else will be done. And it gets the attention of the agents.

Bluffing Games

In negotiation, if you bluff you may be thousands of dollars better off; or you may end up with nothing. It all depends on the risks you want to take. If the home is exactly what you want, the safe option is to declare your maximum price in writing in the beginning. Make it clear that you will not pay a cent more. And *mean* it. If the sellers refuse your offer and you then increase your offer, you will look like a liar.

State your walk-away price. And be prepared to walk away

The best way to give yourself the best chance of buying the right home is *not* to bluff. State your walk-away price. And be prepared to walk away.

With many agents, it may be safe to bluff. It depends how good the agent is at negotiation. The best way to discover the agent's negotiating ability is to ask the agent some direct questions before you make your offer.

Two Questions for the Agent

Despite their rhetoric, the best price is rarely the aim of agents. Their aim is a sale. If you are serious and if you are the only buyer interested, the agent will be keen to make a sale at any price. To obtain a lower price, there are two questions you can ask. The first is, 'Why are they asking this price?' Incompetent agents will suggest you offer a lower price. The second question is, 'How much will they take?' Incredibly, many agents will suggest a price to offer. This price will often be less than you are prepared to pay. Thousands of buyers save thousands of dollars by asking incompetent agents these two questions.

Sometimes you don't even have to ask anything other than the price. If you say, 'How much is this home?' many agents will tell you the asking price followed immediately by the lowest price they think the sellers will accept.

In Werribee, Victoria, a salesperson from Westwood First National Real Estate, writes two prices beside the address of each home – the price the sellers want and the lowest price he thinks the sellers will take.[10] He gives buyers his lists. He is not alone. Many agents betray sellers by suggesting that buyers make low offers. Of course, sellers are furious when they discover what their agents are doing. But buyers are amazed at how easy it is to pay less than their maximum price.

Betraying sellers means nothing to some agents if it gets them a sale.

Mystery Shopping

Before you choose an agent to sell your home, you should 'mystery shop' the agent by asking about the homes the agent has for sale. See if the agent is loyal to the sellers. This will tell you if the agent is going to betray you or protect you. Don't sign anything to sell your home with any agent until you mystery shop the agent's office.

If you have already signed up with an agent and you suspect the agent is encouraging buyers to offer less for your home, have a friend do some mystery shopping for you. You may be shocked at what you discover. A journalist who was selling her home had a friend mystery shop her agent. She was appalled that the agent was disclosing her personal details and suggesting she was 'desperate' to accept a lower price.[11] Almost no one is immune from the tricks of agents. A few minutes research can save you thousands of dollars. Mystery shopping is excellent research.

'Fire Ant' Agents

South American fire ants are nasty creatures. When they take hold in an area, they are almost impossible to eradicate. Fire ants get their name because their sting feels like a severe burn. Colonies of fire ants invaded parts of Brisbane in 2001. Professor Andrew Beattie of Macquarie University believes they may invade southern states. 'No one will want to buy a house infested with fire ants,' he said. He said this was happening in some parts of Queensland.[12] Queensland is also infested with agents using a nasty negotiating sting. It's the sting of deliberately misleading consumers about prices. It is done to attract more buyers to homes and to assist in conditioning sellers. So, if a home is advertised for $250,000+, remember the words of one buyer, 'They don't tell you how much the 'plus' is. It's so misleading.'[13]

A real estate trainer from South Australia, David Pilling, claims to have 'invented' methods similar to this sting.[14] Perhaps, by the time you read this, agents will have been prosecuted and this sting will be eradicated. If not, it is vital that you know how to recognise this real estate 'fire ant' which now infests many areas in Australia and New Zealand.

The sting works like this. Buyers are shown homes that are well above their price range. They are told they have a strong chance of buying these homes. Of course, many buyers fall in love with these homes. Then the fire ant agent stings the buyers *and* the sellers. The agent will ask the buyers to make their offer and sign a contract. Many buyers spend money on inspection reports and legal fees. As one stung buyer said, 'We paid for a pest report on a home we had no chance of buying. The real pest was the agent.'[15]

The reason the agents do this is so they can say to the sellers, 'This is what the market is saying your home is worth, therefore you should lower the price of your home.' Most sellers reject these offers, but as more offers are made from more stung buyers, sellers become more conditioned. Finally, they weaken and lower their prices. The following story is typical of how thousands of buyers are hurt by this negotiation sting.

Tanya and her husband were from Melbourne. They began their search for a home in Brisbane in January 2001. 'We are absolutely appalled at the way the system is allowed to run here,' said Tanya. 'When informing agents of the limit we can spend ($250,000 to $290,000) we have been deceived continuously by agents showing us properties they say are in our range. If the property is a For Sale property, the agent cannot say the price. Rather, they say the market will inform them as they conduct the open for inspections etcetera. They encourage us to put in a written offer and it could take a good day or two before our offer is given to the seller, which is submitted with many other offers. The seller takes the highest offer without us being able to offer any higher if ours is not accepted.'

Tanya and her husband were often shown homes that sold for more than $100,000 above their limit. Tanya said, 'These properties are not auction properties!' But just like a fire ant plague, auction tricks spread to all types of sales.

In another case, they were told a home was in the range of '$250,000 to high 200s'. Fed up with the lies, and desperate to buy something, they offered $285,000. The agent then said they would have to offer 'over $300,000'. Furious with a system they could 'do nothing about', Tanya felt they had no choice but to offer $305,000. Although it stretched their finances, they reasoned that, at last, finally, they would have a home. To their disbelief this offer was rejected. The home later sold to someone else for $352,000.

Thinking this was even worse than the Melbourne auction system, they decided to look at auctions. When they found a home that was being auctioned, they told the agent their price limit was $300,000. 'If we cannot afford the home, please tell us,' Tanya pleaded. The agent 'strongly advised' them to have a look, saying they had an 'excellent chance'. With their hopes up again, they arranged an inspection. And again, they loved the home. Back in the agent's office, they said they would pay their maximum price of $300,000. But the agent said they had to offer 'over $310,000 to secure it'. So angry she could barely speak, Tanya spat, 'Okay, I will pay $310,000.' Somehow she would find the money if only to end the trauma. The next day the agent said, 'Sorry, but the owner wants to take it to auction and see what happens.' Tanya was too upset to attend the auction. The home did not sell. Later she saw it advertised for $400,000. 'We are a busy self-employed couple with three children and the amount of time, money and stress we have been put through is outrageous,' said Tanya.

Later in the year, while her husband was in London on business, Tanya found another home. It was owned by an elderly lady. Tanya offered $250,000. The agent faxed the contract to her husband in London to sign. This time things looked good. But, once again, the offer was declined. A few days later, as Tanya was about to attend an auction for yet another home, the agent said the lady had reconsidered. 'Do you want to resubmit your offer?' asked the agent. Tanya was thrilled. Finally, it was all over. There was no need to attend the auction for the other home. The agent congratulated her. It was smiles all around. The agent promised to give her a copy of the contract so she could arrange finance.

But suddenly the agent began avoiding her. Time was running out. In desperation Tanya's husband flew home from London to help arrange the finance. Just before their finance was approved, the agent terminated the contract, saying they had not complied with the finance clause. 'There was nothing we could do about it,' said Tanya. The agent said there was another buyer at a higher price. The home sold to someone else.

Tanya was now desperate. 'We will have to find

somewhere to rent and be locked into another lease, pay for double removalist costs, phone connections and redirections of mail. We had enrolled our children into a school close to the home we thought we had bought. It is a busy time of the year at our work, school holidays are coming and Christmas is only four weeks away.'[16]

Each year thousands of buyers endure similar traumas. The real estate institutes infer that 'bad incidents are isolated', and that the 'majority' of consumers are happy with agents. But the opposite is true – thousands of buyers experience frustration, lack of courtesy, loss of money and emotional pain because agents do what suits agents, not what suits consumers. The 'isolated' excuse works because, for most consumers, their real estate dealings are isolated. They don't buy or sell real estate every day and so they don't realise that what is happening to them is also happening to thousands of other consumers.

In Queensland, the real estate institute commissioned an independent research company, AGB McNair, to discover 'what buyers wanted' from agents. The research showed that '99 per cent of buyers wanted to see a [truthful] price on a home.'[17] As in other states, thousands of homebuyers are not told truthful prices in Queensland. Most agents use systems that suit agents, not consumers, no matter what the research reveals.

The real estate group First National discovered that homesellers (especially women) disliked the stress of open inspections and wanted to be heard on issues such as security. And yet First National continues to recommend open inspections, even going so far as to promote a 'national open for inspection day'. Their new corporate slogan is, 'We're listening'.[18]

Honest and competent agents are the exception not the rule. And the rule for sellers and buyers who meet dishonest and incompetent agents is to use methods that protect them from such agents.

PROTECTION FROM NEGOTIATION TRICKS AND TRAPS

The things we fear most in life are the things we don't understand. But, having read this far, you understand more about real estate than most people. You can recognise tricks. You know the difference between the appearance and the reality. As you venture into the real estate world, remember, don't sign anything until you are sure you are safe. And here's how to be extra safe.

Don't Sign Anything

It is better to offend someone by saying no, than to fight someone because you said yes too soon

People get hurt because they sign the wrong things. Sure, at the time they sign, they may not realise they are doing the wrong thing. But later, when thinking about their mistake, what stands out most was that moment of signing. 'If only I had waited. If only I had not succumbed to the pressure – or the guilt – or the feeling of obligation.'

It is better to offend someone by saying no, than to fight someone because you said yes too soon. Of course, you can't say no forever. There comes a point when you have to sign to sell or buy a home. But that point should only come when you are absolutely certain you are safe.

The Higher Authority

This technique is your ultimate protection. Here's what you do. Select someone with whom you check decisions that need your signature. Someone such as your lawyer, accountant, a relative or a trusted adviser. This person should not be with you at the negotiation. He or she is your 'higher authority' to whom you are committed to referring any decision.

When an agent, or anyone, wants you to sign something, just say, 'Yes, that's good, but before I sign anything I have a rule. I always speak with [name of person], so I'll do that and get back to you. Thanks very much. Goodbye.' The higher authority technique is your constant negotiating companion. Use it all the time.

Do not mention this higher authority person when you *begin* a negotiation. If you do, the agent may insist on having the higher authority present. First, listen to what is said. Ask lots of questions. Get plenty of information. And then, at the end, when you are being 'closed' for a signature, mention your higher authority. It doesn't matter how important it may seem for you to sign, don't do it. Even if you are at an auction and you are the highest bidder, you could still say, 'I have to check with someone before I sign.' Don't be intimidated. Don't sign anything without checking *everything* with your higher authority.

When Ray and Rachelle found a home to buy, the agent asked them to sign a contact. He said it was 'totally safe' and 'standard procedure'. The contract was 'conditional' on their loan being approved; so they signed. They also paid a deposit of $15,000. Four days later, they were told that 'finance was approved' and the contract then became binding.[19]

However, a week later the lender said their mortgage insurance was refused because of power lines near the home. This meant that the loan was now rejected. Ray and Rachelle claim they were not told their loan was 'subject to mortgage insurance'. They were stuck in a contract with no loan and the prospect of losing their $15,000 deposit. They called the Real Estate Institute of Victoria and were told they 'should have read the contract' before they signed it.[20] Ultimately, their parents helped, but they came close to losing all their savings. A terrifying experience, just because they didn't use a 'higher authority'.

The message for all buyers is clear. Don't sign anything until you get legal advice from an independent lawyer. It doesn't matter if the agent says that signing a contract without legal advice is 'standard'. Agents sell real estate. Lawyers do legal work. That's the way it should be.

With the higher authority technique, if an agent says it is

'standard procedure' to sign a contract, you should reply, 'That's *your* standard procedure. My standard procedure is to always check with someone before I sign anything.'

The Pause Button

When you are under pressure, when you are being influenced, when you have 'fallen in love' with a home, that's when you need the most caution. You should always be able to do what is known as 'pushing the pause button'. Have another person with you (not your higher authority). Say to this person, 'Hold on to the pause button and if we are about to sign something, push it for me.'

Remember this: agents want you to sign for their benefit more than yours. Some use clever lines to trick you into signing. One of the slickest is to make you think that signing is 'no big deal'. Another is to point out the minor obligations and ignore the major obligations. For example, an agent trying to persuade you to sign a selling contract (softly called a selling agreement) may say, 'This gives us permission to bring buyers to your home.' This is known as lying by omission. The agent is not telling you that you will be locked in for a certain period of time. If your home is sold to any person (even if the agent has nothing to do with the sale), you must pay the agent. Some agents will say 'The law says you have to sign.' The perfect reply to such a statement is, 'Then you won't mind if we check that with the person who advises us about the law – our lawyer.'

> **Agents want you to sign for their benefit more than yours**

Earnest and Annie were born in 1917. After 61 years of marriage they were thinking of selling their home in Hopper's Crossing. When the L.J. Hooker franchised agent at Werribee approached them and asked them to sign 'this standard paper', they signed.

Earnest was deaf. He and his wife did not realise the agent now had exclusive rights to sell their home for six months. They were 'locked up'. When they complained, the agent threatened legal action saying, 'It is not our policy to release you.' The agent reminded them of their 'legal obligations', saying that if their home sold, by any means, within the six month period, they would have to pay the agent.[21]

When Susan's marriage fell apart, the same agent came to her home. He 'chatted casually' while he recorded some details so 'if she decided to sell he would have all the relevant information on file'. Susan signed his 'form' without reading it. When she wanted to sell, she decided not to use this agent. But the agent told Susan that if she sold her home in the next six months, he was 'entitled to his full commission'.[22]

These cases are common and occur all over Australia and New Zealand. The people who are most vulnerable are the elderly or those selling for traumatic reasons. These people have little hope with crooked agents who act with almost total impunity. In real estate a handshake is almost meaningless. As the Real Estate Institute of Victoria stated when criticising a suggestion that a handshake should have meaning, 'Commission can not be claimed on a handshake'.[23] But that's the point. If agents were *forced* to honour their words, many would not get paid.

Always use the pause button when an agent asks you to sign anything

Always use the pause button when an agent asks you to sign anything. The pause button looks after your interests. It protects you. Honest agents will gladly give you time to consider what you want to do.

NEGOTIATION IDEAS TO HELP YOU

The three most important rules for safe real estate negotiation are information, caution, and advice. Get plenty of information before you decide. Use extreme caution and never take a short cut for any reason. If you don't make the time to get information and advice, you could be forced to live with your mistake for many years.

The Best Advice

The people who advise you should be totally independent and not connected in any way to the real estate agent. Also, the agent should not be receiving payment from the person who gives you advice. Some lawyers pay agents for referring clients to their law firms.[24] Agents can also receive payments from banks, mortgage brokers, valuers, conveyancing firms, building inspectors, pest inspectors, furniture hire companies, removalists, maintenance people. Wherever you spend money when selling or buying a home, the agent could be pocketing some of your money. That one-stop real estate shop often means the real estate agent 'cops the lot' in kickbacks, commissions, volume discounts or rebates. Obviously, businesses associated with agents can never give you objective advice.

Courtesy and Respect

Don't let an agent's treatment of you be a reason to get upset with the other party – the seller or the buyer. If you show respect and courtesy for the person on the other side, you will have a much better chance of success.

When a retired doctor sold the 'lovely cottage' he had owned for 30 years, the agent had three buyers interested.

> **Never underestimate the power of courtesy and respect**

Two of the buyers offered $216,000. The third buyers, a young couple, offered $205,000. When they made their written offer, they wrote to the doctor saying how much they loved his home, how they wanted to raise their children in it and how they would look after his 'beautiful garden'. They explained that $205,000 was the most they could afford. The doctor accepted their offer instead of the higher offers.[25] Despite what many people may think, there are a lot of such 'doctors' in this world.

Never underestimate the power of courtesy and respect. The best negotiators are rarely tough or loud. They are softly spoken and kind. If someone likes you, it can make a big difference.

Meet the Other People

It is easy to say no to someone you don't know. If the sellers know you as 'the buyers' or if you think of the sellers as 'the sellers', everything is mathematical. It's numbers instead of faces. When you consider there are two groups of people, both making perhaps the biggest financial decision of their lives, and they seldom meet each other, it is no wonder there is antipathy in negotiation.

If you are buying, ask the agent if you can meet the sellers. The same applies if you are selling – ask to meet the buyers. Once people see each other, feelings change and negotiations often come to a successful conclusion.

There is one time when you *must* meet the other people; that's when an agent is obstructive. If you are buying and you can't get straight answers, in a reasonable time, go and meet the sellers. You must never use this meeting to cheat the agent out of commission, that's similar to shoplifting; however, you must not suffer bad treatment in silence. Being fair means you expect fairness in return. It does not mean you accept unacceptable behaviour. Being fair also means being firm.

Terms

If you are having trouble reaching an agreement on price, you may find a solution in the terms. Is there something you can do to help the other side achieve their goals? You could agree to let the sellers stay in the home for a short time after you buy it. Or you could offer to settle the purchase in a shorter or longer time. The biggest headache for many people is juggling the moving and travelling to another home. For example, many people need the money from a sale to build a new home. Often they have to move twice, from the home they sell to a rented home and then to their new home when it is completed. If you allow the sellers to rent their home back from you until their new home is complete, they may accept a lower price in return for the convenience.

You can be creative when you focus on terms instead of price. Money is not everything. It's what can be done with the money that matters. Look at what the other people want to do and see if you can help.

Concessions

Negotiation is about concessions. The other party asks you for something and you agree. Each concession brings you one step closer to success.

You should never give a concession without receiving one in return. If you want the buyers of your home to wait an extra few weeks before they move in, then give something in return for this concession. If you do not give a concession in return for one given to you, you will build resentment. Some people seem to ask for everything but give little in return. The negotiation then collapses. Negotiation is about trade-offs, one side gives and so does the other side. It's about fairness.

Hold Back

Sometimes you can hold back on your best price. This assumes, of course, that you have decided to take a risk and not offer your best price up-front. How much you hold back depends on how much you want to risk losing the home if you are a buyer, or losing the buyer if you are the seller. It may also depend on the state of the market.

Real estate, like any commodity, is influenced by economics. Sometimes it's a buyers' market and other times it's a sellers' market. This influences the risk you take. Will you find another home? Or will you find another buyer? What are you prepared to hold back so that, later, if there is some haggling to do, you can offer something extra?

If you are selling, it can be an excellent idea not to offer too many inclusions of your home, such as white goods or furnishings, in the asking price. These can be added in later, during the haggling stages. It depends on the conditions and the price points in the negotiation.

Price Points

If you are a buyer, you may want to offer less than you are willing to pay. As a seller, you may hold out for a little extra.

Just don't let the other side see you as greedy. Sometimes, as sellers, it is best to sell and get on with your plans rather than risk your home going stale and selling at a lower price later. As buyers, often it is best to pay your best price for the home you love.

If you are haggling, at some stage you may encounter the 'split the difference' proposal. Let's say the difference between what the seller wants and what the buyer is offering is $10,000. The suggestion will be made that one person goes up $5000 and the other person comes down $5000. The person who first suggests splitting the difference is usually in the weaker position. The other person can 'anchor' the price at the point of the split. For example if the sellers want $260,000 and the buyers are offering $250,000 and want to split the difference, the sellers can say, 'So you are prepared to pay $255,000?' The price is anchored at $255,000. The difference is now $5000. It may be time to push the pause button because the sellers can then say, 'We are only $5000 apart so what we will do is split *that* difference.' The original difference is then split 75/25, not 50/50.

The Discovery Question

There is a question you should ask whenever you are negotiating anything. It places a moral obligation on the other person. It makes it hard for someone to hide something you are bound to discover later. It's a 'discovery' question with just seven words: 'Is there anything else I should know?' When you ask it, you will often feel the mood change, especially if something is being hidden from you. The response may be, 'What do you mean?' You can then say, 'Well this is a big decision. I want to make sure I know everything I should know.' You then *repeat* the question, firmly and directly, 'Is there anything else I should know?' Many times the response will be, '*Well, yes there is.*' The information you discover can make you glad you asked this question.

'Is there anything else I should know?'

It's probably the most important question to ask as the negotiation concludes.

HOW TO BRING FAIRNESS
INTO PRICE NEGOTIATION

There are many problems with pricing a property in a manner which is fair to everyone. The first problem is that sellers often expect too much for their homes. This problem grows when agents use the Quote Lie to sign up sellers. The agents create more problems with dozens of devious methods to make sales. They cause enormous financial and emotional problems for thousands of real estate consumers.

And yet, whatever solution is made or whatever system is suggested, if it doesn't favour the agents, many will use standard phrases to scare and trap inexperienced consumers. 'You've got to advertise.' 'Auctions are the best way.' 'You get more buyers if you use a price range.' 'Let the market decide.' 'You might buy it for a low price.' 'You might sell it for a big price.'

The truth is that real estate is riddled with deceit: auctions, bait pricing, advertising, kickbacks, inspections, conditioning and negotiation – so often, it all involves lies, tricks and traps for consumers.

An Honest For Sale Price

Selling or buying real estate can be fair and simple. There is an honest For Sale price. Genuine buyers inspect the home. If they want it, they pay the price. If they think the price is high, they make an offer. Finally, the sellers and buyers agree on the price and the terms. The contracts are signed with smiles and handshakes. What a wonderful way to buy or sell a home.

With an honest For Sale price, agents can give buyers an honest explanation of how fairness can occur by saying, 'This is the price the sellers will accept for the home, *if it is the best they are offered*. However it is not the price at which the sellers *must* sell. If there is more than one buyer for the home, each buyer is given the opportunity to declare their best price. The sellers then accept the best price.' It's simple and fair.

Buyers have to compete for homes by being the best paying buyers. But sellers also have to compete for buyers by making sure their homes are priced to attract the best buyers. This is the economics of real estate prices. Homes should be sold to the buyers prepared to pay the best prices – but without the typical duplicity which hurts so many sellers and buyers.

Buyers are outraged when they are quoted prices at which they can *never* buy a home. With an honest asking price, they can buy the home at this price. Yes, there is a risk that another buyer may offer more – but they are told this in the beginning. This is not gazumping. This is real estate economics. Sellers have the right to accept more for their homes just as buyers have the right to offer less. An 'offer' for a home does not have to be a lower offer. It can be higher.

> An 'offer' for a home does not have to be a lower offer. It can be higher

As long as this is pointed out to sellers and buyers, there can be no arguments against the truth. Deception is eliminated when the truth is told from the beginning. If agents followed the ethical principle – *don't hurt anyone* – most typical real estate systems would be eliminated. Honesty would return to real estate. And then, maybe, trust would return and agents would not be among the least trusted of all professions.[26]

Gazumping

One of the worst things to happen to buyers is being told they have bought a home and then, later, being told the home has been sold to someone else. This is especially distressing if the price offered by the losing buyers was less than they were prepared to pay. This is why buyers should be encouraged to *declare their highest price*. They should be told that nothing is certain until a legal contract is signed by the sellers. But if they have offered their highest price and another buyer pays more, at least they had their best chance to buy. It also means the sellers get the best market price.

If an agent says to buyers, 'The home is yours', and then, later, someone else buys the home, the buyers have been gazumped. If this happens, the buyers should receive compensation from the agent. Sadly, no such remedy exists. The New South Wales Department of Fair Trading says that gazumping is 'not against the law, but is not good ethics'.[27] However, in 2002 some agents began to offer 'Gazumping Compensation'. If they say to buyers, 'The home is yours,' and another buyer buys the home from the agent, these agents will give the entire commission on the sale to the buyers who were gazumped.[28] Having a few thousand dollars towards their next home eases the pain of being gazumped.

Economics

The most basic economic research would reveal that the typical real estate methods are deeply flawed and cause great social harm. Such research would also reveal solutions that would benefit consumers.

William Vickery won the Nobel Prize for Economics in 1996.[29] He supported 'socially beneficial' methods of price negotiation. Vickery spent decades studying selling methods, including auctions. He designed a method to encourage buyers to offer their maximum price and not fall victim to paying too much. He said all buyers should offer their maximum price in private. The highest paying buyer wins, but pays the price offered by the *second* highest buyer. This means all buyers will offer their maximum price, but will be protected from paying above the true market price.

All buyers should offer their maximum price in private

In their award speech, the Nobel Committee praised Vickery's method for being 'socially efficient'. While it is hard to see homesellers accepting the *second best* price for their homes, it is also hard to argue with a professor of economics who won a Nobel Prize for a selling method based on social fairness.

The solution for the real estate industry can also be simple and fair. Sellers should be shown how to ask an honest For

Sale price. Buyers then declare their highest price. This price can be at, above or below the price asked by the seller. If the price offered is acceptable to the sellers, a sale is made. Everyone is treated fairly and everyone is happy. This would create an honest real estate society.

HOW TO SELL AND BUY WITHOUT AGENTS

In thousands of cases, sellers and buyers would be better off if they bought and sold without agents. They would save the huge commissions, they would avoid the unnecessary expenses of advertising and they would avoid the trauma caused by agents and their socially harmful methods.

In the United States, around 16 per cent of homes are sold without agents.[30] But in Australia and New Zealand that figure is around two per cent. The real estate industry has the public bluffed. It has created a myth that real estate is complicated. In reality, it's only the tricks that are complicated. Buying or selling honestly is easy. There is no special skill to what most real estate salespeople do. To become a salesperson, all that's generally required is no serious criminal record, and the ability to sit through a few days training. Until recently, in many states, budding salespeople could apply for a job in the morning and be selling homes in the afternoon.

Even a shady past may not prevent someone from selling real estate. In 1999, a man was released from a West Australian jail. Within a year, he was the Real Estate Institute of Western Australia's second highest selling salesperson.[31] In 1999 the Real Estate Institute of Queensland fined a salesperson for unethical conduct. In 2000 they voted this person 'Salesperson of the Year'.[32] In 2001 the Office of Consumer and Business Affairs in Victoria offered a real estate award for customer service. They couldn't find anyone among the nominees who was worthy of the award. Today, the award no longer exists.[33]

In New South Wales, in 2001, the President of the Real Estate Institute said sellers who tried to sell without an agent were guaranteed to lose money.[34] The opposite would be more truthful.

In July 2001, the President of the Real Estate Institute of Victoria, Valda Walsh, reportedly compared selling your own home with 'pulling your own teeth' and said, 'I prefer to go to the dentist, thank you.'[35] To compare selling real estate with performing dental surgery is misleading. It fosters the myth that selling real estate is difficult and best done by agents. This is nonsense.

If you have ever met an agent and thought you could do better yourself, you are probably right. It's not hard. If there is no agent in your area worth hiring, here's how you sell your own home.

SELLING WITHOUT AN AGENT

You will probably need a lawyer to help you to comply with the real estate laws. Also, you may need documents prepared before you offer your home for sale. Let your lawyer take care of the legal side while you focus on the selling side.

You will have to calculate a fair asking price. Check the recent sale prices in your area, but remember that many homes – especially those sold by incompetent agents – have been undersold. Hire an independent and reputable valuer who is not connected with an agent in your area. Explain why you want a valuation. Unlike real estate salespeople, valuers spend years studying their profession. Their record of accuracy is much better than most agents.

Hire an independent and reputable valuer who is not connected with an agent in your area

Next, you should get a building and pest inspection report. It is prudent to be prepared for anything the buyers may discover. Many buyers will want such reports. You can then honestly explain the condition of your home. Be frank about any faults. Honesty is the foundation of successful negotiation.

Make a list of your home's features and the benefits of your area. You can give copies to interested buyers. Include as much information as possible. A feature you think unimportant could create a sale for you. One homeseller wrote a five-page essay called 'Why we love our home'. It included all the features of her home, the benefits of the area plus a history of the home. It was beautiful.[36]

Once you have chosen your asking price, you need a strategy for working with buyers. Be serious about selling and be fair. All you want is the best market price. You should set a goal to sell within a time range. Make it flexible because you don't want to be locked in to a set date, as happens with auctions. Three to five weeks is usually all you need. Often it is much less. Just be careful your home does not become stale.

The buyers who want to buy in your area will come to your area before they buy. Some will already be living in the area. There are three ways to attract them.

First, have a professionally made sign with simple information and colours. For example, use a light blue colour with white letters which say, *Home For Sale – Call Owner.* And then state your phone number. That's all you need. The buyers who call will have seen your home from the outside which means they are interested in both the home and its location.

The second way for you, the homeseller, to attract buyers is local advertising. There is a big difference between your advertising and that done by most agents. Your advertising has one purpose – to attract a buyer who will buy your home. You are not advertising to increase your profile or to condition yourself down in price. You want to attract the right buyer. You only have one home, so you cannot switch buyers to other homes. Although agents can sell homes without placing specific advertisements, it is hard for you to do the same. Other than from the For Sale sign, buyers don't come to your door as they do with agents. You have to do something agents rarely do – sell a specific home from a specific advertisement.

There are always buyers in your area. Most will be known to the agents. You can attract many of these buyers with your advertisement. However, you must be very careful not to damage the value of your home with advertising. Your advertising has to be short, sharp and clear.

The big secret to protecting the value of your home is *not to identify it* in an advertisement. You do not want anyone thinking there is something wrong with your home. Remember, stale homes get lower prices. A home which is fresh gets the most attention and almost always the best price. Use text, not a picture in your advertisement. Your aim is to attract buyers not to 'sell' your home in the advertisement. Just state the main facts in a clear manner. And never exaggerate or use puffery. You want buyers to be delighted when they see your home, not disappointed. The main facts to include are the price, the style of home, the size of the home, the number of bedrooms and its location. You should also include the words 'want to sell soon for best offer'. This creates a sense of urgency and seriousness. It also allows you to explain to buyers that if there is more than one buyer interested you will sell to the buyer who pays the best price (or the buyer you choose).

Your advertisement must be easy to see. Book it for three weeks. If you decide to sell sooner, you can cancel the advertisements.

The third way to find buyers is to produce your advertisement as a flyer to be distributed in your area.

Do any of these three things and you will attract buyers. All you have to do is speak with the buyers and show them your home. You then negotiate the best price and your home is sold. It's a lot easier than you may think.

How to Negotiate with the Buyers

When buyers call, their first question is usually, 'Is the house still for sale?' If you say yes, it may create the impression that other buyers have rejected your home. So just say, 'At the moment it is, yes.'

Some callers will just want to come for a look, but first you must do some basic qualifying. It saves your time and theirs. Just ask, 'What sort of home are you looking for?' Let them tell you. Or, if they ask you to describe your home, always end with the question, 'Does this sound like what you are looking for?' And then say, 'When do you hope to buy?' This lets you know if they are able to buy now. It tells you if you are dealing with a looker or a buyer.

Some people have to sell their homes before they can buy. Others have to arrange finance. There is nothing worse than showing your home to someone who wants to buy it and then you have to wait while they get organised. You need buyers who can buy now.

Never discuss offers with buyers before they see your home. Some will be quite blunt on the phone, saying such things as, 'Will you take an offer?' Your reply should always be, 'Why don't you look at it before we talk about that?' Be courteous. Try to speak with a smile when you get a blunt question. Deflect hard questions by saying, 'I have to talk to (my partner or whomever) about that.'

Be careful with investors and bargain-hunters. The best paying buyers are usually those who want a family home. They are more interested in finding the right home than in talking you down in price. To identify all buyers before they inspect your home, just say, 'What is your name?' And then add, 'And your phone number?' Never let anyone into your home unless you know who they are. If you don't get a good feeling about someone, just say, 'What's your number, I'll call you back.'

You should never have an open inspection where just anyone can wander through, but you should try to have inspections around the same times, so that you aren't stuck at home all day. If you have enough calls, make the appointments half an hour apart. Some may overlap, but this doesn't matter. The sight of another genuine buyer may increase the desire of those who like your home. But never fill your home with people. Two sets of buyers – one leaving and one arriving – is enough.

When showing people through your home, don't crowd them. Give them space. And don't point out the obvious, such as, 'This is the kitchen.' The best thing to say is, 'Have a look around. If you have any questions, let me know.' And then guide them casually through your own home without acting desperate (even if you are).

When they have finished looking, if they like it, they will tell you. If they don't want to buy, they will be anxious to leave. Just thank them for coming. There is no magic trick to selling real estate. Agents don't sell homes to buyers that don't like the homes. They just show more homes. You only have one home, so just smile and say, 'Goodbye'.

If too many buyers are not interested, find out why. Call some of them later and ask for their help. Say, 'I know our home is not what you are looking for, but from what you've seen in the area, I was wondering if you had any advice for us.' People are much more likely to be frank over the phone than in person. Listen to what they say. If you get many similar comments, you will know the problem you face. It may be the price.

Those who like your home will respond in different ways. Some will come straight out and make you an offer. They may say, 'Okay, what's your last price?' Just smile and say, 'What's your best price?' But then quickly say, 'Look, we are expecting some more people, so why don't you think about it and give us a call later on?' The phrase 'expecting more people' is always the truth.

By telling the buyers to 'think about it', you are doing the opposite to what they may expect. Be sincere. The less you push them, the more interested they become. If it is a good home at a fair price, it will sell itself. Sure, you may get some price haggling, but the way to handle this is to say, 'We are expecting more buyers and we are going to sell to whoever gives us the best offer.' Mention your time frame, saying you hope to sell around a certain date. Don't lock yourself in to a set date. Be flexible – just in case.

Some buyers may ask you to hold the home for them.

While this is tempting, it can trap you. If you hold the home for someone and later they change their minds, you have wasted valuable time, and turned away other more genuine buyers. It is only fair that the buyers who look at your home are in a position to buy now.

If the buyers offer to buy at the full asking price, your decision must be based on how many people have seen your home. If they are the first buyers, they could be the best buyers you will ever get, or perhaps other buyers could pay more. How do you know? Without having a good agent to advise you, here's what you might do. Say, 'We are expecting more people and we want to see as many as possible and see how much they offer.' This will certainly test the sincerity of the buyers. However, it could be dangerous. You may lose these buyers and have to accept a lower price later.

Use your judgement. Rely on your assessment of people. If they seem nice and appear genuine and you are happy to sell now at the price you are asking, then proceed, but with caution. Say, 'I don't want to promise you anything, because nothing can really be certain until it all becomes legal.' To further test their sincerity, you may add, 'What if you find a home you like more than this one, or if we find a buyer who wants to pay more?'

Don't accept any money and don't sign anything. Remember the pause button and the higher authority. Get independent advice *before* you make a final decision. Tell the buyers that you have to speak with your lawyer (or whomever). Ask for their full details including the name of their lawyer or conveyancer. And then say, 'Let's let the legal people work out all the legal details.'

Spend time with people once they are interested. Make them comfortable. Sit with them (in the best spot in the house). Be polite, they may be as nervous and concerned as you. If buyers really like your home, the price will rarely stop them buying. They knew the price before they came to your home, so they can't say they can't afford it.

If they say your home is more expensive than others, don't

be offended. And don't say, 'Well, why didn't you buy one of the others?' Just smile and say, 'That's because we think it's better than the others. We hope you agree with us.'

If they want to make you a firm offer, ask for it in writing. Do not make an instant decision. Say you will consider all offers in writing and sell to the person with the best offer. It is okay to ask them to declare their best offer.

If you have spent many years in your home, if it is a loved home, tell them how much you love it; tell them how and why you first fell in love with your home. If it's true, you can say, 'We know how you feel. We looked at lots of houses before this one. And we have never regretted buying it.' Tell them all the good things about your home and the area. Don't be afraid to share your enthusiasm for your home. Selling is often called the 'transference of enthusiasm'. Natural passion is a great persuader.

Private Sale Companies

Private sale companies claim to show you 'how to save thousands selling your own home'. For a fee, of course. They will compare their fee with an agent's fee, point to the difference and ask you to pay them. In advance. But if your home does not sell, you lose. Worse, you may then have to go to an agent which means you will pay twice.

Like any company that wants your money, ask yourself, 'What do I get for the money I pay?' Typically, you get a For Sale sign, some letterbox flyers and an Internet advertisement. About $150 worth of value, all for an up-front fee of about $1500. You still have to spend money advertising.

Many private sale companies claim a high 'sales success rate'. But the question most sellers don't ask is, 'Why do they want fees in advance?' At the very least they should offer a guarantee.

One of the golden rules of selling a home is *never pay any money in advance* for any reason. All fees and commissions must come from the sale of your home, not before.

BUYING WITHOUT AN AGENT

Most homes are sold with agents and it seems therefore as if the agents have control. The secret is to find a home before the sellers sign with an agent. It is so simple, it's hard for many buyers to accept.

All you do is go to the area of your choice, select the streets you prefer and contact the owners. You can place flyers in letterboxes. Or, for a small fee, the post office will do it for you. If you're really determined, you can knock on every door in the areas of your choice. This is how some agents find homes for sale, and you can do it too. It beats spending months chasing incompetent agents who rarely call you back. It beats trudging around open inspections, listening to agents giving you false quotes about the selling prices.

David lives in Canberra. He says it is easy to buy and sell without agents. 'When we arrived here, we just walked around and put notes in letterboxes of houses that we liked and said if you are interested, please ring us.' It worked. 'When we sell, we just advertise in the paper and sell without agents. I'm not putting agents down, no, some people need them; but if you keep your head and think about what you are doing, anyone can sell and buy their own home without the help of an agent,' he said.[37] It's certainly worth a try if you can't find a good agent.

Three People

Three different people can sell your home. A competent agent, you and, lastly, an incompetent agent. You have to choose the person who will do the best for you. If that's you, choose yourself. You should start by looking for a competent agent. If you can't find one, consider selling with no agent. If you do choose an agent, don't sign anything unless the agent guarantees *in writing* that you will be safe from the common traps of real estate. If you are prepared to stand up to agents and insist on your basic rights, you can take control. It is better to insist that an agent does the right thing than to suffer when an agent does the wrong thing.

Whether you are buying or selling, a good agent is always your best option. Your second option is to do it yourself. If that doesn't work, you can deal with other agents because when you know how to recognise the tricks and traps of real estate, you can protect yourself.

Don't sign anything unless you are sure you are safe. Your home represents most of your wealth. Be careful and you will enjoy selling or buying. You will get the right price and the right home. You may enjoy it so much that, one day, you might decide to invest in real estate.

And then you'll have to avoid some of the most dangerous traps in real estate.

Summary

- Agents usually act for sellers and have a duty to obtain the best market price. This rarely happens.

- Most agents are dreadful negotiators. They cost sellers thousands of dollars and, at the same time, often cause incredible emotional damage to buyers.

- As a seller, beware of 'the endowment effect', the tendency to want an unrealistically high price because your home is special to you.

- Investing in an independent valuation from a registered valuer before you sell can be one of the smartest things you ever do. It is like having inside knowledge.

- As a buyer of a family home, if you love the home and you can comfortably afford it, be prepared to pay your maximum price. Bluffing or offering too low a price increases the risk of not buying the home.

- Make fairness your aim. If you respect others you may be delighted at how you are treated in return.

- When selling, the best you can get is the best price on offer in the market. Whether or not this matches your needs is another issue.

- When buying, decide on the maximum you can afford and then find the area to fit your price. If you can't find a home in your price range, you are looking in the wrong area.

- When selling, if you price your home too high, buyers will buy other homes. Your home will become stale.

- The three most important safety rules in negotiation are information, caution, and advice.

- Always use the seven-word 'discovery' question: 'Is there anything else I should know?'

- Until a legal contract is signed by both the sellers and the buyers, and the contract has become legally unconditional, *nothing* is certain. **Don't sign anything** until you get independent legal advice.

Chapter Ten

Investment Traps

Protect yourself from 'legal' crimes

We are all Alices in a Wonderland
of conflicting claims,
bright promises, fancy packages, soaring words
and almost impenetrable ignorance.

F.J. Schlink, founder of the US's first
independent product testing agency, in 1927

Kidnapping is a simple crime. All that's needed is a victim whose friends or relatives can pay a high ransom. But it's also a high risk crime. Snatching the victim is the easy part. The hard part is 'the drop' – when the victim is exchanged for the ransom. This is when most kidnappers are caught. And punished severely. The maximum penalty for kidnapping is life imprisonment. If no one is physically hurt, if all the money is recovered, if the kidnappers plead guilty and if the crime is a first offence, the kidnappers may receive a discount on their sentences. But they would still get at least ten years in jail. Kidnapping is a serious crime.

Most criminals measure risks against rewards. Just like investors. Kidnapping is a high risk 'investment'. Smart criminals seek crimes with a high return and a low risk of punishment. But imagine if criminals had a high return from kidnapping and no risk. Imagine if there was no punishment, no jail term. At worst, they might have to endure embarrassment as they scurry to avoid television cameras. Now imagine if, somehow, their crimes were legal. They wouldn't be crimes at all. Imagine if their lawyers could sue anyone who called them criminals.

And here's the exciting part for criminals. Imagine if they could keep the money from their kidnapping crimes. It would be a dream come true. They would be in paradise. Surfers Paradise.

A Real Estate Kidnapping Story

Mrs Pope is 60. She works in the public service in a role she performs admirably. At 42 she was widowed and left with three children. She now lives alone. Friends describe her as a 'lovely lady'.

One summer night Mrs Pope was wondering if she would have enough money to retire. Suddenly, a man barged into her home. The man said he would not harm her, but she must do *exactly* what he said. Later, Mrs Pope said she didn't know what to do other than 'obey completely'. Taking her outside, he drove to the airport where, together, they boarded a flight to Queensland.

The man contacted Mrs Pope's children and demanded a ransom of $100,000. The only way to get that much money was to mortgage Mrs Pope's home. In a few days the ransom was paid into a bank account nominated by the man. Mrs Pope was allowed to return home. Within a week, by tracing bank transfers, the police arrested the man.

Although shaken, Mrs Pope was in good spirits. In court, she said the man had been kind to her. She was kept in a motel at the Gold Coast where she was 'very comfortable'. The man was sentenced to 12 years imprisonment. Everyone said she was brave. But Mrs Pope was as modest as ever. 'Aside from being a bit scared, there was no harm done and I got my money back. It could have been a lot worse,' she said.

This story is fiction. The truth is worse. And it's happening to thousands of Australians and New Zealanders.

THE TRUE STORY OF THE 'KIDNAPPING AND RANSOM' OF MRS POPE

Until the part where the man 'burst' into her home, the story is true. The man did not burst in. He was invited in. His name was Murray Cox. He looked and sounded respectable, and he worked for a company with a respectable name – Networth Planning Corporation.[1] He sat and listened to her talking about her retirement and her debts.

Mrs Pope had two homes – a family home and an investment home. Together with superannuation her assets totalled $800,000. Her total debt was $82,000, giving her a net worth of more than $700,000.[2] But she was worried about her debt level and wanted to reduce it as soon as possible. Mrs Pope said she did not want any obligation, especially about buying real estate. The man showed her the Networth Planning brochure. On the cover was a photograph of an elderly couple, a man standing behind a lady with his arms wrapped tightly around her. It was an outdoor windswept look with the couple smiling upwards. So safe, so secure, so happy.

The brochure said 'Networth Planning do not sell properties'. It mentioned two other companies which it claimed had 'impeccable reputations' – Express Mortgage and Ray White Real Estate. The man suggested flying to Queensland to meet Express Mortgage, saying, 'They will do a plan for you.' It was all about 'financial freedom' which was exactly what Mrs Pope wanted. And so, on Sunday January 21, 2001 she boarded a flight to the Gold Coast.

Greeting her at the airport was Gloria Dawson from the Investment Services Division of Ray White Real Estate at Surfers Paradise. Although it was approaching evening, Gloria was kind enough to give Mrs Pope a brief tour of the area.[3] Chatting amicably, Gloria revealed that she had been divorced many years ago. Left with two boys – both of whom were now grown up – she had worked for a charity for several years. Needing a change, she chose real estate. Now she was the proud owner of three properties. Her eldest son had just purchased his first investment property. Talking about investing, Gloria said, 'Express Mortgage are a very experienced and very reputable firm. They have been around for a long time.'

That night, after Gloria dropped her at a motel, Mrs Pope kept wondering why she needed to travel so far just to sort out her finances. But Gloria seemed nice; and, after all, there was no obligation.

The next day, just after 7 am, Gloria arrived at the motel. 'You're early,' said Mrs Pope as they drove to Express Mortgage. 'Yes, but I love what I'm doing,' Gloria replied.

Mrs Pope was about to meet another man for a 'financial consultation'. His name was Glenn Coleman from Express Mortgage. From the beginning, she didn't like him. The 'consultation' began with a question, 'What do you hope to achieve?'

'I want to do all I can to maximise my finances for my retirement. At my age I am not interested in taking risks. My aim is to reduce my debt before I retire.' Mrs Pope was worried that she may have to work beyond the age of 65.

Mr Coleman responded enthusiastically. He spoke of the wonders of the Gold Coast, how it is the 'fastest growth region' in Australia. His knowledge flowed like a gushing tap; it was all positive – the fortunes that had been made 'here on the coast' and the wonderful opportunities unique to the area.

It was Mrs Pope's turn to listen. Growing increasingly nervous and wondering again what she was doing at the Gold Coast – a place she had never much liked – listening to this man talk about investing. All she wanted to do was talk about retiring.

Mrs Pope said, 'I am not interested in any get-rich-quick schemes'.

'Neither are we,' he said. 'We are interested in responsible planning.'[4]

She still wasn't comfortable. She didn't like this man. Something didn't feel right. Later, she said she 'felt guilty at the time for judging him badly' and decided he must be acting in her best interests. Every question she asked was returned with an instant and logical response.

But, as Les Henderson, author of the best-selling book *Crimes of Persuasion* writes, 'No matter what questions you ask, or how many you ask, skilled swindlers have ready answers and their persuasive scripts include retorts for every objection. They typically brush aside questions or concerns with vague answers or assurances.'[5]

Entering her details into a computer, Coleman said, 'You definitely have the capacity to eliminate your debt through real estate. We would set up a loan so you are only paying the interest on the loan. I have done a very conservative plan for you.'

'I don't believe I can afford to do it,' she said.

'You can't afford *not* to do it,' he replied. Coleman then said to Gloria, 'Show her 42 Turtle Beach.'

'Can I look at anything else?' asked Mrs Pope.

'In your situation, that is really the only property you could afford. And even that will depend on us being able to arrange your finance.'

This was the property he had chosen for her. And he was the expert. Impeccable reputation, that's what the brochure said. Or was it Gloria? Or that first man, the nice one, what was his name? Murray Cox, that's right. It was so confusing. And so fast. As if in a trance, Mrs Pope was driven to inspect the property. On the way, Gloria pointed out the Gold Coast landmarks while speaking constantly about 'rising values'.

The property was a one bedroom unit for 'only $178,000'. Mrs Pope wasn't sure. She felt trapped. As many victims describe it, she said, 'You reach the point where you feel foolish or guilty if you say no. It is all so well crafted. I can't really pin-point what happened.'

Victims use words like 'whirlwind' or 'whisk' to describe almost surreal experiences. Often they say, 'It happened so fast. But everyone was so nice, like they'd known me for years and really cared about me and wanted to help me.'

They returned to Express Mortgage. Coleman had great news, 'Your loan has been approved.' Panicking, Mrs Pope said, 'I would only be interested if it was a responsible lending institution.' It was Origin Finance. 'That's the ANZ bank, you know,' said Coleman. He also mentioned the Bank of Adelaide.

'This is what made me feel okay,' Mrs Pope said, 'The well-known banks plus the lawyer they sent me to. I just could not, and still can't, believe that all these people can be so unethical.' It wasn't until months later that Mrs Pope discovered what thousands of other victims discover. She had been conned. She had paid $178,000 plus about $10,000 in expenses and $14,000 for 'furniture and fittings' – more than $200,000 - for a property worth less than $120,000.[6]

And everyone seemed to be in on it. From that nice man who first came to her door, to the lady at the airport, to the finance consultant and the lawyer, right through to the bank lending the money. Of course they approved the loan; they were taking her two valuable homes as security as well as the dud investment property. How embarrassing. It all made sense when she looked back on it. Even the owners of the motel probably knew what was going on.

But, at the time it was happening, Mrs Pope knew none of this. Coleman made an appointment for her with a well-known law firm – Rapp & Yarwood. In the meantime, Gloria took her back for another look at the unit, telling her again about the 'huge demand for property' and how she had 'made the right decision' and 'how capable Mr Coleman is at these matters'.

With nothing to eat since 7 am, they stopped for lunch. They had to be quick; the appointment with the lawyer was at 3 pm. Papers had to be signed before she caught her flight home. The lawyer from Rapp & Yarwood made sure everything was legal.[7] One of his first comments was, 'I am not here to give you advice on financial planning. I am here to go through the contract for the sale of the property.' He asked her to sign a 'Client Agreement' which stated, among other things, 'The work that we do will not involve at all any financial advice or considerations.' Near the end of the agreement were the words, 'You have been informed that you should seek independent advice in relation to this Agreement.'[8]

Even though his agreement virtually admitted he could not be trusted to act in her interests, Mrs Pope signed everything the lawyer told her to sign. She didn't know she was making a mistake. She didn't know the law firm was pocketing thousands of dollars in fees from these scams. He was a lawyer and Mrs Pope trusted lawyers.

It *is* legal for lawyers to act for unsuspecting consumers, even when the lawyers must know, or should know, that these consumers are being ripped off. But, if they protected naïve consumers, the real estate company would not send them any more victims. And so they protect themselves by saying, 'We are not giving you financial or investment advice. We are just here to go through the contract for the sale of the property.'

Mrs Pope was the victim of a 'legal crime', a type of real estate 'kidnapping', much worse than the fictional kidnapping described earlier. She told these people she wanted to reduce her debt by the age of 65. Instead, it was increased from $82,000 to $275,000. Her new loan ends on February 27, 2026. Assuming she lives that long, she will be 85.[9]

WHAT ARE THESE INVESTMENT SCAMS?

These scams are about selling properties to unsuspecting consumers for tens of thousands of dollars above their true value. The prices of the properties are 'loaded', as much as $100,000 above their value. This is often referred to as 'Two-Tier Marketing', meaning there is one price for locals and one price for people who are not locals, those with no knowledge of the area or its values. But people who are not locals are the targets of these real estate con artists.

Units, townhouses and homes are often built purely to sell to interstate investors. Once sold, they are all rented. Some experts believe these properties are destined to be 'the slums of the future', especially the smaller units or those built in the same subdivisions.[10] To make it worse, there is little chance of any capital gain. The only way to get out is to sell at a loss. One study showed that even after ten years, the average loss was $28,640 – and that's just on the prices at which the properties were bought and resold.[11] It does not include the costs of buying, the costs of selling or the costs of holding the properties, all of which would probably increase the average loss after ten years to around $50,000.

Young Victims

In 1990, when he was 28, Gary Solomon paid $75,000 for a unit at Loganlea between Brisbane and the Gold Coast. The company that sold it to him, Looker and Young, showed him all the positive newspaper articles and all the projections. He was told that he 'couldn't lose'. The fact that the Metway Bank was providing finance made him feel confident. Ten years later, his unit was part of a slum with a high rate of criminal activity. It was worth about $35,000. He can't afford to sell and yet, the longer he keeps it, the less it is worth and the more money he throws at it.[12] His total loss is close to $90,000.

In 1994, at the age of 23, Jason from the Melbourne suburb of Brunswick paid $117,000 for a unit. He wanted to secure his future. He and his mother were flown to the Gold Coast on a Sunday morning and flown back that night. They were taken to a Westpac Bank where a man in casual clothes was waiting with loan documents. A mortgage was later placed over his mother's Melbourne home. They were also whisked to an office where a lawyer, alone in the building and wearing jeans, had them sign contracts for their 'magnificent investment'.

Jason was told, 'property values will skyrocket' – a common lie used by real estate crooks.[13] Another lie is that 'real estate doubles every seven years.' Seven years later, in

2001, when Jason wanted to buy his first family home, he discovered that his 'magnificent investment' was worth about $70,000, almost $50,000 less than he paid for it.[14] And, because he was 'an investor', he did not qualify for the First Home Owner's Grant.

The Lenders

What many victims don't realise is that the lenders are using the family homes of the victims as security for the loans on the dud investments. If the victim is buying an 'investment' for $117,000 which, in reality, is worth $70,000, the banks take a mortgage over their family home.[15] In Jason's case, the bank used his mother's home which was then worth at least $300,000.[16] The bank had security of $370,000 (the family home plus the dud investment). It was delighted to lend $117,000.

The lenders know – or ought to know – that their customers are being ripped off. But they are more keen to lend money than to protect customers.

Real estate crooks often say, 'You don't need your own money. You can use the bank's money. That's what smart people do. It's called OPM – Other People's Money.' But the other people are the banks, who are safe while you have increased the amount you must pay and you have lost a large slice of the equity in your home. When you hear the expression 'other people's money' those other people will want their money back, plus more. In the end, it is always your money that you are paying.

Equity Fraud

If you buy a dud investment, you lose a slice of the equity in your home. Equity is the difference between what your home is worth and what you owe on your home. For example, if you have a home worth $500,000 and you owe $200,000, your equity is $300,000. If you pay $100,000 too much for a dud investment and your home is taken as security for a loan, you lose $100,000 of your equity. Just as surely as if crooks had stolen $100,000 of your money.

Those touting a dud investment will tell you that you don't have to pay any money. Well, not from your pocket, you don't. Not really. All you need to do is sign a lot of papers after listening to several slick presentations. It could be years before you discover how your money – your equity – was stolen. Until you decide to sell, you may never know. By that stage, the crooks have long gone. It's like a form of real estate cancer where, until they decide to sell, victims don't know how badly they have been hurt. This is why it can take years for complaints to surface.

In 2001, the New Zealand Commerce Commission said it received very few complaints about real estate scams.[17] But this doesn't mean people are not being conned, it just means people don't know they are being conned. The 'smart' crimes are where the victims don't know they are victims. Real estate investment scams almost define 'the perfect crime'.

This crime – which is a form of 'home equity fraud' – catches thousands of home-owners every year. The builders, the developers, the marketeers, the agents, the banks, the lawyers – they know what's going on. It's a billion dollar industry which takes a terrible toll on the finances of hard working and decent citizens in Australia and New Zealand.

COUNTING THE TOLL

These real estate investment scams are perpetrated by people known as 'marketeers'. Victims come from all over Australia and New Zealand; trusting types, often close to retirement. They are seeking security in their old age. But they are fleeced unmercifully by this form of legal kidnapping. Their lives are ruined at a time when their lives should be most secure.

They are fleeced unmercifully by this form of legal kidnapping

In 1998, approximately 3000 consumers living outside the Gold Coast region were tricked into buying dud investments in the area.

The average amount by which each property was loaded was $50,000.[18] Plus the legal costs and the constant holding costs. Considering that these scams have been part of the Gold Coast real estate scene since at least 1992, as many as 30,000 people may have lost more than a billion dollars. And this is in just one part of Australia. These scams are not unique to Queensland. As you will see, they are now surfacing in many other areas, including New Zealand. As author Terry Ryder says, these disastrous investments are created by 'sellers with no scruples, laws with no teeth and buyers with no idea'.[19]

The New Zealand Consumers' Institute, which was formed in 1959, called these property deals 'probably the biggest scam we've ever reported'.[20] In just one brief study, 15 New Zealand families lost more than NZ$1 million between them.[21] In all, hundreds of New Zealanders have been duped by property investment scams. And it is still going on.

Legal and moral are two different things in the world of real estate

All those who take part in these scams – from marketeers to the real estate agents, the banks and the lawyers – deny they are doing anything wrong. They fall back on that 'legal' line which bears no relation to morality. Legal and moral are two different things in the world of real estate. As the outspoken consumer lawyer Tim O'Dwyer states, 'Many lawyers have their snouts firmly in the troughs of the investment scams, while most of the legal profession remains shamefully silent about it all.'[22]

The heartbreaking tales of savings wiped out, families torn apart, people forced into bankruptcy, depression and even suicide could fill an entire book. How, one wonders, could this be allowed to happen? And why, even with the increasing publicity now being given to these scams, do so many people continue to become victims?

WHY IT KEEPS HAPPENING

After the terrorist attacks of September 11, 2001, the focus of the world was on capturing the mastermind, Osama Bin Laden. But there was a chilling message from many terrorism experts, 'If you kill Bin Laden, there are thousands more ready to take his place.'

And so it is with real estate con artists. Expose one and two more will emerge. Shonky salespeople who see crooked bosses making millions will start their own 'investment companies'. And before too long, the ones who have been exposed resurface elsewhere. They breed like rats and become increasingly cunning, reinventing themselves faster than laws can be passed to stop them.

The profits are so huge and the penalties are so low, it's hard for anyone, other than the scrupulously honest, to resist. They are like drug dealers lured by enormous profits; but without the risk of punishment. In some cases, these crooks are hailed as being good for the economy because jobs are created at all levels of the process.[23] That's similar to making heroes out of car thieves because they benefit the car alarm industry.

The real estate institutes imply that their agents are not involved. But many institute members are involved in investment scams.[24] The real estate industry is more concerned with protecting its image than protecting consumers. Industry codes of ethics bind agents to a code of cover-up. No matter what an agent is doing, no matter how many consumers are being hurt, the code is clear: agents must be 'loyal to the institute'. To speak out publicly can mean expulsion from the institute for 'breach of ethics'.[25]

In today's corporate world where profit at any cost is the focus, the pay-offs have created an industry sworn to a dark, immoral silence; bonded in an unspoken collective conspiracy. In business, morality is rarely the focus. And that's why it keeps happening.

THE STANDARD STING

The classic real estate investment sting works like this. You are invited to a 'free seminar'. The buzzwords are 'wealth creation', 'tax minimisation' and 'negative gearing'. There is a heavy emphasis on fear – the fear of being poor in old age, the fear of missing out on the booms or the fear of working hard for no return. You may be told that most people struggle to survive when they retire. Life's winners are those who invested in real estate. And on it goes. The message will be that you don't have to be 'like everyone else'. You can be rich 'if you know what to do'. You will be shown a series of graphs and charts which 'prove' that real estate is the best investment, especially as a retirement strategy. But Noel Whittaker, one of Australia's most respected financial experts, says, 'I believe basing your retirement around residential real estate is one of the worst retirement strategies because the properties are an aging asset that require continual maintenance.'[26] You won't hear Noel's advice at the seminars.

You will see figures that seem to make perfect sense. You will see how, for just a few dollars a week – all of which is 'fully tax deductible' – you can build a 'property portfolio'. It sounds great. You will hear case studies of people, just like you, who have made more money from real estate than their jobs. The proof is impressive. You will be hooked, especially if you are told it is all 'guaranteed'. And there is no harm in just 'having a look'.

> **The safest real estate investment advice you will ever receive is don't sign anything**

This is how it all starts. You are being set up. No matter what you hear, no matter what you see, no matter who is speaking, you are going to be conned. If you can't accept that these words are true or you just can't believe it can be that bad or that you will get hurt, then just remember the title of this book – *Don't Sign Anything!* At least not until you know how to make certain that you cannot be conned. The safest real estate investment advice you will ever receive is don't sign anything.

At the end of the seminar, you will be offered a 'no obligation home consultation'. A 'trained consultant' will give you some 'personal' suggestions. What they want to look at, of course, is whether or not you have enough equity in your home to steal. They want to rob you and they have a plan to do it in such a way that you don't realise what is happening to you. Much of what you hear will be exactly what you want to hear. Words like 'conservative' and 'caution' and 'protection' will be used constantly. You will forget any negatives you may have heard. You may forget the advice in this book because the person in front of you will seem so different. He or she will really seem to care about you.

These people are *trained con artists*. The more perfect they seem, the more you like them. And the more they are likely to con you. As one Fraud Squad detective pointed out, 'The biggest shock to fraud victims is not the fraud itself, but being cheated by someone nice. But that's why they were cheated. If the con artists weren't nice, they wouldn't be able to con people.'[27] The respected investment writer Marsha Bertrand says that scam victims hand over their money because their adviser (the con artist) is 'personable, confident, articulate, and, most of all, a good salesman. These are the character traits that most swindlers share.'[28]

At this stage, there will be no pressure. You are in the early stages of the scam where your defences are being weakened. The con artist is winning your trust by saying such things as, 'I can't promise we can help you. I will need to recommend an expert.'

Next, the con artists bring in the 'higher authority', someone they glowingly recommend, a person of 'integrity', someone from a 'long established' and 'respected' company. These companies will have names which sound secure. Names like The Epic Group, The Coral Reef Group, Australian Financial Management Corporation, Pioneer Mortgage Services, Advanced Income Planners. These are just a few of the scores of real companies which have made false promises to real people, companies whose directors have shattered the lives of thousands of trusting investors. Don't try to remember these names. By the time you read this book, they may have disappeared. In their place will be other names which sound just as impressive. The directors could be the same, or there will be new players with new companies. Just remember what they do to people. And make sure they don't do it to you. Don't sign anything.

They pretend to be 'experts' or 'financial consultants'. They produce glossy brochures and material with claims such as, 'We research the best areas to invest.' These areas will be far away from where you live. This way you can't be an expert. If you live in Sydney or Melbourne where the average home price is above $300,000, a property at the Gold Coast or in Brisbane for $150,000 can seem great value. It may not occur to you that it is only worth $100,000.

You will be taken to these areas. There will be a shared cost arrangement on the airfare, perhaps a $150 ticket which will be free if you decide to buy. You will be told that there's no obligation to buy and the worst that can happen is that you get a trip for $150.

But that's when the 'whirlwind' begins. You are whisked to the airport, flown to a distant location, met by someone who seems so nice and taken for a tour of the area past all the million dollar homes and the plush hotels. Your head spins. You hear tales of how much money is being paid. You get hungry and then, when you stop for lunch, your new 'friend' will tell you his or her life story. It will be similar to yours. You will hear how investing changed their lives. And how they now 'love helping people like you'. They love showing them how to be financially secure.

You are drawn in. After all they have done for you, after they have been so nice, so kind, so caring, you won't know how to say no. If you hesitate, they will feign surprise, perhaps even look hurt. Here comes the guilt, the after-all-I've-done-for-you look. You will be made to feel foolish for even thinking you could say no. If you are a decent, honest and trusting person, you will do what you think is the right thing. You will say yes, not because you feel it is right, but because you won't know how to say no.

And then, you will have bought a dud investment. You will have lost a huge slice of the equity in your home. You may have lost it all. You may even lose your own home in the years ahead.

How Errol and Wendy Lost Their Family Home

In June 1998, Errol, a motor mechanic in his early thirties, and his wife Wendy, who was six months pregnant, bought a unit for $147,900. A company called Advanced Income Planners worked out their 'investment strategy' based on 'conservative' figures. But over the next two years the payments crippled them. Those 'conservative' figures were now called 'projections'. They discovered the unit was worth $100,000. Desperate for help, they contacted ASIC. 'They told us it was our own fault,' said Errol, who called himself 'Silly Me'.

They couldn't afford the repayments and they couldn't afford to sell. A debt counsellor recommend bankruptcy. They lost their family home in Melbourne. Today, they have nothing.[29]

To dismiss Errol and Wendy as 'stupid', or to say it's 'their fault', is to breach one of the major principles of ethics – that of having empathy for our fellow citizens. Errol and Wendy are hard-working, decent Australians. They wanted a better future for their family. They trusted the 'men in the suits': the financial consultant, the lawyer recommended by the consultant and the building society who loaned the money.

Errol is not a financial expert any more than the lawyer who signed him up is a mechanic. If the lawyer took his car to Errol and the work was faulty, no one would blame the lawyer. Errol would be in trouble. The lawyer would demand his money back. But crooked salespeople, who call themselves experts, and lawyers who are in cahoots with these salespeople, wreak havoc in the lives of thousands of citizens and get away with it. Something is seriously wrong with a society which does so little to punish such conduct.

White-collar Crimes

If kidnappers get life imprisonment and their victims get their money back, it makes no sense that white-collar crimes can be treated so lightly.

In their book, *Profit Without Honor, White-Collar Crime and the Fleecing of America*, the authors say that because 'white-collar crimes do not leave a chalk outline on the sidewalk or a blood spatter on the wall' they are not taken as seriously.[30] The immediate shock of a violent crime stays in our mind for years, even though such crimes may be rare. With white-collar crime we often think that no one gets hurt. Nothing could be further from the truth. As the authors say, 'White-collar criminals cause more pain and death than all "common" criminals combined.'[31]

Compared with the sudden shock of a violent crime, white-collar crime, especially in real estate, may take years to reveal itself. The consumer advocate Ralph Nader called this delay in the discovery of white-collar crime 'postponed violence'.[32]

If a criminal steals an elderly lady's handbag containing $100, the penalty can be ten years in jail. But if that criminal wears a suit and tie and cheats the elderly lady out of $100,000 with a real estate scam, he keeps the lady's money. And he can keep doing it for years to thousands of other citizens. And when these citizens try to complain they are told that everything was 'legal' or that it's only 'your word against theirs'. They not only feel helpless, they are often made to feel stupid.

As the clinical psychologist and expert on criminal behaviour Dr Stanton Samenow says, 'A crime victim may be victimised twice, once by the criminal and then again by the system.' The ease with which crooks can get away with their crimes makes them 'cocky'. According to Dr Samenow, the criminals feel invincible when they realise they are 'unlikely to be confined'.[33] It's paradise for crooks when they can cheat people without fear of punishment.

The people being cheated, of course, are those who most need to be protected. They are rarely wealthy business people. The typical victim is a person with little or no real estate experience who has a trusting nature and can easily be manipulated based on fear of the future. If they are young, like Errol and Wendy, maybe they can recover. But if they are close to retirement, an investment scam can destroy their lives. In the United States, the government has additional penalties for people who rip off the elderly. In 1994, a law was passed which provides for an extra ten years in jail for excessive white-collar crime against people over the age of 55.[34]

The laws in Australia and New Zealand are so flimsy the crooks easily find a 'legal' way around them. As many consumer advocates have been saying for years – the laws rarely go far enough. In his book, *Buyer Beware*, Terry Ryder reported that the laws are 'several steps behind' the scams.[35]

Despite years of publicity, the scams continue. How many stories need to be written and how many television exposés must be done before the laws are changed, or before the full force of existing laws are used? A newspaper article lasts one day, a television program lasts a few minutes. The crooks face a few setbacks but they soon resurface when the heat dies down. In the last half of 2001, there was a lot of talk in the Queensland parliament about how to stop these crooks. New laws were passed; but before the ink was dry on these laws, the crooks were at it again. Some intense media publicity helped to slow them down, for a while. But they will be back.

As these words are being written, crooked real estate people are working out new scams. There are millions of home-owners left to con. All that's needed is a new way to rip them off. A new sting.

One New Sting

One new sting is clever. It starts by acknowledging that there are a lot of crooks in real estate. It praises the government for trying to stamp out the crooks. Watch out for how they get you this time.

Corporate crooks don't look like crooks

You will be made to feel safe because the crooks have all gone or, if they do exist, there are now 'cooling-off periods'. You will be told how the crooks made it bad for all honest business people. Being a fair minded citizen, you will accept this. You may even feel sorry for the person advising you because he had to work in an industry with these crooks. And now, you are safe. But the person telling you all this is probably a crook. Corporate crooks don't look like crooks. They look like nice people, they talk like nice people – that's how they con you.

But the new scams are not new. Only the words are new. The aim is the same – to steal the equity in your home. The areas will also be new. As the Gold Coast becomes too hot, the crooks will move elsewhere.

The Scam Spreads

Paul and Linda Roberts were in their mid-fifties. In August 2001, their family home in the western Melbourne suburb of Melton was worth about $145,000. Although a modest home, they did not owe any money on it. It was their only asset.

They received an invitation to a seminar. They went along and heard a polished speaker talking about the 'advantages of negative gearing' and how it was important to select the right 'growth areas'. At the end of the seminar, they agreed to an 'individual assessment' to see if their situation met the 'needs' for investment. The 'consultant', from a company called National Consolidated Investments, came to their home and went through the usual charade to see if they 'qualified'. With a home worth $145,000 and no debt, of course they were going to 'qualify'. They agreed to fly to Queensland to inspect property.

However, when they read an article in the *Herald Sun* about Queensland investment scams, they told the 'consultant' they did not want to buy in Queensland. His reply may as well have been, 'No worries, we can rip you off in Victoria.' He arranged for another consultant to visit them for a 'more detailed financial assessment' to see if they could 'invest in Victoria'. On a Sunday morning a man from a company called Stamford Lyon International Realtors arrived at their home and drove them into the city to meet another man from Australian Financial Management Corporation 'just to go through the financial side of things'. At this meeting, they were asked to produce everything from birth certificates to their latest tax returns. All this information was 'processed' into a computer so they could get 'the best possible plan worked out'. This, of course, is all part of an elaborate act. The more official and important the appearance, the more the victims are taken in by it all.

Paul and Linda were driven to some units in the suburb of Beaconsfield. Their 'licensed property consultant' adapted the classic Queensland spin to Victoria, revealing his troubled past and how investing in real estate changed his life. According to the consultant, the units were worth $280,000 each. With expenses, the cost was closer to $300,000.

Paul and Linda were nervous. Linda had heard something about the two golden rules of buying real estate – do not buy anything without an independent valuation and stay away from developers. The consultant said 'The bank will not approve finance unless the property is worth the money.' This made sense. And, besides, these properties were selling fast. The consultant's pager kept beeping and he was saying, 'Oh, there's another one sold.' Again, it was all part of the act.

Linda asked if she could look at other properties at another time, but was told, 'No, these have been selected for you.' They were told it was perfectly safe because it came with a 'rental guarantee'. They said yes. They went back to the city where they signed contracts with 'their lawyer' – recommended by the real estate company. By this time it was almost seven in the evening. They had not eaten all day. The consultant took them back to their home and suggested they celebrate with champagne.

A few weeks later they attended a seminar in Melbourne called 'The Inside Secrets of Real Estate'. They were shocked to hear about several real estate scams, including exactly what happened to them. The audience was warned about a company called Stamford Lyon. Paul and Linda realised they had been conned. But maybe it was not too late. Maybe they could still get out. They decided to fight. They arranged for an independent valuer to appraise their 'investment'. They discovered that the unit, for which they had paid close to

$300,000 (with costs), was worth about $190,000. This meant they had lost almost all the equity in their family home. From an asset of $145,000 (their family home), with no debt, they now had 'assets' of $335,000 (their home plus the investment property) with a debt of $300,000.[36]

Although 'legally obligated', they had not yet settled the purchase. In desperation, they went to an 'Approved' agent,[37] Phil Hickmott. It looked hopeless because it was all 'legal'. In real estate terms, they had been 'stitched-up'. They had bought a property, signed a contract and accepted a loan. In legal terms, they had 'consented'.

Phil Hickmott was furious. He was determined to get them out – somehow. He argued that they had been misled and their 'consent' was based on false information. Therefore, in legal terms, he said there had not been 'informed consent'. He pushed a lawyer to take action. He spoke with a television reporter, Karryn Cooper, who was preparing a story on real estate scams.

Karryn was investigating someone dubbed 'King Con'. Enter Dudley Quinlivan, a man who lived in a mansion on the Gold Coast and controlled a network of companies involved in fleecing people all over Australia and New Zealand. Hundreds of overpriced properties were being sold through Stamford Lyon, a real estate agency that was a member of the Real Estate Institute of Queensland. Stamford Lyon made the usual claim of being bound by the Institute's Code of Ethics. The institute was inferring that its member agents were not involved in ripping off consumers and was blaming the state government for failing to stop the investment scams.[38]

The pressure was mounting on Quinlivan and his companies. Finally, Paul and Linda were offered a deal. They could be released from the contract in return for a 'confidentiality agreement'. They had to agree to keep quiet about what happened to them.[39]

Paul and Linda Roberts refused. 'If we remain silent, the same thing will happen to thousands of others,' said Linda. 'I'd rather lose my home than have that on my conscience.'

Paul said, 'We will sign nothing with you. No deal.' Phil Hickmott, the agent who had helped them, was stunned. 'If there was a Victoria Cross for consumers, these two would win one each,' he said.[40]

Karryn Cooper's story was aired on national television. King Con was exposed. It might have slowed him, but it didn't stop him. In the weeks ahead, more stories were aired – each showing Karryn asking Dudley Quinlivan, 'Just wondering if you've got anything to say to those thousands of people that you've ripped off?'[41]

The Mind of a Crooked Real Estate Person

Most people cannot understand the mind of a crook. 'How can they sleep at night?' is the common question. Psychiatrist Dr William Gaylin says that our feelings of guilt are 'the guardian of our goodness'. But con artists seem devoid of guilt. They don't care who they hurt. Dr Gaylin describes crooks as 'beasts of prey' who look at human beings the same way 'trout fishermen see trout'.[42] These investment crooks refer to their victims as 'marks' or 'wood ducks'.[43]

But crooks rarely admit to being crooks. Quinlivan reportedly sees himself as 'squeaky clean', 'totally ethical' and a 'ballsy businessman'.[44] He is a handsome man with a broad smile – a charming type, with ready-made excuses to explain his activities. He admits there are crooks in real estate, but, despite all the evidence against him, denies that he is one of them.[45]

So how does he explain how thousands of people have bought properties from him for as much as $100,000 above their true value? Simple. He says the valuers are wrong. How does he explain why these properties can't be sold for anything near the price paid by his victims? His lawyer answered that question, 'People who believe they have been ripped off may find at the end of the day that they have bought themselves a bargain.'[46]

This is the classic 'real estate is a long-term investment' excuse. When his lawyer says 'end of the day' one has to ask,

'Which day?'. If he sells a property for $280,000 which is only worth $180,000, when will his clients have a 'bargain'? Ten years? Twenty years? Never? His victims are not paying today's prices, they are literally paying future prices in today's market. But even that might be optimistic judging by how some property 'investments' seem to keep dropping in value.

'Investments' that Go Down Over the Years

In 1996, when Daniel and Don, two friends from Sydney, each bought a Brisbane investment property for their families, they were told they would 'double their money in seven years'. They paid $158,500 each for two townhouses. Stan Jenkins, a director of a company called Whitehouse Securities, showed them 'a Citibank valuation to prove the value'.[47] Jenkins said the increase in prices would mean that, every two years, they would be able to buy more property because of the growing equity in their investments.[48] The Whitehouse Securities brochure said, in bold capital letters, 'YOU WILL NEVER GO WRONG WITH BRICKS AND MORTAR'.[49]

That was in 1996. In 1998 their units were worth $145,000 each. Jenkins now said they should look at real estate as a 'ten year investment'. By 2000 the values were down to $135,000 each. Jenkins now said real estate was a '12-year investment'.[50]

In 2001 a townhouse in the same block sold for $117,000. Whitehouse Securities had been deregistered by ASIC and Jenkins had registered other companies. With expenses, Daniel and Don had lost more than $50,000 each. It had a devastating effect on both their families.

Dudley Quinlivan is not Stan Jenkins. And Stamford Lyon is not Whitehouse Securities. But their methods are almost identical. And somehow, like footballers who play the same game, the same names surface in different teams at different times. It's a chain of deceit and trickery.

The Chain of Deceit

Murray and Helen Casey were in their early sixties. Like other victims, their only asset was their family home in Montrose, Victoria, which was worth about $200,000.[51]

In July 2000, on the advice of a 'financial expert' from a company called Greenwich Solutions, they flew to Queensland. It was a Sunday. They were pushed to buy a unit for a total of $178,500 (including costs).[52] When they expressed concern, they were told, 'This is a good investment with great tax benefits and will be ideal to set you up for retirement.' They were taken to a law firm – Richard Ebbott and Co. – where they signed contracts to buy the unit.[53]

Back in Melbourne they told their daughter-in-law what they had done. She discovered that the unit was worth about $110,000. Murray and Helen, on the verge of retirement, suddenly found themselves with their family home fully mortgaged to pay for an 'investment' unit which was worth $70,000 less than they were paying.[54]

The following Sunday, Helen called the lawyer in Queensland whom they had met the previous weekend. She wanted to cancel. It was too late. The lawyer said, 'You have signed and you cannot pull out and if you try to you will be sued by the property owner.' When Helen persisted, the lawyer became annoyed, saying he had just arrived home from a barbecue and did not appreciate being disturbed on a Sunday. He said he didn't want to speak any longer.[55]

Helen and Murray did not sleep that night. The next day, Helen was treated by her doctor for 'extreme distress'.[56]

The Links in the Chain of Deceit

Look carefully at the links in this chain of deceit and you'll often see the same people. Greenwich Solutions used to be known as The Epic Group, which used to be known as The Coral Reef Group. In 1998, The Epic Group sold more than 2000 overpriced properties to naïve investors.[57] In the Queensland parliament, Epic was named as one of the worst of the property scammers.[58] It had ruined the financial futures of thousands of Australians. King Con (Dudley Quinlivan) used to work for Christopher Bilborough, the boss of Epic. The law firm, Richard Ebbot and Co., which signed up Murray and Helen for Greenwich Solutions (previously Epic), was the same law firm that also signed up Daniel and Don for Stan Jenkins and Whitehouse Securities. Mrs Pope dealt with a company called Networth Planning. The director is Jason Paris who used to work for Quinlivan. Mrs Pope was signed up by a law firm called Rapp & Yarwood, the same firm which signs up victims of Quinlivan's companies.[59] Paul and Linda Roberts dealt with National Consolidated Investments. The director is Stephen Quinlivan, son of Dudley. The agent was Stamford Lyon.[60] In New Zealand a company called AFMC (Auckland Financial Management Corporation) bears a striking resemblance to another AFMC which stands for Australian Financial Management Corporation. Both are directed by Dudley Quinlivan.[61] Mrs Pope, who lost close to $100,000, dealt with Ray White Surfers Paradise, a member of the Real Estate Institute of Queensland, as was Stamford Lyon.[62]

An entire book, indeed volumes of books, could be filled with stories of consumers ripped off by these scams. Thousands of investors are yet to discover they have been ripped off. This is why an independent inquiry is needed into the entire real estate industry. It makes no sense for governments to liaise with real estate institutes that claim their member agents are bound by 'codes of ethics'.

In Queensland, the Minister for Fair Trading acknowledged that 'some of those shonks are members of the REIQ.' She questioned why institute members linked to real estate scams were not 'booted out of the REIQ', but then said that 'the vast majority of agents are honest'.[63] But the vast majority of agents support dishonest methods or, at best, do little to remove them.

Protect Yourself

The only way to protect yourself from a real estate scam is don't sign anything until you have taken three major precautions. First, get **independent legal advice**. Never use a lawyer recommended by the agent or the marketeer. Second, arrange your own **independent valuation**. And, finally, **speak with other investors** who have dealt with the same company. In every case where consumers are ripped off, they did not take any of these precautions.

FIGHTING BACK

If you bought a property because you were told it was a good investment and you based your decision on false information, you have been cheated. Do not feel embarrassed or ashamed. You are a victim of fraud. The best way to try and get out of these investment scams is to turn your wrath on those associated with the crooks, the companies and people who are concerned about their image – the lenders, the lawyers and the institutes – the 'respectable set'. These people knew you were being ripped off or, if not, they should have known – and they did nothing to warn you.

There is little point chasing the crooks. If you can find them, they will just tell you that real estate is a 'long-term investment' or the value you have now been quoted is wrong. Find an honest and determined lawyer prepared to fight on your behalf at a reasonable cost. You need to fight back and you need people who care enough to fight with you. Strong, determined people.

You must pursue the lenders and the lawyers. Be determined to obtain justice for yourself. Contact any state and federal body which is supposed to help consumers who have been ripped off. Speak with consumer protection groups. Contact the media. No matter how hard it seems, no matter how much you feel the odds are against you, keep going until someone in authority takes notice of you.

Perhaps you will be worried that you will be sued for defamation if you speak out. And yes, as you will see, some crooks may threaten or bully you. But consider this: the reason so many consumers are hurt in real estate is because other hurt consumers did not speak out.

Think of the courage of Linda and Paul Roberts. By speaking out, they risked losing their own home. They could have remained silent and accepted a 'deal'. They could have saved themselves, but they chose to save others. In the end, they managed to get out of their mess.[64] But if they had never complained, they would have lost almost all the equity in their home.

In the eighteenth century, Edmund Burke said, 'The only thing necessary for the triumph of evil is for good people to do nothing.'[65] You did not get caught because you are greedy, you got caught because you are a trusting person. Even if you can't get out, you can still speak out and help others from being conned.

Real Hope for Victims?

A husband and wife from Cairns could provide hope for thousands of victims of real estate scams. They bought a unit on the Gold Coast for $164,900. Its real value was $100,000.[66]

In December 2001, the Australian Competition and Consumer Commission (ACCC) began action in the Federal Court against those involved in the chain of deceit with this couple. This included: the Commonwealth Bank who knew the property was worth $100,000 yet failed to tell the couple; the marketeer, Oceana Commercial (formerly The Coral Reef Group and then Epic); the finance consultant and King Con, Quinlivan; the developers, Dean Cornish and John Grounds; and the lawyers, Gregory Pointon from Perrin Pointon Solicitors and Rodney Johanson from Short Punch and Greatorix. The ACCC alleged the lawyers failed to tell the buyers that the unit was grossly overpriced.[67]

If the ACCC succeeds on behalf of these two consumers, it will provide real hope for other victims. It will clearly show what many people have known for years – these investment scams are a massive fraud.

In the meantime, if you want to invest in any area, remember three words – don't sign anything. At least not before you get independent legal advice and an independent valuation on the investment you are considering. This advice will help to keep you safe.

GET-RICH-QUICK PROPERTY SEMINARS

They came from the East, fanning across the country, setting up shows with promises of miracle health cures and 'new discoveries'. They were the snake oil salesmen of nineteenth century America, making fortunes from gullible consumers. Today, they still infest America; but their product is no longer health cures, it's wealth cures. Their motive is the same: making money selling dud cures.

Now they are polluting Australia and New Zealand, fleecing millions from naïve consumers eager to find out 'how to do it' in real estate.

THE SNAKE OIL SCAM

The real estate snake oil boys all use similar methods. First, there is the free seminar. Sometimes there is a small charge, with a 'money back guarantee'. There are amazing promises of 'easy wealth' and information guaranteed to be 'life changing'. The purpose of these seminars is to talk you into paying a huge fee for a 'big' seminar, where '*all* the information will be revealed'.

Snake oil salesmen follow two rules to trap you. First, they target your desire and, second, they convince you that they can fulfil your desire. 'If your dream is to create wealth, look at me, I am wealthy. Let me show you how I did it.' But the snake oil boys rarely get wealthy from real estate. They get wealthy from your money.

Like most con artists, they prey on fear. They want you to feel inadequate with your own financial life. They will come out with such lines as 'Job stands for Just Over Broke.' You are supposed to think, 'That's me.' The speaker will tell his story which will be similar to yours. He was once poor, he was struggling, he had no hope. And look at me now. I am young. I am rich. I am confident. Hey, you've gotta like what I've done; and I can show you how to do it. For a fee, of course. And, for tonight, you can have a 'special price'.

In case you are wondering why the speaker is sharing all this 'secret' wealth creating information when, surely, if it were that good, he could do it himself, you will be told, 'I like to help people.'

You will also be told, 'All successful people act fast.' This is nonsense. Successful people rarely act fast. They wait until they gather facts, they assess the risk, including asking that all-important question, 'What's the most I could lose?'

Successful people – and in this case we are talking about *financially* successful people – look for clues before making a decision. They recognise warning signs. One of the biggest warning signs will be the techniques suggested by the snake oil gurus.

The Crooks' Techniques

The 'techniques' of the snake oil merchants range from the barely ethical to the downright deceptive. For example, here's how they suggest you buy property: look for people who are in trouble. It's called 'distress'. Take advantage of their situation.

There will be tricks you can use with valuers, such as getting quotes from several valuers before you employ one or two of them. You ask, roughly, what price they think a property is worth. The technique is to find two valuers – one who gives a low price and one who gives a high price. You then use the low valuation to convince sellers to sell cheaply and the high valuation to convince lenders to give you more money.

And then you improve the property, from simple methods of painting and cleaning to deceitful methods of showing false high rents to increase the 'value' so you can borrow more money and buy another property. And you keep repeating the process, over and over, buying more properties and making more and more money, leap-frogging the fraud.

There will be 'how to buy without using your own money' schemes. Many of these methods also involve fraud. One is known as 'Hydraulicing', where you are taught to create two prices for a property you buy – the real price and a pumped-up price on the contract.[68] If you buy a property for $300,000, you ask for a contract price of $350,000. Inside the contract is a clause giving you a 'discount' of $50,000. You tell the valuer that you are 'paying $350,000'. And you have the contract to 'prove' it. You find a valuer who gives you a valuation close to, or at, the contract price. You then go to a lender and say, 'I am buying for $350,000. Here is the contract for $350,000. Here is a valuation for $350,000. I want to borrow $300,000.' Add on a bit more for expenses and, presto, the guru says, 'You buy properties for nothing.' You are now a real estate cheat.

Hydraulicing is often suggested by developers. Once they can show that units in a building have sold at a certain price, the valuers – who rely on selling prices to set valuations – can often be influenced by these false prices to create inflated valuations. It is almost certain that, one day, people will be prosecuted over these scams.

If you use your home as additional security, you can borrow even more. You can buy a property for $300,000 and borrow $350,000, maybe more. You now have at least an extra $50,000 to put down on another property. And you can keep using the same trick.

To get bargains, you will also be told to look for properties where the owners live overseas or interstate so they don't know the real values. This works well when prices have risen suddenly and you can offer distant owners a price thousands above what they think it is worth, but well below its new value in the booming market. The snake oil boys call this 'smart'. Decent people call it fraud.

These seminar gurus, to whom you are a stranger, will tell you they 'want to help you'. Then they will teach you how to harm strangers. You should remember the saying, 'If a man will steal for me, he will steal from me.'[69] If any real estate 'experts' suggest anything even slightly dishonest, you should avoid them, no matter how much money you can make. There is something inherently sick about seeking to profit from deceit. Don't be swayed by the statement, 'business is business'. That's a common excuse for cheating. People who use investment strategies that involve cheating or preying on the misfortunes of others are crooks. Don't become one of them.

Decent people call it fraud

Their Purpose is to Fleece You

Most get-rich-quick seminars have one purpose – to sell you advice for thousands of dollars. But is their advice ever good? Rarely. Is it ever *good value?* Never. You will be charged thousands of dollars for information you could easily get from a $30 book. The only difference between a good book and most of these courses is the cost.

Buy the books. Do the research. And save yourself thousands of dollars before you invest in real estate.

Checking Out the Snake Oil Experts

Before an 'expert' asks you to buy property, ask to see the expert's personal financial statements with evidence that their 'wealth' comes from the methods they recommend. They will probably say this information is 'private and confidential'. But the words private and confidential are often modern synonyms for 'embarrassing and disgraceful'. It's almost certain that the real estate 'expert' encouraging you to make your fortune in real estate is making his fortune from you.

John Reed is an American expert on real estate gurus. He has discovered that more than half of them, including 'trendy' gurus known to Australians and New Zealanders, are charlatans. Some are criminals. On his web site, John Reed gives his candid opinion of more than a hundred well-known gurus. It's blunt reading.[70]

John lists several ways to detect those he describes as 'B.S. Artists', such as 'an emphasis on a flashy lifestyle'. Many have photographs of themselves standing in front of expensive cars. They also 'claim to do lots of deals themselves'. John believes this is nonsense. 'You can smoke out such gurus by asking them for the addresses of the properties they have owned,' he says. As for the glowing testimonials, John says they are 'almost certainly barefaced lies or they are leaving out pertinent facts like they committed fraud to do the deals.'[71]

John Reed says these gurus target beginners 'because they are predators and predators go after the weakest prey. The bogus material sold to beginners generally overstates the rewards, understates the effort, risk, and time required and gives advice which is incorrect, inadequate or even dangerous.'[72] Although John Reed is talking about America, his comments apply equally to Australia and New Zealand. 'Get-rich-quick gurus have no interest in helping you. They are only interested in helping themselves to what little you have in your bank account.'[73]

The real estate industry has many gurus who operate in a dark and murky world. In 2001, an ex-employee of one of Australia's biggest gurus approached the media to blow the whistle on the flashy guru's methods. Before the story went into production, he had a sudden change of heart. The television producer claimed the whistleblower 'feared for his life'.[74] These gurus are a variation on the snake oil salesmen from years past. Go and have a look, if you must; but, whatever you do, don't sign anything unless you are certain the advice you are given is honest, profitable and worth what you pay for it.

BEWARE OF PROPERTY 'SOURCERERS'

Be wary of companies that offer to 'source' properties in return for a fee. As with the investment scammers, these companies will have safe sounding names. Names like 'The Investment Institute'.

The Investment Institute places large advertisements in major newspapers with the heading, 'PROPERTY INVESTORS BEWARE – Never pay full price for your investment properties'. The advertisements promise to show you how 'to purchase well below the true market value' and to use an approach that makes it 'impossible not to succeed'. And then, in bold type, this promise: **We are regularly saving our clients between $10,000–$50,000 by locating and negotiating properties on their behalf. We can do the same for you.** With our help, you could make a profit of up to $50,000 immediately.'[75]

The advertisement also claims, 'You can buy at such a low price that you can quickly 'on-sell' your property for an immediate profit. We can even handle the resale for you.'[76]

Let's take that more slowly. The Investment Institute says it will find a property for you to buy up to $50,000 below its value. It says it will then resell this property for you. And give you $50,000 profit. If true, this is the best real estate offer of all time. You could stop work and become rich as a client of The Investment Institute. They even offer 'proof', such as one advertisement[77] with the following 'success examples':

Market Price	Valuation Price	Purchase Price	Savings
$590,000	$575,000	$530,000	$60,000
$320,000	$298,000	$280,000	$40,000
$275,000	$250,000	$230,000	$45,000
$393,000	$385,000	$345,000	$48,000
$515,000	$505,000	$450,000	$65,000
$530,000	$510,000	$460,000	$70,000

The 'savings' are the 'profits' you can make immediately. But why would they find you a property which gives you an instant $50,000 profit? Why wouldn't they just make the $50,000 profit for themselves? According to Nigel Kibel, a speaker at one of their seminars, 'I do this because I care about you. It might sound corny, but I really do.'[78]

In a one-hour seminar, The Investment Institute explains how it 'helps' people. First, there are the usual statistics about how elderly people struggle; about how 'wealth begins in the mind' and about how you too can be wealthy. Gordon Gekko, the infamous character played by Michael Douglas in the 1988 movie, *Wall Street*, is quoted. (Gekko's most famous quote was, 'Greed is good.') There are statements such as 'Property will go up by 10 per cent next year'. And 'the profit you make is in the buying'. If you buy well, you can create 'instant profit'. It's like 'creating equity out of thin air'.

Again, there is the 'proof' – figures where people had made huge instant profits. And the statement that it's all simple. You just 'buy a property worth $300,000 for $250,000'. Easy.

According to The Investment Institute, some of the ways to buy properties for less than their value are: 'death, divorce, distress, developers, dealing directly, disenchanted owners, debt problems.' To show how easy it is, Nigel says, 'Go to a solicitor and see if Aunty Bess has died.'[79]

And how do you discover how to do all this? Just attend one of their advanced courses – for a fee. Or you can have The Investment Institute do it for you – again for a fee. 'Anyone who wants to know more can speak to one of our consultants.' The seminar ends with the words, 'You can't afford not to use our services.' From the back of the room, the 'consultants' appear, eyeing the audience with beady eyes, like circling sharks, ready to speak privately with all those who are interested.

Inside The Investment Institute

'I beg you not to use my name,' said one 'client' of The Investment Institute who told what happened to her family. In respecting her wishes, we will call her Jane. An Asian immigrant in her late forties, Jane's father was seriously ill and the costs of caring for him were crippling her. Also, her four-year-old daughter has Down Syndrome. Her husband had been employed by the Australian public service for 30 years. After cashing in her superannuation from her country of origin and paying outstanding bills, she wanted to invest the balance of her money for her family's future.[80]

In May 2001, Jane's husband had contacted the First National Real Estate Group requesting a booklet on real estate. He received the booklet together with a letter from the CEO of First National, Ian Bremner, saying that First National had over 550 offices and was 'committed to providing the best in real estate service'.[81] Jane and her husband felt secure dealing with such a big company. A few weeks later, Jane saw an article in her local paper about investing in real estate. A seminar, run by The Investment Institute, was being sponsored by a real estate agency called Frank Facey – a member of the First National Real Estate group. The article said that people could make 'spectacular profits' in a short time by investing in real estate. People were urged to call Frank Facey First National Real Estate to book in for the free seminar.[82] Jane attended the seminar where she was urged to sign up for a four-day course at a cost of $4700. A few days later, she and her husband signed up.

During the four-day course, Jane was told that The Investment Institute charged a flat fee of $2500 to source properties. The presenter told her about some apartments where the owner, a development company, had been persuaded to take $55,000 off the price.

Two days later, Jane and her husband were taken to inspect an apartment in Melbourne. When they were asked to sign a contract, Jane said she wanted more time to check everything out. The director of The Investment Institute, Mr Paul Murphy, said that because they were paying him $2500 to 'source' a property, they should 'trust his judgement'. He said he was 'staking his seventeen years' reputation as a financial planner' on this apartment.

The listed price was $633,000. A valuation was produced showing the apartment as being worth $630,000. But Jane and her husband could buy it now for only $570,150, with a 'guaranteed rent return'. With such proof that they had picked up a bargain and made an instant 'profit' of $63,000, they were hooked. The next day, after a brief call from a law clerk at a legal firm recommended by Murphy, they paid a deposit of $50,000 and signed the contract.[83]

There was confusion over the date the balance of the money had to be paid. Jane had believed it was 60 days, but later discovered it was 30 days. When she protested, she described the reaction, from the sales manager at the development company, as 'bullying and vehement'. She became suspicious and wondered what else might be wrong. She employed a valuer who valued the apartment at $515,000, almost $60,000 below the price she was paying.[84] 'I had been conned,' she said, using words such as 'fraud' to describe what happened.[85]

Jane was distraught. A businessman from her local church wrote to the development company stating that Jane and her husband said they were the victims of 'a scam that must be exposed'.[86] Jane's husband received a call from an outraged Paul Murphy demanding that the sale proceed. According to notes made by Jane's husband, Murphy said, 'I am warning you, I am ruthless and I will fight you to the end. I will win.'[87]

Murphy had a powerful ally. He had already recommended and sent Jane and her husband to a lawyer who was involved with The Investment Institute, giving lectures at their seminars and acting for their clients. The lawyer agreed with Murphy, telling Jane and her husband that their allegations were 'ill conceived and unfounded' and The Investment Institute was 'taking the matter very seriously'. Jane and her husband were told they must proceed with the purchase. The lawyer proposed that they also apologise to the development company and The Investment Institute. The lawyer then prepared a written apology for them – just what Murphy wanted. Jane and her husband were terrified of Murphy. Both Murphy and the lawyer indicated that Jane and her husband could lose their family home as well as their $50,000 deposit (and more) if they resisted. And so they took what they believed was expert legal advice and signed the prepared apology letter. They bought the apartment. Later, when they received their legal bill, the lawyer had reduced the fees, saying that Jane was a 'valued client'. Jane then sent the lawyer a thank-you note for helping her family avoid a defamation suit. In June 2002, the lawyer denied there was any conflict of interest in acting for Jane and her husband while, at the same time, having a relationship with The Investment Institute.[88]

A Not-so-obvious Experience

You may think this could not happen to you. Such a scam seems obvious. But it's rarely obvious, at least not at first. Many well-educated and otherwise intelligent people get caught. Most of our biggest mistakes in life are obvious only when we look back on them. When you make these mistakes, you get swept along by statements designed to trap you. The people who want to cheat you are experienced at cheating. As the saying goes, 'When a person with money meets a person with experience, the person with the experience gets the money and the person with the money gets the experience.'[89]

Jane is an intelligent person. In 1998, she narrowly escaped being ripped off in a Queensland investment scam. Three years later, The Investment Institute gave her the worst financial experience of her life. The approach might have been different, but the motives were the same: pretend to be an expert, pretend to be safe, pretend to care and then put on a good show. It's the same result – more trusting and inexperienced consumers conned in real estate.

In March 2002, Paul Murphy commented on the Queensland real estate scams, 'It makes me want to puke what goes on.' When asked about his own methods, he said, 'We don't sell properties that don't stack up. I am not in this business to rip people off.' As for the satisfaction of The Investment Institute's clients, Murphy said, 'We have never had a client who has bought a property and been dissatisfied.'[90] Four days after paying $570,150, Jane and her husband were told by a Melbourne estate agent that their apartment was worth $480,000. 'You've been had,' the agent said.[91]

Beware the Second 'Burglary'

When a home is burgled it often gets burgled again. Burglars know that the stolen goods will be replaced with new goods. They know the layout of the home, maybe even the routine of the owners. And so they come back. It makes perfect sense; if a person can be a victim once they can be a victim twice.

In the United States, thousands of people are ripped off by con artists selling bogus investments. Many get caught twice. The con artists wait a few months – sometimes years – and then the victims receive a call offering to help them recover their lost money. It's a different person, of course, from a 'different' company, with a very caring tone. Because they seem to know so much about the scam, and they are so 'sympathetic', they win the trust of the victims who then hand over more money to help with the 'recovery'. Nothing happens. This 'second burglary' scam is almost certain to occur in Australia and New Zealand.

Another company tied to Dudley Quinlivan is called Australian Fraudwatch Services.[92] One may wonder why the man dubbed King Con is a director of a company with such an honest name. Maybe he intends to repair the social damage his companies have caused. Maybe he intends to call the victims of investment scams and offer to help them. Maybe not.

Mrs Pope, the 60-year-old lady who was caught in an investment scam in February 2001, received a phone call in November 2001. A man offered to sell her a report about how she could improve her finances with her investment. It wasn't much money to pay, just $89.00, and, after all, he 'sounded like a nice man'. Mrs Pope paid the money.[93] In January 2002 she was approached by a law firm offering to fight her case on a no win/no fee basis. They asked her to fill in a form and send it to them. She did. And then she received a letter asking for $500. She didn't pay.[94]

In 1999 a couple in their mid-fifties became classic investment scam victims when they bought a unit for $154,900. In 2001 it was worth $85,000. They were contacted by a company that offered to buy their unit for $230,000. Fantastic. All they had to do was pay $14,000 now, and wait seven years to get their $230,000. It was 'guaranteed'. But they had learned their lesson. They did not sign anything and they sought independent advice before making a decision. They discovered that the directors of the company were former bankrupts with a dubious past.[95]

INVESTMENT SCAMS: A SUMMING UP

Again, one has to ask how can this happen? Why do so many people get caught? And why are they usually such nice people? And, even when they discover they have been caught, why don't they complain – *really* complain? In Australia and New Zealand there are enough victims of real estate crooks to form a protest march to rival any public demonstration.

The majority of victims are embarrassed, even ashamed. Many blame themselves. They feel stupid to have been caught. They are not the sort of people who make a lot of noise. Some don't even tell their friends or relatives. They suffer in silence. They are good people and, mostly, they are easy to manipulate. And they rarely fight back, even though they have been cheated out of a huge slice of their assets. They are easily intimidated by threats and the thought of a lengthy court case.

These manipulators are difficult for the ordinary person to understand because they are devoid of conscience. They target their victims carefully, choosing some of the most decent people in our society, people who are no match for their manipulative skills and, as stated, people who rarely fight back. Aldert Vij, author of *Detecting Lies and Deceit*, says that such manipulators 'show little concern for conventional morality, and openly admit that they will lie, cheat and manipulate others'. He also says that they are 'scheming but not stupid. They do not exploit others if their victims might retaliate, and they do not cheat if they are likely to get caught.'[96]

And this is why these scams are so common. Victims rarely fight back and there is little fear of punishment for the crooks. It's the perfect 'crime', a form of financial and psychological kidnapping – with no risk.

These scams have been going on for years, with almost no action from governments. As far back as 1974, real estate con artists were using a variation of today's scams. Outside the town of Lake Cargelligo, in far western New South Wales, blocks of land were reportedly being bought for as little as a dollar each. These blocks were then offered to Sydney investors for the 'bargain' price of one thousand dollars each.[97] Just like today, they were sold by 'investment experts' or 'wealth specialists'. And just like today, the prices seemed cheap in comparison with the prices in the victims' home areas. It was so easy to make money that even real criminals became involved.[98] Fleecing real estate consumers was easier than street crime. And a lot less risky. The victims poured in from the big advertisements for these bargain investments. It was like sale time at a major department store. The salespeople, huddled in little booths in their offices, were signing up dozens of eager victims. A young man was about to sign when he said to the salesman, 'I just want to do two things – speak to my lawyer and call someone at Lake Cargelligo.'

The salesman leaned forward and whispered, 'Mate, this is not for you. Get out of here while you can.'[99]

The same rule applied then as applies today – don't sign anything without getting independent legal advice and an independent valuation.

If you remember the title of this book, you will *never* get caught in an investment scam.

But, as already discussed, if you have been caught, you must not suffer in silence. You are a victim in a sophisticated chain of deceit, where everyone involved in the chain, from the marketeers to the salespeople to the banks to the lawyers, probably knew you were being ripped off. And yet, they did nothing to protect you. Don't be silent. Speak out. Loudly. Do your part to stop these predators from destroying more lives.

As the American ethics lecturer, Carol Bly, says, 'A well organised predator can commit some injustice for a number of years before the law weighs in.'[100] Real estate predators and their silent conspirators have been committing injustices for too long.

As you read this, someone, somewhere is being ripped off by a real estate crook. Someone just like you. Thousands of future victims need to be warned. Governments must be shamed into action to punish these crooks and protect thousands more people from being hurt. These crooks will not stop unless their fear of punishment exceeds their thought of reward. Real estate crimes have to be made high-risk crimes to deter criminals from stealing the equity from thousands of decent home-owners in Australia and New Zealand.

The words of Mrs Pope, whose story began this chapter, sum it up well: 'Unfortunately, there seem to be as many unscrupulous people out there as there are trusting souls.'[101]

The best advice for trusting souls is don't sign anything until you are sure you are safe.

SAFETY IN THE REAL ESTATE MARKET

There are three types of real estate consumers – sellers, buyers and investors. No matter what role you play, you can be safe. All you have to do is know what to do before you do it. Until then, don't sign anything.

Safety for Sellers

The safest advice when selling real estate is don't sign anything with any agent unless you get a *guarantee* which protects you from the common traps of real estate. Chapter Twelve will show you how to receive a guarantee *before* you sell.

As for when you sell, it depends on what you intend to do. If you are selling your home and buying another home in the same market, it makes little difference when you sell. You should look at the entire 'package' – the selling *and* the buying. Always overestimate your buying costs and under-estimate your sale proceeds. Not too much, but just enough to make sure you have more money than you planned to have.

If the market is going up and you intend to buy a more expensive home, the longer you wait the more it will cost you. For example, if your home is worth $500,000 and prices jump by 20 per cent, your home's value increases by $100,000; your home is now worth $600,000. But if you want to buy a better home which was worth $800,000, that home will also increase by 20 per cent, and will now be worth $160,000 more ($960,000). Therefore, the more the prices rise, the more you have to pay to buy a better home.

If you are buying a cheaper home, the longer you wait the better off you will be. But waiting is always dangerous, especially if you sell and don't buy or buy but don't sell in the same market. The market can change and you may be financially caught short. However, provided you sell and buy in the *same* market you will be fairly safe.

Safety for Buyers

The right time to buy a family home is *when you find the right home*. This may not mean the best home, it means the *right* home. And the right home is one you can *safely* afford.

The happiest people are those who need the least, not those who have the most

Be careful of the trap of over-commitment. If there is any risk, consider lowering your price bracket. Buy a cheaper home, even if it means you do not buy in your preferred area.

If you are borrowing, consider what will happen to you when (not 'if') interest rates rise. As a safety margin, you should always add four percentage points to the cost of your loan to see if you could still afford the loan. If not, don't buy.

Consider your needs instead of your wants. The happiest people are those who need the least, not those who have the most. Be careful of the desire to appear successful. Don't make the classic mistake of spending money you can't afford in order to impress people you don't like. Thousands of people get up early and drive to work in a nice car which they are paying off, so they can earn a big income to pay for a big mortgage on a nice home which is empty all day because they have to work so long to pay for it. It doesn't make sense. As the psychologist, David Meyers, said, 'More than ever, we have big houses and broken homes, high incomes and low morale, secured rights and diminished civility. We excel at making a living, but often fail at making a life.'[102]

One study showed that most couples are so busy trying to pay off their debts, they spend an average of 12 minutes a day talking to each other.[103] Your personal, financial and emotional safety should be your first priority. Today, the amount people are borrowing is growing faster than the amount they are earning. In the future, those who don't earn enough to cover their repayments are headed for trouble. They will get caught in the 'negative equity' trap, meaning they will owe more on their homes than their homes are worth. For example, there will be people who owe $400,000 on homes that are worth $350,000 and they will be struggling to meet their repayments. Most people won't have savings to help them. Our national savings rate is close to zero. In some cases, it's negative. Because of easy credit, many people now spend more than they earn. In 1995, total consumer debt was about half the annual income of an average family. By 2002, it was more than 105 per cent.[104] As Elizabeth Warren, the co-author of *The Fragile Middle Class*, wrote, 'The next time the economy contracts, bankruptcies will explode.'[105]

> There are few sadder sights than home-owners who are forced to sell

There is only one end to an explosion in debt – an explosion in misery as families buckle under the weight of repayments. There are few sadder sights than home-owners who are forced to sell. In Australia, in the Home Fund debacle of the 1990s, falling prices and high interest rates crippled many families. The more they paid, the more they went backwards.[106] In 1991, when the real estate market collapsed in England, 80,000 families lost their homes through mortgage foreclosures.[107]

If you buy a home you can easily afford, it won't matter what happens. Whether the real estate market goes up or down, you will be safe. And you will be thankful for this advice. If things go well, you can buy a more expensive home later. When you can *easily* afford it.

Always make your financial safety a major priority.

The Return to a 'Safe and Sound' Society

Safety is becoming a major concern for society. And it's not just physical safety we want, it's emotional and financial safety. We are becoming more safety conscious as we realise that the best things in life are not *things,* and that it's hard to be happy unless we feel safe.

The baby boomers, those born between 1945 and 1960, were the primary consumers in the 1980s and 1990s. And they were big spenders, often giving little thought to their

> It's a proven formula:
> low debt and careful living equals happiness

future. It was as if they really believed the song about being 'forever young'. But soon the baby boomers will be the funeral boomers. And this will make them scared. They may remember their parents, those who were born in the 1920s and 1930s, who were the primary consumers of the 1950s and 1960s. These people belonged to the 'safe and sound' generation. Two wars and a Depression led to a safe and simple life. And a happy one. According to research, the time when people said they were most happy in the last century was 1957.[108] It's a proven formula: low debt and careful living equals happiness.

The baby boomers considered their parents old-fashioned and conservative. They thought increased happiness came from increased possessions. Today the average family is smaller but the average homes are twice the size of the homes in the 1950s. The baby boomers have had wealth increases from property booms. They have appeared to get rich without effort. But they have failed to see the real cost of greed – a growing sense of insecurity. As Dr Patch Adams said, 'Greed has infected our society. It is the worst infection.'[109] And Harvard University economist Juliet Schor says that 'Sixty per cent of families could only exist for about a month if they lost their jobs'. [110] The corporate collapses of 2001 and 2002 saw many people forced to sell their homes. They had not prepared for the worst.

The only thing saving many baby boomers from bankruptcy is the wealth they are inheriting from their parents – the safe and sound generation. But the baby boomers will not be passing on much wealth to their children – their inheritances will barely last their own lifetimes. There is only one solution for the future. 'Safe and Sound' will come back into fashion.

Safety Factors for Investors

If the people who gave real estate investment advice were accountable for their advice, there would be less people giving advice. As you have seen, many real estate 'experts' are just unscrupulous salespeople earning fat commissions from selling dud 'investments'.

The two reasons for investing in real estate should be capital growth – the amount by which a property goes up in value; and return – the amount you receive while you own a property.

Always check the past capital growth of a property with similar properties in the same location. The same location means same *street* or same *building*. Check the prices of family-owned homes, not investment properties. Do not make comparisons between cities. A dud investment in Brisbane may look good compared with Sydney. But Brisbane is not Sydney.

Anyone who says real estate always goes up does not know much about real estate. Often, the so-called experts quote '10 per cent increase per year'. They tell you that the wealth of millionaires is in their real estate investments. They don't tell you about the auction of a Gold Coast penthouse in 2001. Its highest bid was $1.31 million. The owner paid $4.2 million for it in 1996. And they won't tell you about the investor who paid $1 million in 1982 and sold for $960,000 in 2001.[111] Millionaires often become ex-millionaires because of real estate. And, as you know, thousands of small investors wipe themselves out with real estate investments that give poor capital growth and poor returns.

Anyone who says real estate always goes up does not know much about real estate

You should seek a return of at least seven per cent gross. If the property is worth $200,000, it should rent for $14,000 a year. From the rent, you have to deduct mortgage payments, rates, insurance, maintenance costs, agent fees and a vacancy allowance. If you don't do the sums on gross returns before you invest in real estate, you will have to endure the pain after you invest. If the sums look terrible based on return, don't buy.

Discover the 'vacancy factor' – the percentage of rental properties that are vacant. If the vacancy factor is high, it's a sign that prices could be too high.

And then there's the 'replacement cost' – the cost of the land plus the cost of building the home on the land. When the total replacement cost is *above* the selling price, that's a good sign. If a home costs $200,000 to build and the land value is $100,000 but the total selling cost is $250,000, that is a sign that prices may rise. But if the replacement cost is below the selling price, that's a sign that prices may fall.

The factor of location is important, but not nearly as important as many experts believe. There are factors as equally important, such as: the price, a history of capital growth and a good return. All should be considered. A weakness in any one of these could mean trouble. Location is not the only rule of real estate investment. For example, there are few better locations than Melbourne's Southbank. A check of the prices of many Southbank apartments will show huge price falls.[112] Do your research before you buy. Employ an independent valuer and get independent legal advice. A salesperson who is paid a commission when you buy is not independent. Be careful.

And finally, here's a tip that will upset some experts – never buy in a location you don't like. The reason is simple: you need to feel good about your investments. Life and happiness is all about feelings. It's hard to feel good about something you don't like. If the price is right, if the sums stack up, if you like the location and the property, then buy.

Protect Your Family Home

Be wary of any 'expert' who tells you to use the equity in your home to buy an investment. Yes, lots of people do it; and yes, it can look good on paper. But the whole purpose of investing is to give you more security. And security is owning your family home with no mortgage. Your family home is precious. It should be sacrosanct.

Your home's equity is your greatest asset. It is also the greatest target of real estate 'experts', shonky salespeople and lenders who lick their lips at the thought of having a slice of your equity. The experts who tell you to 'free up the equity in your home' or that 'renting is more economical than buying' are missing an important point – the *feeling* that comes from a home of your own. A home with no debt is one of the best feelings in the world. Be careful of excess debt. Better still, become paranoid about it.

> **Security is owning your family home with no mortgage**

As the playwright, Ibsen, once wrote, 'Home life ceases to be free and beautiful as soon as it is founded on borrowing and debt.'[113] The Ancient Greek philosophers decreed that the major goal in life is to be happy. The happiest people are those with no debt on their own homes and with safe investments that give them financial security. They may not be the most 'financially successful' people, but they are the happiest people. And that makes them the most *successful*.

The people who buy millions of dollars of real estate by using the equity in one property to buy more properties seem really smart. But not many have been around for a long time. Such strategies often end in disaster. The 'keep-borrowing' advice is coming from two types of people – young self-proclaimed seminar experts and those earning fat commissions from 'investment' sales. You will be far safer to take note of the older and wiser investors – those sneered at by many of today's 'experts', but those who have been around for a long time.

The Safe Investors

The safe real estate investors do it this way: they work hard; they always save their money; they are obsessed with saving. They buy a family home and work hard to pay it off. Once their home is fully paid, they *never* borrow on it again. They just save more money. When they have a big enough deposit, they buy another property – usually in their local area where they know the values and they can watch over their investments.

They make sure that *all* the costs – mortgage, rates, the whole lot – are covered by the rent from the property. They never use negative gearing. This way, if they lose their jobs, they are safe. They are always playing it safe. They keep saving and buying, saving and buying, usually for many years. Sure, they break the investment rules of 'experts'. But here's the irony: these investors are worth a lot more than most 'experts'. There's a clue here.

If you think this advice is too conservative or it will take you too long to acquire wealth, then perhaps you should ask yourself why you want to invest in the first place. Keep asking why and you will keep coming back to the same answer – you want to be financially secure. Well, there are few short cuts to financial security. If there were, most real estate 'experts' would not be earning their money as 'experts', they'd be using the strategies they tell you about.

We should be prepared for the worst and if the best

happens, no harm done. But if the worst does come, there also will be no harm done. And the only way to avoid harm and to maintain prosperity is to play it the way they used to play it. That's what history tells us. The happiest time of the past hundred years was in the 1950s. The way we played the game in those days was *safe and sound*. And that's the best advice for you. Play it safe and sound.

Honest Experts

One of the characteristics of honest experts is admitting their mistakes. After the stock market fall in October 1987, several economic experts said, 'The real estate boom is over.' In the next twelve months, prices soared. In 2000, one of the country's most well-known forecasters said real estate would fall in 2001.[114] Again, prices soared.

If honest experts can be wrong, how do consumers predict the market? If they listen to real estate agents, they will almost always be told it's a 'good time' to sell or buy. The real estate writer Terry Ryder says that a huge meteor could be plummeting towards Earth and agents would still be saying 'now is the time to buy'.[115] So what do you do?

You should ask the most important real estate question of all, 'What is the worst that can happen in my situation?' This does not mean all risk is eliminated, but it does mean that safety should be your main concern. Risks must be kept to a minimum. If the worst case doesn't happen, then all will be well. You will be extra safe.

Some real estate experts will not like this advice. They will tell you it is 'advice for losers'. But avoiding loss is something you must do before you make a profit. Survival is your main aim. Play it safe. You may not get rich quickly. But you won't go broke quickly either.

David Potts is the business editor of the Sydney *Sun-Herald*. In a competition to see who could earn the most money, he and nine others had a mock $100,000 to invest in shares of their choice. Emily Knox was in first place. She was in Year 12 at North Sydney Girls High School. The person running second was not a person at all, but a dartboard. And third place went to the paper's astrologer. The business editor was running last.[116] But, unlike many experts, David Potts was honest enough to show that his advice, on this occasion, was not the best. And that's one way to pick honest experts – they admit their mistakes. They are not super-confident and all-knowing.

And finally, a story about another so-called expert. On October 3, 2001 in the Sydney suburb of Castle Hill, a lady saw a snake at her laundry door. She called a snake expert. 'Stand back everybody,' he said, 'I know what I am doing'. An hour later, the snake expert was in hospital.

Be careful you don't get bitten, or kidnapped, by a real estate expert. Don't sign anything until you know exactly what you are doing and you are sure you are safe.

Summary

- The signs of an investment scam are a 'free seminar' with buzzwords, such as 'wealth creation', 'tax minimisation' and 'negative gearing'.

- Properties are sold to unsuspecting consumers for tens of thousands of dollars above their true value.

- These scams are often called 'Two-Tier Marketing', where there is one price for locals and one price for people who are from out of town.

- Victims are encouraged to 'free up the equity in your home'. They are told they don't need 'any money'.

- If you buy a dud investment, you lose a slice of the equity in your home. Lenders use the homes of the victims as security for the dud investments.

- The lenders, many of them major banks, know – or should know – that their customers are being cheated.

- Typical victims have little investment experience, trusting natures and are easily manipulated based on fear of the future.

- When new laws are passed or investment scams are exposed, be extra careful. The people who welcome the news laws are often the worst crooks.

- Investment crooks sound nice. They make you feel safe and secure. That's how they con so many people. Crooks don't always look like crooks.

- Always get **independent legal advice**. Never use a lawyer recommended by someone selling something to you.

- Always get an **independent valuation**. Ignore any valuation shown to you by someone who is selling something to you.

- **Don't sign anything** – especially if it seems like a great opportunity. In real estate investing, more people go broke quick than get rich quick.

- Play it safe. You may not get rich quickly. But you won't go broke quickly either.

Chapter Eleven

Inside Real Estate

Dishonesty, incompetence, greed, persecution and cover-ups

*In this age in which everything
is held to be permissible so long as it is freely done,
repugnance may be the only voice left*

*that speaks up to defend
the central core of our humanity.*

*Shallow are the souls that have
forgotten how to shudder.*

Leon Cass

The real estate industry is like a well-organised criminal network, where few criminals are ever caught. They can steal a lot more money with pens and contracts than with knives and guns. Unless you are involved in real estate, it is hard to understand the extent of the deception. The tricks are so slick, the propaganda so perfect and the self-interest so endemic that an entire society has been fooled.

By the time sellers and buyers realise what has happened to them – if they ever do realise – it is too late. They are caught. Those who complain are often told that 'nothing illegal' has happened. To unravel the webs of dishonesty, and to fight the 'nothing illegal' excuses, is too hard for most consumers. It is also beyond the comprehension of most legislators. It is like a stampede of deceit where the government agencies that should protect honest consumers and punish dishonest agents are trampled into submission and acceptance. Mostly, only blatantly illegal 'crimes' are punished.

When Kandiah Bojan from the L.J. Hooker franchise at Epping pleaded guilty to stealing more than a million dollars from his trust account, the case made headlines. Bojan lost the money at the Sydney Star City Casino.[1] But his victims were entitled to compensation from a government fund.[2] However, it's the less obvious crimes for which there are no compensation funds. These crimes are rampant, yet described as isolated. On the surface, such deceits appear innocent. Underneath, it's another story. Whether they are legal or moral crimes, they are still crimes. Collectively, they cause consumers to lose tens of millions of dollars every year.

> **Whether they are legal or moral crimes, they are still crimes**

INSIDER TRADING: REAL ESTATE ROBBERY

The penalties for robbing banks are severe. Even if no one gets hurt and all the money is recovered, bank robbers can expect lengthy jail sentences. The law is tough. But when it comes to agents robbing people of the value of their family homes, the law barely notices. These robbers not only get away with their thefts, they are often seen as clever – 'astute business people'. And their victims rarely get their money back.

Agents who buy the homes of trusting homesellers for thousands of dollars below market value and then resell them and make huge profits are not clever, they are thieves. The common real estate saying, 'If it was that cheap, I'd buy it myself,' has a lot more veracity to it than frivolity. Given the chance – and there are plenty of chances – plenty of agents will buy a home from their client at thousands of dollars below its value. There are laws about agents buying homes from their clients, but most of these laws are so weak that crooked agents rarely have trouble getting around them. If there is a loophole in a weak law, greed will find it. Although the law varies in different states, it basically says that agents have to 'declare' if they are the buyers of the homes they are employed to sell. This is similar to making it mandatory for bank robbers to announce, at the start of their robbery, 'This is a hold-up.'

Insider trading in real estate is not usually as brazen as buying a home from a seller and reselling it immediately for thousands of dollars more. This is too risky for agents, too obvious that they have stolen their clients' money. To its credit, the law will most likely take action – either by having the sale cancelled or by ordering the agent to repay the loss to the sellers. But that's if the sellers complain or if they even realise what happened. Many sellers don't realise, and many who do realise don't complain. The victims of insider trading are often elderly, and they are either too embarrassed or too proud to admit what happened to them. They are also honourable, the sort who believe that 'a deal is a deal'. They keep their word – never mind that they were unaware of what was happening when they made their 'deal'. Some are too frail to understand what happened, especially those who are in nursing homes or retirement villages – which is one of the places suggested by the Real Estate Institute of Australia's published manual on how to find business.[3] In many cases crooked agents will have a relative or a 'mate' buy the home. Other times, and this is quite common, agents arrange for a developer or investor to buy the property. A deal is made between the agent and the developer that when the property is resold or developed, the agent will get the new business. Such deals are common.

> **If there is a loophole in a weak law, greed will find it**

Brian, a 71-year-old single man, lived in the Melbourne suburb of Hawthorn.[4] His next door neighbour was a real estate agent.[5] The agent's wife bought Brian's home for $200,000.[6] Three weeks later, the agent resold Brian's home through his real estate office for $307,000.

The agent prepared a brochure for the home which said, 'Such a good investment, it's almost beyond description!' That was true. In the 23 days, from the time Brian sold his home until the agent resold it, its value increased by $107,000.[7]

The legal loophole? The agent was not acting as Brian's agent. 'Absolutely at no stage did I wear my hat as a real estate agent,' claimed the agent. It was 'a private sale between neighbours'. Although Brian said he felt 'diddled', he also said, 'A deal is a deal'; and besides, his neighbour was his 'friend'.[8] He didn't want any trouble.[9]

This sale became the topic at a real estate licensing course conducted by the Real Estate Institute of Victoria. One of the students described what happened. 'The tutor passed around a copy of the newspaper report about the old man who sold his house to the wife of the agent. There was some discussion about whether the agent had acted improperly – the class was somewhat divided on this point. The tutor said that the agent had made two mistakes: he should have 'splashed some paint around and said the place had been renovated' and he 'shouldn't have sold it so quickly' – that way no one would have noticed his profit margin.[10]

Perhaps the tutor meant that the agent should have done something like this. When John sold his home in the Sydney suburb of Castle Hill to move into a retirement village, his home was also bought by the wife of the real estate salesperson. The home was *not* resold. It was rented as an investment. According to other agents, John's home, which the salesperson's wife bought for $262,000, was worth 'well over $320,000' – perhaps as much as $350,000.[11] When questioned, the owner of the agency said: 'We have met all the requirements of the *Property, Stock and Business Agents Act 1941*, the Real Estate Institute Code of Ethics and the Department of Fair Trading.'[12] All nice and legal.

A couple of streets away in the same suburb, another elderly seller, Walter Clift, had much earlier sold his home with a real estate agent called Peter Pilkington.[13] At the time Pilkington was the owner of the local Ray White franchise, displaying the slogan 'The Right Advice'.[14] Mr Clift was ill and confined to a nursing home when he was visited by Pilkington and asked to sign all the legal papers to sell his home. The buyers were the parents of Monique McLaughlin, one of Pilkington's salespeople. The home was resold almost immediately for an extra $135,000.[15]

Insider trading in real estate is widespread and little is being done to stop it

Insider trading in real estate is widespread and little is being done to stop it. On the contrary, it is often considered 'clever' or 'astute' to buy homes on the cheap, to pick up a 'steal' as it's called. And if any agent dares to speak out, that agent risks ridicule, even hatred. The official industry response is that insider trading is 'isolated'. But to the victims of insider trading these 'isolated' incidents are the worst financial incidents of their lives. One agent hinted that it doesn't really matter because elderly people don't really need much money at their time of life.[16]

Protecting Yourself

To protect yourself, or your loved ones, from insider trading, here's what you must do. Don't sign anything with any agent, no matter how much you like the agent, unless the agent signs a guarantee that if your home is bought by the agent or anyone closely associated with the agent, either in a personal or business capacity, and you later discover that your home was sold well below its true value, then you will be entitled to receive an immediate refund of any commission, together with payment of the difference between the selling price and the true value. If the agent has resold the home, then the profit on the resale plus the commission should be returned to you.[17]

The agent should also advise you if your home is being sold to an investor or developer with whom the agent has had prior dealings. If your home is being sold for redevelopment, the agent must advise you if there is going to be an arrangement between the developer and the agent for future business between them.

LYING BY OMISSION

In ethics there is a concept known as 'lying by omission'. Liars claim to tell the truth but leave out information which hides the whole truth. As you have seen, a common example is when auctions are described as a success when homes sell 'above the reserve price'. The missing information is the price the buyers were prepared to pay.

A home in the Melbourne suburb of Cheltenham had a reserve price of $300,000. It sold for $305,000.[18] The impression was that the sellers got an extra $5000. But the buyers were prepared to pay $323,750.[19] The sellers sold for $18,750 less, not $5000 more. It's one of real estate's cleverest scams – sellers think they win but they are actually losing. They were probably quoted a figure of $350,000 when they first signed up for auction. The agent lies by omission and then blames the market to cover up the lie. It's dishonesty and incompetence working in tandem. And it's rampant.

In just one example in one suburb, Eastwood, collectively three homes sold at auction for more than $100,000 less than the buyers were prepared to pay. One home sold for $301,000. The buyer had offered $310,000 before the auction. Another sold for $725,000. The buyer would 'gladly' have paid $800,000. A third buyer paid $402,500 when she was prepared to pay between $420,000 and $430,000.[20]

Lying by omission is done to manipulate consumers into making decisions which suit agents but harm consumers. There are only two reasons these lies exist: either agents do not understand what happens, which means they are incompetent; or they deliberately conceal the truth, which means they are dishonest.

Another widespread example of lying by omission occurs with advertising. Many sellers are duped into believing that advertising is 'essential' to sell their home. If this were true, there would be little need for agents or the agents should receive less commission because, according to the agents, the *advertising created the sales*. And yet sellers are asked to pay twice – once for advertising and once for commission. It doesn't make sense. There is no fund to compensate the tens of thousands of homesellers who are tricked into wasting millions of dollars on advertising.

Not only is this a moral crime, it may well be a legal crime. Peter Macmillan is a lawyer specialising in Trade Practices legislation. He is a former assistant director with the ACCC. In examining why agents encourage sellers to spend money on advertising, he says, 'It may be arguable that such a service is not needed by the seller and that a false and misleading representation has been made to say it is needed.' Mr Macmillan says that not only is this a breach of Section 53 (f) of the Trade Practices Act, it is also 'a criminal offence'.[21]

THE PREDICAMENT OF NEWSPAPERS

When the interests of newspapers conflict with the interests of consumers, it creates both an ethical and a commercial predicament. If newspapers exposed the whole truth about the real estate industry, they would lose millions of dollars in advertising revenue. Such predicaments are not unique to real estate and newspapers; they affect media organisations around the world. To be stifled by commercial interest is one of the greatest frustrations of any ethical journalist. Their choice is often brutal – give up the story or give up their job.

In 1996, Roberta Baskin from the CBS program, *48 Hours*, reported on the inhumane conditions in Nike 'sweatshops'. In 1998, when Nike was sponsoring CBS's coverage of the Winter Olympics, Roberta was horrified to see CBS reporters wearing the Nike logo. Her follow-up stories on the sweatshops had been stopped. CBS denied there was any connection with their multi-million dollar sponsorship deal with Nike.[22] But as columnists Russell Mokhiber and Robert Weissman wrote in their book *Corporate Predators*, often journalists 'who have the gall to question the practices of Nike and other global corporations will be shown the door. Goodbye Roberta.'[23]

Several journalists who have written stories exposing crooked real estate practices have told how their stories have been 'cut to pieces' or never been published. One freelance journalist could not believe that she was 'told' what to say. 'I have never been so hijacked on any project I have ever worked on,' she said.[24] 'If I write the whole truth, I will be out of a job,' said another journalist.

Terry Ryder was a property journalist for *The Courier-Mail*, Brisbane's major daily newspaper. In February 1997, he wrote two articles criticising the auction system. He explained how agents promote auctions because they benefit agents, not consumers. He also exposed how sellers were exploited with advertising expenses which give 'enormous exposure' to agents. He said he was 'amazed' that sellers allowed this to happen. Of course, as Ryder revealed, most sellers did not realise what was happening to them.

According to Ryder he was placed under 'extreme pressure' because of these articles. 'The boss of a big real estate chain was furious. He threatened to withdraw his multi-million dollar advertising account.'[25] A few weeks later Terry Ryder resigned.[26] Today he is the author of three real estate books where he says he is 'free to write the truth about what goes on in real estate.'[27]

Granted, newspapers do print unfavourable real estate stories, but rarely do these stories harm the interests of agents *and* newspapers. Stories supporting auctions far outnumber those opposing auctions. And honest stories about advertising are almost non-existent, especially in newspapers which receive millions of dollars from real estate advertising.

No journalist of integrity wants to be influenced by advertisers. But the huge real estate advertising dollars are a persuasive force. The real estate industry often expects that its advertising patronage entitles it to 'special treatment'. The advertising staff are keen to please agents.

The American real estate trainer, Mike Ferry, who has many agent devotees in Australia and New Zealand says, 'Whenever a newspaper runs articles damaging to agents, I suggest [agents] write to the editor to complain about the articles, and further state that they will never run real estate classified in that publication again.'[28]

Ted Lake, the publisher of a real estate newspaper[29], said, 'This industry helps to keep the mainstream press alive with advertising, yet they [the media] are oh-so-quick to put the knife in at any opportunity.'[30] When stories about power lines and their links to cancer appeared in the media, Lake referred to journalists as 'media vultures', because such reports lowered the value of homes near power lines. Lake's home is 50 metres from a power line.[31]

In Queensland, the Raine & Horne network said, 'How can you understand newspapers allowing attacks against agents when they rely heavily on advertising to keep them profitable?'[32]

When Sandy Nelson failed to sell her Adelaide home at auction, the agent sued her for advertising expenses. Sandy said, 'The newspaper was interested in the story until they heard it was Brock Partners – then backed away, saying they could not print anything bad about them because they are one of their biggest advertisers.'[33] Sandy won the case but nothing was mentioned in the newspaper in which the agent was the big-spending advertiser.[34]

Real Estate News Reports

Many property writers believe that auctions are good or that advertising is important. They do not realise their advice is wrong. Often it is not really 'their' advice. Terry Ryder explains it this way, 'Property writers spend most of their time speaking with real estate networks, institutes and agents. Journalists can't help being influenced. It happened to me. I would call an agent about something which seemed really bad and the agent would give me a convincing excuse. I'd then write the excuse.'[35]

Most property writers talk to agents more than consumers. Many are friends with agents. This is why they sound like agents. The most accurate real estate stories are written without the influence of agents. Often, these stories are written by columnists or general news journalists, usually from a consumer's perspective.

Paul Sheehan is an award-winning writer, the author of the best-seller, *Among the Barbarians*.[36] He is a senior writer for *The Sydney Morning Herald*. He is not a property writer, and yet, when he wrote about auctions, he managed to clearly explain, in a brief article, what few property writers ever explain – the 'pervasive' and 'ritualised' lying with auctions.[37] His words were those of an unbiased observer, free from polluted real estate spin. He even exposed the classic myth that auctions get better prices when buyers are competing against each other. His answer to that was, 'If more than one buyer wants the place, then the silent auction begins.' (Meaning that buyers are asked, in private, to declare their best price.) In one sentence, Paul Sheehan exposed the auction trap that catches many property writers. Another person to make similar comments about auctions, without the influence of estate agents, was Professor William Vickery. He won a Nobel Prize.[38]

Real Estate Censorship

This book will almost certainly be banned from being advertised in many newspapers. The author's previous book, *Real Estate Mistakes*, was released in January 2000. It was advertised in many suburban newspapers owned by News Limited. The response from consumers was totally positive. Not so with real estate agents and newspapers. On March 6, a memo from the administration manager of the News Limited owned Cumberland Press in New South Wales was sent to staff urging them to be 'on the lookout' for any advertising for *Real Estate Mistakes*. Staff were told not to publish any advertisement for the book.[39]

In the weeks that followed, similar bans occurred in other states. Earlier bans had been placed on the advertising of two other booklets by this author, *18 Costly Mistakes Made by Homesellers* and *14 Common Mistakes Made by Homebuyers*.

Following are some of the reasons for banning these

advertisements: in Queensland it was 'due to the nature of the material'; in New South Wales, 'They have something in them which is contrary to what other agents think', and, 'detrimental to other agents'; in South Australia, they thought 'it would compromise our strong relationship with all real estate agents', and, 'We have this company policy[40], which in fact is a national News Limited directive.'

In Victoria, the reasons included such statements as the newspaper's duty to 'protect readers'. The real estate advertising manager explained that local newspapers are different from daily newspapers because they are delivered free to homes. He said, 'There is a higher degree of ethical responsibility on the content in the local newspaper before it is placed in a letter box.'[41]

Advertising material which warns sellers and buyers about the traps of real estate is not 'ethically acceptable'. But advertisements with statements such as, 'Sexy young ladies seek affairs with single or married men', are acceptable.[42] Readers need to be 'protected'.

One reader tells the following story, 'My phone bill was extraordinarily high. Calls to sex lines had been made. My children confessed to making the calls. When I asked how they had got access to such numbers, they told me it was from the local paper. Has the paper such low morals and such a desperate need for the advertising dollar? I don't feel comfortable trying to explain to my nine-year-old what is meant by ads saying "sex with the best transsexual", "male to male sex", "busty blonde beauty" or "sexy hands". I urge you to call or write to the publisher and object to them accepting this disgusting advertising from smut peddlers.'[43]

According to some newspapers, they have 'the right to reject any advertisement we consider unsuitable for publication for any reason at our absolute discretion'.[44]

In May 2001, an agent in Victoria said he was told by the advertising manager of the local newspaper, which is part of the News Limited owned Leader Newspaper Group, 'Anything with Jenman on it will not be printed.'[45]

In a conversation six months earlier, the real estate editor of Leader Newspapers said 'Real Estate Mistakes is a fantastic book. I wish I had read it earlier. Next time I buy or sell I will only use an agent that uses this method.'[46] But what they believe and what they print can be different things. As the US politician, Adlai Stevenson, once remarked, 'Newspaper editors are people who separate the wheat from the chaff, and then print the chaff.'[47]

In October 2001, an agent from Sydney's Northern Beaches area was not allowed to publish an advertisement in the Manly Daily.[48] The agent was offering a guarantee that homesellers would not have to pay commission if their homes sold below the price quoted by the agent.

In January 2002, a Launceston agent, Peter Lees, joined a national campaign against advertising kickbacks or, as they are often called, 'rebates' or 'volume discounts'. Leaflets were distributed promoting an article on kickbacks. The article included the statement, 'many newspapers refuse to accept advertisements promoting material which protects consumers'.[49]

Lawyers for Launceston's The Examiner newspaper wrote to Peter Lees accusing him of defamation and demanding that the article 'not be distributed to any person by your firm'. The lawyers said if the article was distributed in Launceston, it could 'only be interpreted as a reference to the Examiner'.[50]

A year earlier, The Examiner had refused to accept an advertisement from Lees headed 'DON'T SIGN ANYTHING'. The newspaper's lawyers now said, 'the Examiner newspaper is not a party to any such practice [refusing to publish advertisements beneficial to consumers]. It does of course offer marketing packages and volume discounts to real estate agents.'[51]

In hundreds of areas, due to the power of the agents and the newspapers, consumers hear only one side of the real estate story. They don't hear the inside story.

THE DARK SIDE

Ray Peattie was a crooked cop. Like most crooked cops, he didn't start that way. In the beginning he surely had noble intentions. It was three years before he became a crook. It was so easy – a group of cops sharing a bribe, it was just natural to accept his share. At this point, Ray's life changed. As he admitted, 'Once you are on the dark side, you are always on the dark side.'[52]

Twenty-four years after he joined the police, Ray Peattie was in charge of an 'anti-corruption plan' for Manly Police in Sydney. The results of his findings showed that only six per cent of officers had ever seen acts of corruption. Fortunately, there were some police officers with enough nobility left in them to expose Peattie and his dark companions.

The police force is like any institution. If they set their own codes, if they police themselves, if they issue their own findings, the dark side can take over. It's the same in real estate. In 2000, the Real Estate Institute of Victoria set up an 'ethics committee'. On the committee were agents who had crossed over to the 'dark side' of real estate. One consumer lawyer said, 'That's like putting the fox in charge of security at the chook house.'[53]

REAL ESTATE INSTITUTES

The impression that real estate institutes are the police for the real estate industry is a myth. The motive of any real estate institute is to *protect the interests of agents*. The institutes' members are agents. But when it comes to creating legislation to protect consumers, the legislators spend more time speaking with institute representatives (agents) than with consumers.

When the Queensland government proposed new legislation to protect consumers, the Real Estate Institute of Queensland spent months liaising with legislators.[54] The Office of Fair Trading then held a series of public seminars to explain the new laws. The seminars were co-presented by the Real Estate Institute.[55] Astonishingly, the Queensland

Office of Fair Trading has a link on its web site directing consumers to the Real Estate Institute. This means that a potential buyer, in search of advice, can dial into the Fair Trading web site, click on the link to the real estate institute and be directed to real estate agents who have been raided, charged or are being investigated by the Office of Fair Trading for ripping off consumers.[56]

A few days before the state election of 2001, the Real Estate Institute of Queensland sent a fax to its members outlining the benefits for agents if the Coalition of the National and Liberal Parties was elected.[57] When the Coalition lost the election, the institute welcomed the Labor Party and said it was 'looking forward to working with the new Beattie government'.

The most notorious offender in these heart-wrenching multi-billion-dollar scams was a member of the Real Estate Institute of Queensland

A few months later, in an amazing act of hypocrisy, the Real Estate Institute of Queensland blamed the Beattie government for the thousands of consumers caught by the notorious Queensland investment scams. The institute's president, Mark Brimble, said 'It's time every aspect of this scam was laid open to public scrutiny.' He also said that the institute was concerned at the possibility of a 'cover-up' by those who benefit from the scams.[58]

Public scrutiny? Cover-up? Blame? What the institute did *not* say was that the most notorious offender in these heart-wrenching, multi-billion-dollar scams was a member of the Real Estate Institute of Queensland – as were several other institute members. The institute suggested that if the government could not stamp out these practices, the 'regulatory responsibility' should be given to the real estate industry bodies. As Terry Ryder commented, 'That's similar to saying that if the government cannot stamp out crime, it should seek the assistance of the Mafia.'

In New South Wales the institute met several times with the Department of Fair Trading about new legislation to protect consumers. The institute was trying to persuade the government to scrap a proposed cooling-off period on selling agreements and a time limit on agency agreements. The institute told its worried agents, 'You are assured we will continue to promote your interests.'[59]

Cover-ups, Denials and Reprisals

Many agents want to see real estate improved for the benefit of consumers. But these agents are the silent minority. If they suggest changes that do not help agents, no matter how much consumers are helped, they are likely to be ignored. If they expose bad practices they face abuse. There is a cone of silence about what really goes on inside real estate.

Only eight per cent of Australians considered real estate agents to be honest

William De Maria, in his book *Deadly Disclosures – Whistleblowing and the Ethical Meltdown of Australia,* talks about organisations 'hell-bent on reprisal' against those who speak out. He laments that most people find it hard to believe that 'whole institutions can be corrupt'. They accept bad incidents as isolated.[60] De Maria says we can seldom grasp 'the idea of whole-of-system corruption'. But that's the real estate industry – riddled with deceit, dishonesty and corruption. Such a claim, of course, will incur the usual denials from the institutes.

The Real Estate Institute of Victoria, in response to a television report about unethical real estate conduct said, 'The overwhelming majority of vendors are very satisfied with the service provided.' The wry grin of the presenter was not lost on viewers.[61]

A survey conducted in November 2001 showed that only eight per cent of Australians considered real estate agents to be honest.[62] But the industry says 'only a minority' of agents are dishonest. A common ploy to prove that agents are honest is to compare the number of sales with the number of complaints. As already stated, most consumers can't be bothered complaining. Many more don't even realise how they have been cheated.

The denials, the cover-ups and the persecution of those who speak out has turned the real estate industry into a moral wilderness. Powerful forces of self-interest have seen the most basic of consumer rights sacrificed for the sake of profit.

In New Zealand, the power of the Real Estate Institute is so strong that agents are required by law to be members. And the institute's 'law' forbids agents from speaking out about bad practices.[63] When Malcolm Cox from Napier publicly criticised common real estate practices he felt the full force of retaliation. One of his statements concerned 'commission only' schemes for salespeople. He said paying no salary was 'a shameful way to treat new recruits, many of whom experience enormous financial suffering and leave the industry feeling very bitter'. This is the truth. But agents are not allowed to speak the truth if it does not 'reflect well on the industry'.

In a form of kangaroo court, Malcolm was found guilty by his 'judges' – agents seeking to protect their image and profits. He was fined NZ$3368.75.[64]

The Real Estate Institute of New Zealand's mission statement reveals the purpose of the institute: 'To be the recognised authority on real estate in New Zealand by providing real estate related services and products to a level of quality and competence that will ensure the sustained growth of the company through the provision of exceptional value to members and where appropriate the public.'[65] Value to members first and then, if appropriate, the interests of the public.

Real estate institutes infer that consumers are protected with their 'Codes of Conduct' and 'Codes of Ethics'. But these codes have no force at law. They are words with almost no meaning. As Mike Iveson from the Australian Property College points out, the institute Codes of Ethics are 'more about relationships between agents'. There is little mention of consumers.[66]

There is no evidence that agents who are members of real estate institutes are more honest than agents who are not members. Several past presidents of the Real Estate Institute of Victoria were receiving kickbacks on advertising money before, during and after their terms of presidency. One boasted about taking $14,000 in advertising money from an elderly lady when he already had a buyer for her home.[67]

One of the basic rights of consumers is the right to have companies compete fairly to win their business. Anything that opposes this right is anti-competitive. It is against the law. Despite this, institutes and their members regularly breach consumer protection laws. Such breaches are so common they have become almost 'accepted' industry practice.

In October 1999, the Federal Court in Perth declared that Michael Griffith, the Executive Director of the Real Estate Institute of Western Australia (REIWA) was 'knowingly concerned' in anti-competitive breaches of the Trade Practices Act.[68] In his judgement, against both Griffith and the institute, Justice French said there was almost a 'righteous belief' that the Real Estate Institute was entitled to behave in ways that were in 'blatant contravention' of the law. Because of what he called the institute's 'entrenched culture of non-compliance', the institute was ordered to commence a Trade Practices Compliance program.[69]

Two years later, in 2001, when dummy bidding was news across Australia, the Real Estate Institute of Western Australia opposed changes. Like other institutes, it supported dummy bidding. It just called it vendor bidding and said it was 'misunderstood'. It also said it had not had any 'formal complaints' and therefore, it was 'not a problem in Western Australia'. The Minister for Consumer Protection reportedly made an almost identical statement, saying, that 'dummy bidding is not enough of an issue to warrant banning in Western Australia'. He added that no formal complaints had been made.[70]

The ABC invited the institute to debate the issue on radio. The institute refused. And so the ABC interviewed an agent who was opposed to dummy bidding. Although the agent sounded nervous at speaking out, he made many points about how auctions hurt consumers. He said agents like auctions because of the extra advertising money which promotes the agents.[71]

Finally, a vice-president of the institute, Greg Rossen, called the ABC to defend the institute.[72] Rossen began by referring to the announcer, Liam Bartlett, as a 'shock jock'. Bartlett, one of Western Australia's most respected broadcasters, listened patiently as Rossen said, 'What I want to know is are you going to wind me up and beat some meaningless admission out of me. Are you a truth and justice seeker, a raconteur or an egomaniac?'[73]

Bartlett asked, 'Are you speaking on behalf of the Real Estate Institute?'

'Yes, I am. And I'm speaking on behalf of auctioneers. Are we going to have a meaningful discussion or are you going to beat some meaningless admission out of me?'

Rossen said Bartlett could 'press the button' to get rid of him and for the third time, Rossen mentioned 'meaningless admission'. Finally, Liam Bartlett said, 'You are running out of time. If you have anything meaningful to say, I would suggest you get into it.'[74]

And get into he did. Grabbing 80 per cent of the time – and constantly talking over Liam Bartlett – Greg Rossen, the Vice-President of the Real Estate Institute, attempted to defend the indefensible. Bartlett then made one point which destroyed everything Rossen had said. He told Rossen that a dummy bidder was someone 'masquerading as a buyer'.

Rossen's response was, 'Don't use coloured words.'

In an obvious reference to calling dummy bids vendor bids, Bartlett said, 'Well that's what you're doing. If stockbrokers indulged in making phantom bids for stock and they were caught out, they would be in jail.'

Liam Bartlett thanked Rossen for calling and added that it was 'a shame we had to apply the blow torch to flush somebody out from your institute'.[75]

Listening to the interview was Tony Rees, a senior lecturer in journalism at Curtin University. He was 'appalled' at the way Rossen bullied and abused Liam Bartlett. Tony Rees could have been referring to all the institutes when he commented on radio that Rossen was 'someone who makes a lot of money' out of auctions. He said, 'If that is the representative of the real estate industry in Western Australia, then I certainly wouldn't buy a used house from him.'[76]

If stockbrokers indulged in making phantom bids for stock and they were caught out, they would be in jail

In 2001, the Real Estate Institute of Victoria launched a campaign called 'Stamp out Stamp Duty'. It accused the government of 'ripping off' homebuyers. The Treasurer, John Brumby, questioned the institute's motives. He inferred that agents wanted lower stamp duty so they could increase commissions. Institute spokesperson, Enzo Raimondo, described the Treasurer's comments as an 'outburst'. He urged agents to demand an apology from the Treasurer.[77]

The institute said its motive was to obtain a 'fairer deal' for homebuyers. The real estate boom had been a bonanza for the government. More sales at higher prices meant more stamp duty for the government. This was why the institute said the government was ripping off consumers. The institute did not mention that the boom meant more commission for agents. There was no suggestion from the institute that agents lower their charges.

The institute said: 'Victorians pay more in stamp duty than in any other state.'[78] The impression was that the institute cared about consumers. But the Real Estate Institute in South Australia said the same thing. Speaking on radio, their president, Barrie Magain, claimed that South Australian homebuyers pay the highest amount of stamp duty in Australia.[79] Magain said stamp duty was 'unfair'. He, too, wanted a fair deal for real estate consumers. Two weeks later, in his column in Adelaide's major newspaper, he was explaining why homesellers, not agents, should pay for real estate advertising.

Consumers are being ripped off by a multitude of schemes that do far more financial harm than stamp duty

If the government launched a full independent inquiry into the real estate industry, it would discover that consumers are being ripped off by a multitude of schemes that do far more financial harm than stamp duty.

Perhaps the Victorian Treasurer might look more closely at the government funding given to an institute that misleads consumers on such a grand scale. In the 2000 financial year, the Real Estate Institute of Victoria received $1,128,620.00 from the government. One of the main purposes of this money is to provide a real estate 'public information service'.[80] And this is just one state. Millions of dollars of taxpayers' money is being paid to real estate institutes that support and cover up methods that cheat taxpayers of more millions of dollars.

Responsibility

When a former president of the Real Estate Institute of the Australian Capital Territory, John Roden, received a suspended jail sentence for dishonesty[81], the institute's general manager, Adam Moore, reportedly said it was 'not a reflection on the institute'.[82] When a magistrate described dummy bidding as 'evil', Mr Moore said the magistrate had 'gone overboard'.[83] Moore also admitted that the only qualifications needed to become a real estate agent in Canberra was 'a pulse and a phone'[84], a far cry from the qualifications of a magistrate.

The institutes often respond to critics by saying, 'They don't understand the industry.' When presented with evidence of wrongdoing, institutes say such incidents are 'isolated' or caused by agents who are 'non-members of institutes'. Such arguments no longer stack up. As Peter Lowenstern, a senior research lawyer with the Law Institute of Victoria wrote,

'What has been accepted as standard industry practice in the past is no longer good enough in an era when consumer rights are to be taken very, very seriously indeed.' He said agents should cease their 'plaintive mewings' and stop 'hiding behind a legal skirt' to justify unethical conduct.[85] His remarks upset several agents, one of whom described his comments as 'peevish'.[86]

They should back up these claims by offering consumers a genuine and meaningful guarantee

If the real estate institutes were as honest and ethical as they claim, they should back up these claims by offering consumers a genuine and meaningful guarantee.

REAL ESTATE NETWORKS

Despite their offices all being painted in the same colours, agents who belong to networks can be very different – some good, most mediocre and some appalling. Customers can go to one branch and get wonderful service and then go to another branch and get dreadful service. The outside image has no bearing on what happens behind the image. One New Zealand businessman quipped, 'They are like mudguards – shiny on the outside but dirty underneath.'[87] Almost all networks battle to disguise the mediocrity of many of their members. They are more intent on preserving their 'corporate image' and improving their profits than on improving their service. Self-interest sets their culture.

The story of the First National network shows how the best intentions can collapse under the weight of self-interest. First National began in 1981. Its founders had a noble aim: to approach the best agents in every area. By charging a small fee instead of a crippling percentage of turnover, and by focusing on quality members, they attracted some of the finest agents in Australia and New Zealand. Within ten years they had more than 500 members.[88] In 1991, their future looked wonderful.

However, a culture of self-interest began to replace the noble intentions. One example occurred in 1994. A member from the Sydney suburb of Thornleigh, Tony Andrea, was bribing a government official for the rights to sell homes owned by the Roads and Traffic Authority.[89] He said the payments were 'spotter's fees'.[90] But the Independent Commission Against Corruption (ICAC) called them bribes. Despite his dishonesty, he remained a member of the network.[91] In 1996, Phil Hickmott from Melton in Victoria, whose office had been one of the founding members, warned that the network was becoming 'just like all the rest'.[92] His warnings were ignored. Over the next five years, the early noble intentions seemed to disappear. In November 2001, the First National Board moved against many of its members who publicly supported ethical reforms in real estate. In what was described as 'a thinly disguised excuse' the board accused some members of 'co-branding' the network.[93] These members wanted to display their association with an ethical accreditation system, a system at odds with the 'interests' of many First National agents. Members were forbidden from using a small 'Ethics in Real Estate' logo. However, they were still permitted to display a Real Estate Institute logo.[94]

In the same month that the board opposed members wanting to be associated publicly with a group protecting consumers, it moved privately to increase its own interests at the expense of consumers. The CEO of First National, Ian Bremner (who was once CEO of the Real Estate Institute of Victoria) wrote to members about how much extra they could earn on home loans. Members were told they could get 'increased referral fees above the current $150' plus 'higher trailer fees' plus 'income derived from the provision of insurance services'. He said that financial benefits for First National agents would be 'significantly enhanced' because they could 'take advantage of new opportunities'.[95] As is common in the modern real estate world, this was just another way to pocket more money from kickbacks. Many members were appalled at what they described as 'hypocrisy'.

By 2002, First National had become what Phil Hickmott predicted in 1996 – 'just like all the rest'. With the decline in quality came a decline in members; some of the best, including Hickmott, had resigned. In June 2002, First National lost one of its most respected members when a former chairman and co-founder, Sam Pennisi, resigned calling it one of the saddest business decisions of his life. 'I cannot remain in a group that has so lost its way that it barely resembles the one we formed 20 years ago,' he said.[96]

'Into the Act': The Real Estate Gravy Train

Years ago, the comedian Jimmy Durante used a line that became world famous, 'Everybody wants to get into the act.'[97]

Agents are clambering aboard the real estate gravy train in order to pocket money at every stop along the home buying and selling journey. They justify this ride by saying that consumers 'use these services anyway', so 'we may as well get something from it'. This argument ignores the conflict of interest from the temptation to refer consumers to whoever pays the biggest kickback.

Everybody wants to get into the act

Dr Simon Longstaff is the Executive Director of the St James Ethics Centre, an independent non-profit organisation promoting business and professional ethics. He argues that there are economic as well as ethical concerns with bribes or 'grease payments'. In his book, *Hard Cases, Tough Choices,* Dr Longstaff says, 'Where bribery flourishes, the wrong goods go to the wrong people at the wrong prices. There is a gross distortion of the market as economic benefit flows to those who bribe, rather than those who produce the best goods and services at the best prices.'[98]

There are economic as well as ethical concerns with bribes

The New Zealand based network, Harcourts, which has several branches in Queensland, receives commissions from referrals to lenders, lawyers and insurance. Each comes under the heading of a 'service'. There is Harcourts Financial Services with a $100 up-front fee on each loan. Later, there is a 'trailer fee' – a monthly payment to the agent for the entire period of the loan. There is Harcourts

Legal Services with a fee of $50. And then there is Harcourts Insurance Agencies where agents receive five per cent of the insurance premiums.[99]

Harcourts say that 'no part of any fee is paid by the buyer'.[100] But if these fees did not exist or if they were given back to consumers, the costs of home buying and selling would be much lower. Agents get commission for selling homes. To pocket additional money from advertising, conveyancing, lending, insurance, removalists, building inspections and a host of other services, does two things: it gives agents more fees and it increases the costs to consumers. Kickbacks become built in to the total costs of selling and buying.

Kickbacks become built in to the total costs of selling and buying

Some professional people who refuse to pay kickbacks to agents are struggling to survive. In Victoria, the owner of a conveyancing company wrote, 'Some operators who run their businesses in an ethical and professional manner are being pushed out of the market as the client is being steered towards the operator who will financially benefit the agent.'[101]

These commissions and kickbacks are increasing as more networks 'get into the act'. The Ray White network has Ray White Financial Services where agents can earn five times the amount earned by Harcourt members. Documents obtained by this author show up-front home loan commissions to Ray White agents of more than $500.[102] Again, on top of this are 'trailer fees'. Every month when consumers make a loan payment, agents get a slice of their payment.

But agents aren't the only ones getting kickbacks. Many lawyers are now clambering aboard the real estate gravy train.

LAWYERS

In December 2001, Lawform, which calls itself a 'financial services group' for lawyers, wrote to Queensland lawyers with what it called 'really good $$$$ news' that could 'triple or quadruple' their income.[103] It was described as a 'ground breaking' method of making money from commission on home loans and many other services which a lawyer may recommend to clients. Services such as insurance, pest reports, building reports, surveys, valuations. Each can mean a 'spotter's fee' to the lawyers. The scheme began in New South Wales and, according to Lawform, is going to be extended Australia wide.[104]

Lawform said that lawyers have the 'commercial confidence' of nearly 100 per cent of homebuyers. Consumers trust lawyers. And with trust comes what Lawform calls 'potential'. Lawyers are told that their income from commissions (kickbacks) is 'unlimited'. It promises lawyers that the money they can make is far more than they could ever make in their normal law practices.[105]

For example, on a typical $300,000 loan, lawyers are being offered an immediate commission of $1260 and then a $600 'trailer' commission every year – for as long as the loan exists. It's all spelled out in a simple chart. If a lawyer arranges just one home loan per week, then, in eight years the lawyer can be earning $1,503,360 just from kickbacks.[106]

And this is conservative. One suburban lawyer, described as 'enterprising', averaged ten loans per week for five months in 2001.[107] At this pace, in two years, he will be getting $1,188,640 a year in commissions. In five years, he will be making $5,000,000 annually. Plus legal fees. Lawform calls this 'the most significant commercial advantage for solicitors in decades'. It says, 'You will be able to provide yourself with an income well into retirement'.[108] While home-owners are still battling to pay off their loans, their lawyers will be relaxing in retirement on kickbacks from these loans.

Again, it is all 'legal' because the commissions are 'disclosed' to the clients. It's in the paperwork the clients willingly sign because they trust their lawyers. Or as Lawform puts it, lawyers have the 'commercial confidence' of their clients. Many lawyers are appalled. But Lawform claims to have received 'overwhelming response' with 'more than 50 per cent' of conveyancing law firms wanting to participate.[109]

The argument to justify this scheme is the same as the one used by agents: 'Consumers are not paying any more than if they approached the lender direct. The lenders are paying the commissions to the lawyers.' This argument is an admission that the interests of consumers come second to the 'commercial interests' of these law firms. If lawyers can arrange for lenders to pay millions of dollars in commissions to lawyers, they could just as easily arrange for this money to be given to their clients – those people who trust lawyers. In their various 'legal' guises, kickbacks are adding hundreds of millions of dollars to the cost of buying and selling real estate. The conflict of interest makes it almost impossible for sellers and buyers to be treated impartially. The solution for real estate consumers is simple: don't sign anything unless all kickbacks or commissions are passed on to you. If a lawyer, or an agent, or any person suggests you use a company or person, ask the question: 'Are you getting paid from this recommendation?'

> **Kickbacks are adding hundreds of millions of dollars to the cost of buying and selling real estate**

The built-in cost of kickbacks is one of the greatest traps for real estate consumers. Without government intervention, kickbacks, incentives, rebates, commissions – whatever they are called – will keep increasing. There will be no stopping the appetites of some business people.

A company called Asset Buying Corporation[110] is searching for 'distressed sellers' who need to sell property in a hurry. They want big deals – multi-million-dollar properties. And they are prepared to pay big incentives to lawyers who send them desperate clients. Incentives such as ten years of the lawyer's salary or a brand new Mercedes SLK, or a $50,000 home-theatre, or first-class air tickets to anywhere in the world or real estate to the value of $350,000. It depends on how cheaply the lawyers' clients can be persuaded to sell their properties to Asset Buying Corporation.[111]

Most consumers go to lawyers expecting to pay for advice which protects them and saves them money. But, today, such expectations can be optimistic and naïve. At every point in the real estate line, there is the potential for so-called 'professional people' with 'commercial interests' to give advice that benefits the people giving the advice more than it benefits the consumers.

The reality of business in the twenty-first century is that self-interest and greed often takes the place of honest advice. It's called 'commercial reality'. But changing the word 'greed' to the words 'commercial reality' does not make it respectable. Greed has become so common in business that many professional people aren't just being paid; they are being bought.

> **Many professional people aren't just being paid; they are being bought**

GOVERNMENTS

The Australian Competition and Consumer Commission (ACCC) is a federal government commission. One of its aims is to 'protect consumers from unlawful anti-competitive and unfair market practices'. In a handbook for agents, the ACCC says, 'You must not say or do anything that could mislead your clients or customers.'[112]

The role of the ACCC is to 'protect consumers from unfair market practices'[113], which involves making sure that businesses comply with the Trade Practices Act. Section 52 of the Act is clear: a corporation shall not engage in 'conduct that is misleading or deceptive or is likely to mislead or deceive.'[114] This small sentence could be applied to thousands of real estate sales where deception is a deliberate part of the sales strategy.

> **Self-interest and greed often takes the place of honest advice**

When Stewart Walls and his partner went house hunting, they found the conduct of agents to be 'negligent at best' and 'deliberately misleading' at worst. Their biggest shock was the trick of deliberately underquoting prices. One home was advertised for 'low 200s'. Stewart and his partner offered $268,000. Their offer was rejected. The home later sold for $321,000.[115] The agent blamed the market. But Stewart did not accept this common excuse. He believed homes should not be advertised at prices for which they will never be sold.

> Homes should not be advertised at prices for which they will never be sold

The agent told Stewart that advertising false prices is done to attract buyers who can then be talked up in price.[116] Many agents are almost jovial about it. It goes on all the time, 'everyone does it', so what's the problem?

Stewart wrote to the ACCC urging that action be taken to stop this 'widespread' deceit.[117] The agent he was complaining about was a member of the Real Estate Institute of Queensland. He received a reply saying the ACCC was 'unable to assist'. They suggested he contact the Real Estate Institute of Queensland.[118]

The voice of the lone consumer is no match for the collective voice of thousands of agents all saying everything is fine. The real estate industry with its abundance of excuses and years of experience at disguising deceit can easily mislead governments.

If the deceit in real estate really was isolated, it would be easier to prevent. The reason it is so hard to stop is because it is everywhere. And governments are being deceived too, not

> If the deceit in real estate really was isolated, it would be easier to prevent

just when they look at how to improve real estate, but when they sell real estate. Governments are auctioning property and losing millions of dollars of taxpayers' money. And they are being caught up in the same tricks. When Rockdale Council in Sydney sold a property by auction, the agent quoted a bait price 'from $300,000'. But the reserve price was reportedly more than double what the agent was quoting to potential buyers.[119]

Deceit is so entrenched in real estate that it has become accepted. Exposing the deceit may lead to tough questions for governments, such as: Why has it been allowed to go on so long? Why has all the evidence been suppressed or ignored? Why has there not been an independent inquiry?

David Hindley, a senior research writer for New Zealand's *Consumer* magazine, said that consumers had been 'let down by our laws and bodies'.[120] He said the New Zealand Commerce Commission had investigated the mislabelling of sausages, but not real estate scams which are 'wiping out people's retirement savings'.

It's a similar story in Australia. Rare incidents, such as failing to renew a licence or not including the GST in selling fees[121], get more attention than common incidents, such as bait pricing, false guarantees from a real estate institute and the myriad of deceit and misrepresentation. It goes on every day, right under the noses of the government bodies. As criminologist Paul Wilson pointed out in 2002, corporate prosecutions 'represent only a fraction of the corporate crime and malpractice infecting Australian business'.[122] In real estate, the investigations carried out by government bodies can sometimes defy belief.

Persecution

Ron Heyne is a real estate agent in Stirling in the Adelaide Hills. When he warned local residents that open inspections were 'dangerous', he received a letter from the Office of Consumer and Business Affairs asking for 'evidence'.[123] Ron told them where he had obtained his information, which included the Real Estate Institute. Not good enough. He was then asked 'How many open inspections take place in South Australia each year and what percentage can be directly related to any crime proven in the courts?'[124]

He received a visit from two government officials whom he described as 'smirking' as they pointed to the word 'dangerous' in a dictionary.[125] The officials said 'dangerous' had not been used by the Real Estate Institute. Technically, that was correct. What the Institute had said was: '... burglars are raiding the homes of people who are selling their house by open inspection.'[126] They had also expressed annoyance that the South Australian Police had recommended that sellers should not have their homes open for public inspection.[127] But the word 'dangerous' was not mentioned by the institute.

'It felt like a persecution movie,' said Ron. When he insisted on knowing who made the complaint, the officials reluctantly admitted that it was 'other agents in town'.[128] Ron was outraged that he was being investigated at 'the request of his competitors'. He spoke with his solicitor. And then he wrote to the Office of Consumer Affairs telling them that their attempts to 'suppress information which was clearly in the interests of consumers and to do so at the request of my competitors' was, in itself, a breach of the law. He challenged the Office of Consumer Affairs to 'commence proceedings' against him. He believed he would receive 'a much better chance of a fair hearing' from a magistrate. The investigation ceased.[129]

Another incident in Stirling involved an elderly lady, a retired school principal who chose an agent she had known for years – someone she considered 'a family friend'. Her home was reputedly worth 'at least $300,000'. It sold quickly for $220,000. The agent, who normally charged two and a half per cent commission (and often charged two per cent) had a different rate for the elderly lady – four per cent.[130] There was no complaint lodged, probably because, like thousands of elderly sellers, the lady did not realise she had been cheated.

In most states, agents can charge whatever they like. And many charge the most they can get away with. One real estate trainer writes to agents with headings on his letters saying, 'Fed Up with Low Commissions – Get Up to 6%'.[131]

If the governments can enact legislation allowing agents to charge whatever they like, surely they can enact legislation to protect consumers from crooked agents who charge too much and deliver too little. The real estate industry is a dangerous place for consumers.

William and Christine Brewer migrated to Australia from England after World War II. Before they sold their home in the Sydney suburb of Gymea, they attended this author's consumer information seminar, 'The Inside Secrets of Real

Estate'. Mrs Brewer said, 'I felt safer running the gauntlet of aerial bombing in World War II when I was a child than I do when in the company of real estate agents.'[132] If a real estate agent had made a similar statement, the agent could face persecution from an industry that denies the harm it causes to consumers. The network of cover-up in real estate is like an octopus with its tentacles around the entire industry. Anyone who speaks out gets squeezed.

Denial

When the then South Australian Attorney-General, Trevor Griffin, was asked about dummy bidding he reportedly said he did not believe it was a problem, but he would consult with the institute about it.[133] The institutes, which support vendor bidding, say it is not a problem. And so the deceit continues.

When $50,000 worth of jewellery was stolen during an open inspection in Melbourne, the agent was held liable.[134] However, at a Real Estate Institute meeting, the main concern was to stop the story from spreading to consumers.[135]

Real estate issues that harm consumers are rarely mentioned. Those which do receive publicity soon fade away. The industry is skilled at getting the spotlight off itself by issuing denials or giving complex explanations. In December 2001, the television program, *A Current Affair*, aired a story on advertising kickbacks.[136] It explained how agents profit from the losses of sellers and how real estate institutes train agents to make these profits. The Real Estate Institute of Australia refused to comment. This was an issue too dangerous to debate. Christmas was coming and, if left alone, perhaps it might fade away. But behind the scenes, the industry was nervous.[137]

The L.J. Hooker network sent an 'urgent' and 'important' message to its agents saying it did not want to be 'caught'. However, before it issued a reply it needed to be 'sure of its facts' and wanted to know who exactly was receiving 'monetary kickbacks' from newspapers.[138] In an astonishing written admission, the message said, 'It is our firm belief this practice ceased for L.J. Hooker agents around 1996.' The message mentioned the difference between 'monetary kickbacks' and 'bulk discounts'. But to homesellers, whether the agent receives a kickback or a bulk discount, the effect is the same. The agents profit from the sellers' losses. The tricks are still there, but with a new name – 'bulk discounts' instead of 'kickbacks'.

Like most networks, L.J. Hooker imposes a condition on its agents – no advertisement can appear without the network logo.[139] The biggest feature of most advertisements is the name of the agency. The sellers pay to advertise real estate offices. The L.J. Hooker office at Mona Vale in Sydney's northern beaches is renowned in the industry for the huge amounts of advertising money collected from sellers. But, in 2000, the franchisee of the agency admitted that the buyers for all but one home sold in one area had been known to the agency before the agency started advertising at the expense of the sellers.[140]

But agents have an excuse for taking advertising money from sellers when they already have a buyer for a home: 'We might get another buyer who pays more.' The fact that this money is totally wasted is of little concern to the agents. Most people in the industry know what's going on, but those who want to help consumers – including those within government departments – are a tiny minority alongside the vast majority who profit from the harm done to consumers.

In Western Australia, warnings about finance brokers were ignored for years while consumers were losing millions of dollars. It took a Royal Commission in 2001[141] to reveal the deceit and cover-ups. The commission was told that a government official had been taken off an investigation because he 'upset too many real estate agents'.[142]

Whistleblowing

Queensland lawyer and consumer advocate Tim O'Dwyer wages a crusade to clean up the real estate industry. In a two-year period he lodged 354 written complaints with the Department of Fair Trading about the conduct of agents.[143] He has appeared several times on state and national television. He calls radio stations and journalists constantly. He pays for 'protest ads' in local papers (which get censored, like a soldier's letters from a war zone, if they are too critical of agents who advertise in the papers).[144] He writes letters to editors. Faxes and emails pour from his computer to anyone he feels will listen.

O'Dwyer's critics call him obsessed. This might be true. They also accuse him of trying to drum up business for his law firm. This is not true. Like most crusaders, he could earn more money if he remained silent. He might be a 'troublemaker', but his attacks are aimed at anyone who hurts, or fails to protect consumers. As the novelist, Graham Greene, once described a troublesome character, 'I never knew a man who had better motives for all the trouble he caused.'[145]

In 2001, O'Dwyer himself became the subject of a complaint. The Queensland Commissioner for Fair Trading, Matt Miller, wrote to the Queensland Law Society complaining that O'Dwyer was making too many complaints.[146] One of Miller's concerns was that it was not consumers – the clients of O'Dwyer – who were making most of the complaints, but O'Dwyer. However, this is the point government officials often miss – many consumers don't realise they have been ripped off, that's why they don't complain.

O'Dwyer might be a thorn in the side of the government departments. He might insult them (on hearing the Commissioner for Fair Trading on radio, O'Dwyer once quipped, 'Does the Real Estate Institute write his script?').[147] He might go 'over the top' at times. He might be unpopular with agents. But for a commissioner of fair trading to accuse *him* of misconduct and for politicians to describe him in parliament as someone 'seeking to push his own barrow and line his own pocket through shallowly disguised campaigns'[148], is enough to discourage others from coming forward to protect consumers.

Shallow is not a word to describe Tim O'Dwyer. Outspoken, erratic, dogmatic or 'notorious troublemaker', perhaps. But not shallow. He has the frightening ability to strip back quickly shallow layers of hypocrisy in the business and political world. It is O'Dwyer who has felt the effect of what Oscar Wilde called 'the supreme vice of shallowness'.[149]

In his book, *Whistleblowers,* Quentin Dempster writes, 'It is the individual who suffers the most – from not being believed or trusted, from a shattering of self-esteem, from harassment, from intimidation, from being publicly discredited or abused.' To speak out about unethical conduct is fraught with personal risk, not reward. Dempster refers to the 'devastating personal consequences' of people who 'blow the whistle on corporate authority'. He believes that 'without the courage of the whistleblowers we would not be informed about what really goes on in our sometimes very uncivilised society.'[150]

> To speak out about unethical conduct is fraught with personal risk, not reward

The consequences of speaking out in the real estate industry can be severe. This author has been abused in person by agents, had hate mail from agents, had his signature forged on bogus training material which was then leaked to the media, had advertisements banned from newspapers and been physically threatened both directly and indirectly. As far back as 1995, the training officer of the Century 21 network in Australia said, 'What Jenman needs is an assassination.'[151]

And then there are the legal letters with the defamation threats, such as one from (King Con) Quinlivan's solicitors, Quinn & Box, writing on behalf of Stamford Lyon, the real estate agency ripping off consumers in investment scams. The lawyers said that assertions about their client amounted to 'criminal defamation'. But can it be a crime to speak about crime?[152]

The letter said that if their client 'became aware of any further attempt by you to cast any assertions [sic] upon our client's business activities whatsoever, that are derogatory in nature, our client will have no hesitation to immediately commence proceedings against you without further notice.

We advise that the proceedings will consist of injunctive relief restraining you from engaging in any such conduct, together with an action for damages, to recover any loss and damage sustained to our client, as a result of any such conduct engaged in by you.'[153]

This letter demanded a 'retraction' within seven days. No retraction was given. Instead, it was read out to consumers at a series of seminars called 'The Inside Secrets of Real Estate'.[154]

By speaking out about the activities of a company responsible for ripping off consumers, the company 'suffers a loss'. This is because the company can no longer profit from the losses of consumers who are warned about the company.

Wise people, who have nothing to do with property, are asking potent questions and making strong statements

Readers of this book are warned: don't sign anything with Stamford Lyon or any company owned by Dudley James Quinlivan. Or a man called Andrew Adolf Tamandl who, at the time of writing, is a director of Stamford Lyon. Always get independent legal advice first – not from one of the agent's 'recommended' lawyers, but from your own lawyer. And make sure you get the right lawyer.

HOPE FOR THE FUTURE

The real estate propaganda machine is struggling to justify its methods. Too many people of intelligence, influence and compassion are starting to look closely at the industry. And they are seeing what the Irish statesman Edmund Burke described as one of the greatest threats to a society: the inability of people to 'place moral chains upon their own appetites'.[155]

The real estate industry can no longer keep deceiving people on such a massive scale and expect to get away with it. Many people in government departments do care. They are appalled at what goes on in real estate. Journalists, too, especially those with more editorial freedom than many property journalists, are beginning to understand how badly consumers are being hurt. Wise people, who have nothing to do with property, are asking potent questions and making strong statements. The evidence of widespread deceit is so compelling that even the most defiant deniers have little defence left.

The best investigators are those who discover and uncover danger to consumers, not those who cover it up or say they have not had complaints

Almost 200 years ago the poet George Crabbe wrote, 'Deceivers are the most dangerous members of society. They trifle with the best affections of our nature and violate the most sacred obligations.'[156] Deceit in real estate causes consumers to collectively lose millions of dollars when they sell or buy their home. As the journalist Paul Sheehan said about real estate deceit, 'When deceit costs people money it is fraud.'[157]

Many states are reviewing their real estate laws. All it will take is a few courageous government officials to stand up to the real estate industry and its powerful connections, and to push for real protection for consumers. It will only need one state to set the example. Perhaps it will be Tasmania where Roy Ormerod, the Director of Consumer Affairs and Fair Trading, is keen to use the review of real estate legislation to 'tighten up the laws'.[158]

Good law-makers do not wait for the damage to consumers to surface. They seek to discover where consumers are in danger and to protect them from being hurt. The best investigators are those who discover and uncover danger to consumers, not those who cover it up or say they have not had complaints. There was a time when only a few people complained about cigarettes. Even when people began dying, little was done. Laws are usually passed after the damage is done, when everyone knows that people are in danger. In real estate, anyone who buys and sells a home is in danger of being ripped off. Today's real estate laws are woefully inadequate to protect consumers.

Most people who buy and sell real estate are not rich. They are not featured in social columns trading in million-dollar mansions. They are decent people from the 'mortgage belts' of cities and towns. Naïve young couples buying their first home, migrants trying to build a better life, mums and dads raising families, elderly folk who have made a major contribution to society. They deserve safety. They deserve a government that protects them. They do not deserve the real estate industry that exists today.

Today's real estate laws are woefully inadequate to protect consumers

You have rights as a consumer. Although these rights might be missing from real estate, it does not mean they have to be missing when you buy or sell real estate. The next chapter shows you how to claim your real estate rights. It shows you how to protect yourself.

Don't sign anything until you read it.

Summary

- It is hard to grasp the extent of the deception in real estate. An entire society has been fooled.

- Only blatantly illegal real estate crimes – such as trust account thefts – are usually punished.

- There is no fund to compensate thousands of sellers who collectively lose millions of dollars through flawed real estate systems and dishonest agents.

- Real estate is a multi-billion-dollar industry. Powerful forces of self-interest mean consumer rights are sacrificed for the sake of profit.

- Information that helps consumers is often suppressed. Instead, consumers are fed a barrage of misleading information which causes them to lose tens of millions of dollars annually.

- Real estate institutes protect the interests of agents at the expense of consumers, many of whom never realise how badly they are being hurt.

- Legislators spend more time speaking with institute representatives than with consumer representatives.

- If real estate institutes and networks used honest methods, they would offer a genuine and meaningful guarantee. There are few guarantees in real estate.

- If deceit in real estate were isolated, it would be easier to prevent. The reason it is so hard to stop is because it is everywhere.

- Kickbacks add tens of millions of dollars to the costs of buying or selling a home.

- What goes on in real estate is probably the greatest hidden consumer scandal in Australia and New Zealand. There should be an independent inquiry into the entire real estate industry.

- You can help by writing to your local member of parliament requesting an inquiry into the real estate industry. In the meantime, spread the safety message: **Don't Sign Anything.**

Chapter Twelve

Safety in Real Estate

How to get the guarantees you need

We've fabricated a society of wolves and coyotes.
Why does anybody think that we are better than
we were in robber baron days?

Louis Auchincloss

Back in the days when doctors made house calls and pizza companies didn't, things were different. In those days, business was often done on a handshake. Consumers were more trusting. And more business people were worth trusting. There was a spirit in our society which accepted that 'your word was your bond'. Today the spoken word means little. Instead, what counts is the written word. It doesn't seem to matter what you were told, what matters is what you signed.

In the absence of adequate consumer protection, in the midst of a flood of false information and surrounded by agents with self-interest as their main motive, your best protection as a consumer is: don't sign anything unless you are guaranteed that you are safe.

Signing Legal Contracts to Sell or Buy

No matter what an agent tells you, no matter how excited you feel, don't sign anything until you get quality independent legal advice. Four words – Quality Independent Legal Advice – with the emphasis on *quality* and *independent*. Independent means a lawyer chosen by *you*, not the agent. Do not become another victim of the real estate gravy train by using a lawyer recommended by the agent. If you could hear what goes on behind the scenes, you'd realise the importance of this advice. 'There's another wood duck on the way,' says the agent to that 'independent' lawyer.

Choose your own lawyer, one whose job is to protect only you. If you are buying a property in another state and you are told you need a local lawyer, don't sign anything until you speak with your own lawyer. Many people in business, and especially in real estate, are evil. Evil is very seductive. Don't be seduced.

The First Real Estate 'Contract'

Before a home is sold, the sellers have to sign a contract with the agent who handles the sale of their home. This contract, which, as you know, is called a 'Selling Agreement', is the starting point of almost all real estate deceit. If the deceit is stopped at this point, then, like a dam that holds back water, the deceit will be prevented from flowing on to the entire selling process.

That sounds really good. Do you guarantee what you are promising?

Don't be frightened to ask agents to honour their words. When an agent makes one of those glowing promises, just say, 'That sounds really good. Do you guarantee what you are promising?' Honest agents will answer, 'Of course.' Dishonest agents will give you excuses. They will say it is 'not possible to guarantee everything'. They will say you do not 'need' a guarantee, or 'this is the way it is done'. Don't fall for it. Don't sign anything unless the agent's promises are in writing and the agent gives you a guarantee that your basic rights will be protected.

Your Basic Rights

The four most basic consumer rights are safety, information, competition and redress.

1. Safety

In real estate consumers do not get safety. There is more safety at a supermarket than a real estate agency.

2. Information

British management consultant Philip Holden says, 'For a business transaction to be ethical the consumer must have sufficient information about the product, its potential costs and benefits and how it compares with the competition.'[1] Alex Bruce is a solicitor with the ACCC and a lecturer in law at The Australian National University. He says, 'Consumers need accurate and complete information about goods or services.'[2] He also says that 'market distortions can occur when producers limit the information consumers need to make their purchasing decisions'.[3] This is what happens in real estate. Consumers are given a barrage of false information that causes them to make decisions that cost them dearly.

3. Competition

There is a deliberate attempt to stifle competition in real estate. As already mentioned, this book will probably be banned from being advertised in many newspapers. The information you need to make a *well-informed* decision is hidden from you.

4. Redress

There is one unanswered question in real estate circles: if agents claim their systems are the best, if institutes claim their members are so ethical, why don't they offer a guarantee?

Don't sign anything until you are guaranteed that these four basic rights – safety, information, competition and redress – are available to you.

The Myth of 'Standard' Contracts

No matter what you are told, there is no such thing as a 'standard contract'. You can add conditions to a contract or you can remove conditions. You can adjust a contract to suit you or, more importantly, to protect you. If an agent won't agree to your conditions, don't sign anything.

Once sellers sign up to sell their homes, the agents have what they call a 'controlled listing', and the sellers lose control of their most valuable asset. These selling agreements – which agents call 'standard' – are designed by agents, or their representatives – the real estate institutes. They protect agents. They don't protect you.

No matter what the agent tells you, once you sign up to sell your home, the written words take over from the spoken words. Once you sign their 'standard' agreement, you're locked in. If you get a lower price than you were quoted, too bad. If the agent puts you under pressure, too bad. If you don't like how the agent treats you, too bad. You can't control what happens because you are locked in to what was written in that standard agreement which is a legal contract.

When you sign up with an agent, you give the agent the keys to your home. Most people do not give their best friends the keys to their home. The least you can do is make sure you have control over the agent, not the other way around. You do this by making sure that any agreement you sign is based on your standards, not the agent's standards. If not, don't sign anything.

YOU EMPLOY AN AGENT

As a home-owner, you *employ* an agent to sell your home. The relationship should be the same as an employer and an employee. You are the boss; you set the 'conditions' of employment, not the agent. If the agent won't accept your conditions, hire another agent. You must have control. As the employer, you instruct the agent in your requirements. The agent must follow your instructions.

Your three major requirements are these: first, the best

market price for your home; second, protection from the typical tricks and traps of real estate; and third, the right to dismiss the agent if the agent is dishonest or incompetent. These requirements must be non-negotiable. If the agent will not guarantee to give them to you, don't sign anything.

YOUR 16 SAFETY REQUIREMENTS

Here are the sixteen points which will give you control of the sale of your home and protect you – financially and emotionally – from the typical tricks and traps of real estate.

1. A Cooling-off Period

Insist on a cooling-off period of at least two business days after you sign the selling agreement. Say, 'I want the right to change my mind with no obligation within two days.' If you wish, you can make it longer. The period should be enough time for you to feel comfortable with your decision.

Don't sign anything unless you are given a cooling-off period.

2. Period of Agreement

The maximum time for a selling agreement should be seven weeks. If your home is not sold in this time, you control what happens next. You can re-employ the agent or you can hire another agent. It's up to you, not the agent. A short-term agreement gives *you* control.

The maximum time for a selling agreement should be seven weeks

Don't sign anything that locks you up with the agent for more than seven weeks.

3. Estimated Selling Price

You do not want to be caught by the Quote Lie. You need a guarantee that if the agent sells your home below the lowest price you are quoted, you will not have to pay any commission. Ask the agent, 'What is the lowest price you feel my home will sell for?' This is the opposite to what most sellers ask. Insist that the agent gives you this lowest figure. And then say to the agent, 'Will you accept no commission if my home sells for less than this price?' If the agent refuses to agree, this tells you that the agent has been lying to you to entice you to sign the selling agreement; or the agent is incompetent.

This condition is one of the best tests of the honesty of agents. Crooked agents will give you all sorts of excuses. Don't accept any of them. House painters have to stand by their quotes. So should real estate agents. Agents may say they 'do not know what the market' will do. This is nonsense. Agents know the likely selling price of your home. If they don't, they are incompetent. Sure, they may not know an exact price, but they can give you a range within about 10 per cent of their quoted price. For example, an agent may quote a homeseller a selling range between, say, $500,000 and $550,000. If the home sells below $500,000, the agent should not get paid.

A quote guarantee is fair to you as the seller – and that's what matters most.

Don't sign anything unless the agent gives you a guarantee on the quoted selling price.

4. Bait Pricing

Make sure the agent never offers your home to buyers at a price lower than you will accept. Do not fall for the trick that a lower price attracts more buyers. It attracts buyers at a lower price and lowers the value of your home. To sell your home for the best market price, you need a buyer who can afford the best market price. It's fairly simple. Do not fall for the bait pricing trap.

Don't sign anything unless the agent guarantees never to use bait prices to attract buyers.

5. Conditioning

Should you find yourself the victim of conditioning, you must have the right to immediately dismiss the agent. The classic symptom of conditioning is when the agent praises your home before you sign up and then, as soon as you sign, the agent focuses on the faults of your home. Thousands of sellers are the victims of real estate conditioning. It's part of the typical real estate sales process. The Real Estate Institute of New South Wales even had a course called, 'How to Condition Sellers'.[4]

Don't sign anything unless the agent guarantees you will not be conditioned.

6. Final Selling Price

A competent agent will discover the buyers' highest price and obtain a declaration that this price is the highest they will pay. If the agent does not obtain a declaration from the buyers and you later discover that the buyers were willing to pay more than the price at which you sold, the agent must agree to charge you no commission. If the agent says this is harsh, consider how harsh it is for thousands of sellers who have their homes undersold by dishonest or incompetent agents. Good agents will gladly guarantee that they have made every effort to ensure that the final selling price is the best market price.

Also, if another buyer (whom the agent knew about) later proves that your home was sold without this buyer being given a chance to make an offer, and he or she would have paid more than was paid by the buyer who bought the home, you should not pay the agent. Before the agent urges you to sell to any buyer, the agent must make sure there is not another buyer willing to pay more. This condition makes the agents very careful. A loss to you means a loss to them.

Don't sign anything unless the agent guarantees that the selling price is the best market price.

7. Cancelling the Agent's Agreement

Make sure you can dismiss the agent, at any time, if the agent does anything unethical. If the agent applies pressure to you, if the agent tells buyers that you may accept a low price, you should have the right to dismiss the agent. For example, let's say you decide to mystery shop the agent while your home is for sale. If you are asking $500,000 and the agent says, 'They want too much for this home, it's not really worth it', you do not want to be stuck with such an agent. You need a fair right of dismissal.

Don't sign anything unless you have a guarantee that you can dismiss the agent if the agent does anything unethical, dishonest or illegal.

8. Marketing or Advertising

Advertising can turn your home into a lemon. Your home should only be brought to the attention of buyers who can buy it. There is a big difference between lots of buyers and the right buyer. As most buyers spend many weeks looking for a home, the agent should have the marketing skill to attract the right buyer to your home. A competent agent keeps accurate records of buyers and knows how to find the right buyer without damaging the value of your home.

If the agent uses any marketing or advertising method which damages the value of your home, you should have the right to immediately dismiss the agent.

Don't sign anything unless the agent guarantees to protect the value of your home.

9. Fees and Costs

You must only pay the agent when you are satisfied that your home has sold for the best market price. No excuses, no exceptions. You pay at the end, when the job is done, not before. The reason many agents want you to pay money in advance is because they know – once you realise what they are really like – that you will not want to pay them. Do not pay, or agree to pay, any fees or costs, for any reason, until your home is sold.

Don't sign anything unless the agent guarantees that you pay nothing until your home is sold and you are satisfied.

10. Confidentiality

Many agents betray the confidence and trust of sellers. If you catch the agent revealing your personal details to buyers, you must have the right to dismiss the agent. For example, the agent may tell buyers that you have bought another home which infers that you are desperate. Many investors search for desperate sellers because desperate sellers often mean lower prices. If your agent betrays your confidence you must have the right to dismiss the agent.

Don't sign anything unless the agent guarantees to protect your personal details.

11. Insider Trading

If the buyer of your home is the agent or a close relative or associate of the agent, you should not pay any commission. Insider trading in real estate is more common than most people suspect.

Russell and Marilyn Wilde are one of many victims. They sold their home with PRD Realty at Narangba on Queensland's Sunshine Coast. The buyer was Julie-Anne Hills, the daughter of Phillip Hills, the owner of the real estate office. The home, which was worth close to $250,000, was sold for $194,550. Five years later, Russell and Marilyn were awarded compensation of $53,625 by a court.[5] Most victims cannot afford a legal battle. Some never know what happened.

Many agents sell properties to investors or developers and the agents then handle the resale of the property when it is developed. This gives agents the incentive to get the property at a cheap price for the developer. If your agent has had past dealings with the buyer for your home, or if the agent intends to get a future benefit from the development of your property, the agent should make sure you clearly understand what is happening. If not, the agent should forfeit the right to a commission.

Don't sign anything unless you are protected against insider trading.

12. Security at Inspections

If your home is robbed as a result of an inspection, the agent should accept responsibility if the agent has not taken every care to protect your home. Many agents will say they have 'never had a problem'. If this is true, they should not mind giving you a guarantee that they will accept responsibility. By insisting that the agent is responsible for any loss or damage to your home, the agent will be careful.

Don't sign anything unless the agent guarantees to protect your home from bogus inspections.

13. Rebates or Kickbacks

The simple way to protect yourself from having an agent pocket extra money from kickbacks or rebates is to make it a condition that any kickbacks are paid back to you. Honest business people do not accept kickbacks and they never use the legal excuse by saying kickbacks are 'disclosed' or that they are referral fees or rebates or discounts. You should be the beneficiary of any discounts.

Don't sign anything unless the agent guarantees to pass any kickback money to you.

14. Other Agents

The agent you choose should be the only agent to handle the sale of your home. If another agent becomes involved, this agent must also be bound by the conditions placed on the first agent.

Don't sign anything unless the agent guarantees that any other agent will also be bound by the same guarantee.

15. Buyers Found by You

If you sell your home to one of your relatives or close friends at a price which makes you happy, you should not be forced to pay the agent. You need a condition that you do not have to pay the agent or that you can elect to pay the agent whatever you feel is fair in return for the agent's efforts. However, a good agent who knows how to negotiate will be able to protect your interests if he or she acts for you in a sale to someone you know. But, the choice should be yours as to whether or not you still wish to engage the agent in such circumstances.

Don't sign anything unless the agent guarantees not to charge you if you sell your home to a relative or close friend and you do not wish to use the agent's services or pay the agent for any services rendered.

16. Withdrawing from Sale

If your circumstances change and you decide not to sell, then you should be able to withdraw your home from sale with no charge or obligation from the agent.

Don't sign anything unless the agent guarantees that you will be under no obligation should you decide not to sell your home.

And, finally, always get independent quality legal advice before you sign anything at all. No exceptions.

Summing Up the 16 Safety Points

What you have just read is an almost perfect way to protect yourself from the most common tricks and traps of selling real estate. How do you convert all this information into something which controls the agent? You can prepare your own list of conditions and make sure the agent signs your conditions before you sign anything with the agent. Remember, any contract can be changed to suit your needs (provided it contains the prescribed requirements set out by legislation in your state). Do not let any agent bluff you. You are dealing with the sale of your most important financial asset. You cannot have too much protection. If you wish you can use a guarantee which is already available to any homeseller at no charge. (See Appendix.) You can then attach the guarantee to the agent's agreement.

THE REAL ESTATE CONSUMER PROTECTION GUARANTEE FOR HOMESELLERS

In 2001, a guarantee to protect homesellers was prepared by this author in conjunction with legal experts and consumer advocates. It was made available to all sellers at no charge and with no obligation. The message was simple: don't sign anything until the agent first signs this guarantee which becomes an attachment to the agent's agreement. This is a *non-negotiable* condition of the agent's employment.

Homesellers loved it. Here at last, in a simple document, was the protection they needed. The guarantee forced agents

A 'lie detector test' for agents...

to keep their promises. It was described as 'a lie detector test' for agents. Sellers said to agents, 'I will not sign with you until you sign with me.' Naturally, many agents did not like it. It robbed them of the one thing they value most – their ability to control the sellers. In one television program an angry agent was seen tearing it up.[6]

The opposition to the guarantee from the real estate industry was fierce. Agents who supported it were abused by other agents. Sam Pennisi, a real estate agent from Essendon in Victoria, appeared on television supporting the guarantee. He was a member of the First National network, but many members did not want their network associated with the guarantee. Sam who, as mentioned earlier, was a past chairman of First National, was stunned at the reaction. 'This is great for consumers,' he said. 'I can't understand why any agents could possibly object to it if they are doing the right thing by their customers.'[7]

And there, in a few words, is the reason so many agents do not want to give guarantees to consumers – they are not 'doing the right thing'.

One journalist said that 'few agents would sign it' because consumers could take advantage of agents.[8] But agents have been taking advantage of consumers for years. The risk was now reversed. Instead of the sellers having to trust the agents, the agents now had to trust the sellers. One seller chuckled as he recalled saying to an agent, 'It looks like you're going to have to trust me, doesn't it?'[9] The agent signed the guarantee.

Be warned. Many agents will give you excuses why they should not sign a guarantee. However, as long as you remember this – don't sign anything unless the agent first signs a guarantee with you, then you will be safe. You will have control when you say, 'If you want to be the agent to sell my home, then before I sign anything, you have to sign a guarantee for me.'

Excuses

Like the tobacco institutes that denied the harm caused by smoking, the real estate institutes deny the harm caused by agents. Real Estate Institute of Victoria spokesperson Enzo Raimondo gave several reasons why sellers do not need the Real Estate Consumer Protection Guarantee. He said, 'The guarantee is a marketing gimmick.'[10] If the guarantee was only available from one group of agents or from one network, this might be true. However, sellers can use the guarantee with any agent. There is no obligation to choose a certain brand of agent.

He stated that the guarantee was not designed by qualified estate agents.[11] Exactly. Just as the Real Estate Institute Selling Agreements are designed by agents to protect agents, the Consumer Protection Guarantee is designed by consumers to protect consumers. If you are a consumer, use it.

He said, 'The guarantee merely restates existing legislation.'[12] As many agents routinely breach current laws, this is all the more reason agents should guarantee that they will follow the laws. Sure, there is 'existing legislation' but this is cold comfort for consumers who did not have a consumer guarantee clearly restating some of this legislation and who then face the monumental task of having to fight agents in court.

He said, 'The guarantee may generate a feeling of mistrust

between the agent and the homeseller.'[13] Mistrust? In any business, offering a guarantee leads to more trust. Consumers do not trust companies that do not offer guarantees. Most consumers do not trust agents.

The Real Estate Institute also said, 'Why would agents sign so-called 'guarantees' when they are obliged to act in accordance with such guarantees by the law in any event?'[14] One agent responded by asking: 'Why would agents *not* sign?'[15] That's an easy question. The only reason some agents will not sign a guarantee to protect consumers is because the agents have no intention of protecting consumers. This failure to protect consumers breaks one of the fundamental rules of ethical business conduct.

The first principle of ethical conduct is 'do no harm'

The first principle of ethical conduct is 'do no harm'. To refuse to obey this principle and to attempt to thwart a guarantee which protects consumers falls into the worst realms of unethical conduct.

If an agent will not offer you a guarantee that you will be protected and that you will get the best market price for your home, don't sign anything. Find an agent who will give you a guarantee. Or sell your home yourself.

Good Agents

Good agents and bad agents can seem similar. Both may appear honest, both may seem competent and both may be persuasive. It is not until after you sign with an agent that the quality of the agent is apparent. If you have chosen a bad agent, it's too late. You are stuck. This is why, no matter how honest and competent any agent appears, don't sign anything unless you are given a guarantee.

With good agents you rarely have to ask for a guarantee. They offer it as part of their service. When they give you a quote on your selling price, they guarantee it. They make it clear that you will not have to pay any commission until your home is sold and you are satisfied.

Good agents do not use clichés about 'the market', they do not talk about 'exposure'. They talk about what you want and they show you how to get it with safety and efficiency. They place your interests first. The only sure way to know if an agent is honest and competent is if the agent is prepared to guarantee that the service you are being promised is the service you will receive. If this agent does not offer you a strong guarantee, don't sign anything.

Control

One of the hardest things for many sellers to do is to stand up for themselves. Agents can be so persuasive that, before you know it, you can find yourself being drawn in to what they are saying. As one seller said, 'I could feel the agent pushing all my buttons. Although I was determined not to make a decision, I found myself losing control. When the agent suggested I might get a price above what I was expecting, I said to myself, "Maybe he's right." I didn't like him, but his words were so tempting.'[16] Some agents will even make you feel guilty if you question their word. But, if you don't, the next thing you know you will have signed the agent's 'standard' agreement. And you will be caught. It's called being 'stitched up'.

With good agents you rarely have to ask for a guarantee. They offer it as part of their service

You must not let the agents 'push your buttons'. You must keep telling yourself that the only way you can be safe is with a guarantee. You must keep control. Don't sign anything unless you get a guarantee. Do not think, 'This agent is different,' or that you are too clever to be caught. Professional people are deceived just as easily as anyone – often more easily. These people do not expect to be ripped off. In their professional lives, their clients trust them because they deserve to be trusted. They expect that real estate agents, also being professional people, are similar. Big mistake.

When veterinary surgeon Dr Sue Briggs sold her home in Adelaide she thought she was safe. Big name agent, member of the Real Estate Institute, plus the salesperson was a client of hers.[17] It all looked good. A few weeks later it was a different story. Dr Briggs was crunched to sell below her written reserve price. Describing how she was caught, Dr Briggs said, 'At the time of the auction, I had clients in the waiting room and I was in the middle of a consultation when I received a phone call from the agent. I was told to "hurry up" as I was holding things up. The agent placed immense pressure on me to place my property "on the market" and my home was sold. Those agents cost me $80,000. I did not get a chance to have the law protect me because I couldn't afford it.'[18]

Following the sale, Dr Briggs could not believe 'this sort of thing can go on in Australia'. She is convinced that auctions, in their present form, should be 'outlawed or at least have a cooling-off period, so that other sellers do not have to go through what happened to me'.[19]

When a retired doctor, Gladys Watkins, sold her Melbourne home, the pressure to lower her price was so fast and so severe that she said she felt 'numb' (just as the Real Estate Institute of Australia's book describes the state of consumers, when teaching agents to 'move quickly' at auctions and not give them time to 'dwell on the price').[20] Immediately after the auction, having sold her home for far less than she was promised, the auctioneer left in a hurry. Like Dr Briggs, she could not believe that other 'professional people' could be so deceitful.

Kym Power is a successful business woman with 75 employees. When she signed with an agent to sell her home in Brisbane, she couldn't believe how easily she was caught. 'I know I am not stupid, although I now feel very dumb,' she said. Kym met an agent who 'pushed all her buttons' with the standard lines about the best way to sell. Later she said, 'I should have listened to my "little voice", but I just didn't know there was another way.'[21]

There *is* another way – your way, by your rules, not the agent's rules. All the financial and emotional pain felt by thousands of consumers could be avoided if they all did just one thing – refused to surrender control to agents. Real estate is safe when you have control. It is easy if you are prepared to do just *one* hard thing: keep control until your home is sold.

The advice of one determined consumer is almost perfect. 'State clearly what you expect and what you will not tolerate. We gave the agent four weeks to sell our home. He protested loudly, but I went into what I call "Mrs Bitch" mode (hubby lowered his head and retreated to poor little Mr Henpecked at this point). If the agent claims to be a good agent, tell him or her to prove it. From the moment you call an agent for an interview, you are in charge – they are working for you so choose somebody you would want to employ or work alongside.'

> **Real estate is safe when you have control**

This woman also checked up on the agent by sending friends to inspect her home with the agent. She discovered 'he was loyal and did not reveal our reason for selling, nor did he quote a lower price'. Her home was sold in four weeks for a great price.

When buying, she suggests the following, 'We made a list of *precisely* what we wanted and what we *absolutely* did not want. We presented this list to agents and said not even one item was slightly negotiable. The first three agents tried to show us the wrong properties. We left at once. But the fourth agent read each point, ticked them off and said he had just the place for us. And he did! Everybody was happy.'[22]

This is how it can be. If you insist on a written guarantee and get competent independent legal advice, it will be hard for any agent to harm you. You will have control.

And you will be safe.

OUR ETHICAL SPIRIT

Ethical behaviour is about caring for others. It is about compassion – feeling with others. It is about helping people when they need help, especially when they are vulnerable. Ethical behaviour means protecting people. It means not taking advantage of those who are in a weaker position. Look at how we protect each other from physical harm – bushfires are a fine example. Thousands of people volunteer to fight fires. They don't do it for money, they do it to help others. Their satisfaction, their sense of pride is greater than any pay cheque.

Whenever there is a physical threat such as fires, floods or even wars, we often risk our lives for each other. This is our ethical spirit. It goes all the way back to our Anzac spirit. But rarely does this ethical spirit exist in business. Thousands of home-owners are burnt by business greed. But there are no television images of burning homes. There are no insurance companies handing out cheques to the victims of dishonesty. A form of corporate arson has spread through our society burning thousands of victims. If we all knew what was going on, there would be a national outcry. We would rush to help. But we don't relate to corporate crimes the same way we relate to bush fires. And so the corporate arsonists continue to burn the financial security of thousands of people. All on the basis that it's business. This is not the true spirit of business no matter how it is justified. It is not ethical to make profits by hurting others. It is evil.

The economist Milton Friedman said that the most ethical thing a company can do is make a profit because it gives more money to shareholders.[23] This is a dangerous concept for society. Profit is essential but there must be limits on what companies can do to make profits. They can't be allowed to commit financial arson on society purely because it's legal.

Higher profits should not mean lower ethics. Agents should not take advantage of people who, through lack of knowledge or experience, are in a weak position. Not only is this behaviour unethical, it is cowardly. It does enormous damage to our society. Years ago, the missionary surgeon Dr Albert Schweitzer put it this way: 'Ethics is the name we give to our concern for good behaviour. We feel an obligation to consider not only our own personal wellbeing, but also that of others and society as a whole.'[24]

The novelist Bertha Von Suttner believed that after the verb 'to love', the verb 'to help' was the most beautiful verb in the world.[25] Verbs are *doing* words. But few people in the business world are doing anything other than helping themselves. This does not lead to happiness. It is against the nature of our spirit. Greed kills happiness because it removes our ethical spirit.

The greatest happiness in our jobs, indeed our lives, comes from helping people, from acts of kindness which create meaningful and ethical profit – in dollar terms and happiness terms. Near the end of his life, the author of *Brave New World*, Aldous Huxley, said, 'It is a little embarrassing that after years of experience, study and research, all I can tell you is to be a little kinder to each other.'[26]

There are few greater sources of happiness than to see smiles and know you caused those smiles. 'Thank you' is a wonderful pay cheque. It may not always show on a financial balance sheet, but it shows on the balance sheet of happiness. And that's what drives us all – the desire for happiness. Happiness does not come from making profits by hurting others. It comes from helping others. It comes from having the right ethical spirit.

The battle for consumer protection and ethics in real estate needs the help of people with the spirit and the compassion to care about others. And that means most of us. If you feel this book will protect you from the tricks and traps of real estate, please tell others what you know. Let's put that great protective and caring spirit into everything we do.

General John Monash, who led the Australian troops in World War I, believed Australians had the greatest spirit of all. This spirit is part of our nature. We must not store it away, to be used only in times of physical danger. We need it in our entire lives – both business and personal. It is our human duty to protect others, to be true to our highest values. Or, to use the Australian expression, to be 'staunch'. We must not shirk from that duty no matter how much the business world tempts us with its justification of dishonest profit.

Each year at Anzac Dawn Services across Australia and New Zealand, thousands of people gather closely, like kindred spirits, all remembering the Anzac spirit; sharing the emotion of our national spirit. We love and admire the Anzacs because they were 'staunch to the end'.[27]

Today's business people could learn much from the three qualities that shaped the Anzac spirit: courage, comradeship and unselfishness. Imagine if this spirit was part of our entire society. What a wonderful society it would be. We wouldn't have to sign anything.

We could just shake hands.

Afterword

THE real estate industry is rotten to the core. However, such a statement is hard for many people to grasp. From the outside all appears well, but this is the nature of evil. It looks safe, it's inviting, it seduces you. But once you cut through its first layer, and if you know what you are looking for, you begin to see the rot. The more layers you cut through, the more rotten it becomes. When you are deep within the industry the rot is obvious. It's putrid. By then, if you are a consumer, it is often too late. You are caught and you can't escape.

In writing this book I have, many times, gone deep into the real estate industry. Like a miner with a light on his helmet I have shone that light on some of the darkest places in real estate. I have seen lovely families terribly and deliberately hurt. Most times, I have been alone, far away, at least mentally, from family and friends. What I have seen has affected me deeply. Several times the evidence has moved me to tears. At other times, I have felt a level of anger I didn't know I possessed. At one stage – while researching the investment scams – I became so gloomy my wife said my personality changed. She asked what had happened to her 'happy husband'. Another time, while interviewing one of the worst real estate crooks, I was making notes in my journal and my hands began trembling. I was seized by an urge to lean across his desk and grab him by the shirt front. Fortunately, my size stops me from becoming physically violent. On another occasion, shortly after discussing real estate scams at one of my consumer seminars, I developed a rash. The next day, lying in a motel in Coffs Harbour, I was covered in blotches. When I arrived home, my wife cried. Since then I have tried to become less emotionally involved. But it is not easy. So much of what I know has consumed me. I cannot understand how so many business people can do such things to consumers. And I am appalled at the apathy of so many supposedly 'good' real estate people; those who could do something about it but choose, instead, to do nothing – unless, of course, their interests are threatened or their integrity is questioned. And then you see them rage. Selfishness is such a vile quality.

I wondered who was ever going to believe me. I spent hours trying to find the right words to describe what was going on, to make you, the reader, understand the risks you face in real estate, to make the authorities take action. What, I asked myself, was my main purpose? That's easy. I want the real estate world to be safe. I want to be able to go home to my family and grow old knowing that people are safe when they buy or sell a home. Home is the second most emotive word in the English language (after the word 'mother'). Home-life is the fabric of our society, it is something to cherish. Anyone who threatens that fabric needs to be stopped.

Please help. Contact your local state and federal members of parliament. Write letters to the media. Contact the authorities, not just for your sake, but for every decent citizen who is at risk from such a rotten real estate industry. As already stated, the Irish statesman Edmund Burke said it perfectly, 'The only thing necessary for the triumph of evil is for good people to do nothing.' Do something, please. The more people who speak out, the more chance there is that something will be done. Real reform will come if enough people demand it.

Real Estate Reforms

As this book goes to press, the real estate industry is abuzz with talk of reform. In New South Wales and Victoria, new legislation is getting closer. The politicians are saying real estate will be cleaned up. 'The most sweeping changes in decades,' some say. But, at the dirty front line of real estate, these changes barely protect consumers. On the contrary, they are almost certain to cause even more harm to consumers who, thinking they are now protected, will discover, too late, that they were as vulnerable as ever. The current reforms have the footprints of the real estate industry all over them. It's like putting filters on cigarettes and saying smoking can't harm you. Today's real estate chiefs who deny the evils of real estate are like yesterday's tobacco chiefs who denied the evils of smoking.

In Queensland the government – and the Real Estate Institute – say their new state laws are the best in Australia. But one journalist described the Queensland laws as 'the best of the worst'. And that's right. The real estate crooks are now saying 'it's all safe'. One is reportedly showing consumers an old headline about property sharks and saying it has all stopped now. The current real estate reforms have not stopped, and will not stop, real estate deceit. It is still far too easy for the crooks to flourish. As you have read in this book, the real estate industry itself has played a huge part in drafting the new laws. If it wasn't so tragic it would be funny.

Real Estate Crooks

At my consumer seminars, I ask the audience a dramatic question, 'Do you know what a real estate crook looks like?' I take it slowly, pausing for effect so they remember what I am about to say. And then I point to myself and say, 'A real estate crook looks like me.' Many wonder where this is going. I then say: 'Real estate crooks dress nicely and speak well. They say all the things they know you like to hear. They talk about caution and about doing the right thing. They have an abundance of facts to support their statements. It all makes sense. They win your trust, just as I have done. And then they strike. Yes, a real estate crook looks like Neil Jenman.' I pause again before I tell them the difference between someone who is going to help them and someone who is going to hurt them. 'A major difference,' I say, 'between me and a real estate crook is that I have a three-word slogan – "Don't sign anything" – and a crook has a two-word slogan – "Sign here".' It's basic but brilliant advice.

Here is a harsh statement: if, having read this book, you sign anything with any real estate person without first getting quality independent legal advice, you almost deserve to be ripped off. If that's the only way you are going to learn the most important point in real estate – don't sign anything – then, sadly, that's the price you will pay. Don't do that to yourself. Please. Most people do more research for their holiday plans than for their real estate plans. Perhaps the term 'bricks and mortar' sounds safe, but a mortar is also a cannon for firing destructive shells. Be very careful.

Real Estate Responsibility

Many corporate slogans could be replaced with four words, 'It's not our fault'. Blame and excuses abound in today's corporate world. The hypocrisy is amazing. That wonderful word 'responsibility' barely exists in real estate. But it should exist. Agents should be responsible for the claims they make. Real estate networks and institutes should be responsible for their slogans. Words should not be used as magnets to lure consumers; they should be vows of responsibility by which a company stands. The chiefs in the real estate industry should be responsible for the actions of their members. Most real estate consumers are making the biggest financial decision of their lives. They need to know, for sure, that they can trust the person with whom they deal. If something goes wrong, they need to know that someone will help them, not give them excuses or blame 'the market'.

When I had my real estate office, I made sellers a simple but powerful promise: If you are not happy, you can leave me and go to another agent; or, if we sell your home and you are not delighted you don't have to pay us. To buyers, I promised: If we mislead you and it costs you money, we will reimburse you that money. To landlords, I promised: If we fail to take care of your investment, we will refund lost rent to you. And to all our staff, I made this pledge: You will be paid a secure salary regardless of whether or not you make a sale. If you take care of our customers, the sales will come. These promises were unheard of in real estate. Many agents sneered and said I would go broke. But I didn't. My business thrived. Sure, I made mistakes but those mistakes cost me, they didn't cost my customers. Our real estate office was the most popular in our area. Each year, it was the number one office in its network.

Soon I was presenting seminars to agents all over Australia on how to create a more profitable real estate agency. But the more I travelled, the more appalled I became at the methods used by most agents. When I opposed their methods – on the basis that not only were they bad for consumers, but also bad for the agents' profits – I was ridiculed. Many times I was told I was 'commercially unrealistic'. And then, when I began to speak out publicly, many agents began to despise me. I was accused of 'commercial exploitation' or of 'dobbing' on my mates. It was said that I was making huge profits from seminars and agents who paid to use my methods.

Yes, my seminar business was profitable, but as my only income came from agents it didn't make good commercial sense to criticise agents. But it did make ethical sense. It made me feel better about what I was doing. I have lost thousands of agents – both as clients and potential clients – because of my comments on the real estate industry. Today, my profits are far lower than they could be. But financial profit is not the sole measure of success. Success, surely, is about feeling good about what you do.

My 'mates' are not agents who deceive consumers; they are not chiefs of the real estate industry who don't accept responsibility for their slick slogans. My 'mates' are consumers who sell or buy real estate. I have had far better treatment from consumers than from most agents. Yes, I still teach agents and yes, my income comes from agents. But I do not see agents as my clients. Rather, I see myself as a coach to agents showing them how to provide a service their competitors will not provide. Perhaps it is my background in real estate, but I still see my first duty as being responsible to the consumer. And this, I tell agents, should also be your duty. Accept responsibility for your methods and your actions. This will attract more sellers and buyers. And then you will make more profit than you ever imagined. You will also feel better. And that is the essence of what my work is about – take care of consumers first and profits will come later. It works.

These days, one of my biggest problems is agents pretending to be associated with me – agents who say they can 'do what Jenman does' or that they are 'Jenman agents' – and so lead consumers to believe they will be safe. Some of these agents are indeed associated with me, in as much as they have attended or do attend my courses. But then, later, when they meet consumers they only do selective parts of what is known as 'The Jenman System'. Usually, of course, the parts they select are the parts that benefit themselves, not consumers. For this reason, we have introduced an accreditation system called 'Jenman APPROVED'. What it means is this: *I will accept responsibility for the service you receive from an 'approved' agent,* just as I did when I owned my own real estate office.

To the chiefs in the real estate industry I say this: If your methods are as honest and ethical as you claim, if your slogans are genuine, why don't you do the same as me? Accept responsibility for the actions of your member agents. No excuses. The consumers want to know one thing – who can they trust? If it's you, then accept responsibility. It's really quite simple.

Responsibility. I love that word. I will accept responsibility for the service you receive from a Jenman APPROVED agent. I will put my home on the line to protect yours. Thank you for your trust.

And thank you for reading this book.

Neil Jenman

Acknowledgments

Without help, I would never have started, let alone finished this book. My wife, Reiden, has been wonderful. Not just in reading the manuscript dozens of times but for tolerating the days and nights when I have disappeared into my little 'writing room'. Writing, by necessity, is self-imposed solitary confinement. So thank you for buying our lovely dog that, with the patience that only a dog possesses, has kept me company during my 'confinement'. But thank you, most of all, for making our home a 'happy home'. My son, Lloyd, who wrote me the nicest father's day card is making me proud. You are a fine young man. Ruth and Haley, my beautiful daughters, even though you don't like my boring music, you always make me smile. And then Grace and Alec: on the night you were born my writing output dropped substantially. But what a trade-off. You're the stars of the new millennium in our family.

Although you never ask for it, thank you to Gary and Kerry Pittard, Gerald and Margaret Crough and Kerry and Suellen Rowley for your friendship and dedication. So, too, my dear friend Michael Johnston who, after the shattering loss of your (and our) beloved Lesley, showed me what it means to have the character to face both the beauty and the cruelty of life. Your leadership and courage astounds me. I'd follow you anywhere.

And to the team at our office, who rarely see me: thanks for keeping it all going and especially for your devotion to the consumers who contact us. You're better than I often give you credit for.

To the thousands of real estate agents I have spoken with at my courses over the past decade, thanks for coming along, whatever your reasons. To the few who have stuck with me – and believed that the high price of consumer protection on your own profits was a price worth paying – you have my admiration and respect. Soon you will have the admiration and respect of every real estate consumer. And that will lead to the most vital ingredient in any relationship – trust. Any agent who is prepared to place ethics before profits is an agent destined for magnificent profits, both personally and financially. But you know that. So I thank you for your courage and your loyalty to the people who matter most – the real estate consumers.

To all those who have willingly allowed me to tell their stories or to quote their words, thanks so much. Your good wishes have been a surprise and an inspiration. I hope you are pleased with the result. If I have missed anyone, I am sorry.

To those I have mentioned in this book in an unfavourable light, please don't spend your time attacking me with threats or law suits. It will just give me more material for another book. Instead, spend your time destroying methods that will one day destroy the current real estate industry – and your business or career if you use these methods. The word is spreading. Your future customers are getting wiser. People want ethical conduct. Give it to them. That's the secret to business success.

I was told not to trust journalists because on the scale of consumer trust, they ranked with real estate agents. This worried me. I expected to be derided, but it didn't happen. Since the publication of my first book, *Real Estate Mistakes,* I have spoken with hundreds of journalists. At first, many were sceptical, which I also expected (and even welcomed). But all I wanted was the chance to explain. They gave it to me in ways I never expected. Every journalist who read my book or heard me speak about ethics in real estate was more supportive than I ever dreamed. Maybe I am lucky or maybe the people who don't like journalists have something to hide. I don't know but journalism, I have learned, is ethically one of the toughest of all professions. Sure, they don't get it right all the time. But who does? And yes, there are bad ones; it's just that I haven't met them. Those I have met, I liked. Some of you had a profound effect on me. To any who are still sceptical, let me make you this offer. Investigate me. Ask me anything you like. And, once you have done that, do the same to the rest of the real estate industry. If you ask the right questions, it will surely lead to a full independent inquiry into the real estate industry.

It is easy to blame public servants for the ills of our society. I have been guilty of such prejudice. But there are people in government agencies who care deeply about consumers. Perhaps they are in the minority, but it is uplifting to meet them. They often battle bureaucracy and apathy along with corporate and political pressure. With budget constraints and poor staffing, they barely cope with the complaints they do receive, never mind scams which are yet to be realised or discovered. To those good ones – who are often unfairly criticised – if I have created the impression in this book that you are incompetent, I apologise. If you are doing the best you can with all that you have, as I know many of you are, thank you. Keep going, please.

The people I thank most for the creation of this book are the homesellers and homebuyers of Australia and New Zealand. Those who gave me the honour of helping you sell or buy a home during my years in real estate, thanks. I miss you. To the thousands of others who have read my books, attended my consumer seminars or contacted me, I can barely believe how supportive you have been. As I write these words, I have just finished presenting the seminar, 'The Inside Secrets of Real Estate', to more than a thousand of you. As I walked out to speak with you, you paid me more than any commission cheque I ever received. You smiled. You have not just changed my life, you have made it.

Thank you.

APPENDIX I
Organisations & Addresses

To locate a Jenman APPROVED agency,
call toll-free 1800 1800 18 or visit www.jenman.com.au

To contact the author, write to:

Neil Jenman
c/- Rowley Publications
25/7 Anella Avenue
Castle Hill NSW
2154 Australia

Or email neil@jenman.com.au

If you have a real estate story to tell or a question to ask,
please email it to comment@jenman.com.au

We will be pleased to hear from you.

IMPORTANT MESSAGE

Please help all citizens. Please speak out about the lack of ethics in real estate.

Contact radio and television stations.
Write or email to 'Letters to the Editor' at newspapers.
Write to politicians, including your member of parliament.

By speaking out, you will help to create laws to benefit every real estate consumer.

Your voice will count.
You can make a difference.

Thank you.

To find an Independent Valuer, contact
The Australian Property Institute

WARNING: Do NOT take any notice of valuations shown to you by anyone associated with an investment that you are considering. **Don't sign anything until you get an independent valuation.**

Australian Property Institute

API NATIONAL SECRETARIAT 6 Campion Street **DEAKIN, ACT. 2600.** Tel: (02) 6282 2411 Fax: (02) 6285 2194 Email: national@propertyinstitute.com.au	**API - ACT Division** 6 Campion Street, **DEAKIN, ACT. 2600.** Tel: (02) 6282 5541 Fax: (02) 6282 5536 Email: act.div@propertyinstitute.com.au
API - WA Division 27 Charles Street, **SOUTH PERTH, WA. 6151** Tel: (08) 9474 2784 Fax: (08) 9474 1157 Email: admin@propertyinstitute-wa.com	**API - SA Division** 1st Floor, 187 Fullarton Road, **DULWICH, SA. 5065.** Tel: (08) 8431 9411 Fax: (08) 8431 9422 Email: API@maccoul.com.au
API - TAS Division Floor 3, 18 Elizabeth St **HOBART, TAS. 7000.** Tel: (03) 6224 1324 Fax: (03) 6224 3441 Email: sandrakemp@bigpond.com	**API - VIC Division** 10 Beach Street, **PORT MELBOURNE, VIC. 3207.** Ph: (03) 9646 1977 Fax: (03) 9646 4635 Email: apivic@vic.propertyinstitute.com.au
API - QLD Division 2nd Floor, Suite 202, 131 Leichhardt Street, **SPRING HILL, QLD. 4000** Tel: (07) 3832 3139 Fax: (07) 3839 0438 Email: qld@propertyinstitute.com.au	**API - NSW Division** Level 3, 60 York Street, **SYDNEY, NSW. 2000** Tel: (02) 9299 1811 Fax: (02) 9299 1490 Email: api@nsw.propertyinstitute.com.au

The author has no financial interest or connection with The Australian Property Institute.

Government Departments that assist consumers

The author has no affiliation with these departments.

New Zealand
Ministry of Consumer Affairs
PO Box 1473, Wellington NZ
Phone: 64 4 474 2750
Fax: 64 4 473 9400
Web site: www.consumer-ministry.govt.nz

Australian Capital Territory
ACT Office of Fair Trading
GIO House
Cnr Akuna Street and City Walk
Canberra City ACT 2600
Ph: (02) 6207 0400
Fax: (02) 6207 0424
Web site: www.fairtrading.act.gov.au

New South Wales
Department of Fair Trading
1 Fitzwilliam Street
Parramatta NSW 2150
Ph: (02) 9895 0111
Fax: (02) 9895 0222
Web site: www.fairtrading.nsw.gov.au

Northern Territory
Department of Justice
66 The Esplanade
Darwin NT 0801
Ph: (08) 8999 5184
Fax: (08) 8999 6260
Web site: www.nt.gov.au/justice

Queensland
Department of Tourism, Racing & Fair Trading
50 Ann Street
Brisbane Qld 4000
Ph: (07) 3246 1500
Fax:(07) 3246 1504
Web site: www.fairtrading.qld.gov.au

South Australia

Office of Consumer and Business Affairs
91–97 Grenfell Street
Adelaide SA 5000
Ph: (08) 8204 9777
Fax: (08) 8204 9763
Web site: www.ocba.sa.gov.au

Tasmania

Office of Consumer Affairs & Fair Trading
15 Murray Street
Hobart Tas 7000
Ph: (03) 6233 4555
Fax: (03) 6233 4882
Web site: www.justice.tas.gov.au/ca/

Victoria

Consumer and Business Affairs
452 Flinders Street
Melbourne Vic 3000
Ph: (03) 9627 6000
Fax: (03) 9627 6007 (complaints)
Web site: www.consumer.vic.gov.au

Western Australia

Department of Consumer & Employment Protection
219 St Georges Terrace
Perth WA 6000
Phone: (08) 9282 0777
Web site: www.fairtrading.wa.gov.au

Australian Competition and Consumer Commission (ACCC)

Canberra (National Office)
470 Northbourne Avenue
Dickson ACT 2602
Ph: (02) 6243 1111. Fax: (02) 6243 1199

New South Wales
Level 7, Angel Place
123 Pitt Street
Sydney NSW 2000
Ph: (02) 9230 9133. Fax: (02) 9232 6107

Northern Territory
Level 8, National Mutual Centre
9–11 Cavanagh Street
Darwin NT 0800
Ph: (08) 8946 9666. Fax: (08) 8946 9600

Queensland
Level 3, AAMI Building
500 Queen Street
Brisbane Qld 4000
Ph: (07) 3835 4666. Fax: (07) 3832 0372

South Australia
14th floor, ANZ House
13 Grenfell Street
Adelaide SA 5001
Ph: (08) 8213 3444. Fax: (08) 8410 4155

Tasmania
3rd Floor,
86 Collins Street

Hobart Tas 7000
Ph: (03) 6215 9333. Fax: (03) 6234 7796

Victoria
Level 35, The Tower
360 Elizabeth Street
Melbourne Centre
Melbourne Vic 3000
Ph: (03) 9290 1800. Fax: (03) 9663 3699

Western Australia
3rd floor, East Point Plaza
233 Adelaide Terrace
Perth WA 6000
Ph: (08) 9325 3622. Fax: (08) 9325 5976

Consumer Organisations
Non-Government

The author is not associated with these organisations other than as a subscriber to their services. A minor financial contribution has been made by the author to the Western Australian based Real Estate Consumers Association.

Australian Consumers' Association
CHOICE Online
57 Carrington Road
Marrickville NSW 2204
Fax: (02) 9577 3377
Email: ausconsumer@choice.com.au
Web site: choice.com.au

Real Estate Consumers' Association
A non-profit organisation set up in Western Australia
PO Box 2041
North Carlisle WA 6101
Fax: (08) 9355 0806
Email: denise@reca.com.au
Web site: www.reca.com.au

Consumers' Institute of New Zealand
Private Bag 6996
Wellington 6030
New Zealand
Fax: (04) 385 8752
For editorial correspondence: editor@consumer.org.nz
For general correspondence: chiefexec@consumer.org.nz
Web site: www.consumer.org.nz

APPENDIX II
Jenman Consumer Assistance & Opportunities

• Emergency Consumer Assistance

Should you require urgent help on any real estate matter, you can toll-free 1800 1800 18 and someone will be available to assist you without cost or obligation. This service is sponsored by Jenman APPROVED member agents. However, no consumer details are ever passed on to an agent without your express consent. If you require the services of a Jenman APPROVED agent, we will give you the agent's details and it is up to you to make contact with the agent at your convenience.

• Real Estate Consumer Alert

To receive regular alerts and updates on consumer matters, please visit www.jenman.com and register your email address.

• The Inside Secrets of Real Estate

If you would like to attend a free consumer seminar presented by Neil Jenman, please visit www.jenman.com for details or call 1800 631 995.

• Real Estate Careers

If you wish to consider a career in real estate using the ethical principles of Jenman APPROVED, please call 1800 22 11 25 or email careers@jenman.com.au for an information booklet and details.

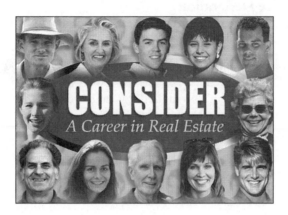

• Real Estate Business Opportunities

If you wish to consider opening your own real estate agency using the ethical principles of Jenman APPROVED, please call 1800 1800 18 or email enquire@jenman.com.au. Real estate with ethics can be a very rewarding business, both personally and financially.

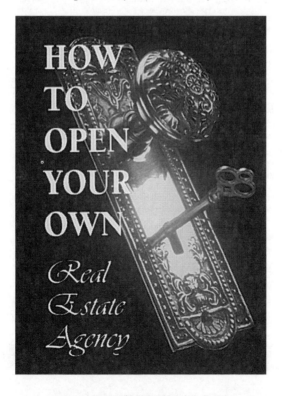

APPENDIX III
Guarantees & Agreements

•Buyers' Price Declaration

If you would like a complimentary copy of this Declaration please call 1800 1800 18.

Buyers' Price Declaration

1. We have inspected the property located at:

....
Address of Property

2. Following discussions with the seller's agent, we advise that we are **interested in buying the property** subject to any further independent advice which we may seek.

3. The HIGHEST price we are prepared to pay for the property is...

.... $..................
Price to be written in words as well as in numbers.

4. We also advise that should someone else offer a price for this property that is HIGHER than the price stated above (in Point 3), we will NOT increase our price. The price stated is the **Highest Price** we are prepared to pay.

5. In order to demonstrate both the sincerity and the FINALITY of our price, we declare that we do NOT require notification should another buyer offer a price higher than that offered by us. In such event, we understand that the property may be **immediately sold to the other buyer**. We will NOT pay more than the price already stated, therefore we do not require an opportunity to increase our price.

6. This declaration does not place any legal obligation upon us to purchase the property, even at the price stated above. Until such time as a formal contract has been signed by both the seller and us, there is no legal obligation for us to buy or for the seller to sell. We also understand that the amount of our maximum price will not be revealed to any person other than the agent and the seller.

Name: ....

Signature: .... Date: ....

By signing this declaration, I acknowledge that:

a) I have been given a copy of it; and
b) that I have been advised to seek independent advice.

JENMAN
APPROVED
ETHICS IN REAL ESTATE
1800 1800 18
www.jenman.com

© Neil Jenman 2001

THE REAL ESTATE CONSUMER PROTECTION GUARANTEE FOR HOMESELLERS

WARNING TO CONSUMERS

This Guarantee is to be attached to and form part of the agent's agreement. Where there is any inconsistency between the clauses in this Guarantee and other clauses in the agent's agreement, the clauses in this Guarantee shall have priority.

Your home is probably your greatest financial asset. When you sell, you must be very careful. In just a few minutes, a simple mistake can cost you tens of thousands of dollars. The equivalent of years of your savings can be gone in an instant.

You must **be very careful**, especially with **what you sign**. My advice is simple – DO NOT SIGN ANYTHING – until you know you are safe.

All licensed estate agents will ask you to sign an agreement before you sell your property. But remember that you are being asked to sign *their* agreement. Although the law requires agency agreements to be in writing, and that certain words must be in the agreement, many sellers bitterly regret signing the agreement given to them by the agent. The solution is simple: if they want you to sign their legal agreement, you must demand that they sign *your* legally binding Guarantee first. Just say to the agent,

I will not sign with you until you sign with me.

This Consumer Protection Guarantee has been designed following consultation with a legal team and advocates who are committed to consumer protection in real estate. Until improved consumer protection legislation comes into effect, you are welcome to use this Jenman APPROVED Consumer Protection Guarantee without cost or obligation to The Jenman Group.

Be warned – DON'T SIGN ANYTHING
unless the agent signs with you first.

And, make sure, once the agent signs this Guarantee, that you keep a signed copy. If you would like a complimentary copy of this Guarantee please call 1800 1800 18 or visit www.jenman.com. Best wishes for a safe and successful sale.

Neil Jenman

1. Cooling-Off period
The agent agrees...

The sellers can cancel the Agent's Agreement any time within two business days of signing and receiving an executed copy of the agreement, by handing to or sending (by fax or mail or e-mail) the agent a notice to rescind. If an agreement is signed on a weekend or public holiday, the right to rescind shall commence on the first business day thereafter and end 5pm on the second business day. The sellers may **cancel the agent's agreement** without reason and without any obligation during this cooling-off period.

The agent accepts that this is a condition of the agent's appointment.

2. Period of Agent's Agreement
The agent agrees...

The maximum term of the Agent's Agreement will be 49 days from the date the Agent's Agreement was signed by the sellers (and a copy of the agreement is provided to the sellers) or the date when the agency is first legally able to offer the property for sale, whichever is the later.

The agent accepts that this is a condition of the agent's appointment.

3. Estimated Selling Price
The agent agrees...

The agent promises that the likely selling price has not been 'over-quoted' in order to entice the sellers to 'sign up' with the agent.

To ensure that any estimate given by the agent is as honest and accurate as possible, the agent must provide, in writing, a likely selling <u>range</u> to the sellers. This range must include one specific price (which the seller understands is an estimate) which will be the middle point of the agent's range.

To assure the sellers that the agent is not deliberately quoting a high price in order to win the rights to sell the property, with the intention of talking the sellers down in price after the agent has been appointed, the agent agrees that if the home sells below the lowest price on the agent's range then **the agent will forfeit any right to commission** and the sellers will not be liable for any advertising or marketing costs whatsoever.

Should the market conditions change substantially during the term of the agreement, the agent will advise the sellers about such changes together with an explanation of why the agent could not have known about such changes at the time the sellers entered into the agreement with the agent. Any decision to vary this condition of the Guarantee will be at the sole discretion of the sellers.

The agent accepts that this is a condition of the agent's appointment.

4. Bait Pricing
The agent agrees...

The agent will not market or promote the property by use of a lower price than what the sellers are willing to accept. The agent understands that under-quoting the value of the property in order to attract buyers on the basis that these buyers can then be talked up in price, is contrary to the interests of the sellers because it attracts buyers who can only <u>afford</u> the low price, or buyers who only want to pay the low price.

The agent accepts that this is a condition of the agent's appointment.

5. "Conditioning"

The agent agrees...

The agent promises not to engage in the practice commonly known in the real estate industry as 'conditioning'. If the agent praises the property and mentions its good features <u>before</u> the agent is appointed and then, <u>after</u> the agent is appointed, the agent criticises the property and points out its bad features, the agent will be considered to be attempting to 'condition' the sellers. In this case, the sellers will be **entitled to immediately dismiss the agent** and no further obligation will exist from the sellers to the agent. This condition excludes honest comments to keep the sellers informed during the selling period.

The agent accepts that this is a condition of the agent's appointment.

6. Final Selling Price

The agent agrees...

The sellers are engaging the agent to obtain the best available selling price. Should it be established that the buyer for the property was willing to pay more than the final selling price – even if the sellers accepted this price (without being aware that the buyer was prepared to pay a higher price) - then the agent will agree to forfeit **the commission** payable by the sellers.

The same condition also applies if it can be established that a second buyer, who was known to the agent and had inspected the property, had made a written offer to the agent for more than the price paid by the buyer who purchased the property.

This condition will not apply if the sellers knowingly choose to accept a lower price from a particular buyer.

The agent accepts that this is a condition of the agent's appointment.

7. Cancellation of Agent's Agreement

The agent agrees...

The sellers will have the right to cancel the Agent's Agreement at any time during the period of the agreement if the sellers are not satisfied that the agent has acted in a manner which is in the best interests of the sellers. If the agent has introduced a ready, willing and able buyer who enters into a binding contract as negotiated by the agent, then the sellers acknowledge that a commission is payable to the agent. This commission, however, is **forfeited** if the agent is found to have carried out any of the following:

- Breached confidentiality, especially disclosing the sellers' "bottom line" price.
- Failed to act in the best interest of the sellers.
- Breached any state or federal consumer legislation, such as false advertising or misrepresentation.
- Acted unethically towards either the sellers or any potential buyer.
- Used harsh or unconscionable tactics against either the sellers or buyer to effect a sale at an unfair price.

The agent accepts that this is a condition of the agent's appointment.

8. Marketing/Advertising

The agent agrees...

The agent will clearly explain to the sellers the agent's plan for the marketing of the property so as to ensure that the maximum price is obtained. The agent will not deliberately use any marketing strategy, which has the potential to lower the price of the property. Should the sellers become aware, after the agent has been appointed, that the agent is using a marketing strategy for any purpose other than to attract as many genuine buyers as possible, then the sellers will have **the right to dismiss the agent** and no commission or marketing costs will be due to the agent or any publication in which the agent has placed advertisements.

All costs of marketing are to be included in the agent's commission.

The agent accepts that this is a condition of the agent's appointment.

9. Fees and Costs

The agent agrees...

All fees and expenses claimed by the agent, including advertising, will only be due and payable upon an unconditional sale at a price not below the range as stated in this Guarantee. The sellers acknowledge that if the value of the premises is decreased due to information beyond the agent's professional and local knowledge, such as termite infestation or building defects, and the sellers agree to sell at a lower price due to these defects, then the above clause cannot be relied upon. The agent shall, in such a situation, before the sellers commit to sell the property, provide the sellers with a revised written estimate of the selling price.

The agent accepts that this is a condition of the agent's appointment.

10. Confidentiality

The agent agrees...

Any personal details of the sellers that do not affect the value of the home must NOT be revealed to any person unless instructed by the sellers. The agent will not discuss the sellers' reason for sale.

The agent accepts that this is a condition of the agent's appointment.

11. Insider Trading

The agent agrees...

Should the sellers discover, at any time in the future, that the buyer for the property was the agent, a close relative, personal or business associate, or employee of the agent, or any company in which the agent, relative, employee or associate had any interest, and the agent has not made full and proper disclosure in writing to the sellers prior to the sale, then **the agent will forfeit the right to a commission from the sellers.** If the commission has already been paid at the time of the sellers' discovery of such "Insider Trading", then the agent will immediately **REFUND the full amount of the commission** plus interest calculated at the rate of 10 percent per annum, calculated from the date of settlement.

Should the property have been on-sold within 24 months at a profit, then, in addition to the commission and interest to be refunded, the agent will pay to the sellers the difference between the price the sellers received and the price at which the property was later re-sold by the agent, relative, associate, employee or any company in which the agent had any interest. The term 'associate' will be viewed with common-sense and the agent will not be expected to be bound by this condition for being 'associated' with buyers through the normal business of the real estate office.

If the buyer of the property is an investor or developer and the agent has had past dealings with the buyer, the agent will advise the sellers in writing that such dealings have occurred. The agent will also disclose to the sellers any pending or current arrangements made with any buyer (who is a developer or an investor) in respect of future business between the agent and the buyer in respect of the property.

The agent accepts that this is a condition of the agent's appointment.

12. Security at Inspections

The agent agrees...

All people who inspect the sellers' home will do so in the presence of the agent who agrees to qualify all people to ensure they are genuine home-buyers, not 'lookers'. If the agent conducts 'Open for Inspections', the agent agrees to accept responsibility for the correct identification of any person who enters upon the sellers' premises. If the sellers' insurance company does not cover loss, damage or theft arising from Open Inspections then **the agent agrees to accept full responsibility for any loss,** damage or theft occurring during an 'Open for Inspection', or which can later be shown to have been caused by having had the premises open for inspection to strangers.

The agent accepts that this is a condition of the agent's appointment.

13. Rebates (Kickbacks)

The agent agrees...

If the agent receives a fee, rebate or financial advantage from any company or supplier used for and on behalf of the sellers, then the total amount of any such fee, rebate etc, will be deducted from the agent's commission. The agent agrees NOT to receive any rebates, bonuses, incentives, inducements, rewards or any form of kickback from any company or person in relation to the sale of the sellers' property except as disclosed and reimbursed to the sellers.

The agent accepts that this is a condition of the agent's appointment.

14. Other Agents

The agent agrees...

The sellers will employ one real estate company only. This agent is NOT permitted to pass on any details of the sellers' property to any other agent without the express written permission of the sellers and only after the sellers have been provided with the details of the other agency, and written confirmation that the co-joined agent co-signs this Consumer Protection Guarantee.

The agent accepts that this is a condition of the agent's appointment.

15. Buyers found by the owner

Although the agent will be granted the rights to be the agent for the sale of the property, the sellers reserve the right to sell or transfer the property to a close relative or partner should the opportunity occur, or if directed by a court. In this case, the sellers will not be liable for any commission to the agent, but will reimburse reasonable expenses incurred on the sellers behalf. The sellers agree to refer all other enquiries to the agent – especially those who approach the sellers directly, either from a sign or from the agent's efforts.

The agent accepts that this is a condition of the agent's appointment.

16. Withdrawing from Sale

The agent agrees...

Should the sellers decide to withdraw the property from sale for any reason, there will be no charges payable by the sellers to the agent (or any company or service provider directly connected to the agent). Under no circumstances is the agent entitled to place a 'caveat' or claim a 'lien' on the sellers' property.

The agent accepts that this is a condition of the agent's appointment.

PLEASE NOTE

The Jenman Group is a real estate education company committed to promoting ethics in real estate. Thousands of agents have attended our courses. However, only those who carry our official accreditation, APPROVED, can use the Jenman APPROVED System. Acceptance or use of this Consumer Protection Guarantee does not obligate you to use a Jenman APPROVED agent. This Guarantee is copyright and permission to use it is granted to any genuine home seller. The Jenman Group does not accept any responsibility for the actions of any agent unless they are APPROVED by us, in which case we GUARANTEE that our APPROVED agents will honour this Consumer Protection Guarantee.

For enquiries please call our

TOLL-FREE Consumer Support Line 1800 1800 18.

If you have any concerns about any real estate matter, we urge you to seek independent legal advice.

We wish you well with your real estate matters.
Please be careful.

References and Sources

Chapter One

1. Saturday May 13, 2000.

2. Brett Foley, 'Widower's complaint prompts investigation into agents', *Age,* June 1, 2000; Adrian Tame, 'Property games' agents of shame', *Sunday Herald Sun,* June 11, 2000; Tim Hilferty, 'When death comes knocking so does the real estate agent', *Daily Telegraph,* August 19, 1999.

3. 774 ABC Radio 3LO, Tuesday May 30, 2000.

4. *Age,* June 1, 2000. Also, *Sunday Herald Sun,* June 11, 2000 in which Enzo Raimondo, CEO of the Real Estate Institute of Victoria, was quoted as saying that this was 'the first complaint of this nature in four years and he believed the practice was "isolated"'. If agents were discovered to be following up death notices, Raimondo reportedly said that the institute could require them to 'undertake a training course or expel them'.
   The president of the Real Estate Institute of New South Wales, John Hill, was quoted as saying that the agent in Sydney 'could not be punished because [he] was not a member of the institute'.

5. Letter dated July 20, 2000 sent by the Real Estate Institute of Victoria to all member agents announcing the upcoming 'public awareness campaign' with the aim of the campaign referred to as 'simple – to demonstrate that REIV agents are ethical, professional and community minded'. Letter signed by Jeffrey Gole, President, Real Estate Institute of Victoria Ltd.

6. Real Estate Institute of Victoria, half-page advertisement, *Herald Sun* Real Estate Liftout, p.2, Saturday July 22, 2000, saying: 'REIV members must abide by a strict Code of Ethics that establishes the highest standards in real estate practice.' The advertisement, which also appeared in other newspapers, said the institute did 'not condone' agents following up death notices which it referred to as 'intrusion into grief'.

7. Receipt Number 4444 issued by the Real Estate Institute of Victoria Ltd, July 24, 2000.

8. Tony Warren, *A Systems Manual for Residential Property Managers,* Real Estate Institute of Australia Ltd, Canberra (affiliated with the Real Estate Institutes of New South Wales, Victoria, Queensland, South Australia, Western Australia, Tasmania, the Northern Territory and the ACT), ISBN: 0909784647. Chapter 4, 'A System for Growth or

Sixty-nine Ways to Prove your Worth'. Method 44 is 'Follow-up death notices'. Method 59 is 'Visit nursing homes and retirement villages'. The manual says that one agent found many properties by 'calling on the old folks'.

9. Distressed consumers are still complaining about agents hounding them when a relative dies. In November 2001, a man called radio station 3AW saying his father-in-law had just passed away and an agent had called offering to sell the home. As of May 2002 no action had been taken against any agent for following up death notices, although the real estate institutes are apparently no longer selling the manual that suggests agents follow up death notices. In June 2002, a journalist told this author that following the death of a parent several agents had called.

10. The man had seen a home priced at $168,000. He made an offer of $150,000 that was accepted by the owner. He paid a deposit of $15,000 and he and the owner had signed the contracts. Later, he was told by another agent that the home was worth between $130,000 and $150,000. He wanted to cancel the sale, but the cooling-off period had elapsed and he was legally bound to proceed. On March 10, 1999, the man was sentenced to 18 years imprisonment with a non-parole period of 15 years. On October 15, 2001 the Supreme Court of Victoria dismissed leave to appeal, VSCA 183. Records viewed by the author.

11. Incident occurred May 21, 1997. The matter came for trial in July 1998. The tenant, a 40-year-old male, was sentenced to a minimum 19 years in prison with a further term of 5 years. On August 31, 2000, the New South Wales Court of Criminal Appeal upheld an appeal on the grounds that the trial judge had erred in not conducting a fitness inquiry pursuant to the *Mental Health (Criminal Procedure) Act 1990*. The convictions and sentences were quashed and a new trial ordered, NSWCCA 344. Records viewed by the author.

12. Incident occurred June 22, 1999. Peter John Lenane was convicted of manslaughter on August 8, 2000 and sentenced to two years imprisonment on August 25, 2000, by Supreme Court Judge Geoffrey Miller. Lenane was released from prison on April 2, 2001. The case caused controversy in the region. Many people felt Lenane was harshly treated. The victim, 66-year-old Ian Menzies, was angry because the home he bought was infested with fleas and his dog had died a 'horrible death'. Menzies harassed Lenane and, on the night of June 22, entered the grounds of Lenane's home with the apparent intention of tampering with Lenane's car. An altercation ensued and Menzies died from two stab wounds to the chest. Information provided to the author.
Bunbury Herald 29/2/00, 1/8/00, 8/8/00, 10/8/00, 15/8/00, 29/8/00 and 3/4/01. And statement by Bunbury Police District Superintendent, John Watson, in the *South Western Times* 17/8/00.

13. Angela O'Connor, 'How can agents get it so wrong?' *Sunday Age,* July 23, 2000. South Yarra agent Phillipe Batters claimed he 'had to underquote' and that it was 'a commercial reality'.
    Anthony Black, 'Rubbery figures', *Sunday Herald Sun,* December 10, 2000. Batters again was quoted as saying that 'Under-quoting is a widespread commercial reality'. Agent Tim Fletcher was quoted as saying, 'Most buyers expected agents to under-quote a property by at least 10 per cent.' What many government regulators fail to realise is that thousands of prices quoted by many agents are prices at which the properties will not be sold. Therefore, this deceit is illegal. A spokesperson for the Real Estate Institute of Victoria, Enzo Raimondo, said consumers who complained about underquoting 'needed to be able to prove it' and that the institute could fine agents or terminate their membership. Despite thousands of cases of false quoting consistently occurring, this author has been unable to find one case of an agent being fined or having membership terminated by any real estate institute in Australia for giving false quotes. As this book goes to print, one agent is being investigated over false quoting.
    Also, 'Home pain as prices soar', *Herald Sun,* July 18, 2001. Stories of buyers whose hearts were broken when they realised they had no chance of buying a home they were told was in their price range. Home quoted in the 'mid-$200,000 range selling for $420,000'. Or home quoted for $450,000 selling for more than $600,000. Institute spokesperson, Raimondo, claiming the institute was 'quite vigilant' about it and did not 'condone' it. However, institute members are among the worst offenders.
    Also, Mike Bruce, 'Underquoting is real problem', *Herald Sun,* March 16, 2002. Misquoting is described as the 'real evil' of real estate.

14. *Today Tonight,* Channel Seven, March 2, 2001. The journalist's voice-over says, 'Phillipe Batters accepts that underquoting by agents to potential buyers is a widespread practice.' Batters says, 'I don't believe that [underquoting] is a wrong thing to do. Journalist asks: 'Is that just a little lie?' Batters replies, 'It is. Yes. I think it is a ... I don't think ... ah ... I think a lie might be ... well it is a lie I guess. It's one way ... ah ... you can't avoid the word ... ah ... that it is ... ah ... a lie but it's a commercial reality that we need to do it [lie].'

15. Phoebe Cary, American poet born September 4, 1824 at Mount Healthy, Ohio. Died July 13, 1871.

16. Henry Louis Mencken, essayist and critic. Born September 12, 1880 in Baltimore, Maryland. Died January 29, 1956.

Chapter Two

1. Charles V Ford, *Lies! Lies! Lies! The Psychology of Deceit,* Chapter 13 'Effects of Deception', American Psychiatric Press, 1996, ISBN: 0880489979.

2. Chuck Whitlock, *Scam School,* Chapter Two, 'Profile of the Predator', Macmillan USA, 1997, ISBN: 00208621395. See also web site www.chuckwhitlock.com

3. From statement by minister and documents sighted by the author. Date of claim: November 11, 2000. Caveat W744520V. Agent: R. G. Woodard Pty Ltd. A 'charge' against a family home is known as a 'caveat'. It means that a person or company has a financial claim or interest in the property and the property cannot be sold without the claim being paid or the caveat being withdrawn by consent or court order. Although the minister signed up with the agent, he had not noticed the 'fine print' in the selling agreement which gave approval for the agent to lodge a caveat on his home in the event that any money was owed to the agent. This is exactly what happened – the agent gave a false quote, did not sell the home and then refused to allow the home to be sold until he had been paid $4700.

4. Statements to author and documentation sighted by author. Homesellers: Helen and Rodney Godlonton. Property: 4 Brantwood Street, Sans Souci. Agent: Montgomery Real Estate, Kogorah. Salesperson: Nigel McAllister. Agent's written estimate of selling price: $875,000. Advertised by agent as 'Price Guide $750,000'. Agent said this was to 'pull buyers in'. Auction Date: March 3, 2001.

5. Statement to author and Memorandum of Advice from legal counsel sighted by author.

6. Letter faxed May 9, 2001 to Real Estate Institute of New South Wales. Sighted by author.

7. Faxed letter of reply May 9, 2001 from Real Estate Institute of New South Wales. Ref: 95:AG/KB stating institute policy and that the institute 'has no power to award compensation' against its member agents. Letter advises Mrs Godlonton to obtain her own legal advice as to her 'rights' about compensation. Mentions Department of Fair Trading. Sighted by author.

8. Mrs Godlonton, letter to the Real Estate Institute of New South Wales. asking for urgent response about why the institute advertises that its ethics and rules of practice 'guarantee protection' when there is no guarantee. Mrs Godlonton received no reply.

9. 'The Personal Property of Marilyn Monroe', Christie's, New York, October 27–28, 1999.

10. 'Daily News', auctionwatch.com, October 28, 1999. Hammer price: $1.15 million. With Christie's buyer's commission the total price paid was $1.26 million.

11. Julie Keller, eonline.com October 29, 1999. Buyers: Peter Siegel and Bob Schargin.

Chapter Three

1. Dr Craig Franklin, Associate Professor, Department of Life Sciences, School of Zoology & Entomology, University of Queensland. Confirmed to author. The idea for this analogy came from Chapter 14 of John Gordon Davis's novel *Hold My Hand I'm Dying*, Fontana Paperbacks, 1967, ISBN: 0006177360.

2. Chris Walker, 'Under the hammer', *Money Magazine*, March 2001. 'In industry parlance, the entire auction process "conditions" or "crunches" the vendor (more effectively than private treaty), meaning that it brings the price they will accept down, relatively quickly and robustly, to a point where a sale becomes more likely.' Chris Walker once worked as a real estate agent.

3. Edward Guthrie, *Real Estate Practice in Australia*, Real Estate Institute of Australia Ltd, 1988, ISBN: 0909784329.

4. Statement from homeseller, March 13, 2002.

5. Written statement to author from homeseller's daughter, January 31, 2001. Property: 2 Bennett Road, West Ryde. Auction date: October 7, 2000.

6. Summons and Francis First National Real Estate, West Ryde, Summer 2001.

7. Murray Hubbard, 'Real estate row leaves Bernie boiling', *Gold Coast Bulletin*.

8. Murray Hubbard, *Gold Coast Bulletin*.

Chapter Four

1. Edward Guthrie, *Real Estate Practice in Australia*, Real Estate Institute of Australia Ltd, 1988, ISBN 0909784329.

2. Statement to the author.

3. As told to the author by homebuyer and confirmed in writing.

4. As told to the author by salesperson.

5. Student at training course as told to the author.

6. Graham White, *Relax and Sell More Real Estate,* Team Training Pty Ltd, 1986, ISBN: 0947075003. White's credentials as noted in his book are licensed real estate agent, general auctioneer, business broker, Justice of the Peace, Associate of the Real Estate Institute of Australia. After sixteen years of face-to-face selling he was appointed to the position of Training Officer of L. J. Hooker Limited.

7. Written statement to the author. April 2001.

8. Roy H Williams, *The Wizard of Ads,* Chapter 'When the Truth Is Not Persuasive', Bard Press, Austin, Texas, 1998, ISBN: 1885167296.

9. Andrew Pennisi, Essendon, statement to the author.

10. Council board member to the author.

Chapter Five

1. Greg Hocking, 'What do you say to the vendor when the purchaser is about to sign the contract and has a bank cheque for more than the 10%?' (Meaning he/she would have paid more.) Program topic at the Auction Interest Group Seminar, Real Estate Institute of Victoria, July 15, 1997.

2. P.K. Property Search & Negotiators, Real Estate Institute member, advertisement in *Australian Property Investor*, April–May 2001. Advertisement says, in part, 'We know the tricks of the trade. Let us bid at auction on your behalf.' The advertisement lists six homes and the amount buyers saved. The average saving was $58,800 per home, not surprising considering the hidden losses of sellers who auction expensive homes. Also, advertisement headed 'Scared of Auctions?' *Manly Daily,* Saturday June 17, 2000, which showed details of homes sold for less than the buyers were prepared to pay.

3. Written statement to author, April 26, 2001.

4. It cannot be stressed strongly enough – these Selling Agency Agreements are designed by agents for the *protection of agents*. No matter what you are told by an agent or by a real estate institute, you must *not* sign these agreements until you are certain that your rights are protected (see Chapter 12). Some Selling Agreements even allow agents to place a mortgage over your home if you do not pay the agent's expenses. This means you could end up with your home unsold and with a mortgage to a real estate agent. As an example, here are some words from the Real Estate Institute of Northern Territory (REINT) Selling Agreement (which are written in small print): 'The Seller agrees to grant to the

Agent a mortgage over the Property to secure the payment of any contribution to Expenses payable by the Seller under this Agreement. The Seller acknowledges that this Agreement to grant a mortgage may be supported by the lodgement of a caveat over the title to the Property.'

5. James Tostevin, 'The Listing Machine', from written course notes provided to the author.

6. David Pilling, *Six Strategies to Massive Sales and Profits,* CD, Pilling Systems. Mailed to agents on request following promotional letter of February 23, 2001. From transcript provided to author.

7. From salesperson who worked at McIntyre Real Estate, Hampton Park. Tuesday June 13, 2000. Written statement to author. See also, Amber Morrey, 'Real estate scam', *Cranbourne Independent,* Wednesday March 6, 2002.

8. As reported to author by colleagues of seller. And from the author's research.

Chapter Six

1. Sydney's *Wentworth Courier.* In one typical edition (October 10, 2001) this newspaper had 344 pages of real estate advertising from a total page count of 422. The *Melbourne Weekly Magazine,* August 19–25, 2001 had 172 pages of real estate advertising from a total page count of 216. This represented 80 per cent real estate advertising content.

2. Calculation based on the number of homes sold in Australia and New Zealand relative to the population.

3. Claude C Hopkins, *My Life in Advertising and Scientific Advertising,* Advertising Age Classics Library, McGraw Hill – NTC, Reprint edition, 1986, ISBN: 0844231010.

4. Gael Himmah, *The Listing Master,* graphic 'The Expense of Wasteful Advertising', Gael Himmah Publishing Co., Walnut Creek, California, 1982, ISBN: 0960048812.

5. Lesley Springall, 'Let the buyer beware', *Independent Business Weekly,* December 13, 2001. Email from Greg Towers, April 3, 2002 who points out that sellers do not often realise that they are helping the agent with increased 'profile'.

6. *Real Estate Journal of New South Wales,* July 1997, Real Estate Institute of New South Wales.

7. David Pilling, 'Beyond 2000 marketing for buyers', *Victorian Real Estate Journal,* Real Estate Institute of Victoria, December 1998.

8. Ian Watt, *Real Estate Success, Money and You,* Morescope Pty Ltd, 1989, ISBN: 0731678648.

9. Training course notes 1995, Real Estate Institute of Victoria, provided to the author.

10. Statement to the author who, as a young man, worked at this real estate office.

11. Howard Luck Gossage, *The Book of Gossage: A Compilation,* Bruce B Bendinger (editor), which includes 'Is There Any Hope for Advertising?', 1995, ISBN: 0962141534.

12. Andrew Pennisi, Essendon, statement to the author.

13. July 26, 2001. Also, Paul Robinson, 'Royal commission to target union power', *Age,* July 27, 2001.

14. From documents obtained by author from the Melbourne Weekly showing the difference between the casual rates paid by sellers and the 'volume' rates paid by agents.

15. Maurice Dunlevy 'Get agents to "fess up about fees"', *Weekend Australian,* Saturday, July 14, 2001, p. 39.

16. Homeseller to author.

17. 'Sales Inspection Report and Exclusive Agency Agreement, Clause 15', Real Estate Institute of New South Wales, 2000. Source within the institute reported to this author that the most important clauses are deliberately written in small print.

18. The Real Estate Institute of Australia, Code of Conduct, section 2.13.1: 'A member must not demand, retain or receive a discount or rebate which relates to a service by a stocktaker or tradesperson, or to advertising, in connection with a transaction or a service provided by the member unless the member has obtained the written consent of the client to the seeking or retaining of the discount or rebate by the member.' The real estate institutes often refer to their codes of conduct but few consumers realise that these 'codes' offer little or no protection for consumers. On the contrary, as this point shows, the institute's Code of Conduct supports agents being able to profit from the losses of consumers.

19. Statement to author.

20. Told to author by senior real estate institute board member.

21. Part of the content of a letter to institute CEO, Norman Huon, from Garry Nash, obtained by the author. Nash closed his letter by saying, 'Should the Institute remain steadfast in its endeavours to justify and

retain this unscrupulous and deceptive method of obtaining additional income for agents I cannot continue to serve as a Director/Vice President of the R.E.I.V. My conscience will not allow it.'

22. Norman Huon resigned in 1999 and stood down as CEO in March 2000. Although he supported the abolition of rebates, this was not the reason for his resignation. He was CEO for three years. He did not come from a real estate background. He no longer works within the real estate industry. Mr Huon was reported to have urged the Real Estate Institute to become 'a better corporate citizen'. See also, Louise Clifton-Evans, 'Housing the poor – an outgoing executive wants the industry to do more', *Herald Sun,* Saturday January 8, 2000. Also author's conversation with Mr Huon, April 26, 2002.

23. John F Dalton, Associate of the Graduate School of Business, Royal Melbourne Institute of Technology, 'Boardroom Ethics', paper delivered to the Ethics in Business and the Professions Conference, Massey University, Palmerston North, June 1993, published in *Business Ethics in Australia and New Zealand, Essays and Cases,* Klaas Woldring ed., Thomas Nelson Australia, 1996, ISBN: 0170091139.

24. Bruce Bell, Managing Director, Collins Simms Pty Ltd, March 24, 2000. Letter provided to the author.

25. Mr and Mrs Bebarfald, written statement and documents provided to the author, October 17, 2000. In May 2002, Mr and Mrs Bebarfald sold their home with another agent.

26. Documents obtained by the author. Deed of Agreement prepared by lawyers agreeing on rebates payable to agents for advertising for the period June 1, 2001 until May 31, 2002.

27. Lawyer to the author.

28. Keith Moor, 'Inquiry on *Age* payment for ads', *Herald Sun,* March 3, 2000. The article reported that millions of dollars were being paid to agents by way of discounts and rebates and that such payments were keeping advertising rates artificially high. Unlike the *Age,* the *Herald Sun* was not offering real estate advertising rebates.

29. *Media Watch,* ABC TV, Monday March 20, 2000.

30. Antony Catalano, '*Age* gets OK on home ad contracts', *Age,* March 4, 2000.

31. Antony Catalano, *Age,* March 4, 2000.

32. *30 Individuals and 10 corporations in residential real estate industry charged with stealing $4 million through kickback and bid rigging scheme,* media release, City of New York, Department of Investigation, Thursday June 22, 1999.

33. Police Commissioner Howard Safir, media release, City of New York, Department of Investigation, June 22, 1999.

34. Property: 40 Botticelli Street, Fig Tree Pocket. Selling Agreement: May 15, 2000. Auction date: Saturday June 10, 2000. Real estate salesperson: Jason Arnott. Manager of agency: Jason Adcock. Auctioneer: James Callianiotis. Bryan and Anne were told to expect '$1 million plus' for their home. A figure of $1.3 million was mentioned before they signed up for auction. After they signed, the agent advertised their home as '$800,000 plus' and began telling Bryan and Anne that the price range was now '$600,000–$700,000'. This, of course, was all part of the standard auction conditioning method which includes a series of standard letters. In one letter, the agent even forgot to remove the x from the space where he was supposed to write a number. At the auction the highest bid was $745,000. The agent pressured Bryan and Anne to accept. They refused. On the day of the failed auction, the auctioneer, Callianiotis, and the agent, Adcock, had a huge advertising feature in the Brisbane paper the *Courier-Mail* lauding the 'benefits' of auction and saying that auctions 'achieve the best possible price'. Their agency at the time, Raine & Horne Brisbane West, was also described as 'No. 1 Queensland Office' and 'No. 1 Auction Office Australia'. Bryan and Anne paid $16,215. On July 11, in response to vigorous questioning about the advertising, they received a partial refund of $3,040. From documents provided to the author.

35. Real Estate Institute of Victoria, Real Estate Industry Awards for Excellence, Thursday October 29, 1998, Crown Towers, Southbank. Property sold: 47 The Ridge, Canterbury.

36. Real Estate Industry Awards for Excellence, Thursday October 29, 1998. Award category: Best Residential Marketing Campaign (budget greater than $6000). Agent: Karen Gornalle & Associates.

37. Homebuyer to the author October 12, 2001.

38. Michael Meakin, Brian Mark Real Estate Werribee, Victoria. Dozens of agents report identical experiences. The abandonment of typical real estate advertising leads to better prices for homesellers and greater satisfaction from genuine homebuyers.

39. *Renovation Rescue – Get Ready to Sell,* television program, Channel Nine, July 19, 2000. Agent: Ian Dinnerville from Hornsby, New South Wales.

40. Channel Seven, February 14, 2001. Also, *Sun-Herald,* February 18, 2001, and conversation between agent and author, February 15, 2001.

41. Homeseller to the author.

42. Andrew Pennisi, Essendon, to the author.

43. James Tostevin, 'The Listing Machine', from written course notes provided to author.

44. Interview with the author at Lisa's home, June 4, 2001. Agent: Rendina Real Estate. Property: 21 Epsom Road, Kensington. Auction date: June 16, 2001.

45. Lou Rendina, Real Estate Institute of Victoria, Northern Branch President, 'Underquoting ... it ain't necessarily so', *Moonee Valley Community News,* Tuesday July 12, 2001.

46. Letter to the author.

47. Anne Gibson, 'Estate agents feel heat on ads', *New Zealand Herald,* July 25, 2001.

48. Anne Gibson, 'More real estate agents to face court,' *New Zealand Herald,* July 25, 2001.

49. Comment to the author.

50. *Victorian Real Estate Journal,* Real Estate Institute of Victoria, June 1998, p.6.

51. Commercial Credit Control Pty Ltd, facsimile sent to agents, October 2000.

52. From lengthy statements and conversations with the sellers who, several months after the incident, are still terrified of this agent. Confirmed May 11, 2002.

53. Property: 17 Petrel Close, Hallet Cove, South Australia. Agent: Ray White Real Estate West Lakes. Date of Selling Agreement: December 19, 2001. Date of Auction: February 20, 2002.

54. David Pilling, 'The Dynamics of Marketing', *Victorian Real Estate Journal,* September 2000, Real Estate Institute of Victoria.

55. Statutory Declaration provided to author, April 22, 2002, and from documents obtained by the author. The Selling Agreement signed by Jim and Enza is prepared by the Society of Auctioneers and Valuers (SA) Inc. It contains harsh clauses in fine print. But, as the letter from the lawyer pointed out, in large print, these clauses say: 'The vendor shall pay the amount of the expenses and professional fee within 7 days after invoice, or at settlement, whichever is the earlier, and in the event they are not so paid then the agent may issue a notice requiring immediate payment.' (Clause 9.2). And, 'In the event that the monies demanded by notice issued pursuant to Clause 9.2 are not paid within the time stipulated in the notice those monies shall then upon such

default become a charge over the property and any other real property that the vendor may own from time to time. The agent shall be entitled to the Caveat of the property or such other real property owned by the vendor to secure the monies due. All costs incurred by the agent in collecting the monies demanded in any notice issued pursuant to Clause 9.2 including stamp duty shall be payable by the vendor and shall be $200.00 per notice issued.'

This is the sort of agreement that, in this author's opinion, should be outlawed. Few sellers ever understand what they are signing when choosing an agent to sell their homes.

56. Statement to the author.

57. Written statement provided to the author, May 16, 2001. Gordon TAFE, Geelong. Tutor, Wayne McKay, director of Hayden Real Estate, Geelong. In August 2001, the Real Estate Institute of Victoria's journal had this message for its member agents, 'The true value of the Internet to a real estate business is to attract sellers – to get listings.'

58. Pam Walkley, 'Real e-state', *Bulletin,* February 1, 2000.

59. Realestate.com

60. Transcript of audio tape obtained by the author, January 27, 2000.

61. Fairfax has a substantial interest in www.domain.com.au and News Limited has a substantial interest in www.realestate.com.au

62. Homeseller to the author.

63. Results of the author's own research and experience in real estate. Also common sense.

64. Dan Gooder Richard, *Real Estate Rainmaker,* John Wiley & Sons, 2000, ISBN: 0471345547.

65. Dan Gooder Richard, *Real Estate Rainmaker.* Also confirmed by research done in Australia (April 2002) where the average time buyers spend looking for a home in many areas is almost identical to Richard's results.

66. Prepared by GR8 Graphics, Springwood, NSW.

67. Prepared by GR8 Graphics. This advertisement was not accepted for publication by several local newspapers across Australia.

Chapter Seven

1. Written statement from agent to the author about one of the many 'appalling tactics' he witnessed before, during and after real estate auctions. The agent states that it is well known in real estate that auctions are 'a great conditioning tool'.

2. Author's own research and experience. The main reason for the rise in 'popularity' of auctions is because agents push auctions. The word 'popular' is used in real estate as a synonym for 'plentiful'. Consumers who genuinely like auctions are either: one, buyers (usually investors) with plenty of real estate knowledge and experience who know that auctions allow them to buy for lower prices; or two, sellers who have become victims of the real estate propaganda about auctions.

3. Peter Mericka of Real Estate Lawyers Victoria to the author. Also, 'Auctions – more of scam than you know', *Age,* Thursday July 5, 2001, in which Mericka described the auction system as 'one gigantic scam'.

4. Robert Lentz, *Ultimate Secrets of the Country Auction,* New Jersey Plain Citizen Publishing Co, 1973.

5. Robert Lentz, *Ultimate Secrets of the Country Auction.*

6. Alan Fleming, *Real Estate Office Manual,* Real Estate Institute of Australia Ltd, Canberra, with which are affiliated the Real Estate Institutes of New South Wales, Victoria, Queensland, South Australia, Western Australia, Tasmania, Northern Territory and the ACT, ISBN: 0909784620. The book's title page states that 'the author and publisher have full confidence in the information and advice published in this book', however, no warranty is given.

7. Real Estate Institute of Victoria, letter to the author stating 'the REIA is not of that opinion'.

8. Alan Fleming, *Real Estate Office Manual,* Real Estate Institute of Australia Ltd, Canberra, with which are affiliated the Real Estate Institutes of New South Wales, Victoria, Queensland, South Australia, Western Australia, Tasmania, Northern Territory and the ACT, ISBN: 0909784620. The book's title page states that 'the author and publisher have full confidence in the information and advice published in this book', however, no warranty is given.

9. Alan Fleming, *Real Estate Office Manual.*

10. Statement from agent Kyle Watson. While attending the Gold Coast Institute of TAFE in 1998, the subject of VPA (Vendor Pays Advertising) and auctions arose. Kyle asked lecturer Don Power (a licensed agent), 'What happens when you have charged an owner $2000 or $3000 and you know you haven't got a buyer and the property passes in. Aren't they very unhappy?' Mr Power looked at Kyle as if he was a child and said, 'Sometimes it's good to give the owner a kick in the guts.' The agents in the class laughed. The new students were horrified.

11. 'Auctions exposed – the great debate', *Your Mortgage Magazine,* August 2001.

12. 'Auctions "are still the way to go"', *Herald Sun,* Saturday June 17, 2000.

13. Brian Edwards, 'Going, going, still not gone', New Zealand *Listener*, July 22–28, 2000. Dr Brian Edwards, CNZM is a broadcaster, writer and media consultant. He is media adviser to the Prime Minister, Helen Clark, whose biography he wrote in 2001. In 1977 he conceived the television consumer program *Fair Go* which he produced and hosted for eight years. *Fair Go* is still on air and celebrated its 25th birthday in March 2002. It is consistently in the top five New Zealand programs.

14. Alan Fleming, *Real Estate Office Manual*, Real Estate Institute of Australia Ltd, Canberra, with which are affiliated the Real Estate Institutes of New South Wales, Victoria, Queensland, South Australia, Western Australia, Tasmania, Northern Territory and the ACT, ISBN: 0909784620. The book's title page states that 'the author and publisher have full confidence in the information and advice published in this book', however, no warranty is given.

15. Graham White, *Relax and Sell More Real Estate,* Team Training Pty Ltd, 1986, ISBN: 0947075003.

16. Brian Edwards, 'Going, going, still not gone', New Zealand *Listener.*

17. '$675,000 beach "bargain"', *Sunday Telegraph,* February 18, 2001.

18. Written statement to the author from the buyer's agent together with the selling agent's advertisement. Selling agent: J. P. Dixon Real Estate, member of Real Estate Institute of Victoria.

19. Ian Eldershaw, written statement to the author.

20. Marilu Hurt McCarty, *The Nobel Laureates – How the World's Greatest Minds Shaped Economic Thought,* McGraw-Hill, 2001, ISBN: 0071356142.

21. Property: 2 Pioneer Drive, Lake Tekapo.

22. Philip Smith of Ray White Real Estate Timaru, New Zealand.

23. *Timaru Herald,* Monday December 13, 1999.

24. David Slade of Fourways Real Estate Ltd, written statement to author.

25. John Nolan, 'Auctions exposed – the great debate', *Your Mortgage Magazine,* August 2001.

26. Alan Fleming, *Real Estate Office Manual,* Real Estate Institute of Australia Ltd, Canberra, with which are affiliated the Real Estate Institutes of New South Wales, Victoria, Queensland, South Australia, Western Australia, Tasmania, Northern Territory and the ACT, ISBN: 0909784620.

27. Agent: Malcolm Hill. Salesperson: Nicholas Drayson.

28. Sharon Wilkes, written statement to the author. Confirmed June 3, 2002.

29. Alan Fleming, *Real Estate Office Manual,* Real Estate Institute of Australia Ltd, Canberra, with which are affiliated the Real Estate Institutes of New South Wales, Victoria, Queensland, South Australia, Western Australia, Tasmania, Northern Territory and the ACT, ISBN: 0909784620.

30. Financial Planning Association of Australia, media release, Friday March 8, 2002.

31. Names are pseudonyms to protect the family from further trauma. Full written statement made by the widow in a statutory declaration dated April 10, 2002. If ever there was proof that consumers need protection at auctions by way of a cooling-off period, this case should be all that is necessary. The incident occurred in the early 1990s; not only has nothing been done to protect inexperienced consumers from the trauma and traps of auctions, but the number of consumers being financially and emotionally devastated at auctions has exploded in recent years.

32. All details from the statutory declaration of John's widow dated April 10, 2002. Also, record of interview conducted by the author's research assistant.

33. Secret signals from auctioneers to stooges planted in crowds have been used for years. In 1997, the Channel Nine television program, *Money,* used a hidden camera to record an agent explaining to a prospective homeseller how his system of signals worked. The agent also assured the seller that dummy bidders were employed by his firm to make bids at auctions. When the agent was later asked by a reporter if he engaged in such deception, he denied it. Agent: R. Exall, program aired Wednesday August 6, 1997.

34. Fiona Connolly, 'Crackdown on dummy auction bids – agents face legal action', *Daily Telegraph,* Saturday March 3, 2001.

35. Enzo Raimondo, Real Estate Institute of Victoria, interviewed by Derek Guille on 774 ABC Radio 3LO, 2.11 pm, Friday May 12, 2000. From transcript obtained by the author.

36. Enzo Raimondo, interview with Derek Guille, ABC Radio, May 12, 2000.

37. Enzo Raimondo Real Estate Institute of Victoria, interview with comperes Ross Stevenson & John Burns, Melbourne radio 3AW, 7.37 am, July 4, 2001. From transcript obtained by the author.

38. Anita Roddick, *Body and Soul,* Ebury Press London, 1991, ISBN: 0712647198.

39. Larissa Dubecki, 'Estate agent sues over "idiot" jibe at auction', *Age,* Wednesday June 27, 2001. Also, Jon Faine, 774 ABC Radio 3LO, 8.32 am, July 4, 2001.

40. Larissa Dubecki, *Age,* June 27, 2001.

41. Larissa Dubecki, *Age,* June 27, 2001

42. Larissa Dubecki, *Age,* June 27, 2001.

43. Melbourne Magistrates Court, Tuesday July 3, 2001. Magistrate Colin Macleod. Tim Fletcher, interview with Jill Singer, 774 ABC Radio 3LO, where Fletcher said, 'I am going to appeal this to the Supreme Court.' In response to Fletcher's arguments Jill Singer said, 'I've got to say, Mr Fletcher, I suspect the weight of public opinion would not be with you on this one.' From transcripts obtained by the author. Also, Tim Fletcher, interview with Ross Stevenson & John Burns, Melbourne radio 3AW, 7.40 am, July 4, 2001, where Fletcher said he was going to appeal. Fletcher did not appeal.

44. *Today,* Channel Nine, 8.23 am, Thursday July 5, 2001. Also, Toby Hemming, 'Magistrate lashes "evil" bids', *Age,* Wednesday July 4, 2001.

45. *Today,* Channel Nine, July 5, 2001, and Toby Heming, *Age,* July 4, 2001

46. *Today,* Channel Nine, July 5, 2001.

47. Consumer to the author, Channel Nine studios, Richmond, Victoria.

48. From an invoice provided to the author. Sale of a property by agent Castran Gilbert showing a charge for 'auction attendance' for three people: Ted $25.00, Ron $25.00 and Peter $30.00. Invoice dated 20 October 2000.

    Also, Digby Warrington-Smyth of Caulfield, 'Confessions of a retired dummy bidder', 'Letters', *Age,* November 22, 2001, who wrote that over a period of three years he was paid $25 per auction attendance for dummy bidding.

49. Lindsay Curtis, Century 21 Auction Services NSW, Facsimile transmission to 'ALL SALESPEOPLE', September 22, 1995.

50. *Some dummy bids at auction are legitimate,* media release, Real Estate Institute of Queensland, Tuesday July 31, 2001.

51. Commonly quoted. In this case, Jane Howard, 'The tree has it', *Sunday Herald Sun,* July 15, 2001.

52. Peter Lowenstern, Senior Research Solicitor, Law Institute of Victoria, 'IT'S TIME ... to clean up auctions', *Property & Environmental Law Bulletin,* 2001.

53. Mike Bruce, 'Law call to quit faking it', *Herald Sun,* Saturday November 24, 2001.

54. Neil McPhee, 'Vendor bids and the conduct of auctions', *Law Institute Journal,* January–February 1993.

55. Keith Moor, 'Issues of 2001, Your Say', *Herald Sun,* Friday December 28, 2001. Also, 'Home auctions: should dummy bids be outlawed?' Public debate at www.publicdebate.com.au gave an almost identical result (83.95 per cent).

56. Marsha Bertrand, *Fraud! How to Protect Yourself from Schemes, Scams and Swindlers,* American Management Association, New York, 2000, ISBN: 0814470327.

57. Graham White, *Relax and Sell More Real Estate,* Team Training Pty Ltd., 1986, ISBN: 0947075003.

58. Douglas Rushkoff, *Coercion: Why We Listen to What 'They' Say,* Riverhead Books, 2000, ISBN: 157322829X.

59. Tony Pride, Wilson Pride Real Estate. Advertisement given to the author.

60. *Macquarie Dictionary*, 2nd edn, The Macquarie Library, 1991, ISBN: 0949757632.

61. Greg Evans to the author. Confirmed May 15, 2002.

62. Jenny Brown, 'Deborah's back on location', *Woman's Day,* April 9, 2001. Confirmed by Ms Hutton April 4, 2002.

63. Judge Ian Robertson, County Court of Victoria, Monday February 5, 2001. See also, Angela O'Connor, 'Estate agents sued over price estimate', *Age,* August 26, 2000; Angela O'Connor, 'Judge rejects auction claim', *Sunday Age,* February 11, 2001; and Kelly Ryan, 'Barrister loses auction lawsuit', *Herald Sun,* Tuesday February 6, 2001.

64. Kelly Ryan, *Herald Sun,* February 6, 2001.

65. 'Sydney agent's insurers pay $60,000 settlement', *Real Estate Agency News,* January–February 2000; and Kate Parsons, '"Bully" estate agent fined', *Sunday Telegraph,* January 2, 2000. Homesellers Stuart Fowler and Shane Solton had auctioned their home in Addison Road, Manly with estate agent Robert Klaric. They had expected to receive $1.75 million. However, as is common at auctions, the bidding stalled at $1.25 million. The sellers claimed that the agent 'bullied' them into placing the home 'on the market' and that it then sold for $1.3 million. They sued the agent, who defended the claim, for $750,000. The agent's insurers, Real Estate Institute Insurance, agreed to settle the matter for $60,000.

66. *Real Estate Agency News,* January–February 2000.

67. *Real Estate Agency News,* January–February 2000.

68. Gordon Broderick, 'Hammer horror', Home & Garden section, *Sun-Herald,* Sunday April 6, 1991.

69. Tim Fletcher, interview with Jill Singer, 774 ABC Radio 3LO, July 4, 2001. From transcript obtained by the author.

70. Magistrates Court's complaint filed July 5, 2001. Auction occurred May 12, 2001. Fletcher had [bait] advertised the home with an anticipated sale price of '$290,000 plus' which was later changed to '$320,000 plus'. When the bidding reached $400,000 at the auction, Fletcher and his brother reportedly went inside the home to speak with the sellers. And then, despite the alleged protests of the sellers, Fletcher went outside and announced that the home was 'on the market for sale'. He then 'knocked it down' as sold for a price of $406,000. The sellers refused to sign and demanded that Fletcher get out of their home. A report in the *Age* (December 12, 2001) said that the seller, Mrs Perryman, had threatened to 'kill' Fletcher for pressuring her to sell her home too cheaply. Whatever went on in that home, one thing was clear – the price of $406,000 that Fletcher wanted the sellers to accept was too cheap. The sellers refused to sign the contract and later sold their home – without Mr Fletcher – for $427,000. Statement from the seller's lawyers obtained by author. Also, *State Television News,* Melbourne GTV9, Wednesday December 12, 2001: 'A court has heard that a home-owner threatened to kill one of Melbourne's best known auctioneers because he sold her property too cheaply.' Also, *A Current Affair,* National Nine Network, September 21, 2001.

71. GTV9 Melbourne, December 12, 2001; and National Nine Network, September 21, 2001.

72. *Queensland Property Agents and Motor Dealers Act 2000.*

73. Alan Fleming, *Real Estate Office Manual,* Real Estate Institute of Australia Ltd, Canberra, with which are affiliated the Real Estate Institutes of New South Wales, Victoria, Queensland, South Australia, Western Australia, Tasmania, Northern Territory and the ACT, ISBN: 0909784620.

74. Ron Courtney, 'Auctioneers beware!' *Victorian Real Estate Journal,* April 1997, official journal of the Real Estate Institute of Victoria Ltd.

75. Common negotiating expression. Well explained by Michael C Donaldson & Mimi Donaldson in *Negotiating for Dummies,* IDG Books Worldwide, 1996, ISBN: 1568848676. The Donaldsons call it 'the Magic Pause Button' describing it as 'a method of keeping emotional distance during high stress situations'.

76. Notes taken during an auction training course attended by the author.

77. Alan Fleming, *Real Estate Office Manual*, Real Estate Institute of Australia Ltd, Canberra, with which are affiliated the Real Estate Institutes of New South Wales, Victoria, Queensland, South Australia, Western Australia, Tasmania, Northern Territory and the ACT, ISBN: 0909784620.

78. Andrew Pennisi, Essendon, statement to the author.

79. Statement from homeseller provided to the author. Also, letter to the Department of Fair Trading.

80. Statement from homeseller provided to the author.

81. Stewart Moir, Manager Arbitration and Professional Standards, Real Estate Institute of Victoria, 'Complaints, issues, disputes in the auction process', *Real Estate Journal*, March 1997, Real Estate Institute of Victoria, Moir said that the auctioneer had threatened a woman to try and persuade her to 'complete the purchase'. The woman had refused to sign the contract at the end of the auction.

82. Cindy Martin, 'Auction: the pros and cons', *Sun-Herald*, Sunday May 13, 2001; and, Cindy Martin, 'Couple's $250,000 dream turns to $30,000 debt', *Sun-Herald*, Sunday May 20, 2001.

83. Cindy Martin, 'Couple's $250,000 dream turns to $30,000 debt', *Sun-Herald*, Sunday May 20, 2001.

84. Cindy Martin, 'Couple's $250,000 dream turns to $30,000 debt', *Sun-Herald*, Sunday May 20, 2001.

85. *Sun-Herald*, Sunday May 20, 2001, p. 55.

86. Email to the author, June 16, 2001.

87. Commonly attributed.

88. *See* Reference 70 this section.

89. In 2002, the Perrymans were forced to pay Fletcher his commission and expenses even though he did not sell their home.

90. Andrew Pennisi, Essendon.

91. Brian Edwards, 'Going, going, still not gone', New Zealand *Listener*, July 22–28, 2000.

92. 'Auctions exposed – the geat debate', *Your Mortgage Magazine*, August 2001.

93. Brian Sher, statement to the author. The statement also said that 'the buyer practically stole that property' and that eighteen months later it is worth 'in excess of $600,000'. March 5, 2002.

94. 'Driving home a sale', *Victorian Real Estate Journal*, March 2000,

Real Estate Institute of Victoria.

95. Stewart Moir, Manager Arbitration and Professional Standards, Real Estate Institute of Victoria, 'Complaints, issues, disputes in the auction process', *Real Estate Journal,* March 1997, Real Estate Institute of Victoria.

96. Well known in real estate circles. See also Stewart Moir, Manager Arbitration and Professional Standards, Real Estate Institute of Victoria, 'Complaints, issues, disputes in the auction process', *Real Estate Journal,* March 1997, Real Estate Institute of Victoria.

97. George B Allen, *The Fraud Identification Handbook – Fraud Avoidance through Knowledge,* 'Manipulating auctions' in Chapter 'Investment Fraud', P. P. Preventive Press, Colorado, 1998, ISBN: 096691600X.

98. Amanda Hodge, 'Beware the undone deal', *Weekend Australian,* May 5–6, 2001. Confirmed by Ms Hodge, March 2002.

99. The author's own lawyer.

100. Peter Mericka of Real Estate Lawyers Victoria to the author. Also, Stephen Healy of Gadens, quoted as saying, 'Contracts for the sale of land have to be in writing. The fall of the hammer does not create the contract. It is equally open for the vendor or purchaser to elect not to sign.' (From Robert Harley, 'Auction certainty under the hammer', *Australian Financial Review,* Thursday June 14, 2001). See also, Angela O'Connor, 'Contracts not binding on bidders', *Sunday Age,* March 17, 2002.

101. Jeff Hercz, homebuyer, statement to the author, July 19, 2001.

102. Alan Fleming, *Real Estate Office Manual,* Real Estate Institute of Australia Ltd, Canberra, with which are affiliated the Real Estate Institutes of New South Wales, Victoria, Queensland, South Australia, Western Australia, Tasmania, Northern Territory and the ACT, ISBN: 0909784620.

103. Michael Johnston, homebuyer, to the author.

104. As told to the author. One of many similar cases.

105. As told to the author. One of many similar cases

106. Property: 10 Daisy Street, Essendon, Saturday August 18, 2001.

107. Marcello, statement to the author, August 20, 2001.

108. Marcello, statement to the author, August 20, 2001.

109. Homebuyer to the author.

110. Homebuyer to the author.

111. Susannah Petty, 'Real estate for dummies', *Australian Financial Review Magazine,* November 30, 2001.

112. Property: 11 Illalong Avenue, North Balgowlah, Saturday August 11, 2001. Agent: Charles Park First National at Manly. Buyer had given instructions to this author's colleague, Gary Pittard, to bid to a maximum of $650,000. When the bidding reached $615,000 the home was sold, thereby saving the buyers $35,000.

113. Cindy Martin 'A ripper of an auction as Sydney home sales sizzle', *Sun-Herald,* Sunday August 12, 2001.

114. 'Auctions exposed – the great debate', *Your Mortgage Magazine,* August 2001.

115. Cindy Martin, 'This man earns $40,000 in just 20 minutes ... being a pain', *Sun-Herald,* June 3, 2001.

116. Buyers' advocate to the author.

117. Garry Walker, Walker & Associates Real Estate, written statement to the author.

118. David Farmer, chief executive of Cairns council as reported by Marie Lowe, 'Forced sale – home auctioned to recoup rates', *Cairns Post,* front page, Saturday July 28, 2001.

119. From statements provided to the author. Property: 5 Beach Road, Lower Sandy Bay. Auction: Friday December 8, 2000.

120. Property: Lots G & 1 Harkness Road, Melton. December 2000. Sale by Elders Real Estate. Sale price $145,000. On October 26, 2000, Phil Hickmott of Wood's Real Estate Melton wrote to the Department of Human Services saying that 'auctions get lower prices at Melton' and that 'we would be failing in our professional duty to recommend a method of sale that has been proven time and again <u>not</u> to achieve the best price.' Wood's Real Estate had sold more than 7000 properties in the Melton area over a period of 30 years. Despite this advice, the Department of Human Services chose to auction the land selling it for a price that Phil Hickmott – when he saw the published result – believed was a 'misprint'. It was no misprint.

121. Michael Meakin of Brian Mark Real Estate, Werribee, statement to the author. Also, letter to the Hon. Bronwyn Pike, Minister for Housing and Aged Care, in which Meakin stated, 'In Werribee, auction is without doubt the worst method of sale. In the Werribee area 90% of buyers wish to purchase subject to loan approval and therefore cannot bid at auctions. We estimate that the price of each [property] will be damaged by at least $10,000 or a total loss of

$30,000.' Despite Meakin's pleas, the Department of Human Services auctioned the properties. In 2002, Meakin wrote again to the Department and offered to sell their homes for no commission. His offer was refused and again the auction method was used. (March 23, 2002).

122. 'Auctions exposed – the great debate', *Your Mortgage Magazine,* August 2001. Comment in article made by Paul Jensen, Chief Executive Raine and Horne.

123. 'Auctions exposed – the great debate', *Your Mortgage Magazine,* August 2001.

124. 'Auctions exposed – the great debate', *Your Mortgage Magazine,* August 2001.

125. 'Rich 200', *Business Review Weekly,* May 23–June 19, 2002.

126. Confirmed by Harry Triguboff, May 31, 2002.

127. 'Real-estate agents cry foul over *Location* – dubious light cast on industry', *Daily Telegraph,* Napier, New Zealand, Friday July 7, 2000.

128. Michael J Boulgaris, *Location Location,* Penguin Books (NZ) Ltd, 1999, ISBN: 0140289127.

129. Michael J Boulgaris, *Location Location.*

130. Michael J Boulgaris, *Location Location.*

131. Michael J Boulgaris, *Location Location.*

132. Brian Learmount, *A History of the Auction,* Barnard & Learmount, 1985, ISBN: 0951024000.

133. Brian Learmount, *A History of the Auction.*

134. Cicero, *De Officiis* (On Duties).

135. Sebastien Mercier, *Tableau de Paris.* A French Act in 1556 created the 'Huissiers Priseurs' (Bailiff-Auctioneers).

136. Pauline Gregg, *King Charles I,* J.M. Dent & Sons Ltd, 1981, ISBN: 0460044370.

137. Dr Elwood Harvey, letter to the *Pennsylvania Freeman,* December 25, 1846. See also Harriet Beecher Stowe, *A Key to Uncle Tom's Cabin,* 1853.

138. *The Ruinous Tendency of Auctioneering and the Necessity of Restraining it for the Benefit of Trade.* Demonstrated in a letter to the Right Hon. Lord Bathurst, President of the Board of Trade, New York. Published by Eastburn, Kirk & Co. No. 86 Broadway, 1813.

139. John Herbert, *Inside Christie's,* St Martin's Press, 1990, ISBN: 031204609X.

140. Robert Lacey, *Sotheby's – Bidding for Class,* Warner Books, 1998, ISBN: 0751523623.

141. *Boxwell v. Christie* [Cowp. 395] 1776.

142. Magistrate Colin Macleod, Melbourne Magistrate's Court, Tuesday July 3, 2001.

143. *The Ruinous Tendency of Auctioneering and the Necessity of Restraining it for the Benefit of Trade,* 1813.

144. *Reasons Why The Present System Of Auctions Ought To Be Abolished,* printed by Alexander Ming Jr, New York, 1828.

145. *The Ruinous Tendency of Auctioneering and the Necessity of Restraining it for the Benefit of Trade,* 1813.

146. *The Ruinous Tendency of Auctioneering and the Necessity of Restraining it for the Benefit of Trade,* 1813.

147. *Reasons Why The Present System Of Auctions Ought To Be Abolished,* 1828.

148. Robert Lacey, *Sotheby's – Bidding for Class.*

149. Robert Lacey, *Sotheby's – Bidding for Class.*

150. Robert Lacey, *Sotheby's – Bidding for Class.*

151. Robert Lacey, *Sotheby's – Bidding for Class.*

152. Robert Lacey, *Sotheby's – Bidding for Class.*

153. Robert Lacey, *Sotheby's – Bidding for Class.* Nicolas Poussin, *Adoration of the Shepherds,* 1633, oil on canvas, National Gallery, London, UK.

154. James Brough, *Auction!,* Bobbs-Merrill Company Inc., 1963, Library of Congress Catalog Card Number 6311637.

155. 'The Somerset Maugham Collection', Sotheby & Co., Tuesday April 10, 1962. Maugham's 35 paintings, collected over a period of 50 years, attracted 2500 people, all crowded into five galleries linked by closed-circuit television. It was the largest crowd ever to attend an auction at Sotheby's. One painting, Picasso's *Death of a Harlequin,* sold for 80,000 pounds, the highest price ever paid for the work of a living artist. Maugham, who was too frail to attend, was represented at the auction by his secretary, Alan Searle, who called him after the auction. According to the *Daily Express* Maugham said, 'That's rather a lot of money for a single gentleman to get.'

156. 'The Personal Property of Marilyn Monroe', Christie's, New York, October 27–28, 1999.

157. Robert Walpole's collection of Old Masters was sold to Catherine the Great. The negotiation was handled in private by James Christie. The selling of expensive works of art was almost always done by private negotiation until the mid 1900s. See, Robert Lacey, *Sotheby's – Bidding for Class;* also, John Herbert, *Inside Christie's.*

158. Christie's Australia Pty Ltd, Melbourne, 11 am, Monday April 17, 2000. 'Lot 532. Walpole, (Hugh): *A Prayer For My Son, A Novel,* author's autograph manuscript, on rectos in blue and black ink (a few pages at the front in typescript), 947 pages, 3 punch holes in gutter of each leaf, bound in 2 vols, green crushed morocco, covers with gilt-titled spines stamped MS, raised bands, t.e.g., dentelles, by Roger De Coverly, sm 4to, February–June 1935. Author of this book *(Don't Sign Anything!)* was the purchaser who, like all buyers, had no choice in the method of sale.

159. Internet Fraud Statistics, 2000, www.fraud.org/Internet/lt00totstats.htm

160. *Former chairmen of Sotheby's and Christie's auction houses indicted in international price-fixing conspiracy,* media release, United States Department of Justice, Wednesday May 2, 2001.

161. Media release, United States Department of Justice, Wednesday May 2, 2001.

162. Manhattan District Court, April 22, 2002. Judge George Daniels sentenced Alfred Taubman to one year and one day in prison and fined Taubman US$7.5 million. The judge said that Taubman had committed a crime motivated by 'arrogance and greed'. The scam had cost sellers tens of millions of dollars. See, 'Ex-chairman of Sotheby's gets jail time', *New York Times,* April 23, 2002; and 'Sotheby's chief is jailed for auction price-fixing scam', *Times,* London, April 23, 2002. Also 'Sotheby's Taubman gets one-year prison term', Reuters Update 1, April 22, 2002; and 'Former Sotheby's head jailed', *Australia Financial Review,* Wednesday April 24, 2002.

163. Scott D Hammond, Director of Criminal Enforcement, Antitrust Division, US Department of Justice, *US v. Alfred Taubman,* paper presented at the Antitrust Conference 2002, Waldorf Astoria, New York, March 7, 2002. Mr Hammond said, in part, 'for most of the 1990s top officials of the two firms [Sotheby's and Christie's], which controlled more than 90 per cent of the world's auction business, had colluded in secret to defraud the sellers of art, antiques, and collectibles who had entrusted those firms with the sale of their merchandise.' Sir Arthur Tennant, the former Christie's chairman, was indicted along

with Taubman in 2001. Tennant is a citizen of the UK which does not allow extradition on antitrust charges. 'Tennant has refused to submit to US jurisdiction and remains an international fugitive,' said Hammond. If Tennant sets foot in America he will be arrested.

164. An open letter from the Queensland Licensed Real Estate Agents, *Telegraph,* Brisbane, Friday August 6, 1971.

Chapter Eight

1. Sally Richmond, 'Losing my real estate virginity', *Your Mortgage Magazine,* December 2000.

2. Sally Richmond, *Your Mortgage Magazine,* December 2000.

3. Author's own survey conducted nationally in April 2002.

4. Several statements to author from agents who attend Tostevin's seminars. Notes taken during seminars.

5. Graham White, *Relax and Sell More Real Estate,* Team Training Pty Ltd, 1986, ISBN: 0947075003.

6. Alan Fleming, *Real Estate Office Manual,* Real Estate Institute of Australia Ltd, Canberra with which are affiliated the Real Estate Institutes of New South Wales, Victoria, Queensland, South Australia, Western Australia, Tasmania, Northern Territory and the ACT, ISBN: 0909784620.

7. Mike Ferry Seminars. Also, *How to Develop a SIX-Figure Income in Real Estate,* Real Estate Education Company, 1993, ISBN: 0793104904.

8. Tom Hopkins, 'Open House Opportunities', *Real Estate Journal,* Real Estate Institute of Queensland, June 1993.

9. David Pilling, 'The bullet-proof office', *Real Estate Institute of Queensland Journal,* Real Estate Institute of Queensland, April 1996.

10. Terry Eilers, *How to Sell your Home Fast for the Highest Price in any Market,* Hyperion, New York, 1996, ISBN: 0786882247.

11. John, statement to the author, May 9, 2001. Confirmed April 22, 2002. John now works as a sales agent with L. J. Hooker.

12. Homeseller, Balgowlah, New South Wales, to the author.

13. Statement to the author.

14. Alan Fleming, *Real Estate Office Manual,* Real Estate Institute of Australia Ltd, Canberra, with which are affiliated the Real Estate Institutes of New South Wales, Victoria, Queensland, South Australia,

Western Australia, Tasmania, Northern Territory and the ACT, ISBN: 0909784620.

15. Danielle Kennedy, *How to List and Sell Real Estate in the 80s,* Champion Press, 1979, ISBN: 0938636006. Ten years later, another edition of this book was released. The section on how to get the price down by using open inspections had been removed. Danielle Kennedy, *How to List and Sell Real Estate in the 90s,* Prentice Hall, 1990, ISBN: 0134022491.

16. Danielle Kennedy, *How to List and Sell Real Estate in the 90s,* Prentice Hall, 1990, ISBN: 0134022491.

17. Blanche Evans, 'Agent's murder sparks safety fears, safety procedures', *Realty Times,* January 10, 2001. Statistics from National Institute for Occupational Safety and Health (NIOSH) which stopped keeping records in 1992. See also, Mark Spencer, 'Every realtor's nightmare', *Realty Times,* July 29, 1998, who says, 'In recent years, Realtors have become increasing wary about holding open houses'. See also, 'Realtor Safety Tips', Center for Real Estate, April 30, 2002, which includes warnings about the dangers of open inspections. Information from the United States.

18. RE/MAX of Australia. March 3, 2001.

19. Danny Katz, 'The prying game', *Age,* May 18, 2000. With permission from Danny Katz.

20. Senr-Detective Adrian Woodcock, Ringwood Police. As reported in *Maroondah Mail,* June 13, 2000.

21. 'It's a STEAL', *Courier-Mail*, Tuesday February 10, 1998.

22. Scott Palmer, 'Burglars, stalkers haunt AFL stars', *Sunday Herald Sun,* June 3, 2001. Confirmed by Mr Ron Joseph, April 12, 2002.

23. As reported in the *Sunday Herald Sun,* December 17, 2000.

24. Conversation between salesperson at Century 21 Carroll & Partners and the author's researcher, Monday July 8, 2002. Also, Fiona Connolly, 'Fans flock to Cracknell property', *Daily Telegraph,* Saturday July 6, 2002. Ruth Cracknell passed away on Monday May 20, 2002.

25. Helen Wellings, 'Uninvited "guests"', *Australian Women's Weekly,* January 2000. Also, 'Insurance confusion', *Australian Women's Weekly,* August 2001, describing how a homeseller had valuable items stolen during an open inspection and discovered that the insurance did not cover the theft. Also, Ken Dickin, interview with Helen Wellings, consumer affairs expert, Adelaide radio 5DN, 2.19 pm, Friday August 10, 2001. Helen said that someone opened their house for inspection and had several items stolen during the inspection. Warns that homes

are not insured when open for inspection. Also, letter from NRMA Insurance Limited (August 14, 2001) confirming that items stolen during open inspections are not covered.

26. John Douglas & Mark Olshaker, *The Cases that Haunt Us*, Scribner, 2000, ISBN: 0684846004.

27. Research conducted during February and March 2002 by author's own researchers. In all, 98 homes were inspected. In all cities, the security provisions were appalling. Perhaps the worst was Adelaide where only three agents asked for names of people inspecting the homes. The researchers were able to discover personal information about the homesellers, including instances of women living alone. Agents and suburbs surveyed included: **Brisbane** – RE/MAX Carina; Yong Real Estate, Carindale; Harcourts, Carindale; PRD, Norman Park; PRD, Bulimba; Raine & Horne, Park Hill; Ray White, Hawthorne. **Sydney** – Di Jones, Paddington; Laing Real Estate, Potts Point; Richardson & Wrench, Potts Point; Vantage Real Estate, Double Bay; Century 21, Woollahra; Spencer & Servi First National, Darlinghurst; McGrath Partners, Woollahra; Raine & Horne, Bondi Beach; Hayek Real Estate, Potts Point; Ray White, Redfern; L. J. Hooker, Potts Point. **Melbourne** – Rendina, Kensington; Brad Teal, Essendon; Nelson Alexander, Essendon; Avion, Ascot Vale; Barry Plant Doherty, Niddrie; Neil G Anderson, Essendon. **Adelaide** – Ray White, Lockleys; Phil McMahon, Henley Beach; Ray McGrath Professionals, Beverley; Century 21, Lockleys; Cathy Jane Real Estate, West Beach; Toop & Toop, Fulham Gardens; L. J. Hooker, Grange; Brock Partners, Kidman Park; Ken Langley First National, Brooklyn Park; Peter Ravese First National, Lockleys; Metropolitan Estates, Woodville South; Ray White, Mile End; Blue Ribbon Estates, Brooklyn Park. (Note: some agents were surveyed at more than one home).

28. The institute suggested that agents write to sellers before an open inspection and say, 'We will be present for the open inspection, but we must point out that there is nevertheless a risk that thefts from your home may occur.' *Real Estate Institute of Victoria Bulletin*, May 1998.

29. David Pilling, *The Systems Revolution*, Real Estate Institute of Australia, 1992, ISBN: 0909784582.

30. Information readily available from government and private sales records. An excellent reference work is the *Real Estate Yearbook*, Allan Consulting Pty Ltd, Pennant Hills, 2001, ISSN: 13288296, Telephone (02) 9980 8074. Published annually.

31. Kent Nerburn, *Simple Truths*, New World Library, 1996, ISBN: 1880032929.

Chapter Nine

1. Stephen Covey, *The Seven Habits of Highly Effective People – Restoring the Character Ethic,* Simon & Schuster, New York, 1989, ISBN: 1863500294.

2. Max H Bazerman, *Smart Money Decisions – Why You Do What You Do with Your Money (and How to Change for the Better),* John Wiley & Sons, Inc., 1999, ISBN: 0471296112.

3. Max H Bazerman, *Smart Money Decisions.*

4. Max H Bazerman, *Smart Money Decisions.*

5. Statement to the author.

6. Nick and Therese Cowling, purchase of home in Clive Street, Footscray. Interview with author, December 12, 2001. Agent: Miles Dowling, Hocking Stuart, Yarraville.

7. Penny Cooper to the author.

8. Penny Cooper to the author.

9. Bruce Connelly, Beaumaris, Victoria, statement to the author. Confirmed April 2, 2002.

10. On the agent's letterhead with business card of salesperson attached. Listed are the asking prices of five homes with suggested offers or amounts by which the homes can be lowered in price. Robert L Westwood Pty Ltd trading as Westwood First National Real Estate, Werribee Victoria.

11. Statement to the author. 'It shocks one to the core to hear that one's so-called trusted agent, that one has chosen after four quotes and who has promised in syrupy tones to do their "absolute best" for you is openly encouraging prospects to offer $20,000 less than the agreed price – and this is after the auction had failed dismally.' Thousands of sellers would discover similar encouragements to offer lower prices being made about their homes if they were to mystery shop their agents.

12. Kathy Vozella, 'Angry ants threaten Sydney', *Macquarie University News,* September 2001.

13. Penny Cooper to the author.

14. Pilling refers to this method as 'Buyer Ranged', a name which displays the ® symbol to show that it is registered. This method involves advertising a home at a price which the seller has no intention of accepting. It is false and misleading. It attracts buyers who want to pay lower prices, thereby enabling agents to place pressure on sellers

to lower their prices. It is another deceitful method to enable agents to overcome the Quote Lie.

15. Statement to the author.

16. Written statement to author. Confirmed April 30, 2002.

17. Published in a report dated August 1996. According to journalist Terry Ryder the purpose of the survey was to measure 'the effectiveness of selling methods in attracting buyers'. The method which least attracted buyers was auctions.

18. First National Quarterly Marketing Meeting presented by National Training Manager Elizabeth White who was launching the 'We're Listening' campaign, October 23, 2001. From notes and statements provided to author by members who attended the meeting. Confirmed May 6, 2002.

19. Property: 113 Gleneagles Drive, Endeavour Hills. Agent: Barry Plant Doherty. Contract dated July 2, 2001. Price $150,000. Subject to finance being approved by July 9. Finance application to RAMS Home Loans Pty Ltd. The Wilkinsons had 'a clear action against RAMS, due to RAM's statement that it had approved finance on July 6, 2001, and its subsequent withdrawal of that statement on July 13, 2001'. From detailed analysis and Memorandum of Advice by Victorian barrister on September 4, 2001. And from statements to the author together with supporting documents. Confirmed April 9, 2002. The message for homebuyers is clear: no matter what an agent says, all legal documents should be vetted by an independent solicitor before being signed. No exceptions.

20. Mr and Mrs Wilkinson, statement to author.

21. L. J. Hooker Werribee, independently owned by the proprietor Vintel Pty Ltd. Agency Appointment dated July 30, 2001 for the sale of 1/5 Bedford Court, Hoppers Crossing. Letter from L. J. Hooker to Mr and Mrs Godden, August 1, 2001. Further letter from the director of the agency, Vince Cannatelli, to Mrs Godden, October 1, 2001, reminding Mrs Godden of her legal obligations. Letter from Mrs Godden to author, October 18, 2001 asking for help and giving permission for her case to be publicly discussed to 'warn others about such practices'. And from the author's interview with Mr and Mrs Godden, Melbourne, Thursday November 1, 2001. Mr and Mrs Godden eventually sold their property with another agent.

22. L. J. Hooker Werribee, independently owned by the proprietor Vintel Pty Ltd. Agency Appointment dated November 5, 2001, for the sale of 14 Riverbend Cresent, Werribee. Letter from L. J. Hooker to Ms S Christie, November 7, 2001, stating that she had a 'legal obligation' and that if her home was sold, either by herself or by any other agent,

within the six-month period, then the agent is 'entitled to our full commission'. Also, statement from Ms Christie. Homesellers note: the maximum time you should sign up with an agent is 49 days.

23. Legal Counsel, Real Estate Institute of Victoria, August 13, 2001. Letter to the author. Note: the original intention of written agreements was to protect consumers, so there would be no confusion about verbal statements. However, many agents make verbal statements that the agents deny later. It has been suggested to the author by a lawyer that there should, perhaps, be a written statement in bold print on any agreement stating, 'Any representations or promises made by the agent verbally which are not reflected in this agreement, cannot be relied upon.'

24. The practice of solicitors paying agents to send them business has become increasingly common. One of the main causes is the fierce competition between solicitors for the lucrative conveyancing dollars. This, together with the emergence in some states of 'conveyancing companies' has eroded the profits of many law firms. Some have all but abandoned conveyancing as they are unable to compete profitably against firms offering massive discounts. Others have taken to offering financial incentives to agents. A typical example was one letter sent by a lawyer to several agents in Sydney, which said, 'Refer potential vendors or purchasers to me, and *I will guarantee you a finder's fee of 10%* of the fixed legal fee that I charge.' As a further inducement to agents, the lawyer also offered to send business to the agents. 'I will refer work to you from deceased estates,' he wrote. From letter dated April 23, 2002 obtained by the author. In another example a solicitor in Melbourne offers agents free movie passes on every new referral, plus, for regular suppliers of clients, the solicitor offers an all-expenses-paid weekend for two at a 5-star Melbourne hotel (from written statement by lawyer to the author July 11, 2002).

25. Agent, Warlimont & Nutt, Mount Martha Victoria, letter to the author, February 7, 2001.

26. Morgan Poll. In the period from 1976 to 2001, real estate agents have consistently ranked near the bottom of professions on a rating of ethics and honesty.

27. Statement by homebuyer who had been gazumped, November 27, 2001.

28. The 'Gazumping Compensation' is a requirement for agents accredited as Jenman APPROVED.

29. William Vickery was born in Canada in 1914. He was Professor Emeritus at Columbia University, New York. In all, he spent 60 years at the University. He won the Nobel Prize for his fundamental contributions to the economic theory of asymmetric information. The *Economist* said that Vickery won the prize for 'getting people to tell

the truth'. His auction method is a 'mechanism which elicits an individual's true willingness to pay' (as compared with purchases where buyers pay less than they are willing to pay, or they miss out to another buyer because they offer less than they are willing to pay). Vickery's ideas were described as 'momentous for the theory of auctions' and are widely used today. The reason Vickery's method is not used in the real estate industry is because: (a) the real estate industry is ignorant of economic principles or, (b) Vickery's method is 'socially efficient' and would not enable agents to use auctions for harmful social purposes such as conditioning homesellers. William Vickery's Nobel Prize was announced on October 8, 1996. Two days later, while driving to an interview, he pulled over to the side of the road and died. He was 82.

30. Danielle Kennedy, *Double Your Income in Real Estate Sales,* Career Press, 1998, ISBN: 1564143791. Also, National Association of Realtors (US), *Profile of Homebuyers and Sellers,* 2000.

31. From documents provided to the author, including: Record of Formal Hearing, Real Estate & Business Agents Supervisory Board (REBA), Western Australia, Thursday August 23, 2001; *West Australian,* Saturday August 25, 2001; and 'WA Police News', February 2002.

32. Lucy Cole was fined by the Real Estate Institute of Queensland's Professional Standards Tribunal on July 22, 1998 for four breaches of ethics. The breaches were against agents, not consumers. Also, Chris Griffith, 'Top agent's past blasted', *Sunday Mail,* October 24, 1999.

33. Conversation between John Tucker of Finning Real Estate Cranbourne and senior staff member of Office of Consumer and Business Affairs, May 15, 2002. Written notes provided to the author.

34. *A Current Affair,* National Nine Network, Thursday July 19, 2001.

35. 'Soul agent: Jane Howard looks at those who choose life without agents', *Sunday Herald Sun,* July 29, 2001.

36. Homeseller, copy of essay provided to the author.

37. Caller to host Christopher Lawrence, ABC Radio 702, Wednesday October 3, 2001. From transcript obtained by the author.

Chapter Ten

1. Mrs Pope, statements and documents to the author. Murray Cox arranged Mrs Pope's flight to Queensland: departure date, Sunday January 21, 2001; return flight, Monday January 22, 2001. The director of Networth Planning Corporation was Jason Paris.

2. Mrs Pope, statements and documents provided to author.

3. Gloria Dawson, Property Consultant, Ray White Surfers Paradise, Investment Services Division, 23 Orchid Avenue, Surfers Paradise.

4. Glenn Coleman, Finance Consultant, Express Mortgage, Level 5, Corporate Centre One, 2 Corporate Court, Bundall, Queensland. Statements and documents obtained by author which included an 'investment analysis' showing 'projections' of how the property would rise in value (from $178,000 to $318,771) over ten years.

5. Les Henderson, *Crimes of Persuasion,* Coyote Ridge Publishing, 2000, ISBN: 0968713300, www.crimes-of-persuasion.com

6. Property: Lot 42 Turtle Beach Residential Resort. Title Reference: 50138347, RP894840, SP133857, Mermaid Beach, City of Gold Coast. From documents provided to the author and discussions with real estate experts about the property. Among the many charges to Mrs Pope was an 'Investment Establishment Fee' of $8790 (excluding GST) by Express Mortgage.

7. Peter D Presser, Partner, Rapp & Yarwood Lawyers, Level 5, Waterside East Tower, Holden Place, Bundall, Queensland.

8. Mrs Pope to the author. Also, Client Agreement between Geoffrey John Rapp and Michael Dermott Yarwood (trading as Rapp &Yarwood, Lawyers) and Mrs Pope. Section 48 of the Queensland Law Society Act 1952 requires that there be a written agreement between lawyers and clients regarding the work to be performed and the charges involved.

9. Home Loan Centre Management Pty Ltd, Level 4, 400 Collins Street, Melbourne. Letter to Mrs Pope, February 27, 2001 confirming loan details. Account Number 1208-93931. Rate 7.59%. Maturity date: February 27, 2026.

10. Queensland Government Conference, March 1999. Karl Sebastian, real estate salesperson said, 'We now have enormous numbers of one-bedroom dog boxes that are the slums of the future, absolutely unfit to live in.' From Terry Ryder who attended the conference. See also, Terry Ryder, *Buyer Beware,* Wrightbooks, 2001, ISBN: 1876627891.

11. Consumers Institute of New Zealand, Inc., 'Gold Coast Property Scams', www.consumer.org.nz November 6, 2001.

12. Statement to the author. Confirmed April 16, 2002.

13. Jason, statement to author. Confirmed April 28, 2002.

14. Jason, statement to author. Company, Looker & Associates. Property at Edens Landing near Beenleigh.

15. The equity in family homes has become a prime target of con artists. It is so easy for them to access this equity because their victims do not 'see' the money. It is almost as if the con artists place a vacuum cleaner into the equity of people's homes and suck it out. You should be very wary of anyone who suggests you use the equity in your home to buy anything.

16. See note above.

17. Consumers' Institute of New Zealand, Inc., 'Gold Coast Property Scams', Editorial, www.consumer.org.nz November 6, 2001.

18. Queensland Office of Fair Trading. Also, Terry Ryder, *Buyer Beware*.

19. Terry Ryder, *Buyer Beware*.

20. New Zealand *Consumer* magazine, no. 409, November 2001.

21. Consumers' Institute of New Zealand, Inc., 'Gold Coast Property Scams'. www.consumer.org.nz November 6, 2001.

22. Tim O'Dwyer to the author.

23. Queensland Government Conference, March 1999, from Terry Ryder's, *Buyer Beware*, Wrightbooks, 2001, ISBN: 1876627891.

24. The most notorious agent involved in these scams was a member of the Real Estate Institute of Queensland – Stamford Lyon, Director Andrew Adolf Tamandl. Others include not only members of institutes but also members of franchise groups and networks. From numerous statements to the author and cases studied.

25. Article 1. Loyalty to the Institute. 'A Member must always be loyal to the Institute and must never publicly criticise a fellow Member. No instructions or inducements from any person will relieve Members of their responsibilities to strictly observe this Code of Ethics.' From the Real Estate Institute of Queensland web site, May 2, 2002, http://www.reiq.com.au/membership/default.htm

26. Noel Whittaker to the author.

27. New South Wales police detective to the author.

28. Marsha Bertrand, *Fraud! How to Protect Yourself from Schemes, Scams and Swindlers*, Chapter 2, 'You'll Find a Friend in Me: Meet the Con Artists', American Management Association, New York, 2000, ISBN: 0814470327.

29. Errol, statements provided to the author. Confirmed April 28, 2002.

30. Stephen M. Rosoff, Robert Tillman & Henry Pontell, *Profit Without Honor: White Collar Crime and the Looting of America*, Prentice Hall, 1997, ISBN: 0131037226.

31. Stephen M. Rosoff, Robert Tillman & Henry Pontell, *Profit Without Honor.*

32. Stephen M. Rosoff, Robert Tillman & Henry Pontell, *Profit Without Honor.*

33. Dr Stanton E Samenow, *Inside the Criminal Mind,* Crown Business, New York, 1984, ISBN: 0812910826.

34. Marsha Bertrand, *Fraud! How to Protect Yourself from Schemes, Scams and Swindlers.*

35. Terry Ryder, *Buyer Beware.*

36. Mr and Mrs Roberts, statement to the author and from conversation with Phil Hickmott.

37. Phil Hickmott, Wood's Real Estate, 289 High Street, Melton, Victoria 3377, telephone (03) 9743 6866.

38. *REIQ calls for a commission of inquiry into Queensland property marketeering,* media release, Real Estate Institute of Queensland, Friday August 31, 2001.

39. Statement to the author.

40. Phil Hickmott to the author.

41. 'Land Scandal', *Today Tonight,* Seven Network, August 24, 2001. Also, Karryn Cooper to the author, April 3, 2002.

42. Dr William Gaylin, Clinical Professor of Psychiatry at Columbia College of Physicians and Surgeons and co-founder of the Hastings Centre, the pre-eminent institute for the study of ethical issues in the life sciences.

43. Jeffrey H Dalrymple, Manager, Compliance & Enforcement Unit, Queensland Office of Fair Trading, to the author.

44. Greg Stolz, 'A slice between rip off and investment', *Weekend Bulletin,* Gold Coast, September 1–2, 2001.

45. Greg Stolz, *Weekend Bulletin,* Gold Coast, September 1–2, 2001.

46. Greg Stolz, *Weekend Bulletin,* Gold Coast, September 1–2, 2001.

47. Daniel and Don, statements and documents provided to the author. Point 17 of statement. The names of the victims mentioned in this story are pseudonyms.

48. Daniel and Don, Point 3 of the above statement.

49. Whitehouse Securities, 'Property investment made easy! Our

Services. What we do for you'. From a copy of the brochure provided to the author.

50. Daniel and Don, Points 31 and 39 of statement provided to the author.

51. Murray and Helen Casey's daughter-in-law, Jennifer, to the author, Monday August 7, 2000.

52. Jennifer, to the author, Monday August 7, 2000.

53. Jennifer, to the author, Monday August 7, 2000, and documents provided to the author.

54. Expert and independent real estate opinions obtained by the author on behalf of Mr and Mrs Casey.

55. Casey family to the author and others.

56. Helen and Murray Casey, Statutory Declaration, sworn at Mooroolbark Police Station, Victoria to T Pembleton, Senior Constable 26767, May 14, 2002.

57. Office of Fair Trading, Queensland.

58. Queensland Parliament, Questions Without Notice: Property Marketeers, Gold Coast. Hansard transcripts p. 23, March 2, 1999. The directors and associated of companies involved in real estate scams donated money to, and were involved with, the Liberal-National coalition, which held government at the time these scams first emerged and during the period of their most rapid growth.

59. From numerous company searches provided to the author and from numerous documents studied by the author, September and October 2001.

60. Statement to the author and documents sighted by the author.

61. From company searches obtained by the author, July 2001.

62. www.reiq.com.au Real Estate Institute of Queensland, Member Agent as at April 24, 2002. Stamford Lyon web site states, 'All Stamford Lyon consultants are licensed Real Estate Agents and our branch is registered with the relative real estate institute in its state or country of operation. This ensures that they all abide by the guidelines of fair trading and uphold strict industry standards to the Real Estate Code of Ethics.' www.stamfordlyon.com, April 24, 2002.

63. Hon. M Rose (Currumbin-ALP, Minister for Tourism and Racing and Minister for Fair Trading), Queensland Parliament, Property Agents and Motor Dealers Bill, September 13, 2001.

64. Statements to the author and investigations by the author. A few months after Paul and Linda were offered a deal to keep silent, it became widely known that Quinlivan was offering similar deals to

other scam victims. See, Hedley Thomas and Amanda Gearing, 'Property "King Con" tries to buy victims' silence', and 'Scam victims gagged', *Courier-Mail,* Thursday March 14, 2002.

65. Edmund Burke (1722–1792), Irish statesman and philosopher, widely attributed.

66. Hedley Thomas, 'Bank charged over scam', *Courier-Mail,* November 29, 2001. Also, *Two-tier marketers face ACCC action,* media release, ACCC, November 29, 2001. Also, Paul Clitheroe, 'Property deals to face ACCC scrutiny', Personal Finance section, *Sunday Telegraph,* December 16, 2001.

67. *Two-tier marketers face ACCC Action,* media release, ACCC, December 3, 2001

68. Garrick Brindley, State Valuation Office, New South Wales, as revealed to the author, April 4, 2001. Also, *Australian Property Institute News,* February–March 2001; and from documents obtained by the author from 'get rich quick' courses, and from the author's own investigations and discussions with legal experts, several of whom point out that there is often a 'separate agreement' for a reduction in price, thereby ensuring that the 'Hydraulicing' scam does not appear in the contracts for the sale of the property.

69. Attributed to Theodore Roosevelt who, as a young man working on his cattle ranch, observed one of his cowboys placing the Roosevelt brand on a stray cow. The cowboy was fired on the spot.

70. Confirmed by John Reed, April 11, 2002. www.johntreed.com

71. Confirmed by John Reed, April 11, 2002.

72. Confirmed by John Reed, April 11, 2002.

73. Confirmed by John Reed, April 11, 2002.

74. Producer, statement to the author.

75. Text of an advertisement that has appeared several times in Melbourne newspapers.

76. Full-page advertisement, *Herald Sun,* Saturday November 17, 2001.

77. Full-page advertisement, *Herald Sun,* Saturday November 17, 2001.

78. Journal notes taken by the author at the seminar, Melbourne, Thursday November 8, 2001.

79. Journal notes taken by the author at the seminar, Melbourne, Thursday November 8, 2001

80. Interview with the author, Friday and Saturday, March 15–16, 2002. Signed statement obtained on the events in this book.

81. Letter from Ian Bremner, First National's Chief Executive, Monday May 21, 2001. The letter appears to be a standard or form letter. Sighted by the author.

82. 'Investing for the future', *South Eastern Real Estate News*, Thursday June 7, 2001.To book for the seminar, consumers were asked to call the Dandenong office of Frank Facey First National on (03) 9792 0265. Jane said, 'At the seminar, it was hard to tell who belonged to The Investment Institute and who belonged to the First National office.' However, after she attended this free seminar, Jane had no further dealings with First National.

83. Jane, 68 point statement plus documents provided to the author which include a copy of the contract and a copy of the valuation showing a figure of $630,000.

84. Point 41 from above statement. Valuation from Mr Doug Neale of Antony Coady & Associates showing a value of $515,000, July 31, 2001.

85. Point 45 of written statement and conversation with the author.

86. Letter dated August 29, 2001 sent to the owner of the apartment, the development company, Westpoint Corporation Pty Ltd (Mr Norm Carey), claiming that the lady and her husband had been manipulated into signing the contract by both Murphy and the salesperson representing the development company.

87. Murphy to [Jane's] husband, Point 53 of Jane's written statement.

88. Simone Campbell, solicitor of McDonald & Associates, 459 Collins Street, Melbourne. Solicitors recommended by The Investment Institute. Documents and statements provided to the author. In a telephone interview with the author on Friday June 28, 2002, Campbell denied she had acted improperly, saying that there was 'no conflict of interest whatsoever'. When asked about her involvement with Murphy and The Investment Institute, she said there was 'no involvement'. When asked about the disparity discovered by her client between the price paid and the true value of the apartment, Campbell claimed the contract was already binding when she was given instructions to act. When asked why she did not attempt to get her client out of what seemed to be a very bad situation, Campbell said she was merely 'acting on the sale' and had nothing to do with the price paid.

89. Leonard Lauder, Chairman of The Estee Lauder Companies Inc. Speech to the Women's Economic Development Corporation, February 1985.

90. Interview by the author at Murphy's office, 530 Little Collins Street, Melbourne, Friday March 15, 2002. In a further interview with the author on Wednesday June 26, 2002, Murphy was asked about the case of Jane and her husband. At first he denied they were unhappy. When their statements were produced, he became agitated and said that 'values are determined by valuers'. It was suggested that values are set by *buyers* with knowledge of an area and that Jane had only bought the apartment based on claims made by Murphy that she could on-sell the apartment and make an 'immediate profit' to help her family. Murphy used similar language with this author to that used with Jane, namely, 'I will fight this to the end and win.' When asked about his involvement with the lawyer, Simone Campbell, he said she was a 'totally independent lawyer' who had 'nothing to do with him'. When it was pointed out that Campbell was a speaker at his seminars, he said, 'No, she's not.' Upon producing evidence to the contrary, he said, 'She is not a speaker *now*.' He claimed he 'hardly knew' Campbell. The author then reached for his mobile phone in front of Murphy and called Campbell's office. Campbell came on the line, whereupon Murphy began shouting, 'Don't talk to him, Simone. You have to talk to me first. Please, Simone, don't say anything.'

91. Jane, Point 62 of detailed statement. Salesperson from Hayden Real Estate, an agency experienced in selling inner-city apartments, September 2001. On July 12, 2002, in response to written advice sought from this agency it was advised that the apartment should sell for between $450,000 and $480,000.

92. Results of company searches obtained by the author, August 21, 2001.

93. Statement from Mrs Pope and documents viewed by the author.

94. Letter from Brisbane law firm to Mrs Pope, December 12, 2001. While it is 'normal' for lawyers to ask for out-of-pocket expenses, in this case, no mention was made of any expenses at the first contact. Mrs Pope, already reeling from the financial effects of an investment scam, was disappointed to discover that almost every person who contacted her wanted money.

95. Information supplied to the author.

96. Aldert Vij, *Detecting Lies and Deceit – The Psychology of Lying and the Implications for Professional Practice,* John Wiley & Sons Ltd, 2000, ISBN: 047185316X.

97. Advertisement, Sydney's *Daily Mirror* (circa 1973).

98. In the early summer of 1974, the author entered a shop-front office in Victoria Road, Parramatta applying for a real estate position. The business was being used to sell country homes and blocks of land throughout New South Wales. A heated and whispered conversation

between two men was occurring behind one of the petitioned screens. Soon after a man left the premises. When asked, 'What was that all about?' the other man said, 'That was Regan. He wants us to share this business with him' (or words to that effect). The person was Stewart John Regan, a notorious Sydney underworld figure who was found shot dead at Marrickville later that year. (Author's recollections, who did not accept the job).

99. Personal experience of the author at Annandale (circa 1973).

100. Carol Bly, (editor) 'The Brutality of Lucky Predators', in the book *Changing the Bully who Rules the World: Reading and Thinking about Ethics,* Milkweed Editions, 1996, ISBN: 1571312056.

101. Letter to the author, January 10, 2002.

102. John De Graff, David Wann and Thomas H. Naylor, *Affluenza: The All Consuming Epidemic,* Berrett-Koehler Publishers Inc., San Francisco, 2001, ISBN: 1576751511.

103. *Running out of Time,* television documentary, Oregon Public Broadcasting and KCTS-Seattle, 1994.

104. Ross Gittins, 'A risky move by the Reserve Bank', *Sydney Morning Herald,* Wednesday September 12, 2001. Gittins predicted that cutting the interest rates would lead to more borrowing and ensure that the real estate boom continued. As he so often is, he was right. But he also warned that 'a bigger boom leads eventually to a bigger bust' and that some families who have borrowed too much may find themselves in financial trouble later.

105. Elizabeth Warren, Teresa A Sullivan, Jay Lawrence Westbrook, *The Fragile Middle Class: Americans in Debt,* Yale University Press, 2000, ISBN: 0300079605.

106. In 1986, the New South Wales government launched a plan aimed at helping low income earners buy homes. Borrowers could pay a lower amount in the early stages of the loan that would then increase in the future. The early payments were insufficient to cover even the interest on the principal amount of the loan, thus creating a shortfall that was added on to the total amount owing. When house prices fell and interest rates rose between 1989 and 1991, thousands of borrowers struggled to meet their payments. Those who wanted to sell their homes then found that the balance on their mortgages was greater than the value of their homes. It was a classic case of negative equity. Of the 39,000 families who borrowed a total of $4 billion, approximately 10,000 of them were in dire financial trouble.

107. John Hurst (from London), *Australian Financial Review,* January 24, 1992.

108. David G Myers, *The American Paradox: Spiritual Hunger in an Age of Plenty*, Yale University Press, 2001, ISBN: 0-300-09120-6.

109. Dr Hunter (Patch) Adams, subject of the 1998 movie starring Robin Williams. See also, Patch Adams with Maureen Mylander (contributor), *Gesundheit!: Bringing Good Health to You, the Medical System, and Society Through Physician Service, Complementary Therapies, Humor, and Joy*, Inner Traditions Intl Ltd, 1998, ISBN: 089281781X.

110. Juliet Schor, *All-Consuming Passion: Waking Up From the American Dream*. Juliet Schor is the director of women's studies and a senior lecturer in economics at Harvard University. She is also the author of *The Overworked American: The Unexpected Decline of Leisure*, Basic Books, 1993, ISBN: 046505434X.

111. Terry Ryder, *Buyer Beware*, Wrightbooks, 2001, ISBN: 1876627891.

112. Author's research of apartment blocks showed enormous capital losses suffered by investors in several apartment buildings. For example, Southbank Towers: from 48 apartments resold, 26 were sold at a capital loss. The worst was an apartment purchased in November 1995 for $406,000 and resold in May 1999 for $285,000 – a loss of $121,000. From the 48 apartments, 26 resold at an average loss of $24,130 and 22 resold at an average gain of $27,953. This covered a six-year period from 1995 to 2001. These figures are vastly different to 'realistic' and 'conservative' estimates given at a property seminar for Melbourne apartments which was held in Sydney in February 2002. At the seminar, the speaker, Mr Charles Griffin from Central Equity, was extolling the virtues of Melbourne apartments and encouraging consumers to invest in the area. He took a unit priced at $475,000 and 'assumed' a capital increase of seven per cent annually which would mean it would be worth $662,000 after five years. Based on the amount of equity placed in the unit, Griffin said investors could expect a return of '31 per cent per year' over the five-year period. From journal notes taken by author during the seminar, and from copies of slides presented at the seminar and obtained by author.

Also, Scott Keck, 'Medium density housing in Melbourne', *Australian Property Investor*, April–May 2002. Scott Keck, Managing Director of Charter Keck Cramer, one of Australia's most respected valuation companies, said in the article, 'In our analysis there's little doubt that over the next two to three years many of the low to only medium quality apartments – particularly those in larger developments which were sold through mass marketing programs and which have already been surveyed to be poor capital growth performers – may fall in value.' Keck added an ominous warning: 'This is the beginning of a two-tier market which has plagued the

Queensland property market for many years, and which is becoming increasingly out of control in Melbourne.'

See also, Karina Barrymore, 'Capital losses from CBD flats', *Australian Financial Review,* January 7, 2002.

113. Henrik Ibsen (1828–1906), Norwegian playwright and poet, *A Doll's House,* 1879.

114. Dr Frank Gelber, director of Bis Shrapnel quoted in the *Age,* May 10, 2000 as saying that a downturn in 2001 was inevitable. Mr Rod Cornish from Macquarie Property Research was also quoted as saying that house prices would 'plateau' and that home loan interest rates would rise to eight per cent in 2001.

115. Terry Ryder, *Buyer Beware.* 'If it were discovered that a giant meteor was about to hit the planet wiping out all life (as in the movie *Armageddon*), there would still be agents out there telling people: "NOW is the time to buy!".'

116. 'Battle of the share tipsters', *Sun-Herald,* October 21, 2001.

Chapter Eleven

1. *R v. Kandiah Bojan.* Bojan faced fraud charges pursuant to Section 178A of the *Crimes Act,* 40/1900. The charge sheets listed 130 offences. Bojan was convicted and sentenced to a total of six years imprisonment. Sentence commenced July 31, 1997. From court documents viewed by the author, May 2002. See also, Lisa Power and Ian Horswill, '$1.7 million / thief lost it all / clients' cash blown at casino', *Daily Telegraph,* May 15, 1997, p. 1.

2. The Property Services Council Compensation Fund.

3. *A Systems Manual for Residential Property Managers,* Real Estate Institute of Australia Ltd, Canberra, ISBN 0909784647.

4. Property: 24 Broomfield Road, Hawthorn.

5. Richard James, 22 Broomfield Road, Hawthorn.

6. Land Titles Office Transfer of Land, Reference: W973145J. Approval No. 571007L. Consideration: $200,000. August 3, 2000, Sandra Maree James, 22 Broomfield Road, Hawthorn.

7. Hocking Stuart, Camberwell. Auction 12.00 noon, August 26, 2000. Documents and transcript of auction proceedings provided to the author.

8. Antony Catalano, 'Probe into $107,000 profit on house sale', *Age,* Saturday September 9, 2000. The seller, Mr Tracy, said he trusted Mr James because he was 'both a friend and a real estate agent'.

9. Brian Tracy to the author's colleague, Kerry Rowley. Notes taken during the conversation.

10. Written statement from student to the author. Real Estate Institute of Victoria Intensive Licensing Course, module ABH508, 'Real Estate Consumer Protection'. Swinburne University of TAFE, Croydon, Wednesday October 25, 2000.

11. Transfer document 6265867X. Property: 4 Gilham Street, Castle Hill, purchased by Lisa Maree McEnally, wife of Grant McEnally of Elders Real Estate Castle Hill, October 8, 1999. Sale Price: $262,500.

12. Bruce Gilmour, Elders Real Estate, Castle Hill, letter to the author June 24, 2000.

13. Property: 10 Tuckwell Road, Castle Hill, February 28, 1994.

14. Pilkington is no longer the franchisee at this office. (2002)

15. Documents obtained by the author. House bought by Peter and Beverley McLaughlin for $285,000 and resold to D.G. C. Investments Pty Ltd for $420,000.

16. Abusive email sent to the author.

17. Of all states, Victoria probably has the best legislation to prevent insider trading. See Section 55 of the *Estate Agents Act 1980*. Act No. 9428/1980, Section 55 (2) states, 'Any person who is convicted of an offence against sub-section (1) shall, in addition to any penalty imposed by the court, be ordered to account for and pay over to his principal all profits resulting or which in the opinion of the court may result from the purchase and any subsequent dealings with that real estate or business.'

18. Auction Results, *Age,* Monday, December, 18. Auction of 7 Olympic Avenue, Cheltenham, 12 noon, Saturday December 16, 2000. Agent: R Malcolm Pty Ltd. Sold $305,000.

19. Written authority to person bidding on behalf of the purchasers, giving instructions to bid 'to the amount of $323,750'. Copy provided to the author.

20. Research conducted by the author. Statement from buyers via the agent.

21. Mr Macmillan's detailed trade practices analysis of common real estate methods described in the author's previous book, *Real Estate Mistakes,* 2000.

22. Richard Mokhiber and Robert Weissman, 'Goodbye, Roberta: The CBS-Nike Connection', in *Corporate Predators and the Hunt for Mega-profits and the Attack on Democracy,* Common Courage Press,

1998, ISBN: 1567511589.

23. Richard Mokhiber and Robert Weissman, *Corporate Predators and the Hunt for Mega-profits and the Attack on Democracy.*

24. Notes from telephone conversation with journalist, August 16, 2001.

25. Terry Ryder, conversation with the author. Also, Terry Ryder, *Property Smart,* Chapter 6, 'Advertising Games – Getting the Editorial Tone They Favour', p. 131.

26. Terry Ryder, conversation with the author. Also, Terry Ryder, *Property Smart,* Chapter 6, 'Advertising Games – Getting the Editorial Tone they Favour', p. 131

27. Terry Ryder, *Confessions of a Real Estate Agent; Buyer Beware;* and *Property Smart.* All published by Wrightbooks. Terry Ryder is also a regular contributor to *Money Magazine.*

28. Mike Ferry Seminars. Also, Mike Ferry, *How to Develop a SIX-Figure Income in Real Estate,* Real Estate Education Company, 1993, ISBN: 0793104904.

29. *Real Estate Agency News.*

30. *Real Estate Agency News,* February 2000.

31. 'Power lines and cancer', *Real Estate Agency News,* March–April 2001.

32. 'The Whisper', internal Raine & Horne newsletter, July 2000.

33. *Brock Real Estate Pty Ltd v. Sandra Nelson,* Adelaide Magistrates Court. Before Mr GF Hiskey, SM. No. 01/6186, August 9, 2001. Transcript of proceedings obtained by the author. Also, statement from Ms Nelson, which read, in part: 'On Monday August 6, 2001, I called "The Advertiser" newspaper in Adelaide after reading an article in the paper regarding a "Code of Conduct" for Real Estate Agents. It was an article which featured statements from the President of the Real Estate Institute of SA. I asked for the journalist that dealt with these issues and got put through to Andrea Stylianou. I related my story to her and asked her if she was interested in reporting the outcome as a warning to other South Australian consumers. She said she was very interested. This all changed when she found out that it was Brock Partners who were taking me to court. She said something along the lines of: "We can't write anything negative about Brock Partners in our paper because they are one of our biggest advertisers." I replied that this was an outrageous situation to which she replied something like, "Well, I know but that's just the way it is, I'm afraid."'

34. *Brock Real Estate Pty Ltd v. Sandra Nelson,* Adelaide Magistrates Court. Before Mr GF Hiskey, SM. No. 01/6186. August 9, 2001.

35. Statement to the author. Confirmed February 17, 2002.

36. Paul Sheehan, *Among the Barbarians,* Random House Australia, Sydney, 1998, ISBN: 009183636.

37. Paul Sheehan, 'False profits a blight on Sydney's religion of real estate', *Sydney Morning Herald,* Wednesday December 5, 2001.

38. Professor William Vickery, Nobel Prize for Economics, 1996.

39. John Walters, Administration Manager, Cumberland Newspapers, memo to staff, March 6, 2000. Sent to the author by a Cumberland Newspapers staff member.

40. Daniel Canny, Eastern Regional Manager, Messenger Newspapers, letter to estate agent, July 3, 2001.

41. Statement to the author from the agent, Saturday May 5, 2001.

42. One of thousands of sex advertisements in local newspapers.

43. Letter from consumer believed to have been sent to several agents, October 11, 2001. Provided to the author.

44. Standard phrase used by newspaper managerial staff in identical letters sent to different agents during 2001.

45. Heather, manager for *Berwick News,* to Grant Real Estate, Narre Warren, May 5, 2001.

46. Edgar K D'Souza, Real Estate Editor, Leader Newspapers, to the author, November 17, 2000, at the conclusion of the Australian Real Estate Awards, Melbourne.

47. Adlai Stevenson (1900–1965). When he was governor of Illinois he was a tireless campaigner against corruption. Quote from *Environment Writer,* vol. 7, no. 12, March 1996.

48. John Vumbaca, Michael Bridge Mathews Real Estate, Dee Why, statement to the author with a copy of the banned advertisement, 'If a real estate agent won't offer you a **guarantee on the selling price** of your home, ask one question, **WHY NOT?**' October 31, 2001.

49. On November 15, 2001, at the Australian Real Estate Convention in Melbourne, more than one thousand people who work in real estate signed a petition calling for the abolition of all real estate kickbacks. See also, www.kickoutkickbacks.com.au

50. Letter dated January 16, 2002, provided to the author.

51. Letter dated January 16, 2002, provided to the author. Also, statement to author from Peter Lees.

52. Bernard Lagan, 'Dark side of the force', *Bulletin*, October 30, 2001.

53. Tim O'Dwyer to the author. Also mentioned by Maurice Dunlevy, 'We're not all dummies', *Australian*, Friday July 13, 2001.

54. Queensland's *Property Agents and Motor Dealers Act 2000*, which came into effect on July 1, 2001.

55. Queensland Office of Fair Trading, media releases, June 2001.

56. On Friday January 25, 2002, police and fair trading officers raided a Main Beach real estate agency. On Wednesday May 1, the agent was charged under Queensland's new anti-marketeering laws. This agent was a member of the Real Estate Institute of Queensland and could be located via the Office of Fair Trading web site. On May 4, 2002, the author visited the Fair Trading web site, went to the section for consumers which contains tips and links to other sites, clicked on the links and saw that the first link was to the Real Estate Institute of Queensland. The institute's 'Member Search' section connected to the most notorious agent involved in the marketeering scams, Stamford Lyon, which is involved with Dudley Quinlivan, the person described by the Queensland Minister for Fair Trading as 'King Con'.

57. February 8, 2001. Fax from Don McKenzie, Chief Executive Officer, for and on behalf of the Board of Directors of the Real Estate Institute of Queensland (REIQ). And, media release, REIQ, Sunday February 18, 2001

58. Media release, REIQ, Friday August 31, 2001. Mark Brimble, the real estate agent who was the president of the institute, said that the Premier 'has something to explain to the people of Queensland about why these scams have been allowed to prosper'. He then intimated that a reason for the investment scams was that 'the State Government is receiving millions of dollars each month in stamp duties'. Neither Brimble nor the REIQ mentioned the millions of dollars being earned in commissions by REIQ member agents involved in the scams.

59. Member Update, Real Estate Institute of New South Wales, December 18, 2001.

60. William De Maria, *Deadly Disclosures – Whistleblowing and the Ethical Meltdown of Australia*, Wakefield Press, 1999, ISBN: 1862544573.

61. *A Current Affair*, Channel Nine, Monday July 30, 2001. Host, Mike Munro.

62. Roy Morgan Poll conducted in November 2001 surveying the ethics

and honesty of various professions showed that real estate agents ranked second last. Confirmed by Gary Morgan.

63. Real Estate Institute of New Zealand, Code of Ethics (13.5): 'Members shall never publicly criticise fellow members.' As with institutes in Australia, this code does not consider what a 'fellow member' may do. It is a clear rule – *no* public criticism. Code (13.1) says that 'members shall conduct themselves in a manner that reflects well on the Institute'. In Malcolm's case, this code was not taken to mean that other agents dishonest actions were not reflecting well on the institute, but rather that Malcolm, by speaking out about these actions, was causing the public not to reflect well on the institute.

64. The matter of the hearing held in Wellington under the jurisdiction of the rules of the Real Estate Institute of New Zealand (Incorporated) BETWEEN Real Estate Institute of New Zealand Inc., Hawkes Bay District, and C. D. Cox Ltd, trading as Cox Partners Estate Agents. Decision of Subcommittee, Regional Disciplinary Committee, Region 3, 10.30 am Thursday September 28, 2000. 'We therefore find the defendant guilty', was the decision of the panel of fellow agents. What did Malcolm say that made him 'guilty'? In part, he said, 'Commission-only is an admission by agents that they do not have the ability to effectively train people. It is a shameful way to treat new recruits, many of whom experience enormous financial suffering and leave the industry feeling very bitter. Debit/credit retainer schemes encourage dishonesty as salespeople are forced to focus on making a sale at any price. The welfare of sellers is cast aside due to the salesperson's desire to eat! As the saying goes, "necessity turns even honest people into knaves".'

65. www.reinz.org.nz/main.cfm April 24, 2002.

66. Michael Iveson, founder and Head of School, Australian Property College (www.australianproperty.qld.edu.au). Confirmed March 20, 2002. Also, according to the provisions of the *Trade Practices Act 1974*, s. 51AD, codes of practice have no force of law. In 1994, the Real Estate Institute of Australia's Code of Ethics was revoked by the then Trade Practices Commission. In 1999, the Australian Competition and Consumer Commission (ACCC) again revoked a new Code of Ethics of the Real Estate Institute of Australia (see media release ACCC, November 29, 1999).

67. As reported to the author by agents who attended a lunch at which the then president of the institute boasted about taking advertising money from sellers when he already had buyers for their property.

68. *Court declares REIWA rules anti-competitive*, media release, Australian Competition and Consumer Commission, October 11, 1999.

69. *Court declares REIWA rules anti-competitive,* media release, Australian Competition and Consumer Commission, October 11, 1999.

70. Kelly Girdlestone, 'Bid for clamp on auctions', and 'Auctions under hammer', *Canberra Sunday Times,* December 2, 2001.

71. *Statewide,* host Liam Bartlett, ABC Radio West Australia, 9.18 am, Wednesday November 28, 2001. Transcripts obtained by the author.

72. *Statewide,* ABC Radio West Australia, November 28, 2001.

73. *Statewide,* ABC Radio West Australia, November 28, 2001.

74. *Statewide,* ABC Radio West Australia, November 28, 2001.

75. *Statewide,* ABC Radio West Australia, November 28, 2001.

76. Tony Rees, to host John McNamara, 720 ABC Perth, 4.20 pm, Wednesday November 28, 2001. Opinion confirmed by Tony Rees, March 30, 2002.

77. Enzo Raimondo, by email October 11, 2001.

78. Letter to Hon. John Brumby, Treasurer of Victoria, October 10, 2001.

79. Barrie Magain to host Leon Byner, Adelaide 5AA, 12.10 pm, Monday November 12, 2001.

80. Paul Riccard, accountant, Real Estate Institute of Victoria, May 16, 2001. Mr Riccard described 2000 as an 'unusually high' year for government subsidies. The previous year the figure was $824,723 which he said was 'more typical'.

81. Media release, Australian Securities and Investments Commission. Australian Capital Territory Magistrates Court, Tuesday August 15, 2000. Roden misappropriated $35,750 of trust account funds.

82. Mathew Chandler, 'Suspended sentence for former REI head', *Australian Financial Review,* Thursday August 17, 2000.

83. Megan Doherty, 'Real-estate chief defends vendor bids', *Canberra Sunday Times,* July 8, 2001

84. Megan Doherty, *Canberra Sunday Times,* July 8, 2001

85. Peter Lowenstern, Senior Research Solicitor, Law Institute of Victoria, 'IT'S TIME … to clean up auctions', *Property & Environmental Law Bulletin,* 2001.

86. Mike Bruce, 'Law call to quit faking it', *Herald Sun,* Saturday November 24, 2001.

87. Statement to the author.

88. First National directory of member offices.

89. Independent Commission Against Corruption, *Report on Investigation into the RTA and Property Disposal,* The Hon. BSJ O'Keefe, AM, QC, Commissioner, February 1995. Between September 1990 and November 1993, Mr Andrea (also known as Mr Papandrea) had been bribing a Roads and Traffic Authority (RTA) official, Mr Peter Samuel, with the intention of influencing Mr Samuel to recommend his agency for the sale of RTA properties. Also Paola Totaro and Mark Coultan, 'Bribery in RTA sales', *Sydney Morning Herald,* February 3, 1995; and, Kate Lenthall, 'ICAC urges bribes action against senior RTA officer', *Australian Financial Review,* February 3, 1995, and AAP.

90. Grant Davis of Tony Andrea First National Real Estate, Thornleigh, NSW, to the author. Mr Davis had seen Mr Andrea passing an envelope containing large numbers of twenty-dollar notes to the RTA official, Mr Peter Samuel.

91. Three senior First National (current and past) board members told this author that 'The issue should be "dropped".'

92. Phil Hickmott, and other First National members, to the author.

93. Numerous reports from First National members together with documentation provided to the author.

94. Brett Harrod, National Chairman of First National, memorandum to all members, November 1, 2001.

95. Ian Bremner, Chief Executive of First National, fax to all First National members, November 30, 2001.

96. Sam Pennisi, Essendon, Victoria, letter to the author.

97. Jimmy Durante (1893–1980), American comedian, commonly attributed.

98. Dr Simon Longstaff, *Hard Cases, Tough Choices: Exploring the Ethical Landscape of Business,* Pan Macmillan Australia Pty Ltd, 1997, ISBN: 073290904X.

99. Annexure PAMD Form 27 Clause 7, Disclosure to Buyer. Harcourts Financial Services. Supplied to the author by a Brisbane solicitor.

100. Annexure PAMD Form 27 Clause 7, Disclosure to Buyer. Harcourts Financial Services. Supplied to the author by a Brisbane solicitor.

101. Heather Stevenson, Right Choice Conveyancing, Carrum Downs, Victoria, letter to the author, March 21, 2002. Also, Michael Benjamin, Victorian barrister and solicitor, describing such

commissions as 'morally repugnant' and warning that they are a breach of Section 176 of the Crimes Act unless full disclosure is made to the client.

102. Financial statements showing 'upfront commission' payments and 'trailer commissions'.

103. Contents of letter from Lawform received by Queensland solicitor, December 4, 2001. Also, www.lawform.com.au December 26, 2001.

104. Contents of letter from Lawform received by Queensland solicitor, December 4, 2001. Also, www.lawform.com.au December 26, 2001.

105. Contents of letter from Lawform received by Queensland solicitor, December 4, 2001. Also, www.lawform.com.au December 26, 2001. 'If you decide to concentrate on the business, market it astutely, and manage it well, you can quickly achieve an income that you could never make practicing law alone.'

106. Contents of letter from Lawform received by Queensland solicitor, December 4, 2001. Also, www.lawform.com.au December 26, 2001. Chart showing upfront and trailing commissions that can be earned each year.

107. Contents of letter from Lawform received by Queensland solicitor, December 4, 2001. Also, www.lawform.com.au December 26, 2001. 'One enterprising Suburban practitioner has introduced 200 loan applications in the first 5 months of this year [2001] – an average of 10 loans per week.'

108. Contents of letter from Lawform received by Queensland solicitor, December 4, 2001. Also, www.lawform.com.au December 26, 2001. 'Most importantly, you will also be able to provide yourself with an income well into retirement.'

109. Contents of letter from Lawform received by Queensland solicitor, December 4, 2001. Also, www.lawform.com.au December 26, 2001.

110. Queensland lawyer to the author. Also, Chris Griffiths, 'Ban likely on kickbacks for lawyers', Courier-Mail, Thursday December 6, 2001.

111. Queensland lawyer to the author.

112. Australian Competition and Consumer Commission, Fair and Square – A Guide to the Trade Practices Act for the Real Estate Industry, Chapter 3, 'Play Fair', 2000, ISBN: 0642402590.

113. Commonly known. Also confirmed in ACCC letter to consumer, provided to the author, August 27, 2001.

114. Russell V Miller, Miller's Annotated Trade Practices Act, 21st edition, LBC Information Services, 2000, ISBN: 0455217068.

115. From statements and documentation provided to author. Property: 12 Broadhurst Street, Paddington. Sold August 31, 2001 by Ray White Paddington. Advertisement for property in *Courier-Mail,* Saturday August 4, stating 'Buyers from low $200's'.

116. George Hadgelias, Ray White Paddington, Wednesday August 8, 2001.

117. Stewart Walls, letter to the Australian Competition and Consumer Commission, September 9, 2001.

118. Australian Competition and Consumer Commission, letter to Stewart Walls, September 12, 2001, reference MARS247804.

119. Statement from buyer to the author, September 4, 2001. Agent R. T. Golby. The buyer claimed the reserve price was 'up around $675,000'. The property sold for $705,000 on August 18, 2001.

120. David Hindley, 'Shark warning! New Zealanders are losing millions of dollars in dodgy Gold Coast property deals', cover story, *Consumer* magazine, November 2001.

121. *Federal court finds that Canberra real estate agency engaged in misleading conduct,* media release, Australian Competition and Consumer Commission, November 2, 2001. A real estate agency had quoted a homeseller a flat fee of $5000 and then, once the home had been sold, the agent charged a further $500 for GST. All prices quoted to consumers are required to include the amount of the GST so that consumers cannot be misled.

122. Paul Wilson, 'Ethics? Bah, humbug!' *Courier-Mail,* January 4, 2002.

123. Corporate Affairs and Compliance Branch, Office of Consumer and Business Affairs, South Australia, reference: CINV/99/0695, October 26, 1999.

124. Corporate Affairs and Compliance Branch, Office of Consumer and Business Affairs, South Australia, reference: CINV/99/0695, December 13, 1999.

125. Ron Heyne, to the author.

126. Marlene O'Rielley, 'Warning – open inspections', cover story, *Real Estate Bulletin,* Real Estate Institute of South Australia, December 1990. Marlene O'Rielley, President REISA.

127. Marlene O'Rielley, *Real Estate Bulletin,* December 1990.

128. Ron Heyne, statement. At first, when Ron Heyne asked *why* they were investigating him, the government officials wouldn't answer. He then asked *who* made the complaint against him. They refused to tell him 'because of the Privacy Act'. After pressing his question again

and again, he said he wouldn't continue the conversation until he knew who made the complaint. He asked them to leave. It was then that one of them (Compliance Officer John Radbone) told him it was other agents in town.

129. Ron Heyne, statement. Also, a letter from Heyne's solicitor to the Commissioner for Consumer Affairs, saying, in part: 'We would suggest that it is inappropriate and indeed ultra vires of your powers under the Fair Trading Act to act upon an industry enquiry or complaint where no consumer complaint or detriment is perceived.' It was suggested to that the commissioner should 'issue a public warning statement pursuant to Section 91A of the Fair Trading Act 1987'. The letter concluded by saying: 'Rather than persecute or harass our client we would suggest that you carry out your functions enumerated under Section 8 of the Fair Trading Act and that you apologise to our client.'

130. Statement to the author by the agent from whom the lady bought a home after selling her home in Stirling.

131. Dave Pilling, Pilling Systems, form letter to agents, 'I have developed a simple method that regularly achieves between 4% and 6%. Would you like to know how?' May 9, 2001.

132. Christine and William Brewer, letter to the author, July 23, 2001. Confirmed April 29, 2002.

133. Kate Dorsey, *Seven News*, Channel Seven South Australia, 6.10 pm, July 9, 2001.

134. Member Service Letter, Real Estate Institute of Victoria, June 1996. The County Court found that the agent was 'negligent in failing to provide adequate supervision of the property'.

135. As reported to the author by an institute board member. The Real Estate Institute told its members, 'We would rather not see this publicised in the press'.

136. *A Current Affair*, National Nine Network, 6.30 pm, Monday December 3, 2001. 'Real estate agents are reaping income in kickbacks from advertisers even when the property is not sold.' Rehame newslines.

137. Numerous reports to the author.

138. 'Urgent and Important', email from L. J. Hooker to all member agents, December 4, 2001. Provided to the author.

139. L. J. Hooker franchise agreement, Clause 4.14 and Item 12, Compulsory Advertisement Header.

140. Kathryn Welling, 'Money keeps rolling in', *Manly Daily,* June 3, 2000.

141. Royal Commission of Inquiry into Finance Broking Industry, Commissioner, Ian Temby, QC, commenced June 20, 2001. Report tabled in Western Australian Parliament, February 19, 2002.

142. *News,* 720 ABC Radio Perth, 8.00 pm, Monday November 12, 2001. 'The WA Finance Brokers Royal Commission has heard a top WA Government official investigating suspect brokers had been sidelined because he had upset too many real estate agents.' From Rehame newslines, 5 am November 13, 2001.

143. Matt Miller, Queensland Commissioner for Fair Trading, letter to the President of the Queensland Law Society, August 22, 2001.

144. Tim O'Dwyer to the author. Also, copies of 'censored' advertisements given to author by O'Dwyer.

145. Graham Greene, *The Quiet American,* William Heinemann Ltd, 1955.

146. Copy of the letter dated August 22, 2001 provided to the author.

147. Tim O'Dwyer, fax to the author.

148. Hon. M Rose (Currumbin-ALP), Minister for Tourism and Racing and Minister for Fair Trading, Queensland Parliament, Property Agents and Motor Dealers Bill, September 13, 2001.

149. Oscar Wilde, *De Profundis,* Methuen and Co., London 1905. Oscar Wilde's personal and emotional account of his feelings and thoughts while imprisoned in Reading Gaol for homosexual offences. Wilde, a playwright, was one of London's most celebrated personalities and famous for his wit. He served two years hard labour and was released on May 19, 1897. He spent his remaining years in Paris, a broken man, living under a pseudonym. He died on November 30, 1900. He was 46. *De Profundis* was published after his death.

150. Quentin Dempster, *Whistleblowers,* ABC Books, Sydney, ISBN: 0733305040.

151. Auctioneer Bill Robertson reacting to a challenge made to the real estate industry to debate publicly that auctions were a fraud. Statement to author by the person to whom the statement was made, December 1995.

152. Quinn & Box, Solicitors and Attorneys, acting on behalf of Stamford Lyon, letter faxed to the author, August 22, 2001.

153. Quinn & Box, Solicitors and Attorneys, acting on behalf of Stamford Lyon, letter faxed to the author, August 22, 2001.

154. 'The Inside Secrets of Real Estate' is a consumer information seminar presented throughout Australia. These seminars are for consumers

only. There is no charge or obligation. No names of consumers are given to any agent or company. These seminars are planned to continue until such time as real estate consumers are adequately informed of their rights when buying or selling real estate. Schedule available at www.jenman.com.au or by calling 1800 1800 18.

155. Edmund Burke (1722–1792), Irish statesman and philosopher, 'Letter to a Member of the National Assembly', in *The Works of the Right Honorable Edmund Burke,* Oxford University Press, London, 1925, 4:319. 'Men are qualified for civil liberties in exact proportion to their disposition to put moral chains upon their own appetites ... Society cannot exist unless a controlling power upon will and appetite be placed somewhere, and the less of it there is within, the more there must be without. It is ordained in the eternal constitution of things that men of intemperate minds cannot be free. Their passions forge their fetters.'

156. George Crabbe (1754–1832), English poet. Crabbe began his career as a doctor, but turned to writing and poetry focused on the plight of the poor. He wrote realistic and touching work and is one of the most underrated English poets of the time. He was a friend of Edmund Burke.

157. Paul Sheehan, 'False profits a blight on Sydney's religion of real estate', *Sydney Morning Herald*, Wednesday December 5, 2001.

158. Email to the author, November 23, 2001.

Chapter Twelve

1. Philip Holden, *Ethics for Managers,* Gower Publishing, England, 2000, ISBN: 0566081156.

2. Alex Bruce, *The Trade Practices Act: Consumer Protection and Product Liability,* LBC Information Services, 2002, ISBN: 0455216541. Also, Alex Bruce, email, March 14, 2002.

3. Alex Bruce, *The Trade Practices Act: Consumer Protection and Product Liability,* LBC Information Services, 2002, ISBN: 0455216541. Also, Alex Bruce, email, March 14, 2002.

4. Course details sent by Telstra Faxstream to the agents.

5. *Wilde & Wilde v. Emilaw Pty Ltd,* Judge Samios, District Court of Queensland, August 18, 2000, File Nos: 5027 of 1997. Also, Allison White, 'Protection urged over house sales', *Courier-Mail,* Wednesday August 23, 2000.

6. Rod Morley of Talbot Birner Morley, *A Current Affair,* Channel Nine, Monday July 30, 2001.

7. Sam Pennisi, Pennisi Real Estate, Essendon, Victoria, *A Current Affair,* Channel Nine, Monday July 30, 2001.

8. Robert Harley, 'Agents market vendor comfort pledges', *Australian Financial Review,* Thursday June 27, 2001.

9. Homeseller to the author.

10. Media release, Real Estate Institute of Victoria, in the Property Section, *Age,* August 4, 2001. The release appeared in this weekly column reserved for comments by the Real Estate Institute. When the author forwarded a letter of reply, it was not published.

11. Media release, Real Estate Institute of Victoria, in the Property Section, *Age,* August 4, 2001.

12. Media release, Real Estate Institute of Victoria, in the Property Section, *Age,* August 4, 2001.

13. Media release, Real Estate Institute of Victoria, in the Property Section, *Age,* August 4, 2001.

14. 'CEO's Report', *Victorian Real Estate Journal,* Real Estate Institute of Victoria, August 2001.

15. Andrew Pennisi, Essendon.

16. Homeseller to the author. She resisted the agent's standard spiel and sold her property privately without an agent for a higher price than the agent quoted.

17. Property at 39 Sturt Valley Road, Stirling, South Australia. Auction date: Saturday, October 21, 2000. Agent: Sula Harland of L. J. Hooker Stirling.

18. Dr Briggs, statement to and conversation with the author. Confirmed May 10, 2002.

19. Dr Briggs, as above, confirmed May 10, 2002

20. Dr Gladys Florence Watkins, statement, and from letter of complaint by her lawyer, outlining how Dr Watkins was tricked into placing her home 'on the market' below what she was prepared to accept. Auction of 142 Springfield Road, Blackburn, May 13, 2000. Agent: Barry Plant Doherty (Whitehorse) Pty Ltd. Auctioneer: Tony Bloomfield. Confirmed May 10, 2002

21. Statement to the author. Sale of home in Kelvin Grove, Brisbane, January 28, 2001. Confirmed May 10, 2002.

22. Statement submitted via 'Your Story' section of web site, www.jenman.com January 4, 2002.

23. Milton Friedman, 'The social responsibility of business is to increase its profit', *New York Times Magazine,* September 13, 1970. See also, 'A question of ethics – a spirited discussion on the complex relationship between business and social responsibility', *Stanford Business,* November 2000, vol. 69, no. 1, Stanford University, California.

24. Albert Schweitzer (1875–1965). Schweitzer was a missionary doctor who devoted his life to serving humanity. He settled in French Equatorial Africa after raising money to build a hospital there. He won the Nobel Peace Prize in 1952 and used the prize money to expand the hospital and establish a leper colony. In 1955, Queen Elizabeth II awarded Dr Schweitzer Britain's highest civilian honour, the 'Order of Merit'. He was known as 'the greatest Christian of his time' and based his entire philosophy on a 'reverence for life'.

25. Baroness Bertha Felicie Sophie von Suttner (1843–1915). Von Suttner was born in Prague. A novelist and later a peace activist, she won the Nobel Peace Prize in 1905.

26. Aldous (Leonard) Huxley (1894–1963). Huxley was an English novelist and essayist. He is most famous for his 1932 novel, *Brave New World,* a science fiction work of how human beings were influenced by indoctrination and drugs. There is a story that one day, late in his life, Huxley was walking with the noted historian and humanities professor, Huston Smith, when suddenly Huxley said, 'You know, Huston, it's rather embarrassing to have spent one's entire lifetime pondering the human condition and to come toward its close and find that I really don't have anything more profound to pass on by way of advice than, "Try to be a little kinder".'

27. Anzac Dawn Service, Cenotaph, Martin Place, Sydney, April 25, 2000.

Bibliography

Adler Jr, Bill (ed.), *How to Profit from Public Auctions*, William Morrow & Company Inc, New York, (1989), ISBN: 0688070884.

Aubuchon, Norbert, *The Anatomy of Persuasion*, Amacom, 1997, ISBN: 08144795229.

Badcock, Blair, Beer, Andrew, *Home Truths: Property Ownership and Housing Wealth in Australia*, Melbourne University Press, 2000, ISBN: 0522848931.

Blackburn, Simon, *Being Good: A Short Introduction to Ethics*, Oxford University Press, 2001, ISBN: 0192100521.

Blanco, James A, *Business Fraud: Know It and Prevent It*, Humanomics Publishing, 2001, ISBN: 0966608542.

Bloch, Sonny HI, and Lichtenstein, Grace, *Inside Real Estate: The Complete Guide to Buying and Selling your Home, Co-Op, or Condominium*, Weidenfeld & Nicholson, 1987, ISBN: 1555840302.

Bly, Carol, *Changing the Bully who Rules the World: Reading and Thinking about Ethics*, Milkweed Editions, 1996, ISBN: 1571312056.

Brough, James, *Auction!*, Bobbs-Merrill Company Inc., 1963, Library of Congress Catalog Card Number 6311637.

Bruce, Alex, *The Trade Practices Act: Consumer Protection and Product Liability*, LBC Information Services, 1999, ISBN: 0455216541.

Buchholz, Todd G, *New Ideas from Dead Economists – An Introduction to Modern Economic Thought*, Penguin Books, 1989, ISBN: 01402831370.

Caires, Douglas & Richard, *The World of Auctions, Where and How to Profit from Auctions*, American Auction Service, New York, 1993, ISBN: 1561712817.

Campbell, Jeremy, *The Liar's Tale: A History of Falsehood*, W. W. Norton & Company, New York, 2001, ISBN: 0393025594.

Cannon, Michael, *The Land Boomers*, Melbourne University Press, 1966, ISBN: 0522837883.

Cialdini, Robert B, *Influence: The Psychology of Persuasion*, Quill, 1993, ISBN: 0688128165.

Chomsky, Noam & Herman, Edward S, *Manufacturing Consent: The Political Economy of the Mass Media*, Panthenon Books, New York, 1988, ISBN: 0679720340.

Croall, Hazel, *White Collar Crime*, Open Univestity Press, 1992, ISBN: 0335096565.

Crowel, Thomas Ray, *Dirty Little Tricks: How Salespeople Are Robbing You Blind!* Success Press, 2000, ISBN: 0966991729.

Cohen, William S, (Senator), *Easy Prey: The Fleecing of America's Senior Citizens and How to Stop It,* Marlowe & Company, New York, 1997, ISBN: 1569247366.

Cooper, Jeremy, *Under the Hammer: The Auctions and Auctioneers of London,* Constable & Company Limited, 1977, ISBN: 0094613702.

Daly, MT, *Sydney Boom Sydney Bust,* George Allen & Unwin, Sydney, 1982, ISBN: 0868611646.

Davia, Howard R, *Fraud 101: Techniques and Strategies for Detection,* John Wiley & Sons Inc., 2000, ISBN: 0471373095.

De Graff, John, Wann, David, Naylor, Thomas H, *Affluenza: the All Consuming Epidemic,* Berrett-Koehler Publishers Inc., San Francisco, 2001, ISBN: 1576751511.

De Maria, William, *Deadly Disclosures: Whistleblowing and the Ethical Meltdown of Australia,* Wakefield Press, 1999, ISBN: 1862544573.

Dempster, Quentin, *Whistleblowers,* ABC Books, Sydney, ISBN: 0733305040.

Dominguez, Joe, & Robin, Vicki, *Your Money or Your Life,* Penguin Books, Australia, 1992, ISBN: 0140167153.

Donaldson, Michael C and Mimi, *Negotiating for Dummies,* IDG Books Worldwide, 1996, ISBN: 1568848676.

Dubois, Maurice, *Sold by Owner! Secrets of Selling Your House without a Broker's Fee,* Liberty Hall Press, 1988, ISBN: 0830693165.

Economy, Peter, *Business Negotiation Basics,* Irwin Professional Publishing, 1994, ISBN: 155623841X.

Eilers, Terry, *How to Sell your Home Fast for the Highest Price in any Market,* Hyperion, New York, 1996, ISBN: 0786882247.

Ekman, Paul, *Telling Lies: Clues to Deceit in the Marketplace, Politics and Marriage,* W. W. Norton & Company, 1991, ISBN 0393321886.

Everett, Susanne, *History of Slavery,* Grange Books, London, 1996, ISBN: 1856279634.

Ferry, Mike, *How to Develop a SIX-Figure Income in Real Estate,* Real Estate Education Company, 1993, ISBN: 0793104904.

Fleming, Alan, *Real Estate Office Manual,* Real Estate Institute of Australia Ltd, Canberra, with which are affiliated the Real Estate Institutes of New South Wales, Victoria, Queensland, South Australia, Western Australia, Tasmania, Northern Territory and the ACT, 1993, ISBN: 0909784620.

Ford, Charles V, *Lies! Lies! Lies! The Psychology of Deceit,* American Psychiatric Press, 1996, ISBN 0880489979.

Frank, Robert H, and Cook, Philip J, *The Winner-Take-All Society: Why the Few at the Top Get So Much More Than the Rest of Us,* Penguin Books, 1995, ISBN: 0140259953.

Glink, Ilyce R, *100 Questions Every Home Seller Should Ask,* Times Books, Random House Inc., 1995, ISBN: 0812924061.

Goleman, Daniel, *Vital Lies, Simple Truths: The Psychology of Self-Deception,* Bloomsbury Publishing, 1997, ISBN: 074753499.

Gough, Russell W, *Character is Destiny: The Value of Personal Ethics in Everyday Life,* Prima Publishing, 1998, ISBN: 0761511636.

Hamilton, Charles, *Auction Madness: An Uncensored Look Behind the Velvet Drapes of the Great Auction Houses,* Everest House Publishers, New York, 1981, ISBN: 08969612300.

Handy, Charles, *The Hungry Spirit, Beyond Capitalism: A Quest for Purpose in the Modern World,* Random House Australia, 1997, ISBN: 009922772X.

Henderson, Les, *Crimes of Persuasion: How Con Artists Will Steal Your Savings and Inheritance through Telemarketing Fraud, Investment Schemes and Consumer Scams,* Coyote Ridge Publishing, 2000, ISBN: 0968713300.

Hendon, Donald W, *Classic Failures in Product Marketing (Marketing Principles Violations and How to Avoid Them),* Hardknocks Factory, Malaysia, ISBN: 9839323369.

Herbert, John, *Inside Christie's,* St Martin's Press, 1990, ISBN: 031204609X.

Holden, Philip, *Ethics for Managers,* Gower Publishing, England, 2000, ISBN: 0566081156.

Irwin, Robert, *Tips & Traps When Selling a Home,* McGraw-Hill, 1990, ISBN: 0070321396.

Iversen, Theodore, *Games Real Estate Agents Play,* TI Financial, 1992, ISBN: 0963525913.

Jenman, Neil, *Real Estate Mistakes: How to Avoid Them, How to Save Your Money,* Rowley Publications, 2000, ISBN: 0958651728.

Johnston, JP, *The Auctioneer's Guide and How to Become an Auctioneer,* Hallett Publishing Company, Chicago, 1887.

Kennedy, Danielle, *How to List and Sell Real Estate in the 90s,* Prentice Hall, 1990, ISBN: 0134022491.

Killick, Mark, *Fraudbusters: The Inside Story of the Serious Fraud Office,* Victor Gollancz, London, 1998, ISBN: 0575065451.

Lacey, Robert, Sotheby's: *Bidding for Class,* Warner Books, 1998, ISBN: 0751523623.

Longstaff, Dr Simon, *Hard Cases, Tough Choices: Exploring the Ethical Landscape of Business,* Pan Macmillan Australia Pty Ltd, 1997, ISBN: 073290904X.

Lumley, James EA, *Top Dollar for Your Property,* John Wiley & Sons, 1998, ISBN: 04716361188.

Mackay, Charles, *Extraordinary Popular Delusions and the Madness of Crowds* (1841), Reprinted by Marketplace Books, John T. Wiley & Sons Inc., 1996, ISBN: 0471133124.

Mauer, David W, *The Big Con: The Story of the Confidence Man and the Confidence Trick,* Random House, 1940, ISBN: 00999409992.

Megone, Chris, Robinson, Simon J, (ed.), *Case Histories in Business Ethics,* Routledge, Taylor & Francis Group, 2002, ISBN: 0415231442.

Miller, Peter G, *Inside the Real Estate Deal,* Harper Collins, 1991, ISBN: 0060165251.

Miller, Russell V, *Miller's Annotated Trade Practices Act,* 21st edn, LBC Information Services, 2000, ISBN: 0455217068.

Moon, Chris, Bonny, Clive, (eds,) *Business Ethics: Facing up to the Issues,* The Economist Books, 2001, ISBN: 1861972814.

Nerburn, Kent, *Simple Truths,* New World Library, 1996, ISBN: 1880032929.

Packard, Vance, *The Hidden Persuaders,* Longmans, Green & Co. Ltd, 1957.

Paulson, Morton C, *The Great Land Hustle,* Henry Regnery Company, Chicago, Library of Congress Catalog Card Number: 7280936.

Pipes, Richard, *Property & Freedom,* Harvill Press, London, 1999, ISBN: 1860466796.

Poveda, Tony G, *Rethinking White-Collar Crime,* Praeger Publishers, 1994, ISBN: 0275945863.

Roulac, Stephen E, (ed.), *Ethics in Real Estate,* Kluwer Academic Publishers, Massachusetts, 1999, ISBN: 0792382285.

Rubins, Leona, *How to Defend Yourself at Auctions,* Westover Publishing Company, Virginia, ISBN: 0878580182.

Rushkoff, Douglas, *Coercion: The Persuasion Professionals and Why We Listen to What 'They' Say,* Riverhead Books, 2000, ISBN: 157322829X.

Ryder, Terry, *Buyer Beware,* Wrightbooks, 2001, ISBN: 1876627891.

Ryder, Terry, *Property Smart,* Wrightbooks, 2002, ISBN: 0701636505.

Samenow, Dr Stanton E, *Inside the Criminal Mind,* Crown Business, New York, 1984, ISBN: 0812910826.

Saul, John Ralston, *On Equilibrium,* Penguin Books, 2001, ISBN: 0140293140.

Sennett, Richard, *The Corrosion of Character: The Personal Consequences of Work in the New Capitalism,* W. W. Norton & Company, New York, 1998, ISBN: 0393319873.

Sheehan, Paul, *Among the Barbarians,* Random House, Sydney, 1998, ISBN: 0091836360.

Sifakis, Carl, *Hoaxes and Scams, A Compendium of Deceptions, Ruses and Swindles,* Michael O'Mara Books Limited, London, 1993, ISBN: 1854799037.

Sirmai, Geoff, *The Confident Consumer: A Watchdog's Guide to Smart Buying and Your Consumer Rights,* Allen & Unwin, Sydney, ISBN: 1864487437.

Underhill, Paco, *Why We Buy: The Science of Shopping,* Texere Publishing Limited, 2000, ISBN: 158799044X.

Vij, Aldert, *Detecting Lies and Deceit: The Psychology of Lying and the Implications for Professional Practice,* John Wiley & Sons Ltd, 2000, ISBN: 047185316X.

Walters, Stan B, *The Truth About Lying: How to Spot a Lie and Protect Yourself from Deception,* Sourcebooks Inc., 2000, ISBN: 1570715114.

Watson, Peter, *Sotheby's Inside Story,* Bloomsbury Publishing, London, 1997, ISBN: 0747534438.

Wagenvoord, James, *Cashing in on the Auction Boom,* Rawson, Wade Publishers, Inc., New York, 1980, ISBN: 0892561513.

Warren, Elizabeth; Sullivan, Teresa A; Westbrook, Jay Lawrence; *The Fragile Middle Class: Americans in Debt,* Yale University Press, 2000, ISBN: 0300079605.

Webster, RH, *The Ancient Art of Auction,* Real Estate and Stock Institute of Australia, 1973.

Whittaker, Noel, *Golden Rules of Wealth,* Simon & Schuster Australia, 1996, ISBN: 0731806522.

Yarbrough, Kelly, *Real Estate Agents and Their Dirty Little Tricks,* Great Quotations, 1996, ISBN: 1562452258.

Index